PENGUI

EMPRESS C

Judith Summers is the author of four novels and a prize-winning non-fiction book, *Soho, A History of London's Most Colourful Neighbourhood*. Born and brought up in London, she studied Fine Art in Bristol and Manchester, and trained as a film editor with the BBC. After becoming a tourist guide, she discovered a passion for historical research. She has written widely on London.

Empress of Pleasure

The Life and Adventures of
Teresa Cornelys

JUDITH SUMMERS

PENGUIN BOOKS

PENGUIN BOOKS

Published by the Penguin Group
Penguin Books Ltd, 80 Strand, London WC2R 0RL, England
Penguin Group (USA) Inc., 375 Hudson Street, New York, New York 10014, USA
Penguin Books Australia Ltd, 250 Camberwell Road, Camberwell, Victoria 3124, Australia
Penguin Books Canada Ltd, 10 Alcorn Avenue, Toronto, Ontario, Canada M4V 3B2
Penguin Books India (P) Ltd, 11 Community Centre, Panchsheel Park, New Delhi – 110 017, India
Penguin Group (NZ), cnr Airborne and Rosedale Roads, Albany, Auckland 1310, New Zealand
Penguin Books (South Africa) (Pty) Ltd, 24 Sturdee Avenue, Rosebank 2196, South Africa

Penguin Books Ltd, Registered Offices: 80 Strand, London WC2R 0RL, England

www.penguin.com

Published by Viking 2003
Published in Penguin Books 2004
1

Copyright © Judith Summers, 2004
All rights reserved

The moral right of the author has been asserted

Printed in England by Clays Ltd, St Ives plc

For Joshua

List of Illustrations

Taken from his 1754 trade catalogue, *The Gentleman and Cabinet-Maker's Director*.

23. *The Harmoniac Meeting*, mezzotint, artist unknown.
24. *Trial of the Sovereign Empress of the Vast Regions of Taste*, artist unknown, *Oxford Magazine*, April 1771.
25. *The Macaroni – A Real Character at the Late Masquerade*, engraved mezzotint by Philip Dawe, 1773.
26. The Pantheon, Oxford Street, aquatint by F. G. Byron, 1785.
27. *Cupid Beating up for Volunteers*, artist unknown, 1773.
28. *Cupid Turn'd Auctioneer, or, Cornelys' Sale at Carlisle House*, engraving by Samuel Wade, 1772.
29. Casanova, aged sixty-three, engraving by Berka, 1788.
30. Teresa's daughter Sophie Williams.
31. Carlisle House, drawing by Howard Penton, 1761.

Illustration Sources and Acknowledgements

1, Private Collection/Bonhams, London/Bridgeman Art Library; 2, Galleria dell' Accademia, Venice/Francesco Turio Bohm/Bridgeman Art Library; 3, Dashkov Collection, State Historical Museum, Moscow; 4, 9, 12, 15, 23, 24, 27, 28, endpapers, from the eight-volume *Collection of Cuttings from newspapers, advertisements, playbills etc formed by Fillinham*, The British Library; 5, The Guildhall, Corporation of London; 6, Bayerische Verwaltung der Statlichen Schlösser, Gärten und Seen, Altes Schloss Eremitage, Bayreuth; 7, 8, The British Library; 10, 13, from Charles Pearce, *The Amazing Duchess*, 1911; 11, 18, 20, from Warwick Wroth, *The London Pleasure Gardens*, 1896; 14, National Portrait Gallery, London; 16, 17, from Horace Bleackley, ed. *Casanova in England*, 1923; 19, from Heinz Gärtner, *John Christian Bach*, 1994; 21, 25, from City of Westminster Archives; 22 *left*, from R. W. Symonds, *The Ornamental Designs of Chippendale*, 1949 and *right*, from R. W. Symonds, *Chippendale Furniture Designs*, 1948; 26, Guildhall Library, Corporation of London/Bridgeman Art Library; 29, from John Masters, *Casanova*; 31, from *GLC Survey of London*, vol. 34, *The Parish of St Anne Soho*, 1966; 30, Princess Helena College.

Acknowledgements

I had wanted to write Teresa Cornelys's biography ever since I first stumbled across her story in the late 1980s. Had it not been for a conversation with my friend Graham Anthony three years ago, I might never have done so. He urged me to follow my instinct and go for it, and I owe him a huge vote of thanks.

Countless people generously gave me their help with writing this book. I would particularly like to thank my agent, Clare Alexander; and Eleo Gordon, my publisher at Penguin Books; my editor Hazel Orme; Bridget Marks, who very kindly translated original German texts such as the letters of Marianna Pirker; John Hackworth, who provided me with information on the Fermor family; David Maislish, who explained the ins and outs of eighteenth-century legal jargon; Lynn Mullen, who gave me information about St Sepulchre's-without-Newgate, where Teresa Cornelys was buried; Patrick Bade, who gave me the benefit of his considerable knowledge about the composer Christoph Gluck; and Signor and Signora Barnabo, who kindly allowed me access to the Palazzo Malipiero in Venice.

In addition I would like to thank Anisha Bondy for helping me with the research in Bayreuth; Othmar Barnert, librarian of the Österreichisches Theater Museum, Vienna; David McCarthy of the Corporation of London; Chiara Toso and Anna Bogo of the Casa Goldoni in Venice; Dr Peter Rückert of the Hauptstaatsarchiv, Stuttgart; Roy Harrison and John Sargent of Westminster City Archives; James Lomax of the Chippendale Society; the archivist of Drummond's Bank, whose records are now held by the Royal Bank of Scotland; the staff of the British Library, the National Library of Wales, Sevenoaks Library and the Public Records Office; the publishers F. A. Brockhaus, for allowing me to quote from *Casanova's Histoire de Ma Vie*, Donald Clarke, for sending me his photograph of Sophie Cornelys William's portrait, and the Princess Helena College for giving me permission to reproduce it; and the Department of Manuscripts and Special Collections, University of Nottingham, for allowing me to reproduce extracts from letters held in the Portland Collection.

On a very personal level, David Rodes, Jim Meyer, Steve Johnson and Judy Rodes-Johnson generously provided me with a refuge to work in when my desk overflowed. My son, Joshua, patiently put up with my preoccupation with all things eighteenth century for two years, and kept my nose to the grindstone. Heartfelt thanks to Donald Sassoon, who generously answered my cry for help and gave me the benefit of his advice, both as a historian, a friend and a writer. His painstaking editing of the manuscript was way beyond the call of duty. Above all, I would like to thank my sister, Sue Summers, and brother-in-law, Philip Norman, who gave me their unstinting support during the two years it took me to write this book. Their criticism of the first draft was invaluable, to put it mildly.

Judith Summers

See Madam Cornelys drives on a brisk trade
With her Op'ras, Assemblies, and fine Masquerade!
The Empress of Taste, and Magnificent pleasure,
To whom all the loves and the joys shew their treasure;
With Duchesses four whom she leads by the nose;
Yet they do what they please, and all under the rose;
In Spite of the K—g, & of laws, and of reason,
She stands above all, & to thwart her is treason,
Two guineas and a half for a Ticket demands,
Which is nothing to pay into Empresses hands;
For she breaks through all order, all laws, and all rules;
And gives coals to the poor, – to take coal from the fools.

1771. Upon Madam Cornely's Masquerade at
two Guineas and a Half a Ticket

Prologue

It is early evening when I walk into Soho, that small-scale, densely packed corner of London's West End. Cars cruise the grid of narrow streets, sleek sharks on the lookout for that rare prey, a free parking space. People hurry along the pavements, their ears glued to their mobile phones. Somewhere below the buzz of their one-sided telephone conversations, the purr of taxis, the thrum of engines, and the sudden, discordant screech of a police siren over in nearby Charing Cross Road I can hear the far-off jangle of bells of the Hare Krishna devotees who are dancing their way to Nirvana down Shaftesbury Avenue, oblivious to the corporeal world.

Darkness is falling. Lights – bright halogen spots, white fluorescent strips, a dusty red neon tube bent into the single word *Girls* – illuminate the upper sash windows of what are now shops and offices but, two hundred years ago, were terraces of private homes. No one scurrying past bothers to look up at the old houses. They are far too busy going somewhere. As always at this hour in Soho, there is a sense of anticipation in the air.

When the advertising executives, shop assistants, financial advisers, designers, publishers, agents, producers, bank-tellers and secretaries who work in the vicinity spill out of their offices, they find themselves suddenly and inexplicably in a festive mood. Reluctant to take the Tube home, they slope off in groups to the nearest club, café, pub or bar. Here they are joined by the tourists, ticket touts, theatregoers, thrill-seekers, celebrities and hard-bitten drinkers who, during the next hour or so, drift into the area in their hundreds. Soho is shrugging off its workaday clothes, and donning the carnival cloak it owes to one person and one person alone.

She is the one I have come here to find. In search of her, I cut north-east through a maze of litter-strewn alleyways towards Soho Square. Across its central garden – a small patch of *rus-in-urbe*, just thirty seconds south of the grime-encrusted pavements of Oxford Street – stands St Patrick's Roman Catholic Church. Despite the solid red bell-tower above its double doors, most people pass St Patrick's without even noticing it. From outside it seems but a sliver of a building, sandwiched between a tall, somewhat shabby nineteenth-century presbytery and a narrow brick lane called Sutton Row. But the interior I enter is vast. The lobby is cold, shadowy, and staunchly Victorian, replete with glimmering candles, a stone *pietà* and a printed sign pinned to one wall warning those taking Holy Communion not to leave valuables on their seats. Paintings of Christ and statues of the Virgin Mary nestle in deep niches along both sides of a long nave. Limpid eau-de-Nil walls soar three storeys high to peeling clerestory windows. At the far end, above the altar table, looms a golden apse inscribed with the Latin word '*Sanctus*'. Sacred.

The pews are deserted but for a scant handful of refugees from the outside world: an Ecuadorian office cleaner, who has stopped in on her way to work; an American tourist, his neck loaded with cameras, who bows his head in prayer; a couple of local down-and-outs, stretched out on the seats clutching empty beer cans in their cold-reddened hands. I take a seat at the back. There is an uncanny silence. If I listen hard enough, I can hear echoes of the past. A violin note. Far-off laughter. The pop of a champagne cork. It was not always so quiet here. Once, long before the present church was built, this was the noisiest place in all of Soho. A place of music and masquerade. A place of gambling and gossip. A place of licence and licentiousness, and incense and insensibility. A place called Carlisle House.

When I close my eyes, the twenty-first century bleaches away. It is the year 1770, and I am standing outside, in Soho Square, looking at a five-storey, double-fronted grey brick mansion that stands on this site. A grand masquerade ball is being given here tonight for the nobility and gentry, and all day long a steady procession of tradesmen has been arriving at the back and front doors. Florists staggering under the weight of elaborate flower arrangements. A hairdresser and his assistant weighed down by wig boxes. A silversmith with a bag of polishing cloths. Musicians carrying flutes and violins. A host of bakers' assistants, each bearing a tray of fancy cakes. A vintner's cart with the name Albert Berger written on its side, stacked with bottles of fine wine.

As the daylight fades the servants employed by the countless viscounts, MPs and baronets who live in the other houses on Soho Square fasten their wooden window shutters and draw their curtains. A servant comes out and lights the iron lanterns beside Carlisle House's front steps, and a crowd of onlookers begins to gather on the pavement to watch the partygoers arrive. There are dockers from the Thames-side warehouses, young City clerks and their wives, pickpockets from the slums of St Giles, milkmaids who tend the cows in the Marylebone fields to the north of Soho, and poxy whores from Covent Garden. Soon hundreds of people are standing in the road, jostling for a front-row view, rowdily drinking gin or beer, warming their hands on makeshift bonfires, telling jokes to while away the time.

By now the long sash windows of Carlisle House blaze with the light of a thousand candles. Dozens of uniformed servants flit back and forth behind them, putting the final touches to the preparations taking place inside. One young maid in a mob-cap presses her face against a pane of glass and peers out at the scores of torches that are burning yellow holes in the black night. Like her fellow servants, she has been up since well before dawn, blacking grates, laying fires, washing glasses, endlessly fetching and carrying, polishing and scrubbing, beating and dusting. Her feet ache and her head throbs. She longs for her bed, but knows that she will not see it till some time tomorrow morning for her work has scarcely begun. And yet, despite her exhaustion, she cannot help but be touched by the feverish excitement that has now gripped every occupant of the house, from the cook having hysterics in the basement to their female employer, who is wound up as tight as a clock.

As the bells of nearby St Anne's Church strike ten, the first of a long line of sedan chairs turns out of Frith Street and into Soho Square. The mob lets out a great cry, and parts to let it through. The chairmen pick a careful path across the slippery dung-covered cobbles and stop outside Carlisle House to set down their burden. Out steps a well-known duke in a blue velvet dress coat with gilt-embroidered cuffs, a ruffled lace shirt and diamond buckles on his brocade shoes. A second sedan chair is set down beside him. Since tonight's entertainment is to be a masquerade, its occupant is in fancy dress, disguised as a chimney-sweep with a blacked-up face.

A carriage pulled by six white horses clatters into the square. King Henry VIII steps down from it, then Adam, dressed in a flesh-coloured silk suit decorated with fig-leaves. A mask of gilded leaves obscures the top half of his face, and the crowd, who have surged forward around him, demands in no uncertain terms, but good-naturedly, that he takes it off so they can see who he really is. Adam obliges, to a rousing cheer, and with a wave of his bejewelled hand he then disappears past two uniformed footmen, who flank the front door. Next to arrive is the Pope – or, rather, a well-known rake dressed as the Holy Father – and after him Hercules and, causing an uproar among the mob, a man in women's clothes.

Suddenly a torrent of sedan chairs and hackney carriages is pouring into Soho Square, coming at the mob so fast that they and their occupants are tossed about like stones on a riverbed. Soon the road is blocked by spectators, masqueraders, rearing horses and tipping carriage wheels, and the timid fear for their lives. One coach, bearing a coat-of-arms, forces its way through the mob to what is known as the Ladies' Entrance, which is at the side of Carlisle House, in Sutton Street. The crowd encircles it, their torches waving dangerously close to the carriage door, lighting up the two masked passengers: a Vestal Virgin, and a beautiful Bedlamite dressed in 'rags' of white silk embroidered with dia-monds. 'Take 'em off!' someone yells, so the women good-naturedly remove their masks as they step down. The Vestal Virgin, whose thin muslin dress hides few of her ample charms, is a viscountess, well known for her adventures. The Bedlamite is none other than a perfectly sane and popular royal princess, cousin to King George III.

The mob cheers as the two women enter Carlisle House. But as a female passenger steps down from the next carriage, people gasp and fall back in awe. They have never seen anything like this masquerader before, and probably never will again. For the lady is dressed as an 'Indian sultana' in bright gold thread and silk, and she is dripping with diamonds, rubies, emeralds and sapphires, £30,000-worth of them, the equivalent of £2.5m in twenty-first-century terms. Her conspicuous wealth is almost impossible to comprehend by most of the throng, who could live happily off the worth of just one of these stones for the rest of their lives. There is an uncomfortable moment as a current of envy ripples through the crowd. Then someone yells, 'Nicked the Crown Jewels, have you?', and there is nervous relief on all sides.

The sultana smiles and hurries inside. Far more precious to her than her jewels is her admission ticket to tonight's masquerade, which she now hands to a uniformed lackey who stands inside the Ladies' Entrance. She purchased this ticket last week from Lady Harrington for two guineas. A picture of a Greek goddess is engraved on the front of the dun-coloured paper along with the words 'Carlisle House', and on the back are written the words 'Ninth Meeting', for tonight's masquerade is the ninth meeting this season of the famous 'Society in Soho-square'.

Passing through a candle-lit passage, she enters a suite of inter-communicating reception rooms crammed with people. By now, the crowd in the house is eight hundred strong, and almost as rowdy as the mob in the street. In a heady cloud of sweat, bad breath, hair pomade and Acqua Mirabilis – the perfume of the age – they push their way through the candle-lit apartments, which open one off another like a series of exquisite Chinese boxes. And Chinese boxes they are indeed. The chairs, seats and sideboards have been made by the local furniture designer Mr Chippendale in the fashionable Oriental style. Chinese mirrors adorn every wall. Chinese carpets, as thick and springy as moss, cover the polished wooden floors.

At the back of the house is a huge banqueting hall. Wax from five hundred burning candles drips from the chandeliers suspended from its ceiling. Gilt and crystal candle brackets adorn walls draped in yellow satin to match the sofas and chairs. By ten o'clock there is not a seat to be had, even at the gaming tables in the side rooms. The revellers mill around the sideboards, picking at the exquisite food, drinking champagne and burgundy wine. They do not care three damns that they are hot and half deafened by the noise of their own voices. If they had wanted peace, quiet and open air, they would have stayed at home by a window or braved the pitted roads and highwaymen on the way to Vauxhall Gardens. They feel secure here, in this stuffy heat. They have the satisfaction of knowing that they are where they deserve to be: with their equals, among the *ton*, that most fashionable sector of society.

In loud, braying tones, they flirt and quip with as much wit as they can muster. They admire each other's costumes, and occasionally criticize. A veritable flock of shepherdesses has turned up tonight, and there are harlequins galore, and several Greek goddesses, and a richly dressed running footman with diamonds in his velvet cap, and a quack doctor, and a Highlander in a kilt. One infamous beauty is wearing a nun's habit cut very low at the front. Another is disguised as a hermaphrodite, dressed on the left side as a man and on the right as a woman. There is even a figure representing 'Nobody'.

But nobody is Nobody here in Carlisle House. Behind their masks the people are all very definitely Somebody. Most of the royal family are present somewhere among the crowd, along with half of the nobility in the kingdom. The Lord Mayor is here and so are many of the foreign ambassadors. The government has turned up in such force that the House of Commons adjourned early tonight, just so that the Members might go home and prepare for the ball. Yet the joy of a masquerade is that no one knows exactly who is dressed as what or which masquerader is who.

Among this sumptuously dressed élite, one figure is not in costume. She is a short, slightly plump woman whose thick arched eyebrows and full, upturned lips give her an air of amused surprise. Her head is covered in a mob-cap bedecked with lace and ribbons, from which escapes a single tendril of greying blonde hair. A double choker of pearls is looped around her neck. Her ruffled dress, while showing only a modest amount of cleavage, is both eye-catching and simplicity itself.

This woman is not young – if the truth were known, something she will never allow, she is forty-six years old – and neither is she very beautiful. But despite her strong nose, her worry lines and her slight double chin she is surprisingly pretty and carries herself with a great deal of confidence. Such is the force of her personality that both men and women turn to look at her as she passes among them, greeting them with curtsies or kisses, making them laugh, complimenting them on their costumes in her sing-song foreign accent, putting everyone at his ease.

Mesmerizing those she passes, she walks through the crowded rooms with a busy, proprietorial air. Even though all the guests are wearing masks, she appears to know each by name. They certainly know her. Tomorrow afternoon, when they meet for a late break-fast – the men in their clubs and coffee-houses, the ladies in their mansions or town-houses – they will gossip about her incessantly. But in truth they know little more about her than her name, and that she is a widow, though who her husband was remains to be seen. Born somewhere abroad, she was once an opera singer, and perhaps an actress too – and everyone knows what *that* means. It is rumoured that she once had a high-born lover. Some whisper that he was the king of France, others that he was a Prussian prince. Many people assume it was both.

Perhaps it is because of her steamy reputation that all the men of the *ton* have an itch to bed her. But few dare try their luck. Their wives are equally smitten by her. They wish to smother her in kisses, but end up lavishing them on her pretty daughter instead. She has a coterie of well-connected patronesses – all here tonight, without exception – who patronize her in every sense. She is their heroine and at the same time their plaything. They mistake her for their puppet, but in reality it is she who pulls their strings. Why, she even gets duchesses to sell tickets for her assemblies, as if they were glorified tradesmen! The duchesses do this because, however well married or high-born they may be, they secretly covet this woman's unique position. To them, she embodies the spirit of the Enlightened age.

This female free spirit is at once an object of desire and a mother hen fussing over her chicks. Whatever her guests want, she will make sure to provide it, whether it be a game of faro, a dish of tea or an intrigue. Everyone she talks to or smiles at feels better for the experience, for she has the knack of making each person on whom she turns her attention feel that they are the cleverest and wittiest person in the room.

And yet her attention is not with them. At the same time as she seems to be listening to what they are saying she is silently monitoring whether or not the flow of wine in the room is keeping up with the flow of conversation, or if there is need for more ventilation, or whether her thieving servants are performing all the tasks for which they are getting paid.

Towards midnight, she glances at a young man who hovers nearby, looking uncomfortable on the sidelines of the party. She nods at him and he pouts back. She raises a disapproving eyebrow and, without a word, without even a smile, the young man, her son, walks upstairs, enters a vast candle-lit ballroom almost ninety feet long and forty feet wide, and tells the musicians on a dais at the far end that it is time for them to strike up.

Drawn by the sound of a Haydn string quartet, the brilliant company swarms up the staircase in a crush of silk, perspiration, powder and lace, and pours into the ballroom. The dancing begins. To the annoyance of the neighbours, it will carry on until eight o'clock tomorrow morning. As to what will take place in the small anterooms, and in the bedrooms on the upper floors of the house, well, that is anyone's guess. And anyone's guess it will remain. Masquerade guarantees anonymity to everyone who desires it. When it comes to the private lives of her patrons, *la patronne* of Carlisle House is nothing if not discreet.

Her own life, however, is another matter. A mistress of the art of manipulating the media, she goes out of her way to keep herself in the public eye. If she so much as changes her wallpaper, she makes sure that London's *Public Advertiser* carries a full and favourable report of it. Unfortunately, the public's interest in her does not always stop there. Muckrakers plague her like lice. Her competitors have got it in for her. Her morals are frequently called into question, and her critics regularly publish letters in the newspapers denouncing what goes on in her house. Her extravagance has grown legendary in the capital. A swarm of creditors are forever dragging her before the courts.

No matter. What is important is that, after ten years in business, her masquerades, concerts and assemblies still draw in the right people night after night. That they are still a cut above the competition, far superior to anything at Almack's. That, at a time in life when most people are content to put up their feet on the fireside fender, she is still bursting with sex appeal and boundless energy and fresh ideas. This woman is unique. She is simply indefatigable. She is the extraordinary Mrs Teresa Cornelys, who rose from the back-streets of Venice to become the most famous impresario in London and the Circe of Soho Square.

One

A mantle of fog envelops the city of Venice. A cloud has swallowed the lagoon. The choppy waters of the Canale di San Marco are licking the walls of the Palazzo Ducale and overflowing into the wide, deserted Piazzetta. Leaning against a wall, a group of gondoliers chat to each other about the inclement weather and the subsequent lack of passengers, their voices as muffled as if they were talking into their hands. Half-a-dozen intrepid tourists gingerly pick their way across the flooded Piazza San Marco towards a café beneath one of the colonnades, their cloaks and skirts lifted high above their knees.

It is the afternoon of 24 November 1734. The grey sky that hangs so threateningly over the Republic of Venice darkens into a drizzly dusk, deepening the bruise-like gloom. The maze of narrow lanes and canals which spreads out from the Piazza, penetrating the city like veins flowing out from a human heart, echoes with plashing footsteps and the patter of rain. Water drips from the wooden roof terraces high above, and tumbles over the gutters of churches. It trickles down the peeling walls of dead-end alleyways, and gathers in muddy puddles on the ground.

Venice, which is usually so crowded with tourists, seems oddly deserted. One catches but the occasional glimpse of a shadowy figure on a distant bridge, or a cloaked back disappearing into a covered passage on the opposite side of a canal. But sounds of life drift down from the upper windows: the murmured conversation of two women; a baby's cry; the swish of a closing curtain; the clatter of a cooking pot as it is put on a fire. Neighbours' laughter. Lovers' sighs.

Night falls, transforming the dull canals into rivers of shiny ink. Candle flames flicker between the cracks of window shutters, glimmering in the darkness like a thousand early evening stars.

Flares and lanterns are lit outside the doorways, making the black water dance with their orange fire. Glass chandeliers illuminate the tall upper windows of the ancient *palazzi*. By their light one can see male valets brushing down velvet evening coats, and hairdressers weaving pearls through women's hair, and maids bustling through suites of stuccoed apartments, heavy brocade dresses weighing down their arms. Today is the Feast of St Catherine, and Venice's élite have just returned from spending the summer at their country villas. Helped by their servants, they are now dressing up for a night on the town.

On the right-hand bank of the Grand Canal, midway between the Rialto bridge and the Palazzo Ducale, stands the San Samuele theatre. Though it is not yet time for this evening's performance to begin, welcoming flares burn brightly on either side of its doors. Inside, the building smells of wood and lamp-oil, sweat and candle-grease, and there is a faint whiff of garlic coming from a half-eaten salami, which is nestling in a basket on a table on stage. Below a high Prussian blue ceiling sprinkled with painted golden stars, the theatre's tiers of wooden boxes and seats are as yet empty, but the stage seethes with activity. Huddled together in front of a backcloth of painted trees, three fiddlers tune their instruments. Two actors play out a mock-fight, thrusting at each other fiercely with wooden swords. A man and a woman rehearse a love-scene in loud, passionate voices, until their idyll is interrupted by the piercing wail of a baby crying out to be fed. A male dwarf wearing breeches and a leather jerkin delves into a costume basket in search of his hat. With her long scarf flying out behind her, a young dancer in a red dress swirls across the boards straight into the path of an acrobat walking on his hands.

Out in the auditorium, children play a boisterous game of hide-and-seek between the benches. Barking loudly at them, a small white dog with a brown eye-patch jumps between the rows of seats in the parterre, stops in front of the stage and lifts its legs. Breaking away from the game, one fair-haired young girl yells at it angrily, and shoos it away. Anna Maria Teresa Imer, the future Teresa Cornelys, is just eleven years old, but she already feels proprietorial about the San Samuele theatre. Her mother, Paolina, is an actress here, and her father, Giuseppe Imer, is the impresario. Although Paolina's main concern is her two daughters, the Genoese-born Giuseppe lives only for the stage. The San Samuele is one of four theatres in Venice owned by the powerful Grimani family – the others are San Giovanni Paulo, San Giovanni Christostomo and the San Bernadetta – and it is dedicated to musical comedy; thanks to Anna Maria Teresa's father, in the next few years it will become the most popular venue in the city for light-hearted *opera buffa*. As *capocomico*, or leader of the theatre's troupe of actors and musicians, Giuseppe is responsible for all aspects of running the company, from commissioning new dramas and musical scores to paying the wages, from designing the costumes and the elaborate scenery to directing, and occasionally writing, the operas and plays. Most of the money he takes in rent for the boxes goes straight to his landlord, Michele Grimani. Any profit he makes comes from charging a separate entrance fee for each performance, renting out seats in the stalls and running a gambling-room on the premises, which during the popular winter season are open seven days a week.

Giuseppe, Paolina and their two daughters live just round the corner from the theatre in the Corte del Duca Sforza, a small paved courtyard sandwiched between the narrow Calle della Commedia and the Grand Canal. Both Anna Maria Teresa and Marianna, her older sister, have inherited their father's talent for drama and music, and in time both will make their professional débuts on the San Samuele's boards. But although both girls will have international careers as opera singers, it is Anna Maria Teresa – or Teresa, as she is called for short – who is destined to follow in her father's footsteps and become a famous impresario. In time she will bring the spirit of Venice to London and, for a short while, become exceedingly famous and rich.

All this lies a long way off in a future Teresa can only dream of at the moment – and even in her wildest dreams she cannot begin to imagine the heights she will reach some day. She is still a child, just entering the awkward state between girlhood and womanhood. Her waist is thick, her chin verging on double. The voluptuous figure, which one day will make men unable to resist her, lies hidden beneath a covering of puppy fat, as does her pretty face. Though some of her friends may be better looking, Teresa has a bright glint in her eyes and a narcissistic streak to her nature that make men notice her first when she passes them in the street.

Teresa will never be a real beauty like Zanetta Casanova, the actress who now climbs on to the stage, sits down on the boards, raises her skirt almost to her knees and idly scratches her calf. Teresa's father follows two paces behind her, wearing a wistful smile. Despite his long marriage to Paolina, who is at this moment sitting in the stalls sewing ribbons on to a costume, Giuseppe has loved the widowed Zanetta for years, and he indulges his burning lust for her as often as he can. Teresa looks at her father staring at Zanetta's ankle as if he would eat it. She has often seen them snatching kisses in the corridors. Once she even came across them making love behind the stage. That she is jealous is understandable, for she loves her father with a passion as fierce as a blacksmith's fire.

This afternoon Giuseppe does not have time for Zanetta or, for that matter, for Teresa. In a matter of hours, a new play by a new writer is opening here at the San Samuele, and he alone is responsible for its success or failure. With difficulty he tears his eyes away from Zanetta's all-too-kissable ankle, claps his hands and, in a loud, resonant voice, calls for silence. The response is immediate. The fiddlers lay down their instruments, the children abandon their game, the duellers freeze mid-fight and even the baby stops wailing as the actress rehearsing the love scene picks him up and puts him to her breast. Giuseppe may look unprepossessing – he is short and stout and has no neck to speak of, a thick-set body and beady eyes – but his appearance belies his natural authority and boundless charisma. No wonder Teresa worships her father when he is clever and witty and eloquent, and possesses the voice, if not the face, of a romantic hero. As well as being a great actor, he is a brilliant impresario who loves musical comedy and has a nose for sniffing out new talent, coupled with the ability to nurture what he finds.

The author of the tragicomedy opening here tonight is Giuseppe's latest discovery. His name is Carlo Goldoni, and in the future he will become Italy's most loved and popular playwright. Goldoni met the impresario last summer in Verona, where the San Samuele company was performing at a theatre festival in the ruins of the Roman arena. Imer and his two leading actresses, Zanetta Casanova and Agrese Amurat, 'didn't know a word of music,' the young playwright noted, 'but all three had taste, a good ear and perfect execution'. Honoured to have the young author drop in unexpectedly on the performance, Giuseppe invited him to join them for supper the following night. The food he provided for Goldoni was splendid, and the company charming: the actors made up poems, danced and sang drinking songs. Afterwards, he persuaded Goldoni to give a reading from his as-yet-unperformed play *Belisario*. When he had finished, 'Imer took me by the hand in an authoritative manner and said Bravo,' Goldoni wrote in his memoirs. 'He begged me to accept a single room in the same house, next to his; and also to share his table while the company was in Verona. It was an offer I couldn't refuse.'

Goldoni spent the remainder of the summer in Verona with the actors, and Giuseppe commissioned him to write a short three-act musical interlude for them. Having observed that the impresario was clearly infatuated with his leading lady, Zanetta, Goldoni dashed off a three-hander called *La Pupilla*, based on their love affair. Giuseppe quickly realized where Goldoni's inspiration had come from, but as the playwright later explained, 'The interlude seemed so well crafted to him and the critique so honest and delicate that he forgave me the joke.'

At the end of the season, Giuseppe persuaded Goldoni to join his theatre company on a permanent basis. The two men travelled back to Venice on the same coach, and when they arrived Giuseppe insisted that Goldoni accompany him to his home. Here the playwright met Teresa, Marianna and Paolina. Since that night he has been lodging in their house. Tonight *Belisario* is opening at the San Samuele — it is the first of twelve Goldoni plays that will be premiered in Giuseppe's theatre during the next eleven years.

The cast gathers around the impresario in the otherwise empty auditorium, and he gives them a last-minute pep-talk. The play is brilliant, he tells them. It will be wildly successful and make them a fortune. If they follow Goldoni's words and his directions, and act with their hearts as well as their heads, the first performance is bound to go well.

Sitting on a bench in the front row of the parterre, her arms crossed over her budding breasts, her unruly fair hair tucked behind her ears and her tiny feet folded beneath her, Teresa hangs on her father's every word. Because she shares his passion for the theatre, the manner in which he talks to his troupe and the words with which he inspires them inspire her in turn. As he describes his vision of the play, how the disparate parts, the music, words and action, will come together into one magical whole, Teresa pictures it happening. When he wishes the players good luck and retires backstage to dress for his part, she follows him, close as a shadow. She loves to be near him, to observe him at work.

Half an hour before the performance is due to start, Teresa leaves his side, and runs to the theatre's small landing-stage on the Grand Canal to watch the richly dressed audience arrive in their gondolas. The men sport velvet coats, lace jabots and brocade breeches. Their waistcoats blaze with crystal buttons, their fingers flash with diamond rings. The women's breasts burst from their low-cut dresses like ripe peaches, and their necks are festooned with loops of fabulous pearls. Lapdogs yap at their heels and scrabble at the hems of their sumptuous skirts.

Inside the auditorium the boxes fill up, and the noise becomes deafening. Old and young, rich and poor, exotic foreigners and well-known Venetians, it seems as if the whole world is here at the theatre tonight, greeting their friends with kisses and laughter, shouting to each other from their seats, flirting gaily. To Teresa the audience seems as magical as the actors and actresses who are, at this moment, dressing up in their stage clothes. Everyone is infected with the excitement of the occasion. Only Goldoni looks anxious as he stands alone in the wings, biting his thumb. When it comes to drama, and in particular tragedy, the people of Venice are notoriously hard to please. They shout out raucous cat-calls during the dramatic scenes and fling candle-ends at the players if they are bored. In fact, they are far more interested in chatting to their friends, making new conquests or even making love behind the shutters of their boxes than in listening to the actors' words. 'The taste of these people for spectacle and music is shown more by their attendance than by any attention they pay to them,' writes the Frenchman Charles de Brosses, of the Venetian audiences. 'After the first scene, where there is moderate silence even in the parterre, it is not considered in good taste to pay attention to the stage except for the most interesting passages. The major boxes are well furnished and brightly lit. There one gambles, or more often simply sits in a circle and chats.' As her father's daughter, Teresa is used to this behaviour. The audience's chattering does not bother her because it does not bother him. What is important, Giuseppe tells her, is that people should enjoy themselves and leave his theatre happy. That way, they will be sure to return.

Tonight, however, something extraordinary happens. Almost as soon as the play begins, the audience grows strangely quiet. For the first time Teresa can remember, it is those on stage who win the battle of words. Soon the audience is watching and listening in a silence that is unprecedented in the theatre's history. And when the play ends everyone in the house, Teresa included, leaps to their feet and applauds. Called forward time and again by the deafening whistles, shouts and cheers of the audience, the actors and actresses take so many bows and curtsies that they are quite overcome, and end up in a flood of tears. In the future, Carlo Goldoni will attribute his success to his earthy language: 'My style wasn't elegant, my versification wasn't given at all to the sublime; but that was precisely what appealed to a public accustomed to hyperbole, antithesis and to the foolishness of gigantesque and romanticism.'

Delighted by the play, the audience spills out on to the landing-stage where their servants and gondoliers are waiting for them. Those without private boats walk off into the surrounding streets. Since the rain has stopped and the mist has lifted, Teresa leaves the theatre with them. Venice is her playground, and it is a city even more lively and fascinating at night than it is during the day. The squares, canals and bridges are brightly lit by flares and lanterns, and fashionable men and women 'of every kind' – aristocrats, labourers, middle-class couples, children, pimps, prostitutes, English lords and Spanish grandees – pour through them to the Piazza San Marco, the city's heart. Under the colonnades there, street musicians in gypsy clothes are putting on impromptu performances, and even though it is late at night the inns and cafés are packed. The shops and stalls under their tented umbrellas are still doing good business; many will stay open all night. Groups of revellers are picnicking everywhere – in boats moored alongside the Piazzetta, on benches beside the cathedral, and on the steps outside the Palazzo Ducale – in fact, anywhere they can find a place to sit down. The sound of laughter and song echoes across the glistening water. 'People sing in the squares, in the streets, and on the canals,' Goldoni writes later of his native city. 'Shopkeepers sing while selling their merchandise, workers sing while they work, gondoliers sing while they wait for their masters. The national characteristic is cheerfulness, and the heart of the Venetian language is the joke.'

Venice in the eighteenth century is a sublime but fading beauty, shimmering on the meniscus of a glittering lagoon. To understand its character is to understand Teresa, for the city is in her blood, and it will remain there throughout her life. In the distant past, Venice was a cruel and sinister creature of ruthless self-interest, secret spies and harsh summary punishments. Its citizens ignored Senate decrees at their peril. Suspected enemies of state were to be found in the morning buried head first in the paving stones or hung from columns in the Piazzetta as a warning to others, their teeth crushed, their hands cut off, their eyes gouged out. Poised on the very edge of Terra Firma, midway between West and East, the Republic of Venice had reigned over the Mediterranean for centuries, a law unto itself. At its peak it was a supreme international trader with its own system of government and its own special dialect – the 'sweet bastard Latin' to which Byron referred. Once upon a time its vast shipyard, the Arsenale, had sheltered the largest and most powerful fleet in the world.

But now Venice's power, like its dark past, is only a memory. Its monopoly over trade routes to the Orient was broken back in the fifteenth century, its navy has shrunk to a skeleton of its former self, and its population is in sharp decline. Those who remain are largely 'a commercial people who live solely for gain'. The once omnipotent Senate has become a mere puppet government, accepted by everyone as essential for the smooth running of the Republic, but in reality largely ignored. The ruling Council of Ten, still chosen from the thirty-odd patrician families whose names were inscribed centuries earlier in Venice's famous Golden Book, still meets at the Palazzo Ducale to issue decrees, but nowadays these are mainly concerned with frivolous matters such as banning the import of French silks and dresses or prohibiting the wearing of too many pearls, and no one takes any notice of them.

No longer a power to be reckoned with, Venice has become a fantasy world for the wealthy, complete with singing boatmen, daily street parades and residents who walk around in fancy dress and live in an almost perpetual state of celebration. As an inter-national tourist attraction, the city is without equal. Every winter it is invaded by tens of thousands of foreigners who come to see its sights and have sex with its famously licentious, famously beautiful women – and these include the actresses at the San Samuele. Venice's nickname, La Serenissima, comes from the word *sereno*, meaning light-hearted, cloudless, serene, and Venice is surely the most light-hearted place on earth. Now that it has no political purpose, the city can devote itself to doing what it does best: giving and receiving pleasure. La Serenissima has taken on the reputation its courtesans have had for at least two hundred years – of being a good-time girl.

Teresa Imer was born in Venice in 1723. She has grown up in a world in which giving pleasure is a vocation, a world where nothing is considered more worthwhile or rewarding than helping other people to enjoy themselves. '*Alla mattina una massetta, al dopo dinar una bassetta, alla sera una donnetta*' runs a local proverb – a little Mass in the morning, a little game of cards after lunch, a little woman in the evening – and for the rich and idle this is how life is lived in Venice every day. There is so much fun to be had, even by the plebeian classes, that it is no wonder that few people waste time

9

cooking: instead, they buy ready-made convenience meals from itinerant street-sellers and hoist them up to their windows in baskets tied to ropes. The Venetian show keeps on rolling twenty-four hours a day, and no one wants to miss a minute of it: 'Here they are getting dressed when the rest of the world are going to bed.' Days and nights are passed in a long round of café-hopping, socializing, boat-rides, picnics, gambling and theatre-going. The scantiest excuse is cause for a party, and Venice can party like nowhere else on earth.

No other city in the world has so many splendid fêtes, public entertainments and religious or secular ceremonies. Dominating them all is the mad free-for-all of the Carnival, which officially runs from the day after Christmas to Shrove Tuesday, but somehow manages to last for half the year. *Carnevale*, as it is called, brings wild masquerades, all-night balls and endless celebrations to every *calle*, *canale* and *campo*. Venetian life becomes a non-stop party. Concerts are given every night, in private homes as well as in the theatres. Fireworks split the sky. Mountebanks turn somersaults on makeshift stages in the Piazza. Wrestlers grapple with each other on the corners. Daredevils from the shipyard slide down ropes from the top of the 99-metre-high Campanile di San Marco, and acrobats pile twenty-seven-strong into flat-bottomed boats to perform the breath-taking Forze d'Ercole, clambering shoulder upon shoulder into a towering human pyramid.

During Carnival weeks, Teresa, like everyone else in the city, dresses up in the *bautta*, a white beak-nosed mask surmounted by a black hood and tricorne hat, paired with the *tabarro*, a long black cloak or domino, which ties at the neck and sweeps the ground. Rendered anonymous and sexless by this disguise, everyone from senators to servants, and from children to octogenarians, runs through the torch-lit streets and in and out of strangers' houses. All day long, and all night too, they have unprecedented licence to engage in conversation with whomsoever they wish, to enter any café or *palazzo* they choose, to stay out until dawn dancing the *monferrina* with total strangers, and to seduce or be seduced. Suppressed desires become possibilities during Carnival, subterfuge and deception are the accepted norm, and only reality is considered abnormal. For all Teresa knows, the masked whore she sees an English lord pick up on the Broglio in the early hours of the morning might be a married noblewoman out on the tiles, and the diamond-studded noblewoman she sees kissing a stranger in a dark doorway is as likely to be her own mother as a patrician's wife.

Teresa sees with her own eyes that, in love at least, women are men's equal. Emancipated from their formerly cloistered existence by their Carnival masks and by the disappearance of the once-fashionable high-heeled wooden clogs, which had made it virtually impossible for them to walk unaided, Venetian women of all classes now move freely about the city by day and night in practical flat shoes. They are honoured and respected. Their beauty is talked of throughout Europe. Men go into raptures over their slender necks, their heavy-lidded eyes and their long, carefully highlighted blonde hair. 'The women of Venice are beautiful, but more to the point, they are flirtatious.' Their reputation for liberated sexuality makes them irresistibly glamorous. With makeup and patches applied by their hairdressers, bedecked with pearls and colourful silks, they slip out of their houses either alone or in the company of a *cavaliere servente* or *cicisbeo*, a male companion, often a brother-in-law or family friend, approved of by their husband. No one knows where they go to all day long, or what they get up to, and no one seems to care very much.

There is, so the English traveller Lady Mary Wortley Montagu writes home, an atmosphere of 'universal liberty' abroad in La Serenissima: 'It is so much the established fashion for everybody to live their own way, that nothing is more ridiculous than censuring the actions of another.' About the only Venetian of either sex not free to do as he pleases is the ruling Doge, who is cloistered in his palace for much of the time, paraded through the streets like a wax effigy on State occasions and forced to pay for the privilege of being a prisoner of his exalted circumstances out of his own purse.

Intrigue flows in Venetians' veins. Giuseppe Imer is embroiled in a passionate love affair with Zanetta; and, like most actresses, his wife earns gold *zecchini* or sequins by sleeping with wealthy foreigners. The city's labyrinthine canals, covered passages and twisting lanes provide endless scope for secret meetings and snatched opportunities. Even the gondolas seem to have been purposely designed for conducting illicit love affairs. Who knows what goes on inside their dark, curtained cabins as the rich are ferried between their *palazzi* and their *casini*, the small sumptuous private apartments in which they can discreetly meet their lovers or pursue gambling, the one activity approached with anything like seriousness in Venice? In these private 'temples of luxury and love' and in the more palatial and public *ridotti*, from whose takings the State sensibly takes a cut, foreigners and Venetians of both sexes often pass the entire night playing card games such as faro and *faraone*, *bassetta* and *biribisso* – and, of course, making love.

In the early hours of the morning, those who have been up all night often gather together at L'Erberia, the fruit and vegetable market north of the Rialto bridge. As Giacomo Casanova will write later in his memoirs, they are shamelessly defiant, almost eager to be seen: 'It's as if they want everyone to know that they're not embarrassed to be spotted there. Flirting is out of the question because of the dishevelled state of their clothes. On the contrary, it seems that the women want to look the worse for wear so that people will talk about them. The men whose arms they lean on cultivate an air of worn-out boredom, and don't seem at all concerned that their companions' disarray is the obvious result of their conquest. Everyone at this gathering looks exhausted, and in need of sleep.'

'If a young man is wild, and must run after women and bad company, it is better this should be done abroad,' remarks the English writer Dr Johnson of the Grand Tour, which is so much in vogue in England during the eighteenth century. And with its lax moral atmosphere, gorgeous women and thousands of prostitutes plying what is facetiously called *l'onorato mestiere* – an honourable trade – La Serenissima is considered the perfect place for a young nobleman to sow his wild oats. No Grand Tour is considered complete without an audience with the ruling Doge, a moonlit gondola ride on the Grand Canal, and a dalliance with at least one Venetian *femme fatale*.

No wonder rich foreigners arrive here in such numbers. 'Here are inundations of them broke in upon us this carnival,' comments Lady Mary Wortley Montagu drily of the thousands of young English milords and their tutors who invade Teresa's city in the winter of 1739/40, 'and my apartment must be their refuge, the greater part of them having kept an inviolable fidelity to the languages their nurses taught them. Their whole business abroad (as far as I can perceive) being to buy new cloaths [sic], in which they shine in some obscure coffee-house, where they are sure of meeting only one another . . . I find the spirit of patriotism so strong in me every time I see them, that I look on them as the greatest blockheads in nature; and, to say truth, the compound of booby and petit mâitre makes up a very odd sort of animal.'

The English, in particular, throw golden sequins about as if they were raindrops. Consequently, the city welcomes them with open arms, clasps them to its seductive bosom – and then proceeds to fleece them left, right and centre, but in such a charming way that, far from being angry at being relieved of their money, they are pleased. For although it is as expensive as a high-class courtesan, La Serenissima always gives good value for money. A cup of coffee at one of the delightfully named cafés in the Piazza San Marco – the Queen of the Sea, the Matter of Fact, or Venice Triumphant (soon to be renamed Florian's after Floriano Francesco, its proprietor in the 1720s) – may cost an arm and a leg, but what visitors are purchasing is not merely a drink and the chance to hear a scratchily played violin solo, but a front-row seat to the greatest show on earth – a show that Teresa Imer will one day re-create in her house in London's Soho.

In the winter of 1734, Goldoni's *Belisario* played to packed houses at the San Samuele theatre for an unprecedented three weeks. After the fifth performance, Giuseppe Imer inserted a short interlude in the intermission: *La Pupilla*, the intermezzo Goldoni had written that summer based on Giuseppe and Zanetta's love affair. Appropriately, the actress was cast as the play's heroine.

Paolina doubtless knew about her husband's relationship with the beautiful widow. Given the lax moral climate of the time, she is unlikely to have cared. Soon she would retire from the stage to devote herself to her younger daughter's future, for it was clear from early on that Teresa was destined for a glittering theatrical career. By her seventeenth year she had blossomed into a ravishingly pretty young woman. With her high forehead, her imperious, slightly hooked nose, her thick arched eyebrows and her curvaceous figure, Teresa exuded sex appeal. Provocative, quick-witted, charming and flirtatious, she could already twist men round her little finger. Though she lived to the age of seventy-four, she would never lose this remarkably useful skill.

To top all this, Teresa was blessed with an angelic singing voice, which outshone that of her elder sister Marianna. This was a gift indeed, for Venetians were passionate about music and singing. Thanks to the relaxed moral atmosphere and the number of wealthy people living in the city, opera had flourished there for more than a hundred years. The Republic overflowed with local composers, who included Baldassare Galuppi, Giacomo Maccari, Salvatore Apolloni and Antonio Vivaldi, all of whom worked with Giuseppe at the San Samuele theatre.

Musical education was taken seriously, not just by theatre people but also by the State. Orphans and girls whose parents could not provide them with dowries were trained to play instruments at one of Venice's four orphanages: the Ospedale dei Mendicanti, the Derelitti, the Ospedale degli Incurabili, and, most famous of all, the Ospedale della Pietà, where the girls were taught by Vivaldi. A visit to one of their concerts was on every tourist itinerary. The exquisite music played by their all-female orchestras and choirs, who were often semi-concealed behind an iron grille, frequently sent male visitors into raptures. 'You know, I suppose, it is entirely of the feminine gender,' Londoner William Beckford wrote home, 'and that nothing is more common than to see a delicate white hand journeying across an enormous double bass, or a pair of roseate cheeks puffing, with all their efforts, at a French horn.'

So desirable was a place in one of the orphanages' orchestras that well-off parents sometimes faked poverty simply to get their children in. An engraved stone on the wall of the Pietà orphanage, placed there in 1548, cursed all parents 'who permit their sons and daughters – whether legitimate or natural – to be sent to this hospital of the Pietà, having means and ability to bring them up, for they will be obliged to pay back every expense and amount spent on them'.

The Imers were not rich people, but they were not poor enough for either of their daughters to qualify for a free musical education. If Teresa's mother was not to fail in her maternal duty, she needed to find a wealthy benefactor with an eye for pretty women to take an interest in Teresa's career. She did not have to go far to find him. The perfect victim for her plan, Senator Alvise Malipiero II, lived just one street away.

'Here are no old people in this country, neither in Dress nor Gallantry,' Lady Mary Wortley Montagu wrote home from Venice. However, in 1740, when Paolina hatched her plan to entrap him, Senator Malipiero was undeniably an old man. Aged seventy-six, he was almost a relic from a former century. His family was one of the most noble in the city: the name Malipiero had been inscribed in the Golden Book as far back as 1297; and two of Alvise's ancestors, Orio and Pasquale Malipiero, had served as doges, Orio in 1178, and Pasquale during the mid-fifteenth century.

Alvise Malipiero II had been a governor of the Republic for forty long years, but by the time Paolina set her sights on him he had lost interest in affairs of State. Dogged by ill-health, he spent much of his time at home. The Palazzo Malipiero was an ancient and heavily restored twelfth-century Byzantine building. It was situated on the Campo San Samuele, adjacent to the church where Teresa and her family worshipped and just across from the construction site that would soon become the Palazzo Grassi. Its ground floor contained a vaulted stone-flagged entrance, which led through to a boat-house and a large garden abutting the Grand Canal. A wide stone staircase swept upstairs to the main rooms, which, as in all Venetian palaces, were situated on the first floor or *piano nobile*. Here, in a suite of seven lofty chambers that led off a salon of truly magnificent proportions, Malipiero indulged his two remaining passions: good company and gourmet food. To the chagrin of his cook, he ate only once a day 'and always alone because since he no longer had any teeth he took twice as long to eat as anyone else would have done, and he neither wished to hurry himself in order to please his guests nor have them wait for him while he chewed his food with his hard gums'.

Although he had lost his teeth, Malipiero was still a good-looking man. He was also highly intelligent, sharp-witted and as well informed as ever. Every evening the Venetian cognoscenti flocked to visit him. As he held court to his friends from behind a long table in his enormous and imposing salon, no one who saw him sitting there would have guessed that he was almost paralysed: several times a year Malipiero was plagued by attacks of gout so severe that they left him crippled in every limb. Consequently, he seldom ventured into the outside world.

Despite his popularity, Malipiero had remained a bachelor all his life. This was an unusual state of affairs in Venice, where marriage was easily entered into and could be annulled almost as easily. Yet he loved women. He boasted that he had had twenty mistresses during his lifetime, and insisted that he had only stopped at that number when he realized the futility of trying to please yet another. But one more woman was waiting in the wings – or, rather, just a street away – and she would turn out to be his nemesis.

The Corte del Duca Sforza, where the Imers lived, backed directly on to Malipiero's garden, and from his bedroom the senator could see into their home. He could not fail to notice their luscious seventeen-year-old daughter, who was so often to be seen at an open window. Teresa's frequent appearances there were certainly not a matter of chance. Having made up her mind to arouse the old man's interest in her daughter, Paolina deliberately pushed her in his way.

Her plan involved more than displaying Teresa at the window. Every morning, she took the unwilling girl to the church of San Samuele to hear the local priest, Tosello, say Mass at the red marble altar. Immediately afterwards, she hauled her across the little square and rapped at the heavy iron knocker on Malipiero's side door. Before long, a servant would let the women in to the dark and chilly entrance floor. Without further ado, Paolina dragged Teresa upstairs to the salon where the senator sat conversing with a fifteen-year-old novice priest who had recently become his companion and *protégé*. In front of a bank of high windows overlooking the Grand Canal, and under the stern eyes of Malipiero's ancestors, whose portraits graced the stuccoed walls, Paolina would then proceed to torment the senator by pushing her daughter at him, while at the same time encouraging Teresa to deny him the kisses he craved.

Teresa had no choice but to do what her mother told her, and she did it with a panache that belied her tender years. At seventeen, she was already instinctively manipulative and well aware of her sexual powers. Overseen by Paolina, who at first always chaperoned her at these meetings, she now honed her seductive skills to perfection on the septuagenarian senator.

Malipiero's companion, the fifteen-year-old novice, watched these goings-on with amazement. One day, he would write what are perhaps the most famous memoirs ever produced, and vividly describe the senator's unrequited passion for Teresa:

She came to visit him nearly every day, but always accompanied by her mother, an old actress who had retired from the theatre for the good of her soul and who had, as one might have expected, formed a project to unite GOD with the devil. She took her daughter to Mass every day, she demanded that she take confession every Sunday: but in the afternoon she took her up to see the amorous old man, whose fury astonished me when the girl refused him a kiss on the grounds that, having made her devotions in the morning, she couldn't condescend to offend the same GOD whom she had eaten and might still have in her stomach. What a sight for me then aged fifteen, the only one who the old man allowed to be a silent witness to these scenes! The villainous mother applauded the resistance of her daughter, and dared to lecture the voluptuary, who in his turn didn't dare refute her maxims which were either too Christian or not at all so, and he had to resist the temptation of hurling anything he could lay his hands on at her. He didn't know what to say to her. His lust turned to anger; and after they left, he calmed himself down by having philosophical discussions with me.

From Paolina's point of view, her plan to ensnare Malipiero worked more effectively than she could have dreamed possible. Despite his decision to give up women, and with so many sophisticated beauties for him to choose from, he soon fell head over heels in lust with Teresa, a strong-willed adolescent who refused him a single kiss. Before long the old man was desperate to get his hands on her. He was in for a tantalizing but frustrating surprise. Though most people at that time regarded actresses – and by extension their children – as little better than prostitutes, here was a young woman who could not be bought at any price.

As a last resort, the confirmed bachelor offered to marry Teresa. This was a development neither she nor her parents could have predicted. Marriage to Malipiero would have secured her own financial position for ever, as well as that of her family. But while she had been quite willing to play along with Paolina's plan to get the old man to pay for her education, Teresa did not want him as a husband. Ancient, withered, crippled and toothless, Malipiero was not an attractive prospect as a sexual partner even though he was rich. The ancient grandness of his *palazzo* might well have oppressed Teresa. Time seemed to stand still under the looming high ceilings of the salon, while outside all was movement and light.

To Malipiero's astonishment – and, no doubt, her mother's horror – Teresa refused him, using as her excuse that his family would hate her if she married him. She was right: Venetian society was sexually liberated, but the class divisions were still strict: if a patrician were to marry beneath him – and marrying a girl from a theatrical family certainly qualified as that – his relations would be barred from future office and their name struck from the Golden Book.

The frustrated senator and the novice cleric spent hours discussing strategies for seducing Teresa, most of them unethical, as the youth later recorded:

'Offer her a huge sum of money, some sort of settlement.'

'From what she says, she wouldn't commit a mortal sin to become queen of the world.'

'You'll either have to rape her or throw her out and ban her from coming here.'

'I'm not capable of doing the former, and I can't bring myself to do the latter.'

'Kill her.'

'That's bound to happen, if I don't die first.'

'Your Excellency is to be pitied.'

Suspiciously, Malipiero asked the novice if he ever visited Teresa at her parents' home. He swore that he did not 'for I might fall in love with her, and if she acted towards me in the same way I've seen her do here, I'd be miserable'. Teresa was clearly a dangerous young woman to get entangled with. And despite his sensible words, the fifteen-year-old was attracted to her. Though he professed a resolution to steer clear of her, she was soon to prove his downfall in Malipiero's eyes.

Handsome, charming and highly intelligent, the youth would grow up to become one of the most important figures in Teresa's life, and perhaps the most famous Venetian of all time. Thanks to his posthumously published memoirs, *Histoire de Ma Vie*, his adventures and love affairs would be written about for centuries to come, and his surname – Casanova – would become an international byword for a seducer of women. It still is.

By the time Teresa became closely acquainted with fifteen-year-old Giacomo Casanova in the Palazzo Malipiero, his family had already been intimately linked with hers for at least sixteen years. His father, Gaetano Casanova, had run away as a young man from his home in Padua in pursuit of an actress, and had ended up in Venice where he had joined Imer's company. Soon he had fallen in love again, this time with Giovanna Maria, the sixteen-year-old daughter of local shoemakers Geronimo and Marzia Farussi. Since Gaetano had little hope of persuading the Farussis that an actor was suitable husband material for their beautiful daughter, the couple eloped and were secretly married on 27 February 1724 by the Patriarch of Venice. Marzia Farussi went hysterical when she found out about the wedding and Geronimo literally died of grief.

Soon after this controversial marriage, Giovanna Maria, or Zanetta as she was also called, joined the players at the San Samuele theatre company, where Giuseppe Imer was immediately attracted to her. Giacomo, the first child of her controversial thespian marriage, was born on 2 April 1725 in a house in the Calle della Commedia, a narrow lane that led from the theatre to the Palazzo Malipiero, and which was just round the corner from the Corte del Duca Sforza where the Imers lived.

Giacomo Casanova's start in life was inauspicious, for when he was just a year old his parents quit Venice for England, where the stunning Zanetta took to the boards using the stage name La Buranella. While in London she was rumoured to have had an affair with the Prince of Wales (later King George II), who might have been the father of her second child, Francesco. Left behind in the care of his widowed grandmother, little Giacomo grew into a sickly infant. The perplexed woman 'didn't know what to do with me,' he wrote later. 'I was weak, I had no appetite, I was incapable of concentrating on anything, and I looked like an imbecile.' He was also prone to terrible nosebleeds: his earliest memory was of being taken at the age of eight to see a witch on the nearby island of Murano; she attempted to cure him of this ailment by shutting him in a trunk and chanting incantations over him.

About this time, Casanova's parents returned to Venice and rejoined Imer's theatre. A number of months later, tragedy struck when thirty-six-year-old Gaetano developed what appears to have been a brain tumour and died within a matter of weeks. On his deathbed, he extracted two promises from those around him: the first from the Grimani brothers, who owned the theatre, that they would help protect his children; the second, from his wife Zanetta, that she would make sure none of their offspring ever went on the stage.

Thrust into the position of sole family breadwinner at the age of twenty-six, with four children to support and a fifth on the way, the widowed Zanetta devoted herself to her career. By now, as Goldoni saw in Verona, Giuseppe Imer was her adoring lover. But since Zanetta did not return her boss's feelings in equal measure, their affair, immortalized in the intermezzo *La Pupilla*, might have been one of necessity for her.

Meanwhile, still in poor health and having just lost his father, eight-year-old Giacomo Casanova was packed off to Padua for a change of air, which it was hoped would cure him of his many ailments, and boarded with a Slovenian woman for six gold sequins a month – an inadequate sum, as she said at the time. Six months later, half starved and in a state of extreme distress, he was rescued from her vermin-infested house by his grandmother, who arranged for him to be looked after by his schoolmaster, a kindly man named Abbé Gozzi. At last young Casanova's life took a distinct turn for the better. Under Gozzi's devoted care, his physical health recovered and he developed an insatiable intellectual curiosity. He studied chemistry, and became passionately interested in medicine. Later, he enrolled at the local university to study ecclesiastical law.

By the time Casanova returned to Venice in 1739, aged fifteen, the sickly child once thought to be an idiot had blossomed into a tall, handsome and highly intelligent youth. Marked out for a career in clerical law, he took his initial vows at the church of San Samuele on 17 February 1740. The priest there, Tosello, introduced him to his neighbour, Senator Malipiero, who was immediately seduced by the youth's charm and reasoning skills.

Casanova became a daily visitor at the Palazzo Malipiero. The senator thought so much of him that he allowed him to attend his sophisticated evening *salons*, even though the youth was only fifteen. Here, Casanova learned the social skills that were to stand him in good stead throughout his life – not least, the power of discretion, which he would one day use to his own advantage to manipulate Teresa.

What was the exact nature of Teresa's relationship with Senator Malipiero? Casanova's memoirs provide an eye-witness account of it. At first, Teresa was encouraged to torment the old man while her mother looked on. Later, she made her afternoon visit alone to the *palazzo*. When asked by a third party what the senator was up to with her, Casanova answered cagily that he was 'providing her with an education' – but what that education consisted of he did not say. Although it would later be rumoured that Teresa had been Malipiero's mistress, and had even lived with him, according to Casanova she lived at home. It seems that her uncanny ability to manipulate to her own advantage the men who loved her enabled Teresa to string Malipiero along indefinitely. That did not stop him regarding her as his, and his alone.

To his chagrin, she had many other admirers, including a local doctor named Leonardo Doro. The senator was so jealous of Doro that he made Teresa promise never to receive him. But Teresa was an independent spirit, who did not like being cornered. And, as one of her later lovers would find out to his cost, promises she made under duress were broken, more often than not. Her promise to Malipiero not to see Doro alone was the first such, as Casanova discovered one afternoon when he needed the senator to grant a favour to one of his own female friends.

Realizing that the best way to work on Malipiero was to approach him through Teresa, 'who could pull off anything to the satisfaction of the old man, who was still in love with her', Casanova decided to go and see her at home. Hoping to catch her off-guard, he turned up unexpectedly at the Corte del Duca Sforza and walked unannounced into her bedroom. To his delight, Leonardo Doro was with her. Deeply embarrassed to be found there, Doro pretended that he was visiting Teresa on a professional call. In a flustered manner he took her pulse, wrote out a prescription, then quickly scurried away.

The compromising situation was more than Casanova could have hoped for, and since he was even more manipulative than Teresa, he took full advantage of it: 'Teresa . . . must have been annoyed that I'd caught her breaking her word to the old man,' he wrote in his memoirs. 'She must also have feared my indiscretion. This was the moment when I could hope to get everything that I wanted from her.' Knowing that under these circumstances she could refuse him nothing, he asked Teresa to intervene with the senator on his own friend's behalf, and she promised to do her utmost to help him, even at the expense of another woman for whom she had already agreed to put in a good word. Within days, the favour Casanova had asked for was granted; and his silence about Doro's visit to Teresa's bedroom was guaranteed.

But where Teresa and Casanova's feelings for each other were concerned, discretion and good sense were soon to desert them. Day in, day out, month after month, the two youngsters were thrown together in an atmosphere of heightened sexuality with only the elderly senator for company, and it is not surprising that these circumstances drew them together. As Teresa played on Malipiero's desire for her, in turn pouting provocatively, flirting, and at the same time denying him the sexual fulfilment he craved, she also cast her spell over Casanova. Although he never openly flirted with her, he found her irresistibly attractive. And she returned his feelings. The young cleric's full, sensuous lips, his clear, intelligent eyes and his swarthy, muscular body were all in stark contrast to those of the gnarled and toothless senator who was forever pleading with Teresa to kiss him.

In addition to the desire they felt for one another, the two young people had much in common. Under other circumstances, they would have been a perfect match. They were close neighbours and came from a similar theatrical background. Their families knew each other – intimately so, in the case of Zanetta and Giuseppe. As time would show, both Teresa and Casanova were adventurous spirits, and both were magnetically charming, attractive and easy to talk to: though Casanova's reputation is as a ruthless seducer, he genuinely liked women and took an interest in their life-stories. He seduced them through his conversation, and very seldom used force.

The mutual desire was there. What Teresa and Casanova lacked was the opportunity to express their feelings. This finally came after lunch at the *palazzo* one day, when the senator hobbled out of his great salon into the adjoining bedroom to take a siesta, as was his custom. He had not left Teresa and Casanova totally by themselves:

with them was a girl called La Gardela, a twelve-year-old gondolier's daughter and dance student whom Malipiero had taken on as his third *protégée*, perhaps to provide Teresa with a female chaperone.

After a while, La Gardela went off to her dancing lesson. At long last Casanova and Teresa were alone. They did not waste any time in beginning a dangerous game of mutual exploration. As he delicately phrased it in his memoirs, 'Being seated close to one another at a small table, our backs turned towards the door of the bedroom where we supposed our benefactor was asleep, in the innocent gaiety of our nature we were overcome with the desire to explore the differences between our bodies.'

Neither of them realized that the jealous senator had set them up. Unknown to them, he was watching them from his chamber. The more passionate their game became, the angrier he grew. When he could stand it no longer, he picked up his walking-stick and hobbled furiously back into the salon, but by this time Teresa and Casanova were so engrossed in each other that they did not even notice he was there. Malipiero lifted up his stick and attacked. As Casanova put it, 'We were at the most interesting part of our examination when a violent blow from a cane fell on my neck, followed by another, which would have been followed by more, if I hadn't very rapidly escaped from the hail by making for the door.'

Casanova ran home leaving Teresa to deal with Malipiero, forgetting in his haste to take his hat and coat. A quarter of an hour later, these two articles of clothing were ignominiously returned to his house by a servant. With them came a note from the senator's housekeeper, warning him not to dare set foot in the Palazzo Malipiero again. His formative relationship with the senator was over.

Left alone to face the music, Teresa went on the defensive. As she later told Casanova, Malipiero did not dare to reproach her about her behaviour. He was too frightened of losing her to mention what he had seen. Though he never talked to Casanova again, he continued to want Teresa to come to his *palazzo* every day.

Their game of cat-and-mouse continued, but now there was no handsome youth to liven up Teresa's long dull afternoons. While the outcast novice continued his clerical studies at the St Cyprien seminary, out of sight if not out of mind, she threw herself back into her musical studies. But neither she nor Casanova ever forgot what had happened between them. The nature of their friendship had changed for ever. Their next encounter would change the course of Teresa's life.

Two

Teresa made her professional solo singing début at the San Samuele theatre on 2 May 1742. It was Ascension Day, by far the most important festival in the Venetian calendar, the occasion when the famous ducal ship, the *Bucintoro*, was brought out from its berth in the Arsenale, towed to the Piazzetta, then decorated with red silk banners, sumptuous sofas and some sixty thousand sequins' worth of gold. From here, the huge, ungainly and unseaworthy craft, some thirty-five metres long and seven metres wide, was rowed precariously across the flower-strewn lagoon by its crew of 168 oarsmen with every dignitary in Venice crammed on board. When it reached the church of San Nicola del Lido, the Doge came out on deck and cast a gold ring into the water, in commemoration of the occasion in 1177 when Pope Alexander III had granted the powerful maritime Republic of Venice the right to 'marry' the sea.

To celebrate the festival, and to mark the début of his talented, bewitchingly attractive younger daughter, Giuseppe Imer commissioned a new opera from a twenty-eight-year-old composer based in Milan. Once again, the impresario had chosen his *protégé* well. In a few years' time, Christoph Willibald Gluck would become the man of the moment in serious music circles, and a leading light in the 'Reform Opera' movement, whose aim was to make musical scores subservient to the drama. As he wrote in 1769, in the preface to his opera *Alceste*, Gluck strove 'to restrict music to its true office of serving poetry by means of expression and by following the situations of a story without interrupting the actions or stifling it with a useless superfluity of ornaments'.

Gluck's musical ambitions might have been high-flown, but his origins were simple. The son of a Bohemian forester, he had shown a precocious musical talent as a young boy. But unlike Teresa, who was lucky enough to have been born into a theatrical family, his ambition to pursue a career in music had not met with encouragement at home. On the contrary, eager that his son take up a sensible trade, like forestry, his father had done his best to thwart him. After years of bitter arguments, Gluck left home, found part-time employment as a church organist in Prague and worked his way through university.

At the age of twenty, Gluck moved to Vienna, where he came to the attention of a Milanese aristocrat named Antonio Melzi. When Melzi offered him a job as a chamber musician in his house in Milan, Gluck accepted. For an aspiring opera composer, Italy was *the* place to be at the time. The country produced Europe's finest composers, sopranos and castratos. Vocal chamber music in the forms of aria and recitative had been popular there since the mid-seventeenth century, and the two forms of opera – *opera buffa*, a light-hearted genre born out of the *commedia dell'arte* theatre, and the more serious *opera seria*, which was usually based on classical stories and legends – were flourishing, particularly in Naples and Venice, where the first opera house had been built back in 1637.

In Milan, Gluck came into his own. He played the violin in Melzi's private orchestra and studied composition and counterpoint with local composer Giovanni Sammartini. In 1741 he wrote his first opera, *Artaserse*, which received its premiere at Milan's Teatro Regio Ducale on 26 December that year. Set to a libretto by the Vienna-based librettist Pietro Metastasio, whose happy endings and lively dialogue were always immensely popular with Italian audiences, the opera was a huge success and made Gluck's name.

Always on the lookout for new talent for the San Samuele, Giuseppe Imer lost no time in commissioning the up-and-coming composer to write an opera for Teresa's début. Like *Artaserse*, *Demetrio* (or *Cleonice*, as it was later named) was set to a libretto by Metastasio. Like most of Gluck's early opera scores, the music was charming and melodic, with only a few glimpses of the great dramatic arias that would one day make him such a revolutionary figure in opera. Teresa's strong, pure soprano singing voice and dramatic manner of acting were perfectly suited to his music. According to Casanova, she shone in her role as Barsene.

In what turned out to be a clever career move, Teresa developed a close working relationship with the Bohemian composer. Over the next five years she would work with him in London, Hamburg, Denmark, Vienna and Padua, where in 1743, the year following her début, she performed in his third opera, *Demofoonte*. Whenever they worked together, Gluck made sure that Teresa was given the best roles in his operas, arousing speculation that they were more than friends.

If Senator Malipiero's jealousy was aroused by Teresa's friendship with the young composer, he could do nothing about it. By 1742 he would have had to come to terms with the fact that it was impossible to stop her doing what she wanted. She had metamorphosed from a wilful adolescent into a self-willed and ambitious young woman, and, at seventy-eight, the gout-ridden senator was at last feeling his age. He could not hope to hold on to his young love for ever.

By now, Teresa had already met the man who was to become her first husband. On paper, Angelo Francesco Pompeati sounded like the ideal match for her, a synthesis of the three men who had so far been important in her life. Like Casanova, he was a Venetian. Like Malipiero, he was older than Teresa: his date of birth is variously recorded as 1701 and 1711 – but with only ten, or at most twenty, years between them, this time the age-gap was less extreme. Although his father was a surgeon, Angelo's career was in the theatre. Like Giuseppe Imer, he had many talents, as a ballet dancer, a choreographer and a scenery designer.

In 1739, Angelo was appointed Master of the Venetian Ballet. For the next five years he worked mainly at the Teatro Sant'Angelo, choreographing works such as the Vivaldi opera *Feraspe*. Five years later, he joined the exodus of composers, musicians, artists and singers who left Italy during the eighteenth century to further their careers elsewhere in Europe, when he accepted a post at the Habsburg court in Vienna.

In 1745 Senator Malipiero died. That same year, Teresa joined Angelo in Vienna, where they were married in the grand setting of St Stephan's Cathedral. Signora Pompeati, as she now was, took up a post as a court singer, the first step to establishing her international career.

In Venice, Teresa had learned that women were men's equals in matters of love. In Vienna she saw that they could govern a country and wage war, too. Maria Theresa – the mother of Marie Antoinette – had been Empress of Austria since 1740, when her father, Emperor Karl VI, had died without male issue, ceding his patrimonial lands to her. Since then, her country had been plunged into a war of succession that would not end until 1763. However, the young Empress was clever enough to withstand the pressure. A strong yet gracious woman, with a naturally regal air, she dominated her husband, Franz Stephan of Lorraine, and tenaciously clung to her heritage through two long wars against Frederick the Great of Prussia and his allies in Bavaria, Saxony, France and Spain.

Despite the almost constant state of war, Maria Theresa's court offered huge opportunities to ambitious foreign artists, musicians, singers and thespians. Vienna's streets might have echoed with the rattle of gun carriages, but it was also a thriving artistic centre, particularly for opera. Since 1730 it had been the home of the Italian poet Pietro Metastasio, the librettist of Gluck's *Demetrio* and one of the most popular and prolific librettists of the age (one of his librettos was set to seventy different scores).

Angelo Pompeati would remain in Vienna for the rest of his life, and become a famous ballet director and set designer at its theatres. Teresa, however, chose to leave as soon as she could. Snowy, urban and landlocked, the city was as different from Venice as a place could be. Although the Empress was an inspiration, life at her court was formal, upright and deeply moral, quite the opposite of how it had been in the light-hearted, amoral Serenissima, and the antithesis of Teresa's own nature.

Teresa's marriage might have been a love-match, but even so she was prepared to abandon it at a moment's notice to further her career. Within months of her wedding she was talent-spotted by a visiting librettist named Francesco Vanneschi, who invited her to join Gluck and Teresa's sister Marianna in a season at one of the most prestigious opera houses in Europe: the King's Theatre in

London's Haymarket. It was the opportunity of a lifetime, the chance for Teresa to make her name as a soprano on a far bigger stage than any in Austria, and she had no intention of turning it down. Like any self-respecting would-be diva, she dropped all of her commitments, including her new husband, and travelled to England immediately.

The London Teresa arrived in during the final months of 1745 was as different from the snowy streets of baroque Vienna as they had been from the watery lanes of Venice. It was 'the wonder city' of the eighteenth century – a vast, overcrowded metropolis that, like some gangly and unruly adolescent, was in the middle of unprecedented development. By contemporary standards the sheer number of its inhabitants was mind-boggling: the city's population stood at 575,000 in 1700, and by 1801 it had reached 900,000. The medieval streets had been completely rebuilt since 1666 when the Great Fire had ravaged four hundred acres of the old City, destroying eighty-seven churches and more than 13,000 homes. Consequently, almost every building was now less than a hundred years old, and London had a thoroughly modern appearance. The houses were no longer built of wood but of brick, overhanging eaves had been banned as a fire risk, many streets had flagstone pavements and the skyline was dominated by the dome of Sir Christopher Wren's magnificent St Paul's Cathedral.

Although thousands of tradesmen and merchants still lived in the shadow of this state-of-the-art cathedral, the *beau monde* had long since decamped from the City to the smart new terraces, wide roads and paved squares of St James's, Mayfair and Soho. The West End, as these new suburban districts of London were collectively known, was thronged with carriages, sedan chairs, horses, smoke-filled inns, crowded coffee-shops, dogs, sheep, cows and people of every class. The clatter of thousands of metal-rimmed wheels and iron-shod hoofs against the cobbled road surfaces, the cries of hundreds of street-sellers and the angry shouts of the chairmen warning pedestrians to get out of their way clashed in a cacophony more discordant than forty orchestras tuning up at once.

With modernity had come pollution. London's roads were thick with horse manure and, since few of the new houses had drains, servants still emptied their employers' chamber-pots out of the upper windows on to the heads of those passing by (as they occasionally did even in late-Victorian London). Sea-coal, burned in every domestic fireplace and factory furnace, produced 'a cloud which envelops London like a cloak', and the pall hung over the capital during every season, darkening the sky and creating an effect of an 'eight-month winter'. Soot hung in the air and stopped the sun shining. Soot blackened the pavements and clung to the horses and cattle in the streets. Soot was ingrained in people's skin and clothing. The houses were coated with it, and had to be washed almost every day. This only exacerbated the problem, for the resulting damp inside the buildings necessitated the lighting of yet more domestic fires, even during the summer, which made the smog worse.

Still, to twenty-three-year-old Teresa, London exuded excitement. From the moment the first housemaid rose before dawn and set to work on her hands and knees scrubbing the front steps until the time her master and mistress went to bed, the city pulsed like a fevered body. Its inhabitants swarmed through the streets shouting imperiously and rudely at one another, brawling or, in the case of the street-sellers, crying out their wares. To a foreigner used to the more sedate life of small European cities it seemed as if Londoners seldom stopped moving, except to sup at one of the hundreds of crowded inns or taverns, to pause inside one of the city's 21,000-odd retail outlets, or to lie slumped in a doorway, dead drunk on gin.

That London's rich and poor lived cheek by jowl, precariously balanced on opposite ends of the financial spectrum, made for a volatile atmosphere. Violence was commonplace, street crime was rife. Every day the capital's newspapers reported the most recent muggings: a washerwoman's girl knocked over and robbed of her parcel of clean laundry in Fenchurch Street; a Wapping merchant attacked by footpads near Tower Hill; a man who had his rings ripped off his hands in a back lane of Westminster; an officer in the Excise department who was set upon by a violent gang of thieves in Stepney. The threat of being hanged from the triple gallows at

Tyburn did nothing to quell the rising swell of crime fuelled by poverty and class resentment. London's rich were stinking rich and, despite handouts from the parish churches, London's poor were desperate. They lived in teeming slums and could afford neither food nor basic clothing. Their children frequently died of exposure and starvation in the bustling shopping streets.

Despite London's crime and the high cost of living, Teresa quickly picked up the scent of opportunity in the smog-filled air. The city was a Mecca for foreign artists, musicians and performers. The dangerous streets through which the nobility were ferried in their hired hackney carriages, sedan chairs and private coaches were said to be paved with gold. As the German composer Johann Mattheson had written earlier in the century, 'He who in the present time wants to make a profit out of music betakes himself to England.' The upper classes had plenty of time on their hands, and plenty of money to help them enjoy it. With their bulging pockets, impeccable taste and seemingly insatiable hunger for diversion, they consumed culture with the same relish with which they gorged on fine roast beef.

Londoners' tastes were broad, but they favoured the Continental. For almost forty years, the reins of the city's cultural life had been held by the notoriously ugly Swiss impresario, Johann Jakob Heidegger, who had made a fortune from arranging concerts and private parties for the court and aristocracy. By 1711 Heidegger had become assistant manager of the Queen's (later known as the King's) Theatre in the Haymarket, the only theatre in the city allowed to put on opera (a special licence to produce it was granted to the theatre on an annual basis by the Lord Chamberlain). In 1719 Heidegger had also founded an operatic business venture, the Royal Academy of Music, in partnership with the London-based German court composer, Georg Friedrich Handel.

From 1729 onwards, Handel had joined Heidegger in running the King's Theatre. For a while opera had flourished there. But not everyone had approved of the Swiss impresario's hegemony over London's social and cultural life. The fabulous masquerades he had given in the opera house during the 1720s had earned him the disapproval of the Church and the reputation as England's 'principal promoter of vice and immorality'. This had not, however, stopped George II from appointing Heidegger as his Master of the Revels, responsible for all theatrical entertainment at court.

By November 1745, when Teresa arrived in England, the 'Swiss Count whose Earldom lies in the Land of the Moon', as one contemporary critic described Heidegger, was seventy-nine years old and living in semi-retirement; the musical life of the capital had deteriorated badly. According to the contemporary musicologist Dr Charles Burney, Italian opera, once all the vogue, had become 'a tawdry, expensive and meretricious lady . . . accustomed to high keeping . . . now reduced to a very humble state, and unable to support her former extravagance'. In short, it was unfashionable, unpopular and as exorbitantly expensive to stage as it is today.

Since Heidegger's retreat from public life to his house in Maids-of-Honour Row in the Thames-side town of Richmond, Handel had spent a fortune on trying to keep the King's Theatre going, and he had lost most of it. *Hercules*, an English opera he put on during the 1744/5 season, had been a disaster for lack of decent singers, and his own *Belshazzar*, staged during the spring of '45, had been equally unsuccessful. Ill and in debt, he too had abandoned the opera house, which that autumn had been taken over by an English aristocrat, Charles Sackville, Lord Middlesex.

Middlesex was determined to revive the popularity of Italian opera in England, and he quickly dispatched his partner, the librettist Francesco Vanneschi, to Europe to put together a new opera company. Vanneschi's first priority was to recruit Gluck as the company's new musical director. This was a coup, for by now Gluck was the rising star of the European music scene. Since writing *Demetrio* for Giuseppe Imer, he had produced four full-length operas: *Demofoonte*, in which Teresa had performed at the Teatro Obizzi in Padua; *Il Tigrane*, which opened in the Lombard city of Crema in 1743; *La Sofonisba*, premiered the following year at Milan's Teatro Regio Ducale; and *Ipermestra*, which opened at the Grimani-owned Teatro San Giovanni Cristostomo in Venice in November 1744. Gluck, it seemed, did not come alone but as part of a package: one can reasonably presume that it was he who insisted to Vanneschi that Teresa and her sister Marianna Imer were included in the deal. The sisters were to join a star cast that included at least two other Italian singers already established in London: castrato Angelo Maria Monticelli, who had been *primo uomo* in London since 1741, and the popular soprano Giulia Frasi.

Teresa sailed into London between November and December 1745 with high hopes of success in her heart and the opera house's new musical director in her pocket. If she was to gain the celebrity status of an international soprano, this was surely her best opportunity. To an ambitious woman such as she was, working at the King's Theatre sounded too good to be true.

It was. Fate was not to be with Teresa on her first visit to London. The winter of 1745/6 was a terrible time to be a foreigner, a Roman Catholic or an Italian opera singer in London. To be all three was simply asking for trouble. A Jacobite rebellion led by Charles Edward Stuart, otherwise known as Bonnie Prince Charlie, was raging in the north of England, and consequently prejudice against Roman Catholics, foreigners and foreign art forms was running high. Staging Italian opera in London was considered at best an unpatriotic activity and at worst potentially treasonable.

Even Lord Middlesex anticipated trouble when his theatre reopened its doors. With that in mind, he commissioned Gluck and Vanneschi to write a blatantly pro-Hanoverian, anti-Jacobite opera designed not only to appease public opinion but also to butter up the Lord Chamberlain, who was in charge of granting the theatre's annual licence. The title of this opera said it all: *La Caduta dei Giganti – la ribellione punita*, The Fall of the Giants – the rebellion crushed. The story, which was based on the mythical tale of Jupiter's victory over the rebellious giants Titan and Briareus, was a thinly disguised allegory of the Jacobite rebellion. 'The Giants having rebell'd, in order to dethrone Jupiter, in the Skies, and deprive the other Gods of their Freedom,' read the programme notes in the bilingual libretto. 'Whilst they are piling Mountain upon Mountain, Jupiter darts Thunder from Olympus, and takes due vengeance on their daring Attempt; by bringing them under the ruins of the

Mountains they had raised. Juno's Jealousy, and Jupiter's Amour with Iris, are introduced merely as Episodes.' Billed as Signora Pompeati, Teresa was to play the romantic heroine Iris, while her sister Marianna, who was singing under the name Signora Imer, was to play Juno. And, in a rather odd piece of casting, the soprano Giulia Frasi, usually known for her sweet singing voice, was given the role of the multi-armed, multi-headed male giant, Briareus.

Rehearsals began in December, and at first it looked as if fate had decided to play into Lord Middlesex's hands. Up on the Scottish border, Bonnie Prince Charlie's pro-Catholic forces were in disarray. A garrison of the rebels holding Carlisle Castle was besieged by the Duke of Cumberland, George II's second son, and when they surrendered to him just before the New Year, the troops were sent for transportation and their officers were hanged. While the Young Pretender retreated north into the Highlands to muster his forces for a fresh attack on the British monarchy, Cumberland – whose harsh treatment of the rebels after the battle of Culloden would earn him the nickname 'Butcher' – headed for London in high spirits, the blood of those he had killed still fresh on his hands. News of his victory was universally celebrated. King George ordered that a banquet be prepared in honour of the return of his heroic son. And in case anyone doubted that the dull, dour, Protestant Hanoverians were there to stay, on New Year's Day 1746 two army deserters were publicly flogged on the parade-ground behind St James's Palace.

Despite the Hanoverian victory, which would be mirrored on stage in La Caduta dei Giganti's plot, the members of the new 'Middlesex' opera company still approached the premiere on 18 January 'with fear and trembling'. As Gluck later told Dr Charles Burney, this was 'not only on account of the few friends he had in England, but from an apprehension of Riot and popular fury, at the opening of the theatre, in which none but foreigners and papists were employ'd'.

Teresa looked on with great interest as, leaving nothing to chance, Lord Middlesex launched an advertising and propaganda campaign in the columns of London's newspapers. In the future she would use exactly the same method to publicize her own business. 'HAYMARKET. At the King's Theatre in the Haymarket, on Tuesday Next, will be perform'd a MUSICAL DRAMA, in Two Parts, call'd LA CADUTA DE' GIGANTI, The Fall of the Giants. With DANCES and other Decorations Entirely New' read the first advertisement in the *Daily Advertiser*. Next, a rash of letters mysteriously appeared in the correspondence columns extolling the virtues of *La Caduta* and stressing the patriotism of the management and performers at the opera house. One read:

A Splendid Drama is prepared in Honour of his Majesty, of the Nation, and of our Arms. The sincere Attachment of the managers of the Opera to the present happy Establishment (spite of the very idle Suggestions of Malice) being well known; not to mention that the Performers were born among our Friends and Allies, and not amidst our Enemies as some have falsely insinuated.

As Teresa saw for herself, Middlesex's publicity campaign worked brilliantly. There were no public riots or demonstrations outside the King's Theatre on opening night. In fact, the Duke of Cumberland himself turned up to watch his recent victory over the Stuart rebels symbolically re-enacted on stage by the Italian opera singers. His arrival caused a furore among the audience of wealthy businessmen and titled aristocrats. As she waited in the wings, Teresa heard them cheer their hero's arrival. Then she stepped on stage and made her London début with this aria:

> *Veritiera, o Giove,*
> *Non mendace è la fama,*
> *Evvi chi ardisce*
> *Aspirare al tuo foglio . . .*

> Dread, Imperial Jove! True are the rumours
> Lo, some power audacious
> Fir'd by ambition
> To thy throne aspires

Like the audacious powers of which she sang, Teresa had aspirations of her own that evening. After her successes in Italy and, to a lesser extent, in Vienna, she had perhaps presumed that the London audience, like those elsewhere, would fall into the palm of her hand. However, despite the Duke of Cumberland's presence and Vanneschi's jingoistic plot-line, *La Caduta dei Giganti* was a resounding failure. Although the aristocratic audience had turned up in great numbers, reluctant to miss what was, above all else, a social event, they applauded the dancers more than they did the singers. Gluck's music was not to their taste, and Teresa herself was accused of having a 'masculine and violent manner of singing' in which 'few female symptoms were perceptible'. 'The Performance was received and carried on with great Attention, Tranquillity, and Applause; and not a little enliven'd by the Presence of his Royal Highness the Duke of Cumberland,' stated a review in the *Daily Advertiser* the following morning, thereby damning the show with faint praise.

Teresa's hopes of becoming the overnight toast of London were dashed. And when *La Caduta dei Giganti* folded after only six performances, so were Gluck's. 'You have taken too much trouble over your opera,' Handel remarked shortly, a few weeks later, when the Bohemian composer solicited his opinion. 'Here in England that is a mere waste of time. What the English like is something they can beat time to, something that hits them straight on the eardrum.' Later, at a fund-raising 'benefit' concert on 25 March in aid of 'decay'd Musicians and their Families' in which both composers participated, Handel was overheard remarking in broken English to the actress Mrs Cibber, 'Gluck knows no more of contrapunto than mein cook.'

Wherever Gluck was, Teresa was sure to be close by. During the first half of this benefit concert, she sang an aria from Galuppi's *Il Trionfo della Continenza*, and after the interval she performed an extract from the ill-fated *La Caduta dei Giganti*. While the season at the King's Theatre limped on with performances of *Il Trionfo*, *Alessandro in Indie*, *Antigone* and, on 15 March, the premiere of Gluck's *Artemene*, she did her best to stay in the public eye, performing not only in the operas but whenever and wherever else she could. On 21 April, she sang at another benefit concert at Mr Hickford's Great Rooms, a popular concert venue in Brewer Street, Soho. This time the object of the fund-raising concert was Gluck himself. Two days later Teresa was on stage again, at the Little Theatre in the Haymarket, a small building across the road from the King's Theatre. On this occasion, 'to satisfy the Curious as well as all Lovers of Musick', Gluck performed his party piece, a 'concerto' played on the glass harmonium – twenty-six glasses filled with water.

Europe's most revolutionary opera composer was being reduced to gimmicks to attract attention. And, as the future would prove, the Little Theatre was never a lucky venue for Teresa to play. For the moment it was her person, rather than her voice, that was keeping her in the public eye. Seducing singers was a popular sport for male members of the nobility, almost on a par with bagging the pheasants on their country estates. Provocatively pretty, voluptuously sexy, and desperate to make a name for herself, twenty-three-year-old Teresa was ripe for seduction. Above all else, she was Venetian – and this alone made her irresistible to the English.

La Signora Pompeati would have had to have been strait-laced indeed to have closed her eyes to the opportunities and temptations that presented themselves to her in London. As it was, flirtation was in her blood. The years she had spent keeping Senator Malipiero at arm's length had made her a past mistress at manipulating wealthy men to get what she wanted from them, and she was not averse to using people when she had to.

As Casanova had already learned to his cost, Teresa had a healthy sexual appetite. During her six months' stay in London she had at least one liaison, and possibly many more. Yet in the end she did not profit from it – in fact, quite the opposite: by the end of March, she was pregnant. This effectively put an end to any plans she might have had to stay on in London and make her career there. The thought of bringing up a child alone in a country where she had not immediately succeeded, a country moreover where foreigners were hated and whose language she did not speak, was not an enticing, or even viable, prospect. Humiliated at having failed to make a name for herself, and pregnant by an unknown man, Teresa had little choice but to return to Vienna, and Angelo, when the King's Theatre closed its doors in June for the long summer break.

Three

Teresa had been born into the theatre. Her first child was practically born on stage. On the night of 8 December 1746 she went into labour as she made her way to Vienna's Ballhaus. Since she was about to take part in a gala performance of *Alessandro in Indie*, the timing could not have been more inconvenient. The opera was being staged at the behest of the Empress, who had subsidized the production to the tune of two hundred ducats so that the tickets could be given away free. Count Joseph Khevenhüller-Metsch, her chief master of ceremonies, had high expectations of the evening and was on hand to welcome the court to the concert hall, which was packed with visitors and local dignitaries.

Like the true professional she was, Teresa went on stage and performed. But as her contractions grew more frequent and painful, it became impossible for her to hide what was going on. Once the audience realized what was happening, the performance disintegrated. 'The production was so terrible (apparently the singer Pompeati was overcome as she made her way to the opera house) that I was thoroughly embarrassed on account of the many strangers present,' Count Khevenhüller-Metsch scribbled in his diary late that night. 'But once confusion and a spirit of pettiness has taken hold there is little one can do but to acknowledge it and keep quiet.'

Teresa's son was born late that night. Named Giuseppe after his maternal grandfather, he was given the surname Pompeati and grew up thinking he was Angelo's child. Yet his so-called father never acknowledged him as his own: he did not mention him in his will and when he died in 1768 he left his entire estate – '2572 florins and good clothes' – to his brother.

Throughout her life Teresa remained the quintessential dedicated career woman for whom work always took precedence over motherhood. This was clear even on the night Giuseppe was born. She was far less interested in looking after children than in furthering her prospects. Giuseppe seemed to suffer from this more than her other children, perhaps because his birth trapped her in a role to which she was patently unsuited. Her future, which had seemed so promising just a year earlier, now looked like being hampered by the demands of an infant she did not want or know how to cope with, an infant whose existence must have been a source of marital strife. Had Giuseppe been born in Venice, her family would have helped her to take care of him. Stuck in Vienna, Teresa was isolated, and aware that what should have been the most important years for building her reputation were drifting by without much progress.

It was not until the spring of 1748, when Christoph Gluck arrived in the city to compose a score for Metastasio's new libretto, *Semiramide riconosciuta*, that opportunity flowered again for Teresa. Almost two years had passed since she had last worked with Gluck at the unsuccessful season at the King's Theatre in London, and he had spent part of this time travelling through northern Europe with a well-known troupe of touring singers and musicians. The Mingotti Travelling Italian Opera Company, as it was called, was in reality two separate outfits run by two Venetian brothers. While foreign tourists flocked to Italy to absorb its music and culture, Pietro and Angelo Mingotti travelled in the opposite direction, exporting high-quality *opera buffa* and *opera seria* to the courts of northern Europe. Of the two impresarios, Pietro was the most successful. In the 1730s he had won concessions to perform in Dresden, Brno and Graz, where he was instrumental in building the town's first theatre. Back in Dresden again in 1747, he had been joined for a season by Gluck, whose opera, *Le Nozze d'Ercole e d'Ebe*, was premiered at Pillnitz Castle on 19 June to celebrate a double wedding between the royal houses of Saxony and Hanover.

The following winter, Pietro's company, again with Gluck on board, had been the first Italian opera group allowed into Denmark by the newly crowned Frederick V, who had recently revoked the ban on Italian music imposed by his sternly religious predecessor Christian VI. So successful had this visit been that the company's music director, Paolo Scalabrini, had been invited to stay on in Denmark as court *Kapellmeister*, and Pietro had been asked to return to Copenhagen the following winter, with Gluck taking on Scalabrini's old role.

On 14 May, *Semiramide riconosciuta* was premiered at Vienna's newly reconstructed Burgtheater. The performance was 'exalted to the stars thanks to the excellence of the company and the magnificence of the decoration', according to its librettist, Metastasio, who refused to give any credit to what he called Gluck's 'ultra-barbaric and intolerable music'. The Bohemian composer's increasingly ground-breaking scores were not to everyone's taste, but his sudden reappearance in Teresa's life heralded a change for the better in her fortunes. Aside from any personal rapport she had with Gluck, working with him offered her the best chance of making a name for herself. So when he offered her the opportunity of going on tour with him and Pietro Mingotti, she naturally took it.

The peripatetic artistic life might have sounded exciting when Gluck had told Teresa about it in the relative comfort of Vienna but, as she was to discover, the reality could be gruelling. Days on end were spent travelling from city to city in cramped, unheated coaches, which jolted precariously over dangerously pitted roads. When it rained, the roads became mudbound. When it snowed, they turned to treacherous ice. Accommodation in the coaching inns and lodging-houses was expensive, uncomfortable and chilly, and even when the company performed in royal palaces or the mansions of the wealthy, there was no relief from the finger-numbing, all-pervading cold. Living expenses on tour often outweighed the wages that musicians and singers were paid. And, as the Mozart family would later discover, entertainers were frequently kept hanging around without work or payment for days or even weeks on end by court officials and aristocrats, who had no conception of the practical problems facing travelling musicians, and who would not have cared less if they had.

Because it was so successful, the Pietro Mingotti company attracted a high calibre of singers. That season, as well as Teresa, they included Christopher d'Hager, Francesco Werner, Maria Masi,

Antonio Casati, Giustina Turcotti, Gaspera Beccheroni and Marianna Pirker. With so many would-be divas competing with each other for star parts and the financial favours of their audiences, tempers within the close circle soon became frayed.

Thanks to her close working relationship with the company's new music director, Teresa quickly became the focus for jealousy. This was not helped by her being given the glamorous romantic roles, such as Princess Rosmiri in Domenico Natale's *Arsace*, which the company staged in Hamburg that September. 'This past week the opera of Arsace was performed here with the greatest approval of all connoisseurs,' a local newspaper reported ecstatically on 3 October, 'and we gladly confess never to have seen so excellent a company assembled, four of the most glorious voices in the whole of Italy being met here almost side by side.' One of these was named as 'Madame Pompeati, from London'. By the end of the month, when the company performed Francesco Gasparini's *Bajazet*, Teresa had already become so famous in Hamburg that she was singled out in Mingotti's newspaper announcements. 'This will be the last appearance by Madame Pompeati,' Pietro wrote of the performance, which was due to take place on 4 November. 'We therefore hope the auditorium will be well attended.'

If she lacked self-confidence as a newcomer among her more mature fellow singers, Teresa hid it well under a veneer of pushiness. Combined with her close relationship to Gluck, this infuriated her fellow soprano Marianna Pirker. To complicate the internal politics of the company further, Gluck was soon embroiled in a passionate affair with Gaspera Beccheroni, who was still being kept by her previous lover, a wealthy English diplomat named John Wyche.

With discontent, discord and lust simmering, the company prepared to leave Hamburg for Denmark in the second half of November. Teresa was aware that the Danish court would offer her another good stab at fame: its queen, twenty-three-year-old Louisa Hanover, was the youngest daughter of King George II of England and the sister of the Duke of Cumberland, before whom Teresa had sung in London two years previously. Determined to make the most of this slim connection, and to make a good impression,

Teresa prepared for the trip by commissioning a short work in honour of the queen's approaching twenty-fourth birthday.

But her attempt to get herself noticed looked like being thwarted. The company were to travel to Copenhagen in two groups, and while Teresa remained behind in Germany for a few days with half of the company, Pietro Mingotti set sail for Copenhagen with the rest, including Christopher d'Hager and Marianna Pirker. They arrived on 22 November to find the Danish court in a state of agitation over Queen Louisa's advanced pregnancy. Since her marriage to Frederick V five years earlier, she had given birth to three children: two girls, who had survived, and a boy, who had died at the age of two. Consequently, everyone was now hoping that the child she was currently expecting would be a male heir.

Eager to get in as many performances as possible before the imminent royal confinement, Pietro Mingotti immediately began rehearsals of *Bajazet*. By the time Teresa arrived in Copenhagen two days later with the rest of the company, chilled to the bone after a dreadful sea crossing, she found that her own role in the opera had been severely cut. Never one to sit on her feelings, she made sure that everyone knew how aggrieved she felt. In a letter to her husband Franz, a violinist who was at the time based in London, Marianna Pirker jealously referred to her voluptuous rival as 'the fat one' and noted that Teresa's 'nose is out of joint because she isn't in the opera at the beginning'.

By 3 December, the two sopranos had made an uneasy peace, perhaps because Marianna had turned her malevolent spirit against Gaspera Beccheroni, from whom Gluck had contracted a venereal disease (it was probably syphilis, and might have been the cause of his infertility). 'We are good friends again, the fat one and I,' Marianna wrote to Franz. 'At least that's how she's acting. It serves that sow [Beccheroni] right, because she's ruined poor Gluck; if Waiz [Wyche] knew about it he'd stop the 100 marks he's giving her every month. It would be good if he did find out about it, but absolutely not from us, so be careful what you say, although I'd like to get my own back. Poor Gluck.'

'Don't worry about Gluck's illness,' Franz replied from London, a few weeks later. 'No one here knows about it and I don't gossip with anyone. About Pompeati, [Gluck's] partiality won't help her much, since from what you write about her and what Abacco and Giaccomozzi say, her singing isn't at all threatening, because she has a voice like a grasshopper. And everyone compares her to Holzbaurin, and she also sings like a grasshopper.' (Holzbaurin was the soprano Rosalia Holzbaurin, Abacco was Joseph-Marie-Clément dall'Abaco, a Flemish composer then based in London.)

This was pure jealousy on Pirker's part. Teresa did not sing like a grasshopper: her voice was strong, but pure and sweet. Even Casanova, who heard her sing many times and was in all other matters her sternest critic, described Teresa's voice as 'angelic'. Determined to make her mark at the Danish court, Signora Pompeati began rehearsing the opera she had commissioned in honour of the queen's birthday, which fell on 18 December. But when the Mingotti company was called to the palace to serenade the queen that day, Marianna Pirker was given the honour of singing first. Even so, the German soprano was still dissatisfied with her reception: 'I've received nothing from the Royal household,' she complained afterwards to Franz. 'The difference between this year [and last] is like night and day, there are too many of us . . . Masi and Pompeati sang at the royal table as well as the castrato [Antonio Casati]. Hager played the violin.'

With no sign of the queen going into labour, the court moved to the Charlottenborg Palace at the beginning of January 1749. To liven up the Scandinavian winter of almost perpetual darkness, the opera season was extended well into the new year. On 29 January, Teresa sang Semira in Metastasio's *Artaserse*. On the same day, Queen Louisa gave birth to a healthy male heir, Prince Christian.

The attention she had received during her season with the Mingotti company had somewhat turned Teresa's head but, even so, she could never have anticipated on the day of the Hereditary Prince's birth that when he inherited the throne he would pay her court in her own London home. What preoccupied her at that moment was the size of her salary. Like many a diva since, she wanted a raise. Since few cash handouts or valuable presents were given away by the Danish monarchy, Teresa approached the court *Kapellmeister*, Scalabrini, at the end of February and demanded a fee of six hundred ducats, perhaps for her services as a singer to the Danish court. To her surprise, he would not agree to her terms. A battle of wills ensued in which Teresa used all the skills of manipulation she had learned in Venice in an attempt to get what she wanted. For once, it was to no avail. Scalabrini proved as stubborn as she was.

Finally, Teresa threatened to walk out, hoping that this would force him to cave in to her demands. Instead he called her bluff. Rather than back down, she packed her bags and set sail for Germany, even though she had no job to go to. This was not the last time in her life that she acted in a self-destructive manner rather than lose her pride.

One person was pleased to see the back of her. 'Now, thank God, Pompeati has left,' Marianna Pirker wrote to her husband on 15 March. 'I've never come across such a scheming and conniving woman in all my life. I wouldn't have believed it, but she couldn't get round Scalabrini. She's off to Hamburg to skin Kopp alive and will come to some agreement with Scalabrini from there.' But no such agreement was ever reached. Teresa's rift with Scalabrini and Pietro Mingotti was final. Having failed to establish herself as a leading soprano in Denmark, just as she had failed in London, she was now forced to return empty-handed to her husband in Vienna.

Professional recognition continued to elude her for another two years. When it finally came, it would be in the far-flung Prussian outpost of Bayreuth where she went in 1751 with Angelo and Giuseppe. Then, as Casanova later commented drily, 'her good luck was not entirely due to her talent; her charms had much more to do with it'. As well as the success she so desperately craved, she found two other things in the city: a fabulously wealthy and indulgent lover, and a female role model who would stand her in good stead for the rest of her life.

The city of Bayreuth had grown up around a castle on the banks of the Roter river between the forested mountains of the

Fichtelgebirge plateau and the Franconian Jura. For many years it was a quiet provincial backwater of the Prussian empire but after 1735, when twenty-four-year-old Friedrich von Hohenzollern of Brandenburg-Bayreuth succeeded as the ruling margrave, the city changed. Affable as Friedrich was – he liked to ride bare-headed through the streets smiling at his subjects, and was only known to have resorted to violence once, when he lashed out at a servant who took the liberty of trying on his new Parisian hat – the about-turn in his province's fortunes owed less to him than to his extraordinary wife. Wilhelmine Friederike Sophie, Margravine of Brandenburg-Bayreuth, was the daughter of Frederick I of Prussia and the sister of the future Frederick the Great, to whom she remained close throughout her life. Blessed with charm, beauty and brains – the Enlightenment writer Voltaire was her friend and correspondent for many years – Wilhelmine also possessed considerable artistic talent. Not only was she an accomplished writer, a portrait painter and a garden designer with a great feel for architecture, she was also a first-class composer, librettist and musician. 'My great joy has always been study, music, and, above all, the delights of society,' Wilhelmine wrote, in her posthumously published memoirs. Exiled to the dull streets of Bayreuth from the busy artistic and social milieu of Berlin, a woman of lesser gifts might have suffocated in the parochial atmosphere. Not so Wilhelmine. Just as Princess Grace would one day inject glamour and culture into the provincial principality of twentieth-century Monaco, so Wilhelmine determined to bring refined living and the Enlightenment arts to eighteenth-century Bayreuth.

The pleasure-loving Friedrich supported his remarkable wife's efforts to turn his city into a cultural centre to rival Paris. The parsimony that had typified his father's court was replaced by a policy of free spending, and the couple's castle soon began to resemble a mini-Versailles, with twin establishments for husband and wife and hundreds of staff to cater to their every whim. His father would have turned in his grave at the money the young couple lavished on themselves, on parties for their many guests, and on the arts: in 1750, Friedrich even set up a court shipping department in the landlocked city, the sole responsibility of which was to control a toy naval fleet on the Brandenburger lake.

Composers, singers, musicians and painters flocked to work for Friedrich and Wilhelmine, attracted partly by the hope of their generous patronage and partly by the margravine's close relationship with her brother, who in 1740 succeeded their father as King Frederick II of Prussia. Commerce, the arts and learning flourished. Between founding a university in the small town of Erlangen and starting the first female Freemasonry group (it was named the Mopsas, after her toy dog), the tireless Wilhelmine also found time to build a new palace and create the now-famous Hermitage gardens, pavilions and grottoes.

The margravine's crowning achievement was to build a state-of-the-art opera house of such sophistication that in the nineteenth century it would attract composer Richard Wagner to the city and, even today, make Bayreuth synonymous with the annual festival of his work still held there. The relatively restrained exterior of the Markgräfliches Opernhaus hid an explosion of rococo decoration designed by the famous Italian theatre designer Giuseppe Galli-Bibiena and his son Carlo. White and gold caryatids and cherubs, ornate gilding and a ceiling fresco depicting Apollo and the Nine Muses fought for attention with three tiers of boxes, each one reserved for a separate social class. Carved from wood painted to resemble gold and marble, Bibiena's auditorium possessed exceptionally good acoustics and contained a huge proscenium stage equipped with the latest scene-changing machinery.

Having taken three years to build, the new opera house was inaugurated in September 1748 to celebrate the marriage of Wilhelmine's only daughter, Elisabeth, to the Duke of Württemberg (the unhappy bride left her husband a few years later, having had more than enough of his infidelities). To staff the new theatre, the margrave's Deputy Grand Chamberlain, a Frenchman named Theodore Camille, Marquis de Montpernis, set up a huge permanent opera company under court *Kapellmeister* Johan Pfeiffer. This consisted of twenty-seven German musicians, ninety ballet dancers and thirty-two French actors and actresses. Topping the bill were nine Italian singing stars. By the time Angelo and Teresa joined the company, he as a dancer and she as a soloist, these stars included Giustina Turcotti and Antonio Casati, her erstwhile colleagues from the Mingotti Opera Company.

In Vienna, Teresa had learned that a woman could govern a country and win battles. In Bayreuth, she saw that a woman could set herself up as a cultural leader, and take a proactive role in influencing the taste of an entire city, albeit a tiny one. Intelligent, musical, charming and able, the margravine became Teresa's mentor. But that did not stop her seducing the margravine's husband. By 1751 Wilhelmine was a virtual invalid, who spent much of her time in bed. This left the genial, generous Friedrich footloose. Although she was now a twenty-eight-year-old mother approaching what would then have been considered middle age, Teresa was still as pretty and sexually attractive as she had always been. If anything, her enhanced self-confidence made her even more so. Despite the presence of his wife and her own tolerant husband, she lost no time in captivating the margrave. And she did not stop there. While the besotted Friedrich plied her with expensive lace, fabulous diamonds and the sumptuous low-cut dresses that were the local fashion at the time, she made yet another useful conquest: her and Angelo's immediate boss at the opera house, the Marquis de Montpernis, who was also the margravine's close friend.

Teresa's power was now formidable. With the margrave and de Montpernis at her feet, and the margravine in thrall to her singing talent, she had everything she could have wanted: money, position, adoration and work. Although her situation was undeniably risky, she juggled her husband and her two lovers with an adept duplicity that did not falter when, in the early summer of 1752, she discovered she was pregnant again. Who the baby's father was, even she could not have said, but she probably persuaded the margrave that the child was his.

Teresa's first daughter was born in Bayreuth on 15 February 1753. With extraordinary cheek, she named the baby Wilhelmine Friederike after the margravine, and enlisted her to be the baby's godmother. If Wilhelmine knew of her husband's liaison with her favourite soprano, she kept quiet about it: at the time of the baby's birth, the royal couple were preoccupied with far more important matters. They had nowhere to live. Three weeks earlier, on the night of 26 January, Friedrich had left his private apartments in the new palace, locking the doors behind him. The sentries standing guard outside had soon smelt burning and noticed smoke creeping out from under the door, but when they told the margrave about it, he had been mysteriously reluctant to unlock the apartments and allow them to investigate. By the time he had done so, what had started out as a small fire had caught hold of the palace and there was little anyone could do to put it out.

With lightning speed, the conflagration engulfed the entire building. Fire-pumps and hoses were brought out from the store rooms, but they proved useless: there was such a bitter frost that night that the water had frozen solid. As flames licked the ceiling rafters of the castle, the bedridden margravine was dramatically carried to safety through the burning rooms and taken to the Marquis de Montpernis's house. Outside the building, all was chaos. Instead of rushing to help save the building, the citizens of Bayreuth fled in fear, leaving the soldiers and the musicians and singers employed at the opera house to try to rescue what little they could. In a frantic attempt to save the furniture, they flung chairs, tables, paintings and even mirrors from the windows, only to see them smash to smithereens on the ground.

The inferno raged for twenty-four hours. When it eventually died down all that was left of the palace was a single octagonal tower and a mound of smouldering charred timbers, melted silver and shattered glass. The margravine believed that the fire had been started deliberately and she was heartbroken. 'We are utterly ruined,' she wrote to her brother. 'I have saved my dog, my jewels, and some books, but I do not know what I have kept, or what I have lost. The margrave has saved nothing from his rooms. The whole castle is in ruins, only one wing has been spared, otherwise the whole town would have been destroyed. I am in some house, and don't know where to find shelter, nor where to go to.'

It was not only the royal couple who had been made homeless

by the fire, but the entire court including the heavily pregnant Teresa. With nowhere to live, the opera house closed and her adoring lover the margrave fully occupied with rebuilding his palace, there was little to keep her in Bayreuth. It was the ideal time to pay a visit to her parents in Venice. As soon as she had recovered from Wilhelmine's birth, Teresa packed up the dresses and jewels that the margrave had given her and, leaving Pompeati behind, set off for Italy with her baby daughter and eight-year-old Giuseppe.

Four

Teresa returned to Italy triumphantly toting her fine clothes and jewels, with her son and baby daughter in tow. Watched, she suspected, by the margrave's spies, she relaxed in her old home in the Corte del Duca Sforza while Giuseppe ran free through the streets of Venice as she had done as a child. Much had changed since she had last been in the city. Malipiero was dead, and his palace was no longer open to her. The old San Samuele theatre had been destroyed by fire in 1747, and although it had been rebuilt it was now under new management. Giuseppe Imer had moved to Venice's San Giovanni Christostomo theatre, and Carlo Goldoni had defected to the Sant'Angelo.

For the most part, life in the Republic continued at the same timeless pace it always had. But Teresa had changed. No longer a young *ingénue*, she was a wife, the mother of two children and a soprano of international standing. She was also a sophisticated *femme fatale* whom few men could resist. At the age of thirty, far from feeling that her attractions were fading, Teresa was more self-confident than ever. Perhaps she was over-confident. The experience of successfully juggling her husband and two lovers in Bayreuth might have led her to believe that she could behave exactly as she liked without suffering any adverse consequences.

One evening towards the end of May, a servant delivered a note to the Imers' house. It was from Signora Manzoni, a notary's wife who lived just across the courtyard, begging Teresa to visit her immediately. Fifteen minutes later, taking Giuseppe with her, Teresa crossed over the Corte del Duca Sforza and climbed Signora Manzoni's stairs. She found her sitting with a tall, richly dressed, handsome man. To Signora Manzoni's delight, Teresa did a double-take. He was Giacomo Casanova.

Casanova was no longer the tonsured novice fresh out of university whom Teresa remembered with such fondness from her teenage days. He had changed even more than she had. Since he had left Venice in 1742, a fully fledged doctor of civil and canon law, his adventures had taken him to the Venetian possession of Corfu in the service of Giacomo da Riva, the Governor of the Galleys, then to Calabria, where his mother's influence helped secure him the position as secretary to the Bishop of Martirano, and later to Constantinople and later Rome, where he was employed by Cardinal Aquaviva, the Spanish ambassador to the Holy See. Disgraced after being an unwilling accessory in the attempted elopement of his French teacher's daughter, Casanova eventually abandoned his religious order. By the time he returned to Venice in 1746 he was penniless. Giuseppe Imer took pity on him, and gave him a job as a fiddler at the San Samuele.

On the night of 20 April that year, Casanova had an extraordinary stroke of luck, which completely altered his future. On his way home after playing his fiddle at a wedding, he came to the aid of a wealthy Venetian senator, Matteo Bragadin, who had just suffered a stroke. Convinced that the young fiddler had saved his life, Bragadin invited Casanova to his home. Impressed by his apparent knowledge of 'cabalistic oracle' into which he claimed to have been initiated, the senator subsequently adopted Casanova as his son.

For the next three years, Casanova was nominally employed by Signora Manzoni's husband as a lawyer. In reality he lived the life of a footloose young nobleman, thanks to a generous allowance from Bragadin, gambling, seducing women and getting into scrapes. He also indulged his love of the occult: he was initiated into a Freemasonry lodge and joined the mystical quasi-religious Rosicrucian order, under whose influence he claimed later to have studied the art of alchemy.

In 1750, after a big win on the lottery, Casanova took himself to Paris where he spent two years absorbing the formal manners of the French court. By the time he returned to Venice again, in May 1753, he was a true man of the world: well travelled, confident, sophisticated, and dressed, like Teresa, in fine clothes and jewels, which seemed to signal that he was now as successful and well-off as she appeared to be.

What had not changed was the spark between them. 'Our surprise in seeing one another was equal to the pleasure we had in recalling what happened to us when we were growing up,' Casanova wrote in his memoirs of meeting Teresa again that evening. 'I congratulated her on her good fortune, and she presumed that she must do the same, judging by my appearance; but her good fortune would have been much more solid than mine if this woman had subsequently behaved more prudently. She had much stronger whims than I did, as the reader will see five years from now.'

For two hours Teresa and Casanova sat together, discussing old times they had shared in the Palazzo Malipiero. Teresa told her friend of her adventures since leaving Venice, 'passing over, as one might have expected, those that her pride did not permit her to recount'. No doubt Casanova was just as selective in what he chose to say about his own exploits. Later Teresa returned home, having offered Casanova the use of her box at the opera that evening and invited him to lunch with her the following day. The margrave was having her watched, she confided, 'but being an old friend I would not be suspected of anything. That's the aphorism of all flirtatious women.'

Impatient to see her, Casanova arrived very early at the Imers' house the following morning. He found Teresa lying in bed with Giuseppe, who 'by precept of his education got up as soon as he saw me sitting at his mother's feet'. Obviously, the boy was used to his mother receiving lovers in her bed. Once he had left the room, Teresa and Casanova fell upon each other. They had waited ten years to consummate what they had begun so long ago at the Palazzo Malipiero, and this time there was no elderly senator to interrupt them. 'I spent three hours with her,' Casanova reminisced, somewhat wistfully, 'of which the last was the most important.'

During the fortnight Teresa stayed in Venice, she and Casanova made love on at least one other occasion. When they finally parted, he promised to visit her when she returned to Bayreuth. But he never arrived. Back in the Prussian outpost, Teresa resumed her duplicitous life with the margrave, de Montpernis and Angelo. Before long she realized she was pregnant again. For once she had no doubt of whose child she was carrying: she knew it was Casanova's.

The margrave could not have been pleased at his mistress's second pregnancy, but such was Teresa's sexual hold over him that he did not throw her out. Sophia Wilhelmine, usually called Sophie, Casanova's daughter, was born some time between December 1753 and February 1754. Since her baptism does not appear in Bayreuth's records, one must presume that, anxious to keep the date of her birth a secret from the margrave, Teresa left the city for her confinement.

Teresa's prospects in the principality were not looking good. Due to the expense of rebuilding their castle, the margrave and ailing margravine had little to spend on entertainment and, to make matters worse, early in 1754 the Marquis de Montpernis, Teresa's lover and the head of the opera house, fell seriously ill. This did not stop him going to Paris with the royal silver, which had been ruined by the fire, so that it could be reworked by highly skilled Parisian silversmiths.

Heartbroken at her friend's departure, the increasingly enfeebled margravine began writing an opera, which was to be performed at the reopening of her opera house that June. *L'Huomo*, a 'Féte [sic] en Musique & en Danses', was based on an existing score by Bernasconi, to which Wilhelmine added six arias of her own. She also wrote a French libretto for the music, and had it translated into Italian by her court poet, Louis Stampiglia.

Although only one act long, *L'Huomo* had fourteen scene changes and countless dramatic and expensive special effects, such as fire breaking out of the earth and thunderclaps issuing from hovering stormclouds. Its theme was of love triumphing over evil. Ironically, Teresa's role, that of Animia, personified the quality of faithfulness. The premiere took place that June in front of Frederick the Great, who had come to Bayreuth for six days to see his ailing sister.

Any pleasure Teresa might have taken from performing in front of the Prussian king was short-lived, for soon after his departure it was announced that the Bayreuth court was to be disbanded the following autumn while the margrave took Wilhelmine south for the good of her health. A second blow fell when the court received news that the Marquis de Montpernis had died in Paris. A funeral service was held for him, and a *castrum doloris* (castle of grief) was sung in his memory. The silver he had taken to Paris was never seen again. On 10 October, the margrave and margravine left their cash-strapped city and departed for Italy. Bayreuth's short Golden Age was over. So was Teresa's.

She had never shown her marriage to Angelo much commitment, and by the middle of 1754 it had broken down irretrievably. She had left him before, to go to London and Copenhagen. Now, at the age of thirty-one, and with three children to support – none of whom were his – she was about to cut loose from him for good. While Angelo returned to Vienna and his post at the Habsburg court, Teresa packed up her jewels, her fine dresses, lace and a stack of silver money she had spirited away during her time in Bayreuth. Taking Giuseppe, Wilhelmine and Sophie with her, and posing as a widow, she headed for Paris and one of the most testing periods of her life.

Travelling in grand style, and leaving a trail of debts in her wake – throughout her life she was never diligent about paying bills – Teresa swept into the French capital in the late autumn of 1754. Although she had travelled widely, she had seen nothing like Paris before. With its vast palaces, its endlessly long and busy streets brightly lit by an estimated eight thousand lanterns and candles, its wide squares, its broad river and its extensive formal gardens, it was by far the most impressive city in Europe, a vast stage set upon which the aristocracy paraded and strutted like haughty, bejewelled marionettes.

Parisians were inward-looking and xenophobic, and had a 'lively and frivolous' attitude to life. Immaculately dressed and very slender – they kept themselves thin by drinking vinegar – the aristocratic women were ferried about in sedan chairs, their porcelain-doll faces so thickly painted that one could not tell what they really looked like. The men of the nobility were equally indolent and self-obsessed. Appearance mattered far more than substance. Fashion, which changed rapidly, was all important, and a scant handful of aristocrats dictated the mores. As Casanova had already discovered during his stay in the city, it only took the Duchess of Chartres to declare that she liked a certain inferior brand of tobacco for a queue of people to form around the shop where it was sold.

Behind its glorious and fashionable façade, Paris was a place of rigid formality where short shrift was given to those who failed. It was also filthy. The streets were ankle-deep in horse manure and the elegant-looking *hôtels* were infested with vermin. Rented accommodation came at an exorbitant price, and invariably with tattered hangings, peeling paint and mattresses crawling with lice. Staircases were often strewn with garbage, and the porters' lodges at the gates were used as public lavatories by passers-by. Still, for any foreigner in financial difficulties, an *hôtel* with its own porter's lodge had one huge advantage: since bailiffs were not allowed past the lodge, the residents were free from the fear of being arrested for debt in their rooms.

Around a hundred thousand foreigners lived in Paris, scraping a living on the fringes of Louis XV's court, and Teresa had no desire to be one of them. Still flush with the money and diamonds the margrave had given her, but with an eye on economy nevertheless, her first move was to rent a suite of apartments at the Hôtel d'Entrainge in the rue de Touron just by the Luxembourg Palace where accommodation, though grand, was six times cheaper than it was near the fashionable Palais Royal (one day Casanova, too, would rent rooms in this street).

Here, as one contemporary said of Teresa, '*elle faisait grande figure*', living under a pseudonym, splashing money about and pretending to be a noblewoman who owned a castle in Germany. One can only wonder at how she imagined she could sustain this deception for more than a few weeks. During the last three years she had grown used to being a big fish in a small pool, and now she simply refused to acknowledge that she was nothing but a minnow in a large, inhospitable sea. As one might have predicted, it was not long before the waters were closing over her head and she got into debt. Soon she was forced to flee her lodgings, presumably on quarter-day when the rent was due (this was a popular move among those living in rented accommodation in Paris).

By January 1755 Teresa had re-established herself in more modest furnished rooms in the rue Saint-Marc near the Opéra, where she hired a fifty-five-year-old maid named Madame Poteau and set about earning some money as a soprano. Before long, she obtained work singing at the Concerts Spirituels, an annual concert series founded in 1725 by André Philidor, which had been set up to create work for the musicians of the Paris Opéra during the twenty-four-day Lenten period when the opera house was closed. In order to justify giving concerts on these holy days, the programmes had originally included a great deal of sacred music, such as composer Michel-Richard de Lalande's *grands motets*, which were normally sung at the king's Mass. Over the years, much of the sacred music had been replaced by profane works, while the series itself had grown to thirty-two performances, the orchestra being accompanied by a large choir.

Teresa joined this choir with great success. Her strong voice and dramatic singing, which had failed to please Londoners ten years earlier, went down well with the French. For the first time, too, she tried her hand at being a concert impresario: in a move she repeated later on a far grander scale in London, she gathered together a small group of musicians and held select musical evenings in her furnished rooms.

The success of these concerts brought Teresa to the notice of two influential and wealthy men. The first, Maximilien van Eyck, was the Parisian ambassador of Liège, a principality in the Austrian-ruled Netherlands. Before long, he had become her attentive lover: as Teresa's maid Madame Poteau later told the authorities, the ambassador 'was always at her place'. Teresa's other admirer was Alexandre-Jean-Joseph le Riche de la Pouplinière, Louis XV's Farmer General and the wealthiest patron of the arts in Paris. Both at his mansion in the city and at his château in Passy where he had a private theatre and orchestra led by the influential Bohemian composer Johann Stamitz, de la Pouplinière surrounded himself with a crowd of people 'drawn indiscriminately from good and bad company; court circles, men of the world, men of letters, artists, foreigners, actors, actresses, courtesans'; members of his *salon* included the ageing Madame de Pompadour, the mistress and confidante of Louis XV. De la Pouplinière was passionate about music, and passionate about Teresa. As well as inviting her to sing at his concerts, he offered to take care of her financially. Since he had married a previous mistress (the couple had separated in 1748 after Madame de la Pouplinière's notorious affair with the Maréchal de Richelieu) this might have been a godsend to Teresa who, mindful of her future, was shrewdly playing the field.

In the end, her liaison with de la Pouplinière came to nothing. Pregnancy, then the curse of all sexually active women, yet again scuppered any plans she might have had for an easy life. As her treacherous maid Madame Poteau later reported to the Chambre Criminelle, no one knew who the father of Signora Pompeati's baby was and, not for the first time, that probably included Teresa herself.

Trouble was building up and, as so often in her life, Teresa was its architect. Though tickets to the musical evenings she held at her home were sought-after, her extravagance soon got the better of her. In debt again, she fled the rue Saint-Marc for the more modest Hôtel de Londres on the rue Josephine and, later, the Hôtel d'Hollande on the rue St André-des-Arts.

Teresa had always carried a secret stash of coins with her, 'silver money which she kept in case of need', but now this ran out. Desperate for cash, she borrowed 1800 livres from Madame Poteau and her husband. When she failed to pay them back, they reported her to the authorities. On 21 May a group of bailiffs arrived at the Hôtel d'Hollande, and arrested her for debt.

Teresa was thrown into the notorious For-L'Évêque prison. It was the first time in her life she had been in gaol. Unknown to her, Casanova was in a similar predicament. The previous July he had been arrested in Venice on the orders of the State Inquisitors, ostensibly because of his involvement in occult activities but more likely because his frequent dealings with foreigners and ambassadors made people look on him as a danger to the Republic. Since then, he had been locked up in I Piombi, the Leads, the notorious cells under the eaves of the Palazzo Ducale. His legendary escape on the night of 31 October 1756 would earn him the admiration of his fellow citizens in the Republic, make him famous and provide the subject matter for *The Story of My Escape*, an autobiographical book he wrote in 1787.

Teresa's release from For-L'Évêque was far less dramatic, but it came much sooner. On 5 June 1755, just a few weeks after she had been arrested, she was summarily released, presumably after being bailed out by one of her admirers. Without waiting for the bailiffs to break down her door for a second time, she fled from Paris, leaving behind a rumoured fifty thousand livres' worth of debts.

According to Madame Poteau's testimony, Teresa also left behind her 'three young children, two little girls, one aged five years, the other an infant, and a little boy of about four years old, it's not known who she left them with'. But who were the children she was accused of abandoning? In the summer of 1756, Giuseppe was ten, Wilhelmine three and a half and Sophie two. By now, Teresa had given birth to a fourth baby – the infant referred to. As well as being her maid, the embittered Poteau was also one of Teresa's creditors, and she might well have been lying to the authorities to paint the blackest picture possible of her erstwhile employer: difficult as Teresa found coping with children, time would show that it was not in her character to abandon them.

For the next three years, Teresa's fortunes vacillated precariously between professional success and financial failure. On the run from her creditors and taking her children with her, she travelled north to the Austrian Netherlands, no doubt armed with letters of introduction from her lover van Eyck. These territories on France's north-east border were currently prospering under the regency of a powerful and cultured man, Prince Charles Alexander of Lorraine. The Empress Maria Theresa's brother-in-law twice over (he was her husband's brother and had been married to her late sister,

Maria Anna), Charles of Lorraine was once described as 'close to perfection'. His friend, the Prince de Ligne, wrote of him that he was 'one of the most beautiful souls that I have met . . . His traits were generosity, a lovable disorder of finances, indulgence and kindness.' Graceful despite being tall and well-built, and handsome despite his pox-scarred face, Charles was universally said to be good-natured, unambitious and easily pleased. Though his position as the resident representative of the Habsburgs forced him to maintain 'the exterior pomp of a Sovereign' in the Austrian Netherlands, he remained at heart an extremely sociable *bon viveur*.

Left a widower when his wife died in childbirth in 1746, the prince had quickly earned himself a reputation as a true ladies' man. He adored women, and they in turn worshipped him. On public occasions he communicated with his many lovers using a secret sign language of his own invention, the key to which he noted down in a small green book: for instance, twisting his handkerchief between his hands meant 'I've learned something new', and passing a hand before his mouth was an inquiry as to whether his companion was indisposed.

With his predilection for women and his considerable political clout, Charles was the perfect willing victim for the ambitious adventuress Teresa was fast becoming. The attractive, flirtatious and pushy Venetian who turned up in Brussels armed with recommendations from his ambassador in Paris must have amused as well as enchanted him, and they became lovers. With Charles's help, by the autumn of 1756 Teresa had established herself as a celebrated singer in the province. More importantly, Charles procured for her the directorship of the theatre in the Flemish city of Gand (modern-day Ghent).

If there was any work Teresa was suited to, it was that of the impresario, a craft she had learned at her father's knee. She had already tried her hand at arranging concerts in Paris. Now, using the skills she had acquired at the San Samuele and the eye for detail she had developed while watching the margravine and de Montpernis run Bayreuth's opera house, she turned Gand's 1756/7 theatre season into a huge success and became a local celebrity. When it ended, she was invited to stay on for another season. However, her outgoings far outpaced her income, and by the end of the summer she was broke again. Her seemingly casual attitude towards money did not go down well with Gand's city fathers, who in November confiscated her licence to run the theatre on the grounds that she was late in paying them 435 florins she owed them.

Teresa did not wait around to be arrested. In fact, she had already moved east to the Flemish principality of Liège where, on 19 October 1757, the local council granted Signora Pompeati the right to run the city's popular Théâtre de la Baraque. According to the *Journal Encyclopédique* of April 1758, a magazine compiled by the local intelligentsia, Liège was 'distinguished by its taste in music'. *Concerts spirituels* were given at the town hall, and the ruling prince-bishop held private concerts for the aristocracy in his palace. Teresa divided her time between performing and directing her company of actors. Before long, she was being fêted as the most perfect musician that had been heard for years in the principality.

But yet again her undisciplined attitude to money soon brought her to the brink of disaster. As Teresa would later admit, she had no concept of bookkeeping. In order to maintain standards, she spent far more on her productions than la Baraque's income warranted, and by the turn of 1758 she was deeply in debt. In an attempt to save herself, she arranged a ball for the town's nobility in January, but although the event was a fabulous social success it failed to make money.

Slowly but surely Teresa's savings, such as they were, dwindled to nothing, and she sold the last of the jewellery and lace the margrave had given her to pay the theatre's rent. By that summer, she was on the road again, leaving yet another trail of debts behind her. A veritable army of creditors in northern Europe was now on the lookout for her. Her situation was getting desperate. Not only had Teresa run out of money, she was running out of places to go next.

Five

On the run from her creditors, Teresa moved north-east into the prosperous region of the United Provinces or the Dutch Republic, as the Netherlands were then known. Posing as a widow and living under the assumed name of Madame de Trenti, she rented sparsely furnished rooms on the fourth floor of a dilapidated tenement building in The Hague. From here, she travelled constantly between Rotterdam, Leiden and Amsterdam, singing wherever the concert managers would employ her. Although her voice was still as pure as ever, the impresarios sensed that she was desperate and refused to pay her. Instead, they allowed her to hand round a collection plate after she had performed. This reduced her to little more than a beggar, for as the audiences had already paid for their concert tickets they were not disposed to be generous towards her.

During the past three years life had been harsh to Teresa. Somewhere between leaving Paris and arriving in the Dutch Republic, both her elder daughter Wilhelmine and her youngest infant had died. While infant mortality was commonplace at the time, due to poor nutrition and hygiene, the death of two young children was none the less deeply upsetting, even for a woman to whom maternal feeling did not come easily. Teresa was in a permanent state of mourning, and only ever wore black.

The colour must have suited her, for her looks, like her singing voice, remained undiminished by the double tragedy. At the age of thirty-five, she could still magnetize men. With barely enough money coming in to feed her surviving children, Giuseppe and Sophie, she took three or four lovers to supplement her income. Her admirers included a Dutch businessman named Jan Cornelis de Rijgerbos, and the ill-mannered twenty-two-year-old son of a local dignitary – research by Casanovaists indicates that he was Johan van der Hoeven, the son of Rotterdam's mayor. The dubious reputation that these lovers generated for her, and the air of mystery surrounding her, made Teresa the focus of gossip among the wives and daughters of the prosperous merchants of Amsterdam. It was said of her that she had men in every city, but since none had a penny they impoverished her instead of making her richer.

The perennial problem of living within her means still defeated Teresa, and by now her means were practically non-existent. By late December 1758, she owed at least eighty florins to her creditors in Rotterdam alone, so much that they had insisted she leave Giuseppe with them as a guarantee that she would pay them back.

Hungry, cold, exhausted by non-stop travelling and with her son in pawn to her creditors, when Teresa arrived in Amsterdam on New Year's Day 1759 to take part in a concert she had sunk to the lowest point in her life. Unknown to her, an old friend was in the audience.

Teresa walked out on stage and, after hesitating for a moment beside the harpsichord, she began to sing a recitative: 'Eccoti giunta al fin, donna infelice' – 'You have come to the end at last, unhappy woman'. Her voice was as true and poignant as it had ever been, and when the song ended the audience applauded endlessly. Afterwards as she passed through the rows of seats holding out the humiliating collection plate, with little Sophie trailing close behind her, her eyes were drawn to a broad-shouldered, richly dressed gentleman seated in one of the rows. In an instant of shock, she took in the features she remembered so well from her past – the high forehead, the slightly bulbous eyes, the full, sensuous mouth, the strong Venetian nose – and noted the gentleman's fine jewellery and expensive clothes.

It was Giacomo Casanova. Teresa was taken aback. She had last seen him in Venice in June 1753. Then they had become lovers. The proof of this, her daughter, was standing just behind her. Her life had changed immeasurably during the intervening years – and so had his, judging by appearances. It was clear that Casanova had prospered, while she had fallen on hard times.

Casanova glanced at her, and their eyes met across the seats. A moment later, without betraying that he knew her, he resumed his conversation with a beautiful raven-haired girl sitting next to him. Teresa carried on moving through the rows as if she had not seen him. She had been raised in the same Venetian school of discretion as he had, and she accepted the rules of the game: the rich gentleman did not want it known that he was acquainted with a humble concert singer.

Murmuring her thanks to those who gave her money, she made her way slowly towards the row in which Casanova was seated. At last she stood in front of him. Without looking up at her, he took a paper twist from inside his muff and placed it on the plate. Teresa could see that it contained a large number of coins. She walked on, with Sophie following close behind her. Ignorant of Casanova's relationship to her, the child brushed innocently past his knees.

The irony of the situation was not lost on Teresa. When she reached the end of the row, she could not resist telling her daughter to return to the finely dressed gentleman. Eager to please her mother, Sophie ran back to Casanova, kissed his hand and stared up at him fixedly. Now it was his turn to be shocked, for Sophie's features were identical to his own. To cover his discomfort, he offered her a sweet from his tortoiseshell chocolate box, and when she did not go away he tried to get rid of her by urging her to take the lot. Eventually she ran off, leaving him to face the amused and curious questioning of his female companion and her friend, neither of whom had failed to notice the likeness between him and 'Madame de Trenti's' child. Teresa heard him brush it off as coincidence. Chance, he said, often produced such similarities.

After the concert, Teresa found out where Casanova was staying. She was proud, but she was also desperate for money. Chance, or God in heaven, had thrown this opportunity into her lap and she could not afford to let it pass her by. Five and a half years earlier, Casanova had promised to visit her in Bayreuth, but he had failed to keep his word. Now it was time for her to pay him a visit. If he had not realized the truth already, he would learn it from her own mouth.

Like most foreign visitors to the leading financial centre of Amsterdam, Casanova was there on a business trip. Since his escape from I Piombi on 31 October 1756 and his subsequent flight from Venice, he had become a minor hero. Fêted by society for his daring escape, he had fled to France, where he had been living ever since. In Paris, Casanova had established a reputation as a financial fixer and helped to set up a State lottery to raise money for Louis XV's cash-strapped École Militaire. He had not reached this position through any particular financial acumen, but through being a subtle and brilliant con-man who knew intuitively when to keep quiet about his ignorance, when to listen and when to speak out. Having spent his way through Senator Bragadin's money, he had acquired a new and even wealthier patron – or rather, patroness. Jeanne de Larochefoucauld de Lascaris, the Marquise d'Urfé, was one of the richest women in the city. A gullible middle-aged widow obsessed with chemistry, alchemy and the occult, she let Casanova persuade her that he had an in-depth knowledge of Rosicrucianism, the order he had joined in Venice some years earlier, and also that he was in possession of the Philosopher's Stone, and knew the secret of turning base metal into gold. Casanova played on her belief in his 'mystical' powers and promised to help her achieve her long-cherished ambition: to be reborn by having her soul transferred into the body of a male infant.

Since their first meeting, the marquise had lavished money and gifts on Casanova, and through her generosity he now cut a dash in the best French circles with his diamond rings and watches, his exquisite gold snuff-boxes and his magnificent lace-trimmed clothes. To complement his new look, he had acquired substantial apartments in the centre of Paris and a country retreat on the outskirts. La Petite Pologne, as the villa was called, boasted elegant terraced gardens, stabling for twenty horses, luxurious rooms where he entertained his friends and lovers, and a brilliant chef who prepared tasty Spanish stews, exotic Oriental pilaus, Italian risottos and rice-fed fowl with delectable white flesh. By now, Casanova had become such a trusted figure in French government circles that Louis XV's ministers had sent him to Amsterdam to negotiate the sale of State securities on their behalf. He was also conducting private business on behalf of the Marquise d'Urfé; on his return, she would reward him with a gift of twelve thousand francs.

This being New Year's Day, Casanova had been invited to dine with one of Amsterdam's most successful financiers. Thomas Hope (or DO, as the adventurer referred to him in his memoirs) was a forty-year-old widower who, having no children of his own, lived in a sumptuously decorated house with his niece Esther, a captivating fourteen-year-old nymphet who was the heiress to his fortune. It was Esther who had suggested that Casanova accompany her to the concert after dinner. On the way there, she had told him that they would hear a remarkable and mysterious Italian soprano. Her name was Madame de Trenti, and she had the voice of a nightingale.

When the nightingale turned out to be Teresa, Casanova was not overwhelmingly pleased. Though his heart beat faster at the sight of her, he felt uncomfortable, partly because he had failed to keep his promise to visit her in Bayreuth, but most of all because of her obviously impoverished state. Casanova always prided himself on being generous – giving away money was never a problem for him, particularly when it was not his own – and when he saw that she was in need, he had put the paper twist, containing sixty-two florins, on her collection plate. Although Teresa was still a desirable woman, this patronage was as far as he intended to take their relationship, for that night his sights were set on fourteen-year-old Esther.

Relieved to have got away so lightly, Casanova took Esther home, then returned to his rooms at the Star of the East hotel where he ordered a supper of oysters. But he had not seen the last of Teresa. The moment he sat down to eat, she appeared in his doorway with Sophie by her side. Caught out, he jumped up 'to embrace her ecstatically'. What followed was a scene of exquisite melodrama, in which Casanova pretended to be delighted to see Teresa, whose genuine emotions battled with her sense of the theatrical and her needy, manipulative side.

As Casanova embraced her, Teresa fainted – not on to the floor but picturesquely into an armchair. Unsure whether she had collapsed through hunger or emotion, or merely for effect, he attempted to revive her with eau-de-Luce smelling-salts. When she came to, she stared at him fixedly, so overcome that she was unable to speak. However, when Casanova asked her if she wanted something to eat she revived enough to answer that she did.

By the time the food was delivered, Teresa had recovered sufficiently to attack it with a hearty appetite. While Sophie slept soundly in Casanova's bed, the lovers recounted to each other their good and bad fortune. And since she claimed to have already heard about his latest vicissitudes, it was Teresa who did most of the talking. She spoke candidly about her affairs with the margrave and de Montpernis, the break-up of her marriage, her misfortunes in Paris, her artistically successful but financially disastrous spell in the Austrian Netherlands, and her present terrible predicament.

Yet if Teresa's gruelling existence was exacting a toll from her, it was hard to see what it was. Far from being ground down by poverty, she had lost none of her spirit and nerve, as Casanova discovered towards dawn when, 'saving to the last what was the most important, and would interest me most', she disclosed to him that, as he had suspected, he was indeed Sophie's father. In case he doubted her word, she had even brought along the girl's baptismal certificate, but Casanova had already seen all the proof he needed in the child's face.

Far from trying to wriggle out of his paternal responsibilities, he offered to take the pretty Sophie back to Paris with him and bring her up at his own expense. Desperate as her plight was, Teresa refused. Sophie was her jewel, she insisted, and if Casanova separated them it would be as if he was tearing out her soul. Instead, she suggested that Casanova take Giuseppe. Casanova asked her where the boy was. He recorded her reply in his memoirs:

'He is, I wouldn't say in boarding school, but left in pawn, in Rotterdam, since he'll never be returned to me until I pay back the people who have him everything I owe them.'

'How much do you owe them?'

'Eighty florins. You've already given me sixty-two, so give me another four ducats and my son will be yours, and I'll be the happiest of mothers.

'I'll hand him over to you next week at The Hague, since you said you have to return there.'

Modern sensibilities might be shocked by Teresa's outrageously casual attitude towards handing over her son to a man he had met just twice in his life, but by the standards of the time she was acting as a concerned and responsible parent. The concept of childhood as a special condition scarcely existed during the eighteenth century. If anything, growing up was considered a training-ground for adulthood, a time to acquire the skills that would see one through adult life. Who better to help Giuseppe acquire these skills than Giacomo Casanova? Not only was he a childhood friend of the boy's mother, a fellow Venetian who had worshipped in the same parish church as she had, their families had worked together, and the pair had spent their formative years together in Senator Malipiero's *palazzo* and later been lovers – as had their parents.

Casanova was the ideal person to raise Giuseppe. Teresa knew him to be trustworthy and generous. He knew how to turn circumstances to his own good. Placing Giuseppe in his care was tantamount to placing him in the care of a concerned uncle or step-father, a canny and wealthy one at that. Besides, Teresa had little choice but to find a home for her son. To a woman in her situation, bringing up children was less a matter of nurturing them emotionally than ensuring they were fed. In Daniel Defoe's novel *Roxana*, published in 1724, the eponymous heroine is left with five children to raise, and she described her situation thus: '. . . the Misery of my own Circumstances hardened my Heart against my own Flesh and Blood . . . I began to be reconciled to parting with them all, any how, and any where, that I might be freed from the dreadful Necessity of seeing them all perish, and perishing with them myself.'

If Teresa prevailed on Casanova's generosity, it was for Giuseppe's sake as much as her own. When he agreed to take him on she was so overcome with gratitude that she clasped him in her arms, kissed him passionately and would not let go of him. But on this occasion Casanova was not interested in what she was so blatantly offering him. Her ardent caresses felt excessive, and he responded without enthusiasm. Try as she might, Teresa could not reawaken his desire for her, 'or rather,' he added, callously, and not altogether truthfully, 'the old liking I'd had for her, because I'd never loved her passionately . . . She was pretty, blonde, full of spirit and talent; but her charms weren't the same any more, for if they had been I would have felt their force.' A poverty-stricken thirty-five-year-old mother-of-two was no match in his eyes that night for Esther, the nymphet heiress on whom he had set his sights.

This was the first time that Casanova had shown no interest in Teresa, and his indifference upset her so much that she burst into tears. However, resilience was always one of her finest qualities: she pulled herself together and left with a regretful sigh. Using the money Casanova had given her, she redeemed Giuseppe from her creditors in Rotterdam and took him back to The Hague, where Casanova visited them a few days later, and saw for himself just how low Teresa had sunk.

Her rooms were up four narrow flights of stairs in a decaying tenement. Yet even in these wretched surroundings, Teresa somehow created a dramatic tableau. Looking every inch the tragic heroine – like Medea, in Casanova's eyes – she was seated at a table covered with a simple black cloth, her two beautiful children beside her, and two flickering candles illuminating her pale skin and fair hair.

The evening started well, but the atmosphere soon deteriorated. At first, Casanova sat Sophie on his knee and 'covered each part of her pretty body with kisses, delighted to be the man to whom this little creature owed her existence'. He called Giuseppe his son, hugged him, and was instantly charmed by his intelligence and beauty. However, by the time he had eaten – Teresa had made a great effort to produce a fine supper and wines for him, and insisted that she had not treated the margrave better – Casanova's enchantment had worn off and he had come to the conclusion that the twelve-year-old boy he had agreed to adopt was false, secretive and horribly sly. Constantly on his guard, Giuseppe spoke in a calculating manner, never from the heart, and when questioned on any subject he gave well-thought-out answers, which seemed designed only to please people.

Far from being ashamed of the boy's behaviour, Teresa boasted that it was she who 'had accustomed him [to be discreet], and for that reason she suffered without sorrow his habit of being as reserved with her as he was with everybody else'. Casanova was bitterly critical of her attitude: 'I told her that this was abominable, and that I couldn't conceive how a father could have any fondness, let alone liking, for such a buttoned-up son.' If he took him on, he asked Giuseppe, would he promise to keep no secrets from him? The boy swore that he would sooner die than lie to his new 'father', and Teresa defended her son with pride:

'That's his character,' his mother interrupted, 'such is the horror of lying I've inspired in him.'

'That's all very well,' I answered, 'but you could direct your son towards happiness by a different route. Instead of showing him the ugliness of falsehood, you could show him the beauty of truth. It's the only means of making oneself lovable, and in this world, one must be loved in order to be happy.'

'But,' he answered with a smug little smile which didn't please me at all, but which enchanted his mother, 'isn't not lying the same as telling the truth?'

'Not at all, for you would only have to say nothing to me. It's a question of unfurling your soul, of telling me everything that's going on inside you and around you, and even revealing to me things which make you blush.'

Casanova's sermon in praise of speaking from the heart sounded worthy, but coming from him it was nothing short of hypocritical. He himself thrived on duplicity. He had become an emissary to the French government only by keeping his mouth shut about his ignorance of financial matters, and he lived off a half-crazed, over-credulous widow whom he had brazenly misled into believing that he possessed mystical powers. Teresa, on the other hand, was proud to have taught her children the Venetian skill of pleasing other people, which she had learned as a child. As time would show, giving pleasure to others was her vocation as well as a necessity. Speaking from the heart was a luxury that neither she nor her children could afford.

That evening, Casanova would not stop talking about the importance of instilling the correct precepts in children. Nor would he for the rest of his life. Teresa defended herself against his continuing onslaught, but Sophie disintegrated into tears. Told by her mother that she was silly to cry, she obediently released a peal of laughter and threw her arms round Teresa's neck. This display of false emotion angered Casanova even more, and he made an unsuccessful attempt to persuade Sophie to come to Paris with him. Torn between the warring adults, the child burst into tears again. Convinced that they were only for effect, Casanova took Teresa to one side and lectured her sternly on her child-rearing methods: 'If she'd brought up her children to be actors she'd succeeded, but for polite society they were monsters in the making.'

Now it was Teresa who broke down in tears. She was raising her children the only way she knew how, according to precepts she considered essential for their survival. Yet here was Casanova telling her that everything she was doing was wrong. Torn between standing up for herself and possibly losing Casanova's friendship, she begged him to stay on in The Hague for another day. When he refused, she resorted to a more manipulative strategy: she told Sophie to work on him. But her methods were so obvious that Casanova could not help laughing at them.

In the end, Casanova agreed to dine with Teresa and her children the following night, but only on condition that he was given just one bottle of burgundy and a simple meal for, as he explained to Sophie, he knew they were not wealthy. 'I know that, my dear friend, but Mama said that you'll be paying for everything,' the little girl answered. Casanova burst out laughing again. So did Teresa: getting her own way was one of the skills she had learned as a young girl, and she was proud to be caught out using it, and even in her most desperate moments she retained the ability to laugh at herself. The wines were given to her by one of her admirers, she admitted, and if Casanova did not mind she would invite the fellow to join them for dinner the following night.

Before Casanova left, Teresa insisted on taking him to see the tiny room where her children slept. He sensed that she wanted him, and again he turned her down. Neediness was not a quality he found attractive in women. As far as he was concerned, his sexual relationship with Teresa was over for good.

However, this did not stop him becoming jealous of her lover when he met him the following evening. VDR, as Casanova called him in his memoirs, has been named by Casanova scholars as Johan van der Hoeven, and he could do nothing right in the adventurer's eyes. He was rude, arrogant and useless. His clothes were ordinary and his character was bland. As for his manners, they were intolerable. He criticized the simple food Teresa had prepared at Casanova's request, and lavished praise on the wines that he himself had provided. Worst of all, van der Hoeven failed to show due deference to Casanova.

Teresa's motives in introducing the gauche, conceited young man to her sophisticated ex-lover were, at best, dubious. No doubt, making both men jealous had much to do with it. But once she realized that van der Hoeven was getting on Casanova's nerves she put the young man in his place. Though she took money from many men during her life, Teresa knew her worth and never felt she had to sacrifice her pride in return.

Van der Hoeven left before dessert was served, his nose thoroughly out of joint. Unfortunately, Casanova had not seen the last of him. Their next encounter, in a coffee-house the following evening, nearly cost both men their lives. The young man was playing billiards when Casanova walked in. Intimating that he was a good player, he quietly advised Casanova to bet on him. Moved by this show of friendship, Casanova put a wager on the youth. But after van der Hoeven had lost the first three games, Casanova discreetly switched his bet to the youth's opponents.

Three hours later, the tournament ended with van der Hoeven having lost every one of thirty or forty games. He offered Casanova his condolences for betting on him, whereupon Casanova admitted that he had bet against him for most of the night. Furious that everyone was laughing at his expense, the self-important young man stormed off in a temper. Later that night, sword drawn, he confronted Casanova in a moonlit street and demanded to know whether his point was as sharp as his tongue.

Casanova tried to calm him, but van der Hoeven would not be appeased. He tried to provoke Casanova by hitting him with the flat of his blade. A violent fight followed. Determined to stop the youth before he himself was killed, Casanova wounded him lightly in the chest and invited him to give up. Answering that he was not dead yet, the young man came at him like a fury, whereupon Casanova wounded him four more times. Advised by his host in The Hague to leave the city immediately, Casanova fled to Amsterdam.

As it happened, van der Hoeven had not been seriously wounded, and the following day, terrified that Casanova would go back to France without Giuseppe, Teresa sent him a letter assuring him that he could safely return to The Hague. In an outrageous move, she dispatched it with her other lover, the twenty-eight-year-old Jan Cornelis de Rijgerbos.

Later that week, Casanova left for France, taking Giuseppe with him. When Teresa saw them off in Rotterdam, she told him bluntly that she had heard he had earned half a million francs from his business dealings in Amsterdam. In a blatant bid to get hold of some of it she hinted that she, too, would be able to make a fortune if she could leave Holland and establish herself in London. For good measure, she also made Sophie tell Casanova that he owed his current spell of good luck solely to her prayers.

Casanova laughed at Teresa's blatantly manipulative strategies. He pressed a hundred ducats into her hand and promised to send her an equal amount when she wrote to him from London, perhaps supposing that she never would. Teresa was still not satisfied. As Casanova stepped into his sedan chair, she pleaded for a further hundred ducats. Pulling her to him, he whispered that he would pay her a thousand if she would only let him take Sophie.

Teresa refused. She might trade her own body to survive, but she would never sell Sophie, even to the child's own father. She would find alternative means of leaving the Dutch Republic and making her fortune. They involved a man named John Fermor.

Six

Like Teresa, who had already been known as Anna Maria Teresa Imer, Signora Pompeati and Madame de Trenti, John Fermor was no stranger to changing his name. Born in November 1719 in Sevenoaks, a small town in the southern English county of Kent, he had been baptized as John Boorder and brought up thinking that he was the eldest son of John Boorder senior and his wife Ann. But John Junior, as the lad was known, was not Boorder's natural child: he was the illegitimate son of a successful professional soldier by the name of Colonel John Fermor.

Colonel Fermor was the youngest child of William Fermor, a university-educated barrister who had chambers at Staples Inn, London, and a country seat at Walsh Manor, near the Sussex town of Crowborough. William owned a substantial amount of property in Kent, Sussex and London: in the capital, his estate included the King's Head Inn near St Paul's Cathedral and a large family house in Chelsea. In short, he was a wealthy gentleman, able to provide amply for his three sons: the oldest, his namesake William, who stood to inherit his father's property empire; Henry, who became a barrister like his father; and John, who opted for a career in the army.

In 1694, at the age of twenty, William's youngest son, John, joined Brundell's Regiment of Footsoldiers as an ensign. Gradually he rose through the ranks to become a lieutenant-governor in Menorca, where he commanded the castle of St Philip. After fighting alongside the Duke of Argyll at Malplaquet in 1709 and reaching the rank of colonel in Rich's Dragoons, he resigned from service in 1718 with a reputation for honour and bravery. From his London home in Brownlow Street, near Chancery Lane, the retired Colonel Fermor negotiated to buy a large house and seventy acres of land in Knole Paddock, on the fringes of Sevenoaks in Kent, 'between the horseway and the footway from Sevenoake to Seale'. Soon after moving there, he met a young unmarried woman called Ann Jonson, and had an affair with her. A baby was conceived. Since the colonel did not choose to marry the pregnant Ann, it seems likely that she came from a much lower social class than he did, and that their liaison was brief. Ann's baby and Teresa's future lover was born in November 1719 and named John, after his father. Soon afterwards, poor Ann was married off to a local man named John Boorder; the match might even have been arranged by her lover, Colonel Fermor.

Two years later, aged forty-nine, the Colonel stood for election as the Whig MP for Malmesbury, Wiltshire. He took his seat in the House of Commons on 13 December 1722. His must rank as one of the shortest political careers ever, for sixteen days later he died of smallpox, which he probably caught at Westminster. His bereft brother Henry rushed to Sevenoaks to arrange the funeral, and stayed on to take up residence in his late brother's empty house. By now Henry had lost both his parents, all three of his own children, two brothers and a nephew (William, the heir to their father's fortune, had died young and intestate, leaving a young son who had himself died in 1708). All these deaths had left him exceedingly rich, for Henry had inherited the entire family estate, including substantial shares in the South Sea Company.

In 1725, Henry was created a baronet by King George II. Seven years later, he made his will, setting aside £12,000 – the equivalent of over £1.3 million in modern terms – to erect and build 'a chapel, or church, and a Charity School, in the plainest and cheapest manner, so as it be strong and lasting . . . for the use and benefit of the very ignorant and heathenish people' of Crowborough. With the exception of his father's house, Walsh Manor, which he had already assigned to his elder brother's widow, Sir Henry left the rest of the family fortune to his only surviving male relative, his brother's illegitimate son, named in the will as 'John Boorder, junr. alias Ffermor, of the parish of Sevenoaks'.

While he was growing up, did John Boorder Junior have any

suspicion that he was not the son of both his parents? If so, did he know of the extraordinary prospects that awaited him? Even if he did, it must have come as a shock to him when the local baronet Sir Henry Fermor died in June 1734 and he was named as his sole heir, at the age of just fourteen.

One can only speculate about the boy's living circumstances before his uncle's death, but after it John was brought up in a style appropriate to a wealthy young gentleman. This included education at Tonbridge School, where he was later to send his own sons, followed by a stint at The Queen's College, Oxford, where he enrolled on 17 March 1737 as 'John Fermor, son of John Fermor of Sevenoaks' to study divinity. For there were two provisos in his uncle's will: the first, that his illegitimate nephew and any offspring he might have in the future should bear the surname Fermor, not Boorder; the second, that when he was old enough the youth should become rector of St Paulinus's Church in Crayford, Kent, where Sir Henry had already purchased the advowson for him.

After he was ordained into the Church, the Reverend John Fermor duly took up the living at Crayford. With it came a handsome parsonage along with substantial stables, a coach-house, outbuildings and sixty acres of upland and pasture. In 1747 John moved in with his new wife, Elizabeth Austin. By the mid-1750s, the illegitimate boy had become a wealthy, respectable country rector with a wife and two young sons, substantial business investments, and large property holdings throughout the south-east of England. He was also in charge of running his uncle's charity school in Crowborough, where the nomination of both clergyman and schoolmaster was within his gift.

For a few years, John Fermor lived a settled and predictable life, free from financial worries. Then, in 1758, he gave up the rectorship at Crayford to take up the post of vicar at the private chapel that adjoined the charity school in Crowborough. Between leaving Kent and taking up his new post at the school, he travelled to Holland, almost certainly on business to do with the South Sea Company stock he had inherited. While he was there, a chance meeting with Teresa turned his life upside-down.

In Rotterdam, one of the few Dutch cities that allowed trading in the speculative *winhandel* ('trading in wind') shares, Fermor attended a private concert at the home of a Mr Vanhagen, whose musical evenings were patronized by the most cultured residents of the city. That night Teresa was among the performers. As she would later testify to her attorney in London with atypical understatement, Fermor 'took great notice of (my) singing and seemed generally pleased with (my) voice and skill with musick'.

These qualities were, of course, only a small part of Teresa's attractions. To a man who had spent his entire life in small-town England and who had been married for the past twelve years to a country-bred English rose, the exotic, fascinating Venetian soprano must have seemed like a creature from another world. At thirty-six, Teresa was the antithesis of a demure English lady. Sophisticated, stylish and sexually experienced, she had lived all over Europe, spoke Italian, German and French and, although not conventionally beautiful, exuded charm and sensuality. Moreover, Teresa knew that the best way to interest a man was to appear interested in him. Before the night was over, the Reverend John Fermor was Teresa's.

Fermor was irredeemably smitten. Had he but known it, he was swimming in dangerous waters. To Teresa, he was a godsend. He was wealthy. He was generous. Above all, he seemed sympathetic to the plight of the penniless 'widow', who, she confessed, was finding it hard to earn her living. Since he had plenty of money and she was destitute, it was to be expected that money would change hands during their courtship. In the course of the following weeks, Fermor borrowed nine hundred guilders – over seven thousand pounds in today's terms – from a Dutch businessman and gave them to Teresa, ostensibly to help her re-establish her musical career on a more profitable basis.

The summer was approaching, and Fermor was due to return to England. But he could not bear the thought of parting with Teresa. In a moment of madness, he invited her to join him, and promised to help her relaunch her singing career in London. Teresa demurred. Fermor crossed the Channel without her but wrote to her repeatedly, begging her to come to London and promising 'he would then serve [her] to the utmost of his power and that she might depend that she should not want anything in his power [to provide]'.

Although reluctant to give up her independence, Teresa did not hesitate for long. Giuseppe was now being educated in Paris at Casanova's expense but she still had to support Sophie, and her prospects in Holland looked dire. She was now dangerously close to middle age, and her days as a singer and courtesan were numbered. How long could she continue the precarious hand-to-mouth life she had been leading ever since she had quit Bayreuth? If she wanted a final chance to re-establish herself as an opera singer, where better to try her luck than in London, the largest city in the world and the best place to make money out of music?

Past disasters had not dented Teresa's optimism. Her innate sense of self-preservation told her that she must take decisive action if she was not to end up in prison again or condemn herself to a gruelling old age as a common prostitute on Amsterdam's streets. To start from scratch once more in England, a country whose language she did not speak and where she had failed in the past, was an enormous challenge, and the odds against her succeeding at her age were slim. But rising to a challenge was Teresa's forte. Fermor had presented her with a chance she simply could not turn down, and the more she thought about it, the more irresistible his offer sounded. In October, when he sent money for her passage, she prevaricated no longer.

Travelling under yet another assumed name, that of Mrs Cornelys, which she had adapted from the name of her lover Jan Cornelis de Rigjerbos, Teresa took Sophie and boarded the packet boat for England. All she possessed were her fading charms, her knowledge of music, her optimism and her resourcefulness. These qualities were to be the making of her. Against all the odds, she was on the brink of unimaginable success.

Seven

A wife who to her husband ne'er laid claim;
A mother – who her children ne'er durst name.
Is it a wonder? – more yet may be said –
This wife, this mother, still remain'd a maid.

Verses penned about
Miss Elizabeth Chudleigh by
Dr Douglas, later Bishop of Carlisle

The packet boat docked at the port of Dover on 23 October 1759. The following day, worn out by their long journey, Teresa and Sophie stumbled down the steps of the 'flying coach', which had carried them up to London, and stepped into the crush of steaming horses, servants, street-sellers, thieves, con-men, drunkards and fellow travellers who filled the courtyard of a South London coaching inn.

London was daunting, though not entirely unfamiliar. Teresa's first visit, in the winter of 1745/6, had resulted in a humiliating return to Vienna. Then, her sister Marianna and her friend and mentor Christoph Gluck had been in the capital with her. Now she knew only the Reverend John Fermor. Back in the Dutch Republic they had discussed setting up some sort of entertainment business together. But until such time as Fermor helped her to find employment, Teresa would be dependent on him.

This situation was designed to put a strain on their relationship, and it was not long before the first cracks appeared. Since the showcase concert he had promised to arrange for her at the Little Theatre in the Haymarket was not to take place until the following February, and Teresa spoke no English, it suddenly dawned on

Fermor that he had to keep her and her daughter until then. 'Being intirely [*sic*] incapable from her circumstances of making any attempt to furnish out an Entertainment for the Publick or even support herself in the Mean time,' as he later put it, Teresa quickly proved an expensive liability. Within weeks, money had become a major issue between them, and Fermor began to hint that the guilders he had given her in Holland had not been a gift but only a loan intended to help her start a business. Furthermore, he now wanted this money back.

Teresa was shocked. Fermor had enticed her to England with promises that he would help her, so she had naturally expected him to keep her. Annoyed at the disrespectful way he was treating her, she threatened to return to the United Provinces. To her dismay, he immediately issued a counter-threat: he had left a promissory note for the nine hundred guilders she owed him with a Rotterdam businessman, and if she returned there without first paying him back this money, he said he would ask the man to sue her for it on his behalf.

In an immense stroke of good fortune, Teresa suddenly came to the attention of the most well-connected and notorious woman at George II's court. Thirty-nine-year-old Miss Elizabeth Chudleigh was a phenomenon. Beautiful, charming, haughty, extravagant and immoral, she scandalized society for more than three decades, while being accepted in the highest social circles. Her long tenure as maid-of-honour to the Dowager Princess of Wales gave her easy access to nearly every member of the royal family, and she was on intimate terms with most of them. With a few notable exceptions – among them Horace Walpole – men adored her. The penny-pinching King George II was said to be so enamoured of her that he once bought her a watch worth thirty-five guineas and paid for it out of his private purse.

Elizabeth was descended from solid country stock. Her paternal grandfather was a Devonshire baronet, and her grandmother, Lady Mary Chudleigh, a poet and author of *The Female Advocate; or, a Plea for the just Liberty of the Tender Sex, and particularly of Married Women*. Their son, Thomas Chudleigh, Elizabeth's father, became a professional soldier. By the time Elizabeth was born, Colonel Chudleigh had retired from active service and taken up the post of governor of the Royal Hospital at Chelsea, the famous home for army veterans founded by King Charles II.

It was in the Royal Hospital's magnificent red-brick buildings designed by Sir Christopher Wren that Elizabeth spent the first years of her life. Its extensive Thames-side garden was her playground and the retired soldiers were her playmates, along with the Prime Minister's son Horace Walpole – Sir Robert Walpole's Chelsea retreat, Stable Yard, was next door to the Chudleighs' house. This idyllic chapter in Elizabeth's life came to an end with the death of her father when she was six. Faced with the prospect of retreating to the family home in Devonshire and a life of genteel poverty, her mother decided instead to rent a house in London fit, as one anonymous biographer put it, 'at that less refined time, for a fashionable town residence', and to take in a lodger to supplement her income.

So far, so ordinary. From the time she turned fifteen, however, Elizabeth's life began to resemble that of some fictional heroine. After catching smallpox, from which she recovered miraculously without any scars, she was taken to Devon to recuperate. Out riding there one day, she met William Pulteney, the opposition MP and future first Earl of Bath. The jaded scholarly fifty-six-year-old was enchanted by Elizabeth's fresh beauty and vivacity, and he 'took her up' in the same way that one day she would take up Teresa.

In 1741 Pulteney's influence secured Elizabeth a position in the household of the Prince and Princess of Wales. Prince Frederick Louis was the heir to the throne, but his parents despised him. Having been thoroughly humiliated by his own father, King George II seemed hell-bent on replicating that awful relationship with his eldest son, and Queen Caroline's attitude to Frederick did not help matters. 'My dear son, my first-born,' she once commented, 'is the greatest ass, and the greatest liar, and the greatest canaille, and the greatest beast in the whole world, and I heartily wish he was out of it.' She claimed that Frederick's popularity with ordinary people made her vomit. On catching sight of him from her window one day she exploded, 'Look, there he goes – that wretch! – that villain! I wish the ground would open this moment and sink the monster to the lowest hole in hell.' The king and queen's political allies naturally shared their view of Frederick. Sir Robert Walpole once described him as a 'poor, weak, irresolute, lying, dishonest, contemptible wretch that nobody loves, that nobody believes, that nobody will trust'.

Humiliated, kept permanently short of money (he was allowed access to only a third of his £100,000 annual income) and forbidden to marry one Lady Diana Spencer, the woman he loved, the Prince of Wales had eventually been married off to seventeen-year-old Princess Augusta of Saxe-Gotha. Forced through lack of funds to live at St James's Palace with his parents, the young couple had eventually been expelled for keeping news of Augusta's pregnancy secret from the king, then fleeing from court on the night she went into labour. By the time Elizabeth Chudleigh was employed as one of Augusta's six maids-of-honour, the exiled couple were living with their four children in the Duke of Norfolk's house in St James's Square, Mayfair.

As the hard-done-by son of an unpopular monarch, Frederick was a natural focus for political opposition, and his home was the seat of an 'alternative' court, which included among it Pulteney, the Duke of Marlborough and Lords Chesterfield and Carteret. Though the young royals entertained their guests on a lavish scale, throwing sumptuous banquets, masques and plays, the everyday life of a royal maid-of-honour could be tedious, and, according to Alexander Pope, even miserable:

To eat Westphalia ham in the morning, ride over hedges and ditches on borrowed hacks, come home in the heat of the day with a fever, and (what is worse a hundred times) with a red mark on the forehead from an uneasy hack . . . As soon as they can wipe off the sweat of the day, they must simper an hour, and catch cold in the Princess's apartment; from thence (as Shakespeare has it) *to dinner, with what appetite they may* – and after that till midnight, walk, work, or think which they please.

Though maids-of-honour lost their position as soon as they married (a condition of employment that would prove useful to Elizabeth in a few years' time) there was nothing maidenly about their behaviour. Their intrigues fuelled court gossip. At least one of Augusta's maids, the Honourable Anne Vane, became Frederick's mistress: 'a Maid of Honour who was willing to cease to be so – at the first opportunity', as Horace Walpole described her. But Elizabeth instinctively knew better than to get entangled with Frederick. She seems to have been genuinely fond of Princess Augusta, whom she served loyally for many years and who later repaid her loyalty in kind. During her first few years at court she kept her head down and led a remarkably blameless existence.

The contacts Elizabeth made at this time stood her in good stead for the rest of her life, and were eventually of extraordinary benefit to Teresa. Miss Chudleigh grew close to the prince and princess and their growing brood of children – they eventually had nine. She cultivated every aristocrat and politician of importance, she learned how to manipulate her countless adoring admirers, and she blossomed into a flirtatious young woman who was not afraid to tease even the king. A shallow life made up of gossip, hunting, flirting and partying in luxurious surroundings suited her admirably.

Then in 1743 the Duke of Hamilton came to court, and Elizabeth's troubles began. Good-looking and rich, Hamilton was a catch. Like many other men, he fell in love with Elizabeth. The difference this time was that she returned his feelings. Yet theirs was an ill-fated romance: soon after they met, Hamilton disappeared on a Grand Tour, and in order to recover from the grief of their parting, twenty-three-year-old Elizabeth retreated with her aunt, a Mrs Hanmer, to a cousin's house in Sparsholt, Winchester.

There she waited restlessly to hear from Hamilton, but no letter arrived. For some reason known only to herself, Mrs Hanmer had decided to intercept the duke's letters and to push her niece into the path of Augustus Hervey, a grandson of the Earl of Bristol and a serving lieutenant on HMS *Cornwall*, which at that time was docked at Portsmouth. On 14 August 1744, believing that Hamilton had deceived her and, no doubt, on the rebound, Elizabeth impulsively married Hervey in a late-night ceremony in a chapel in the grounds of Lainston House, Sparsholt.

She would have been wiser to follow her late grandmother's advice to 'Shun, oh! shun that wretched state' of marriage, for it proved an appalling mistake. After just three days, Elizabeth told her husband that she never wanted to see him again – or so she later claimed. The rejected groom sailed for the West Indies and the bride returned to London and her job as a maid-of-honour. From the gaiety of her subsequent behaviour not even her mother would have guessed that the so-called Miss Chudleigh was now Mrs Hervey, living in fear of discovery and the disgrace it would bring on her.

From time to time, Hervey's ship returned to England. Occasionally he would request to see his wife, and even demanded his marital rights. Elizabeth would have nothing to do with him. In January 1747, angry and frustrated by what he saw as her high-handed and unreasonable behaviour, Hervey forced his way into her house in Conduit Street and, finding her alone but for the black male slave who accompanied her everywhere, he locked her in the drawing room and raped her. This 'assignation with a vengeance', as she later described it, resulted in a pregnancy. A few months later, like many a maid-of-honour before her, Elizabeth retired to the village of Chelsea 'for the good of her health'. Here the unwanted fruit of her husband's violent assault on her was born, baptized Henry Augustus Hervey, and immediately handed over to a foster-mother. Elizabeth tightened her stays and returned to court. The baby died a few months later, and for many years only a handful of people knew of his brief existence: Elizabeth's aunt Mrs Hanmer and her maid Ann Craddock, Caesar Hawkins, the surgeon who had delivered him, the foster-mother and Hervey.

By rights the drama should now have been over. But this was a story set to run and run. Before long, the Duke of Hamilton returned from his Grand Tour and offered Miss Chudleigh his hand in marriage. He was a real prospect for a woman of Elizabeth's meagre means and advanced years – she was now twenty-five, practically on the shelf in the opinion of her peers. Yet she had no choice but to turn him down, to the disbelief of her mother, her employers and her acquaintances.

After proposals from other suitors met the same fate, Elizabeth became the focus of much gossip among the fashionable *ton*. She brushed off the rumours with a laugh. However, she was too spirited a woman to succumb to blackmail, and when Hervey threatened to tell the Princess of Wales about their marriage she bravely pre-empted him and told Augusta herself. Elizabeth's past loyalty to the princess now paid off. Reluctant to lose her favourite companion, Augusta promised to keep to herself the proof of what was by now practically an open secret.

From then on, freed from the fear of discovery, Elizabeth allowed herself to be caught up in the social whirl. Along with Lady Harrington, Miss Ashe and Lady Townshend, she formed part of a fast set and was the belle of every London ball. The following year she shocked the *ton* by appearing at a masquerade as the mythical figure of Iphigenia, dressed in a transparent gauze gown. 'Miss Chudleigh's dress, or rather undress, was remarkable,' wrote the hostess and writer, the intellectual Mrs Elizabeth Montagu. 'She was Iphigenia for the sacrifice, but so naked, the high priest might easily inspect the entrails of the victim. The Maids-of-Honour (not of maids the strictest) were so offended they would not speak to her.' Stories and poems about this scanty dress cropped up for years afterwards. The king was so enchanted by it that he granted Elizabeth's mother a sinecure: the post of housekeeper at Windsor Castle.

In 1751, the Prince of Wales suddenly died of pleurisy, and Leicester House was plunged into mourning. If the king shed any tears over Frederick, he did so in private: when told that his heir had died it was said that George merely glanced up from his game of cards, remarked, 'Why, they told me he was better!', then carried on playing his hand.

Elizabeth remained in the service of the widowed Augusta, who was now the Dowager Princess of Wales while her eldest son had assumed his late father's title. From being a strong yet circumspect wife whose behaviour towards her difficult in-laws had always been 'most decent and prudent', Augusta suddenly became the daughter-in-law from Hell. Refusing to be sidelined, 'cette diablesse Madame la Princesse', as George II was soon calling her, kept an iron grip on her son. With the support of William Pitt, she also insisted on being named as regent in the event that the King died before his new heir turned twenty-one.

Publicly a spinster, secretly a wife, admired and gossiped about in equal measure, Elizabeth's position might have been uneasy but her close relationship to the newly empowered Augusta ensured that it was at least fairly secure. By now she was rumoured to be the mistress of forty-year-old Evelyn Pierrepont, the Duke of Kingston, whom she had met three years earlier.

Kingston and Elizabeth were made for each other, for they were both spendthrifts. Although he had come into a fortune when he was twenty-two, the duke now had personal debts of some £70,000 (about £7 million in today's terms). But shortage of ready cash never stopped him doing what he wanted. While deeply in debt, he built himself a new house at Thoresby, Nottinghamshire, for £30,000. In 1752, he blew £2,000 (the equivalent of more than £200,000) during a fortnight's stay in London – and no doubt a good part of this was spent on Elizabeth. Kingston was madly in love with her. Although she was now in her thirties, she was still a devastatingly attractive woman who had lost none of her sparkle. Ravishingly pretty – she had widely spaced deep blue eyes, a high forehead, a voluptuous figure and remarkably pale skin – she oozed self-confidence, moved with all the dignity of a queen and acted as if she was no less than a goddess.

Elizabeth was determined to keep Kingston, and she made herself indispensable to him. She became his companion and friend as well as his lover. She shopped with him, gambled with him and hunted with him; it was said she filled her boots with rum when she was on horseback with him to keep her feet warm. The couple frequently spent their afternoons at the courts in Bow Street, London, watching Elizabeth's close friend, the blind magistrate Sir John Fielding, sentencing criminals to be flogged.

The magistrate was not the only person wielding power during those long afternoons: Elizabeth manipulated her lover with a skill that even Teresa could not have matched. According to Kingston's servant, Thomas Whitehead, who would later write a scurrilous book about her, the duke was so firmly under Elizabeth's thumb that he even agreed to the world's first palimony agreement: 'She had great influence over his Grace; the Duke doted on her; she knew it well, and took the advantage of it, by tying him down, so that whenever she should prove herself a *single woman*, he should either marry her, or forfeit ten thousand pounds per ann. during her life.'

But for the time being Elizabeth could not marry Kingston, and they were sufficiently close for her to confide the reason to him. That she was secretly married seemed to add to her allure, and in 1757 the besotted duke bought her a plot of land in Knightsbridge, on the fringes of London, and built her a beautiful country villa. Kingston House, as it was later called, reflected both his extravagance and Elizabeth's acquisitive nature. Designed by Henry Flitcroft, the architect of Woburn Abbey, Bedfordshire, home to the Duke of Bedford, it was a pretty, symmetrical three-storey building, flanked by two lower wings containing stables and kitchens, and surrounded by formal gardens and a grotto. Both inside and out, the villa could 'justly be called a gem', wrote the Prussian visitor to London Count Kielmansegge after he had visited Kingston House in 1761: 'It contains a quantity of handsome and costly furniture and other curiosities and objects of value, chosen and arranged with the greatest taste, so that you cannot fail to admire it greatly. There is hardly a place in the whole house left bare or without decoration, like a doll's house. Everything is in perfect harmony. The view, over Hyde Park, and at the back over Chelsea, is considered with truth one of the finest that could be pictured.'

Horace Walpole's view of his old playmate's house was not so charitable. Writing to Montagu on 27 March 1760 he described it as

not fine nor in good taste, but loaded with finery. Execrable varnished pictures, chests, cabinets, commodes, tables, stands, boxes, riding on one another's backs, and loaded with terreens [*sic*], filigree, figures and everything on earth. Every favour she has bestowed is registered by a bit of Dresden china. There is a glass case full of enamels, eggs, ambers, lapis lazuli, cameos, toothpick-cases and all kinds of trinkets, things that she told me were her playthings; another cupboard full of the finest japan; and candlesticks and vases of rock crystal ready to be thrown down in every corner.

But what Walpole found most curious were the huge covered chamber-pots that dominated every bedroom, 'great mahogany projections, as big as her own bubbies, with the holes, brass handles and cocks etc – I could not help saying it was the *loosest* family I ever saw! Never was such an intimate union of love and a closestool!'

Elizabeth was living at Kingston House when Teresa arrived in England. The duke stayed there with her most of the time, though for the sake of respectability he also kept a house in nearby Mayfair. He need not have bothered, for the couple were widely presumed to be lovers. (Their sexual relationship might not actually have been fully consummated. According to his servant Thomas Whitehead, when the couple finally married in 1769 Elizabeth told her maid, 'You must know, Sally, the Duke is *now* going to enjoy what he has been many years soliciting for.')

Though superficially Teresa's circumstances could not have been more different from Elizabeth's, the two women were immediately drawn to one another. There were many similarities between the two, not least that they were both living under a false identity. Elizabeth, in reality Mrs Augustus Hervey, was pretending still to be a spinster named Miss Chudleigh so that she could keep her post as Princess Augusta's maid-of-honour. Teresa, whose married name was Signora Pompeati, was posing as the widow Mrs Cornelys, partly for added respectability and status, partly to appeal to people's sympathy, but more importantly because, as a widow, she would enjoy enhanced legal rights. As William Alexander would write in his *History of Women*, published in 1779, 'Widowhood, when tolerable circumstances are annexed to it, is of all other female states, the most eligible: being free from that guardianship and control, to which the sex are subject while virgins, and while wives.'

Both Teresa and Elizabeth had known hard times and short-lived failed marriages. Both knew what it was to be dependent on men to whom they were not married. They were of similar age, and equally attractive, if in different ways. Both were skilled manipulators with ingenious minds, a love of style and fertile imagination. Moreover, both had just what the other needed.

To Teresa, her acquaintance with the powerful maid-of-honour was the best *entrée* into English society she could hope to have. Elizabeth moved in the highest echelons of society, and knew everyone at court worth knowing. She had countless well-connected male admirers, among them many dukes, MPs and earls. As the confidante and long-term employee of the Dowager Princess of Wales, and a favourite of King George II, she had unprecedented influence with the royal family, and was virtually a second mother to George, the twenty-one-year-old Prince of Wales, whom she had helped to raise. Self-indulgent, pleasure-seeking, rich, adept at getting what she wanted and a member of the fashionable élite, Elizabeth was the perfect ally for a friendless foreigner intent on making her mark on the London arts scene.

For her part, Elizabeth was besotted by the exotic sophisticated Venetian opera singer, and so was her coterie of equally racy girlfriends. These included the haughty but clever Elizabeth Percy, Countess of Northumberland; Mary, the rowdy and 'Amazonian' Duchess of Ancaster, whose father was rumoured to have been a Newmarket jockey; and Caroline Fitzroy, the Countess of Harrington, an inveterate gambler 'famous for her credit, and also for her gallantries'. Teresa's knowledge of style, gleaned at the courts of France, Austria, Prussia and Denmark, was truly international. Her mysterious past further enamoured her to the female fast set, who believed that her past lovers included even Louis XV. Yet because she was a widow (or so she claimed), Teresa was respectable enough not to jeopardize the women's reputations, or what remained of them.

Teresa's singing voice, while no longer at its best, was certainly good enough to enthrall this small private audience of wealthy women, and her prodigious knowledge of contemporary Continental music further endeared her to them. Her manners were superb. Her imagination, taste and ingenuity were diversions in themselves. Elizabeth loved throwing fabulous parties and it turned out that Teresa, with her gift for creating magical scenes, which she had discovered as a child in Venice, was brilliant at arranging them. When, in June 1760, Elizabeth hosted a sensational party at Kingston House in honour of the Prince of Wales's twenty-second birthday, the event had all the hallmarks of having been masterminded by Teresa: lamps were lit on the roof and on every stair; pyramids of strawberries and cherries were placed on every table; and the servants' rooms under the eaves were transformed into exotic gambling dens, complete with Indian paintings and Chinese chairs.

Above all, Teresa's highly individual personality bewitched Elizabeth and her friends. Obsequious as she could be when it served her purpose, Teresa – Mrs Cornelys – was not afraid to speak her mind when she felt like it. Her powers of persuasion were formidable. She was a woman of strong feelings and ideas, and since she behaved as if she was going to get her own way people usually gave in to her. Although she was not above wheedling money out of men, and even women, when it suited her, she never behaved as if she was beholden to them. Where her relationship with John Fermor was concerned, she acted as his equal, if not his superior. Compared to the aristocratic Englishwomen who, however freely they might have behaved and however exalted their social position, were still subject to their husbands and to the social mores of the times, Teresa was an emancipated woman who embodied the spirit of the Enlightened age.

As a curiosity in a world where novelty was everything, Teresa was a peacock feather in Elizabeth's cap, and she had enough self-confidence to recognize it. Years of failure had toughened her up. Her very survival – and Sophie's – now depended on her ingratiating herself with the well-connected Miss Chudleigh. Communicating in French, their common language, she threw herself on Elizabeth's mercy, painting herself as the victim of a melodrama of John Fermor's making. She was a penniless widow with no one but Elizabeth to turn to, she said. The clergyman had enticed her to England with promises that he would help her to relaunch her singing career, but he was now threatening her with arrest and making life difficult for her. Her début concert at the Little Theatre was not due to take place until the middle of February, and even then Fermor was expecting her to pay all the expenses of it, which would leave her with nothing. In the meantime, if her daughter was not to starve, she had to borrow more and more money from him.

Luckily for Teresa, charitable causes were highly fashionable among the aristocracy. Delighted to find someone who could distract her from court life, Elizabeth set about rescuing the unconventional and magnetically attractive foreign widow. With the help of an opera singer named Elisabetta de Gambarini, who lived in Golden Square, Soho, she and her friends organized a fund-raising concert in aid of Teresa. 'By the particular Desire of several persons of Quality and Distinction. For the Benefit of a WIDOW and her DAUGHTER. At the Great Room in Dean-street, Soho, on Monday the 11TH of February will be a Grand Concert of Vocal and Instrumental MUSIC,' read the front-page notice for it in the *Daily Advertiser* on 4 February 1760. 'By select performers. With an Assembly, and a Ball. The whole to be conducted by Signora *Gambarini*. Tickets One guinea each, to be had at her house, in Golden-square; at Mr Deard's Toy-Shop, opposite Arlington-street, Piccadilly; at Mr Harrache's, Jeweller, in Pall-mall; and nowhere else. NB There will be a Side-Board of Tea, Coffee, and Sweetmeats.'

Elizabeth's intentions in arranging the concert were good, but her entrepreneurial skills did not match them. One guinea was a prohibitive price to pay for a concert ticket, and although Signora Gambarini sent out scores of invitations to prospective purchasers, few bothered to turn up on the night. The fund-raising evening was a financial disaster, and the one who suffered most was poor

Signora Gambarini: since it was she, not Miss Chudleigh, who had hired the hall and the orchestra, it was she who ended up carrying the financial losses; and soon afterwards she admitted that she had 'greatly suffered by the expences [*sic*]' of the evening.

Teresa's own début concert, arranged by John Fermor, was no more successful when it took place at the Little Theatre in the Haymarket a week later. Advertised as a 'Grand Concert of Vocal and Instrumental Music' with the 'Vocal part by a Gentlewoman lately arrived from Abroad', tickets were priced more reasonably between five shillings and half a guinea. But even this was a hefty amount to pay to hear a complete unknown. To show off her voice, Teresa had chosen to sing arias and recitatives by the Italian composers Jommelli, Manna, Galuppi and Vinci. But, as in 1746, London's audience, more accustomed to listening to Handel's oratorios than to Italian opera, did not take to it. Once again, her voice failed to thrill.

Miss Chudleigh, the Duchess of Northumberland and their friends no doubt swelled the audience in the Little Theatre that night, but there were not enough of them to prevent the evening becoming a financial disaster. This time it was the disgruntled John Fermor who shouldered the losses.

With no hope left of getting work at London's main opera house, and mounting debts to her lover, Teresa's prospects were looking as bleak as they had in the United Provinces. Her decision to throw in her lot with Fermor had been a disastrous mistake. For the first time in her life, she was experiencing what it was to be dependent on a man who was no longer her doting admirer. She had failed to match his expectations and was becoming a drain on his finances. Failure made her less attractive in his eyes. Teresa was aware that the longer she remained in London, the more she would be indebted to Fermor, yet she could not afford to leave him. Wanted for debt in practically every country in northern Europe, she had nowhere to run to any more.

Had she been a person of lesser mettle, Teresa might have given up hope then and there and joined the thousands of prostitutes who scraped a bare living on London's streets. But the resilience she had shown in Paris and the Austrian Netherlands came to her rescue. Instead of cracking under pressure, she picked herself up and bounced back in the most extraordinary fashion. Along with Miss Chudleigh, she hatched a fantastic plan that would marry her own particular gifts with the Englishwoman's sensational contacts.

As Mrs Cornelys, she was about to become the talk of London.

Eight

Teresa's plan was to open a smart concert room in the centre of London, a place where she could re-create the light-hearted atmosphere of Venice.

It had taken her only weeks to realize that life at the Hanoverian court was dull, marred by the royal family's meanness and interminable family squabbling. When the nobility were not obliged to be at St James's or at each other's houses, they roamed the town in search of diversion, not through any real appreciation of culture but rather, as writer Oliver Goldsmith phrased it, 'to indulge an unhappy vacancy'. When it came to their pleasures, the English aristocracy loved to spoil themselves, and there was no shortage of suppliers willing to help them do so at a price.

For the moneyed classes, eighteenth-century London was a culture consumer's paradise. The entertainment on offer ranged from the earthy to the ethereal. The hunting, shooting and fishing set were well catered-for by a host of traditional pursuits. Oblivious to the choking smog, they picnicked by the Thames and took boat-trips down to Greenwich and the Royal Arsenal at Woolwich. They fox-hunted in the Marylebone fields, and walked in St James's or Hyde Park. Traditional sports, such as boxing, cock-fighting and bear-baiting, were held at the riverside taverns. Gentlemen in search of 'country matters' did not have to look far: groups of outspoken whores hung about on almost every street corner, and under the colonnades in Covent Garden, where prospective punters could buy *Harris's List of Covent Garden Ladies, or Man of Pleasure's Kalender*, a publication listing the names, addresses and sexual specialities of around eighty local 'spirited madams'.

During the winter season, which lasted from November to May, the pursuit of high culture took precedence over the great outdoors, and the capital became a magnet for performers, musicians and artists from all over Europe. The streets of the West End were overrun by English and Continental painters to whose rented studios the upper classes flocked to view new works or to sit for their portraits, a social event in itself. In 1766, the beautiful and talented Swiss artist Angelica Kauffman moved to London from Rome, and settled in Soho's Golden Square. Within months the surrounding streets were blocked by the carriages of fashionable people who flocked to her studio to have their portraits painted. At the same time the painter Sir Joshua Reynolds was entertaining seven sitters a day at his home in Leicester Square, Soho.

Sitting for an artist or buying a painting was a relatively private occupation. The theatre and the opera offered more public conduits through which high culture could be acquired, and, more importantly, through which those acquiring it could be seen to be doing so by their peers. The 1759/60 London theatre season boasted no fewer than 541 separate performances staged by more than 230 players, who included among them the famous Mrs Cibber and David Garrick, the actor-manager at Drury Lane. Many upper-class families kept private boxes at the theatres and attended performances two or three times a week. Lest they got bored during the evening, the programmes usually included a short play along with the five-act main event.

Still, as in theatres elsewhere in Europe, the real action did not take place on stage but among the audience. A visit to Drury Lane or the Haymarket was viewed more as an opportunity to display one's clothes and jewels than as a chance to see a new play. 'The quality in the boxes are totally employed in finding out, and beckoning to their acquaintance, male and female,' complained a letter-writer to the *Theatrical Monitor*, in 1768. At the King's Theatre in the Haymarket, which in 1760 was still the only venue in London that held the coveted royal licence to stage opera, the upper-class audiences were equally inattentive. 'As the English in general have no great attachment to this exotic entertainment, and are, for the most part, entirely ignorant of the language, this theatre is treated with the utmost contempt by the more sensible part of the people,' commented the Prussian captain Count Archenholz in his book, *A*

Picture of England. 'The nobility alone support it; and they merely because – *it is the fashion.* There is not any place of entertainment in Europe where the audience *yawn* so much as there.'

When they were not snoring during an aria or talking to each other across the actors' voices, the quality might attend a musical concert. Since Teresa's first visit to London, the musical life of the capital had undergone something of a transformation. The catalyst for change had been the arrival in London in 1751 of the Italian violinist Felice de Giardini, said by Dr Burney, the musicologist, to be 'the greatest performer in Europe'. Throughout the early 1750s Giardini had run a series of subscription concerts at Hickford's Rooms in Brewer Street, Soho, and later in the more fashionable Great Room in Dean Street, and in 1754 he had taken over direction of the opera orchestra at the King's Theatre.

Largely thanks to the high standards Giardini demanded from his players, attending commercial concerts had now become part of the social scene, and interest in music had spread from the riverside taverns and City inns, where organizations such as the Academy of Ancient Music and the Castle Society had previously catered to predominantly male middle-class audiences with a serious interest in the subject, to the less serious if more fashionable West End. However, as backdrops against which to show off one's finery and well-honed wit, the existing concert venues left much to be desired. Even the Great Room in Dean Street was nothing more than a chilly converted chapel at the back of the Venetian ambassador's old house.

For sheer enjoyment and novelty, there was nothing to beat London's pleasure gardens, the only venues in the capital where the aristocracy, male and female, mingled happily with the rabble. The New Spring Garden at Vauxhall, Ranelagh House in Chelsea and, to a lesser extent, the Marylebone Gardens were frequented by 'the most famous beauties in London, from the highest to the lowest rank'. On summer nights, anyone who could afford the modest entrance fee to one of the pleasure gardens could listen to music, dance, eat, drink and, perhaps more importantly, make an assignation or even a conquest. The writer Edward Gibbon called Ranelagh 'the best market we have in England'.

Vauxhall was perhaps the most popular pleasure garden with ordinary people. 'It is very cheap going thither,' Samuel Pepys wrote, when it opened in 1661, 'for a man may go to spend what he will, or nothing, all is one – but to hear the nightingales and other birds, and here fiddles and there a harp, and here a Jew's trumpet, and here laughing, and there fine people walking is mighty divertising.' At the centre of Vauxhall was an orchestra pit surrounded by boxes from which lantern-lit shady paths radiated, terminating in magical vistas of statues, romantic ancient ruins, and a mock-up of an old water-mill, set behind a curtain and supplied with lighting and sound effects.

Ranelagh House in Chelsea, 'the enchanted palace of a genius', according to Smollett, was more genteel than Vauxhall and even more magical. From the moment it opened in 1742, it was the favourite of the fashionable set. 'It has totally beat Vauxhall,' wrote Horace Walpole that year. 'You can't set foot without treading on a Prince, or Duke of Cumberland.' Its grounds boasted a Chinese pavilion, an ornamental lake and a vast rotunda 160 paces in diameter heated by a huge central brazier, which was also used to cook the food and heat the drinks. 'The numbers of people who are generally assembled here, and who are walking round, present a curious sight,' noted the tourist Count Kielmansegge, 'which, together with the quantity of lights and music, astonishes people who see it for the first time, much more even than Vauxhall.'

The atmosphere of the pleasure gardens was the nearest thing London had to the magic of Venice. But the gardens had their drawbacks, not the least of which was England's climate. Closed during the winter months, they were usually open only between early May and late September, and even then they were subject to the vagaries of the unpredictable weather and the awful air pollution. Though admission fees were relatively cheap (the usual cost was between one shilling and half a crown, rising to five shillings on nights when firework displays were held), the refreshments could be costly. After Casanova spent an evening eating oysters and drinking champagne with an old flame at the Marylebone Gardens, he was presented with a bill for ten guineas.

The very popularity of the gardens engendered its own problems. Reaching them usually involved an arduous and often dangerous journey. Coaches overturned on the rutted roads, and highwaymen and footpads hung about the route, eager to relieve the nobility of their valuables. With so many people heading off at night down the same long dark narrow tracks, the traffic congestion was dreadful. When twelve thousand people flocked to Vauxhall on 21 April 1742 for the rehearsal of Handel's 'Music for the Royal Fireworks', it took many of them three hours simply to cross London Bridge. 'Mr Conway and I set out from his house at eight o'clock,' wrote Horace Walpole, of an horrendous journey he took to Vauxhall in May 1769. 'The tide and torrent of coaches was so prodigious that it was half an hour after nine before we got half-way from Westminster bridge. We then alighted, and after scrambling under bellies of horses, through wheels, and over posts and rails, we reached the gardens, where were already many thousand persons.'

Returning home after an evening out could be even more trying. Hackney carriages that had been paid to wait frequently made off with other passengers before their original occupants returned, there were long queues for ferries across the Thames, and people found themselves stranded for hours in the pitch-dark countryside, particularly when it rained. Even those who had their own transport had to wait, as Walpole discovered, when 'we found three strings of coaches all along the road, who did not move half a foot in half an hour'.

To Teresa, who had been used to the more intimate scale of Italian, Dutch and Flemish cities, the array of entertainment on offer in London, and the number of people providing it, was both daunting and dazzling. Yet if she was not going to establish a singing career in the capital – and reactions to her début concert indicated as much – she was going to have to make her mark among them somehow. There were two areas of which she had an insider's knowledge: the latest Continental music, which she had studied in the courts of Europe; and the world of a theatrical impresario, which she had absorbed in Venice. The obvious path for her to take, therefore, was to become some sort of musical impresario.

Teresa's genius lay in identifying a yawning gap in the overcrowded market-place of London's commercial musical-entertainment world, a gap that she alone was qualified to fill. She realized that although the nobility could dance, play cards, eat, party, socialize and listen to opera or music in London, they did all these things in separate places. Vauxhall and Ranelagh came nearest to providing all of these activities at the same time, but the gardens were hard to get to, attended by everyone from princes to prostitutes, and only open during the summer when the nobility had retreated to their country estates.

What, Teresa conjectured, if she were to run a pleasure garden in the centre of London, an easily accessible venue within which she would re-create the magical atmosphere of the Venetian Carnival? What if this 'pleasure garden' was to be indoors, in a private house, for example, protected from the choking sea-coal smoke and the unpredictable weather? Then people would be able to attend it all year round.

The idea went further. What if her premises were not merely situated in a house but in a grand private mansion fit for princes and kings? What if she were to put on exclusive concerts there, as she had in Paris? And what if each of these concerts was to be the focus of a larger assembly, which would include eating, conversation, dancing and gambling? Then attending it would become infinitely more desirable.

Teresa's ingenuity did not stop there. She had already observed that, to the upper echelons of English society, mixing with the right people was the most important item on their social agenda. Well, there were plenty of moneyed people in London – people who could afford to pay top prices for their entertainment – but these were not necessarily the kind of people she wanted to attract as customers. She wanted to aim higher: to royalty, the nobility and the wealthiest members of the gentry – the topmost level of society. If she charged so much for tickets to her concerts and assemblies that only the very wealthiest people could afford to purchase them, and if she forced these wealthy people to be vetted for social position by some of the best-connected people at court – Miss Chudleigh and her circle of friends – then, surely, tickets to her premises would become the most sought-after in London.

To put it in its simplest form, as John Fermor would do later, Teresa's idea was that 'a Concert and Assembly furnished out in an elegant Manner and carried on by Subscription in some commodious house for that purpose would probably meet with Encouragement and be a profitable Undertaking'.

In effect, Teresa planned to launch London's first exclusive membership-only nightclub.

It was a brilliant idea, guaranteed to appeal to the nobility's superficial hunger for culture, their thirst for diversion and, even more important, their obsession with class. Yet how could Teresa pull off the venture? She was a woman with few legal rights. She was a foreigner who spoke scarcely a word of English, and she possessed nothing but a mounting pile of debts.

As in the past, Teresa was unfazed by these seemingly insurmountable problems. Though her attempts to run the theatres of Gand and Liège had ended in financial disaster, past failures never deterred her from trying something new. If anything, they had the opposite effect. All she saw was the biggest picture. If successful, the scheme would provide her with everything she needed: a home for herself and Sophie, independence from Fermor, and free rein for her creative and musical skills. In Elizabeth Chudleigh and her coterie of friends, she had the perfect social contacts for the project. Elizabeth's co-operation was guaranteed, for if she was to be put in charge of the membership list her social status would be enhanced and she would have even more power over her contemporaries.

As for money, Teresa would raise the initial investment somehow, probably through appealing cleverly to Fermor's business sense. What she needed to do first was to find grand yet affordable premises within easy reach of St James's, the City and Westminster.

There was only one place to look, and that was Soho.

The parish of St Anne's, Soho, was situated between the consumers' Mecca of Oxford Street to the north, arty Leicester Fields to the south, the poverty-stricken rookeries of St Giles to the east, and royal St James's to the south-west. Fewer than a hundred years earlier, its streets and houses had been in open countryside owned by the Crown and used mainly for archery and hunting; washerwomen dried clothes there too. The Soho fields, as they were known, derived their name from an ancient Anglo-French hunting cry, defined by the fifteenth-century vocabulary *Promptorium Parvulorum* as 'Sohoe, the hare ys founde'.

Up until the mid-seventeenth century, the only buildings in the fields were a hunting inn, a pest-house and a few shacks, which had been erected illegally in contravention of ancient royal proclamations that had prevented development outside London's city walls. Then, in the early seventeenth century, some of the Soho fields were leased to members of the aristocracy and a handful of large country houses was constructed there, the two most notable belonging to Lords Leicester and Gerrard.

Leicester House and Gerrard House would probably have remained the only large buildings in the Soho fields had it not been for two terrible events that took place in the 1660s: the Plague and the Great Fire. Bubonic plague, brought into the country by shipboard rats, struck the City of London in the winter of 1664. As it spread through the narrow, overcrowded streets, killing between 70,000 and 100,000 people, Parliament was prorogued and the court fled to the safety of Oxford. No sooner had the plague abated than the City was struck by a further disaster: on the night of 2 September 1666, the Great Fire of London started in Pudding Lane. Four days later, it had reduced eighty-seven churches and 13,000 homes to smouldering rubble.

Forced to live and work elsewhere while their houses were rebuilt, Londoners camped outside the city walls, many of them in the Soho fields. Even though the homeless citizens had nowhere else to go, the Crown protested vehemently against their illegally erected 'small and mean habitations and cottages'. In 1671 King Charles II issued a fiercely worded proclamation charging 'all persons to forbear building any more new buildings in the suburbs of London and Westminster' and threatening that 'all such buildings shall be abated and thrown down, and the offenders proceeded against with the utmost rigour of the law'.

Everyone ignored this proclamation. Having experienced the fresh air and open aspects of the countryside to the west of London, few citizens wanted to return to what was by then perceived as a dangerous and overcrowded city. Even the Surveyor General, the man responsible for enforcing the law, built himself a house in the Soho fields. During the 1670s and 1680s, what amounted to a hundred years of restrictive building policies collapsed in a frenzy of development. Speculators such as Richard Frith and Dr Nicholas Barbon bought long leases on the fields, and the grass, trees, wild flowers and shrubs disappeared under a seamless grid of roads, terraced houses and paved squares. Wealthy businessmen, the landed gentry and the aristocracy snapped up the new properties straight off the drawing-board, Sir Christopher Wren's architectural practice was contracted to build a church between Dean Street and Wardour Street, and in 1678 an Act of Parliament was passed creating Soho a parish in its own right.

From the start, the new parish had its own, very Continental character. In 1685, Louis XIV of France revoked the Edict of Nantes, and thousands of persecuted Huguenot refugees fled to England, bringing with them their prodigious craft skills. The silk-weavers settled in Spitalfields in East London where there was a plentiful supply of water to drive their looms, but the goldsmiths, tailors and tapestry-weavers moved into Soho's smaller houses, where the proximity of so many wealthy Englishmen guaranteed them a ready market for their superb luxury goods. By 1693, there were five Huguenot chapels in Soho, and in 1711 a survey of the parish's 8133 inhabitants showed that two in five were French. Describing Soho in his 1739 *History of London*, William Maitland wrote that 'Many parts of this Parish so greatly abound with French, that it is an easy Matter for a Stranger to imagine himself in France.'

This cosmopolitan atmosphere attracted yet more foreigners to the area. Cheaper than nearby St James's, and with easy access to Westminster, Covent Garden and the City, Soho soon became the natural haunt of all visiting Continental artists, singers, musicians and tourists. And when the nobility began to move west into newly built Mayfair, Soho's grandest houses were taken over by foreign embassies.

Of Soho's three large open squares, Soho Square was perhaps the smartest. Situated in the north-east corner of the parish and originally known as King's Square after its architect, Gregory King, it was a large cobbled space with five narrow roads leading off it – Denmark, Charles and Sutton Streets on the east, north and west sides respectively, Frith Street and Greek Street to the south. A wide stone pavement edged with wooden bollards protected pedestrians from passing carriages, and in the middle there was a large garden with lawns, gravel paths and an elaborate stone fountain adorned with virgins and river gods and topped by Caius Cibber's imposing statue of King Charles II.

Right from the start 'the great Square', as the diarist John Evelyn called it, attracted Soho's highest-ranking inhabitants. The parish's first royal resident, James Scott, Duke of Monmouth, the illegitimate son of King Charles II with the Welsh-born courtesan Lucy Waters, had built himself a detached mansion on the south side of the square in the late 1670s, but sadly he only ever stayed there for the odd night. In 1683 James's doting father reluctantly expelled him from court for disobedience, and two years later he was beheaded on Tower Hill for leading a rebellion against his uncle, King James II. But the romance attached to his name attracted a bevy of well-born neighbours. By 1685, the year of his death, they included one earl, three peers, five countesses and four baronets.

In 1759, when Teresa arrived in London, Monmouth House was occupied by Daniel Finch, the eighth Earl of Winchilsea. Other residents of the square at that time included the Speaker of the House of Commons Arthur Onslow, the Bishop of Peterborough, Salisbury and Winchester, the Duchess of Wharton, the millionaire Alderman William Beckford, at least three Members of Parliament, the Spanish ambassador and the London envoy of the Venetian Republic.

It was, no doubt, while paying a call on the Venetian envoy that Teresa first spotted the empty mansion that was to become her home and her obsession for the next eighteen years. Carlisle House, as it was called, was situated on the south-east side of Soho Square, adjacent to Sutton Street. A double-fronted grey-brick mansion some forty-six feet wide at the front, it had substantial outbuildings stretching out 294 feet behind it including stables and coach-houses backing on to Hog Lane (present-day Charing Cross Road). Built in the 1680s, the house had taken its name from its first occupant, Edward Howard, the second Earl of Carlisle, who had acquired a lease on the land from the Earl of Portland, who held the freehold.

In 1753 the Howards left Soho, and their lease was sold on to George Smith Bradshaw and Paul Saunders, eminent tapestry-makers and upholsterers who had premises in nearby Greek Street. The actual mansion did not interest the men so much as its stables and coach-house backing on to Hog Lane, which they wished to use as workshops and storerooms. The grand address, however, was certainly good for their business, which was known thereafter as 'The Royal Tapestry Manufactory, Soho Square'.

For the next four years, Carlisle House itself was sublet to the ambassador of the King of Naples, who turned part of the back buildings into a Roman Catholic chapel where he and his staff could celebrate Mass (this was a privilege allowed to foreign diplomats, though still forbidden to the English). After he moved on in 1758, the building was briefly leased by three envoys of the government of the Dutch Republic, who came to England in the summer of 1759 to settle a shipping dispute involving the Dutch West India Company. By the following winter, when Teresa spotted it, the mansion was empty again. Dust-sheets shrouded the chandeliers and furniture, the fire grates and hearth stones were blackened by fallen soot and the whole place reeked of neglect. But as Paul Saunders showed his prospective tenant round, unhooking the wooden shutters to let in the watery winter daylight, Teresa immediately realized the building's potential.

Though badly in need of redecoration, Carlisle House was vast, and needed little doing to it to prepare it for her public assemblies. The cellar contained kitchens large enough to cater for huge numbers of people. The ground floor boasted a plethora of inter-communicating reception rooms furnished with Turkey and Wilton carpets, mahogany tables and brass chandeliers. The disused Roman Catholic chapel was ideal for use as a concert room. From the stone-flagged front hall, a grand staircase led up to a series of bright, imposing first-floor salons perfect for playing cards, socializing and dancing. The second floor was given over to bedrooms, which would make fine living quarters for Sophie and herself, and tucked under the eaves were attics big enough to accommodate dozens of servants.

Crowning the building was a large flat roof-terrace reminiscent of the wooden roof-terraces of Venice where women were wont to sit out in the sunshine to bleach streaks into their hair. It had breathtaking panoramic views – east across the rookeries of St Giles to the City, south towards the Palace of Westminster, west towards Tyburn and newly constructed Mayfair, and north across open countryside to the distant hill-top villages of Highgate and Hampstead. If Carlisle House had any faults, its position was not one of them. A person travelling here from the City, St James's or Mayfair could reach it easily in a sedan chair or carriage or even, if need be, on foot. And the surrounding Soho streets were packed with wine and food shops whose French owners could be sweet-talked into providing Teresa with all the necessaries, and the credit, she required.

With her heart already set on Carlisle House, Teresa took Elizabeth Chudleigh to see it. Once she had obtained her approval, she took Fermor. Relations might have been strained between them, but Teresa needed money and an English-speaking man to secure the lease for her, and Fermor was the only man she knew who could provide her with both. Assuring him that she would be able to pay him back everything she owed him once her new venture was up and running, and hinting that he would share in the business's profits, Teresa roped her lover into the scheme.

Won over by his mistress's enthusiasm, Fermor went to see Bradshaw and Saunders and negotiated a lease on Carlisle House. On 29 April, a memorandum was drawn up between Teresa and Saunders: Mrs Cornelys would rent Carlisle House at an agreed rate of £180 per annum unfurnished, with a further sum to cover the use of the contents: to be £20 for the first year, £15 for the second, and £10 for the third. Since Teresa was a foreigner and a woman, which made her doubly untrustworthy in his eyes, Saunders demanded watertight security over these payments. Fermor agreed to provide it, and as a consequence it was his name, not Teresa's, that appeared on the lease.

Teresa moved into Carlisle House on Saturday, 17 May 1760. Seven months earlier, she had arrived in England with nothing. Now, for the first time in her life, she had a house of her own, and a house, moreover, that matched her grand aspirations. Soho Square was one of London's best addresses, and Carlisle House was among the largest mansions in the square.

All she had to do now was to turn her business idea into a reality. The challenge was just what she needed. With single-minded dedication, and using Fermor's money, she immediately started to refurbish the property. At the age of thirty-seven, Teresa had at last found her vocation. From now on, Carlisle House would dominate her life.

Nine

By now, John Fermor had taken up his job as the rector of his late uncle's charity school in Crowborough. He divided his time between his family and religious duties there, and his mistress in London. This double life did not make him happy. If he thought that renting Carlisle House on Teresa's behalf would successfully paper over the divisions between them, he was wrong.

The lovers appeared to be nursing very different ideas of what the arrangement between them actually was. Since he had guaranteed to pay the rent of Carlisle House and to finance the concerts and assemblies that would take place in it, Fermor presumed that he was to be at least a sleeping partner in Teresa's business and that he would have a fifty-fifty share in any future profits. Teresa, for her part, looked on the money Fermor gave her as part and parcel of their relationship, simple generosity on his part and 'not at all strange coming from a rich Englishman, since we loved each other and were living together'. Having suffered years of financial hardship, she had made up her mind that from now on she would look after herself and Sophie. And so, even though she was using Fermor's money to set up Carlisle House, she regarded the venture as entirely her own.

As soon as she was installed in Soho Square, Teresa began to express her unhappiness that Fermor's name, not hers, was on the lease. If her concerts and assemblies were to succeed, she insisted that it was 'prudent that it should not be publickly known that [he] or any other person was a partner with [her] in the said undertaking but that it should seem that it was her own undertaking, and carried on by herself alone'. Fermor felt uneasy about this, but his protests were no match for the combined feminine wiles of his mistress and Elizabeth Chudleigh, who was acting as her adviser on every aspect of the project. Against his better judgement, he was dispatched to see Bradshaw and Saunders to draw up a new lease putting Carlisle House in Teresa's name.

Even though he had signed away his rights, as Teresa's guarantor Fermor was still obligated to pay the rent of Carlisle House until such time as she could pay it herself, and he had also promised to fund the house's refurbishment. Because of this, he felt he was entitled to live in Soho Square with her. Teresa was shocked by his presumption. If it were known that she was living with a married clergyman, her reputation would be ruined even before the business got off the ground.

Once again Fermor protested. Once again his protests proved useless against the increasingly watertight Cornelys–Chudleigh alliance. Within weeks, he found himself excluded from what he still regarded as *his* house, and forced to rent rooms in nearby Greek Street. As the summer progressed, he looked on warily from there as, with all the skills for creating magical settings which she had learned both from the margravine and from her childhood in the San Samuele theatre, Teresa transformed the shabby décor of Carlisle House into an exquisitely tasteful jewel-box. By early August, Fermor had grown seriously worried. Teresa was freely spending money – *his* money – on what he still believed was their joint venture; but he had no proof that it *was* a joint venture. After all, his name was no longer even on the lease of the house.

Fermor might not have inherited his grandfather's business acumen, but he was not a fool. During the second week of August, suspecting that he would never see a return on all the money he was laying out, he got his lawyer to draw up a partnership agreement, stating that he and Teresa had entered into a fifty-fifty partnership for a term of six years 'in all Concerts, Balls, Assemblys or any other musicall undertaking whatever'. Any profits that these entertainments made were to be equally divided between them 'Share and Share alike'. The agreement also gave Teresa the power to dissolve their partnership 'when she thinks proper', but only if she paid Fermor every penny she owed him, plus a further thousand pounds.

On 13 August, Fermor and his lawyer took the agreement to

Carlisle House and demanded that Teresa sign it immediately. She hesitated. Fermor's legal document made her as suspicious of him as he was of her. Although she attempted to understand what the agreement said, her English was still poor and the legal jargon was beyond her comprehension.

She understood enough, however, not to want to put her name to the document, and her refusal to do so resulted in a bitter argument. Desperate to secure his investment, Fermor resorted to blackmail: if Teresa did not sign the agreement, he would have her arrested and thrown into prison, he told her. 'Greatly terrified with the threats . . . and looking upon herself as absolutely in his power by being so indebted to him', as she later claimed, Teresa had no option but to put her name to the six-year partnership agreement.

With the focused concentration that always enabled her to carry on working regardless of her anxieties, Teresa put aside her worries about Fermor and continued to prepare Carlisle House for its planned opening in late November. At the same time, she finalized the brilliant concept that would make the place unique. The Soho mansion was to house a very exclusive suite of rooms, and if people wanted to come to them, they would have first to subscribe to an exclusive, expensive private club which was to be known as 'The Society in Soho-square'. Membership of this Society was to be strictly limited to the upper echelons of the nobility and gentry – the kind of people who could afford to pay over the odds for the privilege – and a small committee of women headed by Elizabeth Chudleigh would vet anyone wishing to join. Elizabeth and her friends would keep a list of who was and who was not eligible, by their position and pedigree, to belong to the Society in Soho-square. They would set the rules, promote the organization among their immediate circle and even sell subscription tickets from their homes. Advance bookings for meetings of the Society would be imperative, for admittance was to be by pre-paid ticket only. Once bought, a ticket would not be transferable from one person to another. The rules forbade entrance to anyone except a *bona fide* member of the Society.

Using her unparalleled position at court, Elizabeth began to drum up interest in the Society in Soho-square. Within weeks she had a list of wealthy and powerful subscribers, who included among them Elizabeth Percy, Duchess of Northumberland, the Duchess of Ancaster, wife of the Lord Chamberlain, the Duchess of Argyll, Lady Coventry and the Marquess of Hertford's heiress daughter Miss Conway. Most important of all, Elizabeth signed up Edward Augustus Hanover, the twenty-one-year-old Duke of York, younger brother of George, Prince of Wales. Writing about him after his death, the Duchess of Northumberland described the duke as 'remarkably plain' and claimed that he had 'great Vivacity but with a mind so devoted to pleasure and so little regard to propriety as robb'd him of his Dignity and made him rather a trifling than an amiable Character'. A born social butterfly, he flitted from one social event to another, and frequently attended a concert at court, two plays and an assembly on the same evening – which made him an ideal candidate for membership of Carlisle House.

All was set for a successful launch when the winter season started in late November. But on 25 October there was an unforeseen setback: King George II died suddenly at Kensington Palace. The circumstances of his death were, to say the least, ignominious. 'He went to bed well last night, rose at six this morning as usual, looked, I suppose, if all his money was in his purse, and called for his chocolate,' Horace Walpole reported to George Montagu that day. 'A little after seven, he went into the water-closet; the German *valet de chambre* heard a noise, listened, heard something like a groan, ran in, and found the hero of Oudenarde and Dettingen on the floor, with a gash on his right temple, by falling against the corner of a bureau. He tried to speak, could not, and expired.'

Although the Duke of York was plunged into mourning along with the rest of the court, the death of the 'choleric little sovereign' did not in the end scupper Teresa's plans to open Carlisle House a month later. In fact, it proved something of a blessing to her, for the accession of the late king's grandson ushered in a new, brighter social era. George III was the first Hanoverian monarch to have been born and educated in England, and the first to grow up with English as his mother tongue; his popularity far outweighed that of his German-speaking grandfather. More importantly for Teresa, as his mother's 'confidential favourite' Elizabeth Chudleigh had known the twenty-two-year-old sovereign and his siblings all their lives. Now that he was king and his brother, the pleasure-seeking Duke of York, was next in line to the throne, her standing at court rose immeasurably – and so did Teresa's hopes of success.

The first meeting of the Society in Soho-square was set for Thursday, 27 November. As the day approached, Teresa commissioned elaborate engraved entrance tickets to be printed, and sent them over to Kingston House so that Elizabeth could sell them to her friends. Optimistic that she would have a full house on the night, she bought large quantities of china, high-quality wax candles and playing-cards, and ordered refreshments from Louis Weltje, a well-known German chef (later he set up his own club in St James's and became caterer to the Prince Regent). Next, Teresa engaged five waiters and, at a cost of fifteen guineas, a small orchestra of musicians. Leaving nothing to chance, she tipped the local watch £1 8s. 9d. to ensure the safe arrival and departure of the expected crowd, and hired two constables to keep the peace at the door.

Her costs – all met by John Fermor – also included a budget of fifteen shillings set aside 'for advertising the meeting'. On Saturday, 22 November, a notice duly appeared on the front page of the *Public Advertiser*:

The Nobility and Gentry, Subscribers to the SOCIETY in Soho-square, are acquainted that the first Meeting will be on Thursday the 27TH Instant at Seven, the second the 11TH of December, and the third postponed to the 1ST of January 1761. The Subscribers are desired to send their Subscriptions to those they have subscribed to, and shall receive a Ticket and the Remainder before the next Concert.

This was the first of many hundreds of notices that Teresa would place in the *Public Advertiser* over the next eighteen years. Her use of the expression 'The Nobility and Gentry' at the top was a stroke of brilliance that would soon be copied by all her rivals.

Four days later, another front-page advertisement appeared in the *Public Advertiser*, notifying 'the Nobility and Gentry' that the first meeting of the Society would take place the following day, and inviting ticket-holders to a 'general rehearsal' that afternoon. Carlisle House had not yet opened, but Teresa was already proving herself a marketing genius.

On the morning of the twenty-seventh, the reception rooms of Carlisle House were filled with armfuls of costly out-of-season 'spring branches'. Down in the cellar kitchens, Louis Weltje and his helpers set to work preparing the dozens of fish to be served with imported lemons among the refreshments. Later that afternoon the musicians arrived, set up their instruments and began their rehearsals. Packs of playing-cards were set out on the tables, fires were lit in all the grates, and the brass chandeliers were given a final polish and filled with dozens of expensive candles.

As dusk descended on Soho Square, the level of excitement in the house rose even higher. Teresa's future depended on the evening being a success. Would the nobility and gentry appreciate the musical entertainment she had arranged for them? Would Weltje's food be to their taste? Most important of all, would anyone turn up for the first meeting of the Society in Soho-square?

The answer to all these questions was a resounding yes. By the time the servants opened the front doors of Carlisle House at seven o'clock that evening, hundreds of carriages and sedan chairs were on their way to Soho: everyone was eager not to miss the novel entertainment that had been touted around town by the notorious Miss Chudleigh. In fact, people turned up in such numbers that, large as Carlisle House was, they could scarcely all fit into it.

The crush did not seem to bother the fashionable crowd. In fact, it lent an added intimacy to the occasion. As they pushed through the artfully decorated rooms filled with their peers, talking, drinking, showing off their clothes and exercising their wit on each other, the assembled duchesses, ladies, dukes and earls began to realize that they were participating in something out of the ordinary: the meeting had all the atmosphere of a gay and light-hearted private party, but since they had paid for their tickets they were not beholden to any host or hostess. After a while, the ever-present Teresa discreetly ushered them into the converted chapel at the back of the house for a concert of innovative Continental music, which no doubt included compositions by her old friend and colleague Christoph Gluck. To her dismay, getting everyone into the concert room was impossible. There were not chairs enough for everyone, the ladies' hooped skirts took up an inordinate amount of space, and the old chapel was soon so packed that many of the audience had to listen to the music from the hall. Even so, there were no recorded complaints.

Afterwards, the crowd moved upstairs to the first-floor reception rooms, where a group of musicians played dance music. For those who wished to gamble, card-tables had been arranged in the adjoining rooms. As in a Venetian *ridotto*, the house took a cut of the money that changed hands.

The first meeting of the Society in Soho-square was a sparkling occasion, not least because of its novelty value. The subscribers' list ensured that only the wealthiest and best-connected people attended, and they found to their delight that the elegant house, unlike Hickford's Rooms or the Great Room in Dean Street, Soho's other concert venues, provided a perfect backdrop against which to show off their fine clothes and jewellery. Here, at last, was a public setting worthy of the *ton*'s presence, a place on a par with the best private homes in London. Teresa's formula – which was to provide an assembly, a concert, gambling, dancing and food – immediately won over any sceptics. Her tasteful decoration of Carlisle House, the merry yet decorous atmosphere she created, and her superb direction of the evening's events, made an intoxicating mix.

By the following afternoon the Society in Soho-square had become the talk of the town. To the delight of Teresa, Elizabeth Chudleigh and John Fermor, Carlisle House was not set to be 'a losing adventure' like Teresa's disastrous concert at the Little Theatre in the Haymarket the previous February, but, on the contrary, a roaring success.

Aristocrats who had not yet signed up for membership of the

Society now made a grovelling pilgrimage to Elizabeth Chudleigh's Knightsbridge house to beg her to add their names to the list of subscribers already on her books but, unfortunately, not all of them proved as eager to lay their money on the table. On 9 December Teresa placed a notice in the *Public Advertiser* gently reminding them to pay up, and went on to ask an unheard-of favour from those who proposed to attend her second meeting: 'It is humbly hoped that the Ladies will (if agreeable to themselves) come without Hoops, as it prevents many Subscribers from coming into the Music Room.' As Mrs Cornelys, she had been in business for only one night yet she already felt confident enough of success to dictate a dress code to the haughty English aristocracy.

According to Horace Walpole, Elizabeth Chudleigh – or 'the Virgin', as he ironically called his old playmate – was revelling in her new power, which was to control the membership list. 'Propriety is so much in fashion, that Miss Chudleigh has called for the council books of the subscription concert, and has struck off the name of Miss Naylor,' he wrote to George Montagu on the day of Teresa's second assembly. What dreadful deed the unfortunate Miss Naylor had done to deserve being socially ostracized, he failed to say.

The second meeting of the Society in Soho-square took place on 11 December. Once again, the aristocracy turned up in force. The combination of Carlisle House's socially exclusive entrance policy, its programme of serious Continental music played by top-class musicians, the light-hearted atmosphere Teresa created and an advertising campaign aimed at the Achilles' heel of its target audience – their conceit – ensured that no one wanted to be left out.

To John Fermor's relief, subscription money flooded in. For the first time since Teresa had arrived in England, it seemed as if his investment in her was going to pay off. By mid-December, she had paid him back just over £250, and Elizabeth Chudleigh had given him a further fifty guineas she had collected in subscription fees. Although this was a pittance compared to all the money he had laid out on Teresa since she had arrived in London, Fermor could envisage a time when he might make a profit out of her. Despite their frustrating and increasingly quarrelsome relationship, this convinced him to continue financing Carlisle House, at least for the time being.

The third meeting, held on New Year's Day 1761, consolidated the popularity of the Society. People were clamouring to be allowed in. A hundred years earlier, fox-hunting had been the most popular sport in Soho; from now on it was to be gatecrashing Carlisle House. Soon Teresa's front door was besieged by people claiming that they had 'accidentally' left their tickets at home – and also by genuine paid-up subscribers who, having been sent all their tickets for the season, had either lost them or brought the wrong ticket for that event.

With each new meeting, membership of the Society in Sohosquare became more sought-after, and the 'singular' Mrs Cornelys more famous. Teresa had struggled for years to make her name as a singer. Now, almost overnight, she had unwittingly become a celebrity impresario. She was even in demand as a singer again, and invited to take part in a benefit concert at the Little Theatre in the Haymarket in aid of the Flemish composer Emanuel Siprutini, Elizabeth Chudleigh's close – some said intimate – friend. The irony of the occasion could not have been lost on Teresa. When she had last sung at the Little Theatre she had been an unknown, unable to fill the seats. Now everyone was paying over the odds to see her, and would-be subscribers to Carlisle House were clambering over each other to get into her meetings.

That Teresa's head was turned by all the attention she received was understandable. London was at her feet and, for the first time in years, she had substantial amounts of money in her purse. It did not stay there for long. The idea of saving for a rainy day was simply not on her agenda. Though she had had to rely on Fermor's help to get what she regarded as *her* business up and running, by mid-January she could already picture a time when she would have no need of him. With this in mind, she cornered him at Kingston House on 21 January 1761. After borrowing just under four hundred pounds from him to tide over the business in the short term, she and Elizabeth manipulated him into signing another business

117

agreement, which gave Teresa the right to dissolve their partnership as soon as she wished.

However, in the short term she needed Fermor, and not just to finance Carlisle House on a day-to-day basis. By early spring, she had formulated another plan, even more ambitious than the first. She would spend the approaching off-season summer months turning her mansion into a palace truly worthy of the princes, earls and duchesses who attended it. And, with the help of her lover's money, she would do so in the grandest possible manner.

Ten

In consultation with Samuel Norman, a cabinet-maker who had recently taken over Bradshaw and Saunders's upholstery workshops on Hog Lane, Teresa drew up plans for what she considered were essential alterations to Carlisle House. These included raising the front steps, providing new doors, shutters and hinges, fitting new cornices, replastering and repainting the walls, and replumbing the entire building.

This was just the start of her grandiose scheme for transforming Carlisle House. The back buildings that stretched along Sutton Street, including the old chapel where until now she had held her concerts, were to be demolished and replaced by a new complex of assembly rooms. Designed by Jacob Leroux, a French architect based in Soho, these were to be built to the highest specifications, with a plain brick exterior topped by an expensive Tavistock slate roof and gutters lined with lead at a density of 'not less than seven pounds to the foot'. The ground floor of the new building was to contain a 'Great Supper Room' with Doric-capped columns, a yellow deal floor and a table large enough to seat four hundred. On the first floor there was to be a magnificent concert room with arched sash windows along both sides, a thirty-foot-high ceiling and a coffered semi-dome at the east end looming over a raised dais large enough to accommodate a full orchestra. The scale of this room was astounding: at eighty feet long by thirty-five feet wide, it would be three-quarters the size of Inigo Jones's famous Banqueting Hall at Whitehall Palace.

In addition to this new building, Norman's schedule of works at Carlisle House listed plans for renovating the 'Upper Corridor Passage . . . The Waiting Room Gable end of new buildings . . . The Music Rooms over the Waiting Rooms . . . The Garret on Right hand of Stair Head . . . The Women's Garret . . . Second

Floor Night Rooms . . . Mrs Cornelys's dressing rooms . . . The Great Staircase and Passage . . . The Grand Waiting Room . . . Two Tea Rooms . . . The Large Front Card Room . . . The Yellow Waiting Room . . . The Marble Hall . . . The Hall next the Square'.

Apart from overseeing the building of Leroux's new assembly rooms and the renovation of the old house, Norman was also commissioned to supply all the furnishings, including £730 worth of goods for the Concert Room, £125 worth of tables and chairs for the Great Supper Room, 'Octagonal Glass doors' costing in excess of £100 and, Teresa's *pièce de résistance*, a 'fine large glass seventy-six by forty-four head, forty-four by twenty-four in a glass bordered burnished gold frame' for the Concert Room, which Norman priced at just over £262 – an unimaginable amount for a single mirror.

The contract between Teresa and Norman specified that his work was to be 'Executed Performed Fulfilled and done in a neat good substantial and workmanlike manner', and that the Concert Room was to be finished by 20 September, with the rest of the house ready by mid-November, in time for the start of the 1761/2 winter season. If his men failed to meet this deadline, he would be subject to a £100 penalty clause. Though a substantial sum, this was a pittance compared to the full cost of the building works and furniture, which together amounted to some £3200.

The costs were staggering, even to a wealthy man like John Fermor. Having been brought up simply with the Boorder family in Sevenoaks, he probably could not see anything wrong with Carlisle House as it was. Besides, he had already paid for it to be refurbished once. It seemed to him that Teresa was bleeding him dry of money. Although she had already paid him back some of what she owed him, this had not stopped her asking him for yet more loans, and somehow he always found himself agreeing to whatever she requested. Between the end of January and early May 1761, he gave her a total of £459 1s. 6d. – £383 9s. 6d. on 21 January at Miss Chudleigh's house in Knightsbridge, £23 2s. on 30 March, and a further £52 10s. on 4 May, to pay the man she had hired to become the musical director of her concerts: the

German composer, viol da gamba player and chamber musician to Queen Charlotte, Carl Friedrich Abel.

By now Fermor deeply regretted his naïveté in getting financially involved with Teresa. Within the past year they had gone from sleeping together to being sleeping partners in what was officially a joint business, yet in neither area of their relationship did he have any power. As he watched his late uncle's precious inheritance run like water through his lover's fingers – at least five thousand pounds of it had poured away during the past two years – Fermor feared for his future and that of his wife and children in Crowborough. Teresa seemed to be running rings around him. She always did exactly what she wanted, and she had an uncanny ability to make him do exactly what she wanted, too.

Certainly, when it came to translating her vision of Carlisle House into reality, Teresa was willing to use the full range of manipulative skills she had honed on Senator Malipiero during her youth. Despite Fermor's growing anxieties about money, she convinced him that her – or *his* – or *their* – future long-term profits could only be guaranteed if he made a substantial short-term investment in Carlisle House now. Against his better judgement, Fermor found himself agreeing to guarantee Norman's fees so that the transformation of Carlisle House could go ahead.

Teresa also pointed out that, since it did not make sense to rebuild a property one did not own, she ought to buy Carlisle House outright, and she persuaded Fermor to lend her the money to do so. Accordingly he was dispatched to see John Machin, a businessman who had recently purchased Bradshaw and Saunders's interest in the lease. Machin and Fermor agreed a price of thirty-two pounds per annum for a ninety-two-year lease on the house, offices and gardens, plus a further nine pounds a year for thirty-eight years to rent the stable block. This amounted to £1950, a sum that Teresa promised faithfully to pay back by giving Fermor all the subscription money her assemblies took from then on.

Carlisle House officially became Teresa's property on 16 May 1761, or so she believed. In reality, the building now belonged to John Fermor who, in an underhand last-minute move, put the new lease in his own name. The couple's legal, financial and emotional involvement with each other was growing more complex by the week. On 10 June, Fermor forced Teresa to sign yet another agreement, this one stating that, in return for him standing surety for the furniture that had been ordered in her name from Saunders, the agreement he had signed on 21 January, giving her the right to dissolve their partnership, should be rendered null and void.

Unaware of the underlying tensions between Carlisle House's owners, Samuel Norman immediately set to work gutting the main house and demolishing the back buildings. By mid-June, the foundations of Leroux's new assembly rooms had been laid and Teresa ceremoniously cemented in the first stone. A copper plate was affixed to it, inscribed, 'Not Vain but Grateful In Honour of the Society and my first Protectress Ye Honble Mrs Elizabeth Chudleigh is Laid the First Stone of this edifice June 19 1761 by me Teresa Cornelys.' It was indicative of Teresa's growing self-importance that her name was written in the largest lettering, and equally revealing of her attitude to Fermor that there was no mention of him.

The insult was not lost on him. As the walls of the new building arose over the summer, the lovers' faltering relationship broke down irretrievably. Even so, on 10 September Teresa managed to talk Fermor into lending her a further £286 'pour peyer les necessaires'. By the time the concert room was roofed in mid-October, the IOUs Fermor had amassed indicated that Teresa had borrowed just under £745 from him since January, and they were barely on speaking terms.

This was bad news for Samuel Norman who, now that the roof had been completed, was due a payment of £900, which amounted to half the cost of the building work. In a bullish mood, Fermor, who had given Norman guarantees that he would pay him, refused to hand over this sum until Teresa paid him back everything she owed him. But Teresa claimed to have no money. All the subscriptions she had taken during the previous winter had been spent on running Carlisle House, and she would have no further income until the house reopened the following winter. If Fermor

1. *Il Ridotto di Ca' Giustiniani*, after Pietro Longhi. Gambling and intrigue were an intrinsic part of everyday life in eighteenth-century Venice.

2. *The Concert*, by Pietro Longhi. A private concert in the home of a wealthy Venetian.

3. (*top left, opposite page*) Giacomo Casanova, pastel by Francesco Casanova, his brother. Casanova as a young man was intelligent, handsome and elegantly coiffed.

4. (*top right, opposite page*) The only realistic portrait of Teresa Cornelys in existence. She is wearing the lace-trimmed mob-cap in which she is always depicted in satirical prints.

5. (*left, opposite page*) *The Review.* A crowded street scene in Soho in 1750, showing the hooped skirts that Teresa barred from Carlisle House.

6. (*above*) Margrave and Margravine of Bayreuth. Friedrich von Hohenzollern of Brandenburg-Bayreuth, shown beside his remarkable wife, Wilhelmine Friederike.

7. Soho Square, 1731: the square as it appeared in Teresa's day. Crowned by a large roof terrace, Carlisle House is on the lower right just below the street opening.

8. Carlisle House, *c.* 1764. Behind the main house is Jacob Leroux's annex containing Teresa's new assembly rooms.

9. (*left*) *Lady Fashion's Secretary's Office, or, Petticoat Recommendation the Best.* Subtitled *The Only Known Portrait of Mrs Cornelys,* this print depicts a woman receiving masquerade tickets from her servant. Though doubt surrounds its subject – some sources say she is a courtesan – her bonnet and clothes are identical to those Teresa is wearing in other prints of the time, and the face bears an uncanny resemblance to her.

10. (*right*) Elizabeth Chudleigh, captivatingly beautiful, is shown wearing the transparent dress in which she scandalized society at a masquerade ball in 1748.

11. (*below*) Ranelagh Gardens. The pleasure gardens were Carlisle House's main competitor until the opening of Almack's and the Pantheon.

12. *The Promenade*, engraving, artist unknown. An informal gathering at
Carlisle House.

13. Augusta of Saxe-Gotha, Princess of Wales, was George III's mother and Elizabeth Chudleigh's supporter. Her death plunged Carlisle House into mourning, and prompted Teresa into a rare display of bad taste.

14. Edward Augustus, Duke of York and Albany. The Duke's light-hearted character and constant need for distraction made him an ideal candidate for membership of the Society in Soho Square.

15. *The Female Coterie*, engraving by T. Bonnor. The *ton* exchange gossip, gamble, drink and flirt.

16. Lady Harrington. Part of London's fast set, she sold tickets to Teresa's masquerades and rescued Sophie when she fled from Soho Square.

17. Lady Northumberland. Strong-minded and determined to get her way, Elizabeth Percy was behind Teresa's plan to stage operas in competition with the King's Theatre.

18. Vauxhall revellers. An evening function at the Vauxhall Gardens.

did not honour his obligations to Norman, Carlisle House would remain in a half-finished, almost uninhabitable state, her assemblies and concerts would not be able to start up again, and she and Sophie would be out on the street.

A meeting between Teresa, Fermor and Norman, convened on 17 October to settle the matter of the builder's payment, soon degenerated into a bitter argument. Norman looked on in horror as, without any attempt at propriety, the outspoken Italian female impresario and the married English clergyman quarrelled openly in front of him. Fermor insisted that he and Teresa each had a fifty-fifty share in Carlisle House. Teresa protested that they did not. Next, Fermor produced his pile of IOUs and demanded that Teresa pay him back the £745 she owed him. Teresa refused. Instead, she threw two hundred guineas in cash at him and offered him a deal: if he signed over his entire interest in Carlisle House to her then and there, he could keep the two hundred guineas and she would guarantee not only to pay him back the remainder of what she owed him as soon as the winter season started, she would reimburse the £1950 he had paid to John Machin for the head-lease of Carlisle House, *and* she would take care of Samuel Norman's bill.

Teresa had been cornered, but she had come out fighting. Now it was Fermor who was trapped. If he did not agree to this deal, he stood to lose the £745 Teresa owed him, plus the £1950 he had paid for the head-lease, and he would also have to pay Norman the £900 he was due. If, however, he accepted Teresa's deal, he would lose his interest in Carlisle House but would have two hundred guineas in hand, plus the promise of a further £2475 over the next year. In addition, he would have no liability towards Norman.

At length, after a lot of acrimonious mud-slinging, Fermor decided the latter option was the best he could expect under the circumstances, and he agreed reluctantly to Teresa's terms. A memorandum was drawn up and signed by the three, agreeing that Teresa would 'pay the Purchase Money and indemnify Mr Fermor in respect thereof'. She would also meet him on the following Tuesday, pay him back the remainder of the £745 and at the same time provide him with security for the £1950 he had spent purchasing Carlisle House from Machin on her behalf. If Fermor objected to the security she offered, she would pay him back 'by two payments, one in April next, and the other in October next, with lawful Interest in the mean Time'. In return, Fermor agreed that 'all the Benefit of the Agreement between [him] and Machin bearing the date the 16TH Day of May last for the purchase of Carlisle House shall be and belong to Mrs Cornelys and to her Appointment' and that he would 'have nothing further to do in the Building'. He also promised not to assign Teresa's remaining IOUs to anyone else 'or suffer her to be sued thereon'.

By this brilliant if ruthless move, Teresa succeeded in fobbing off Fermor with a tangled web of promises. Now all she had to do was to pay Norman the £900 he was due. Throwing herself on her builder's mercy, she begged him to help her get free of her lover's power. Since she did not have the £900 he was owed, would he instead accept £1800 worth of subscription tickets to her future assemblies? Emotionally exhausted by the scenes he had witnessed, and with no desire to be involved in any more, Norman agreed.

Teresa never repaid Fermor the remainder of the money she owed him. But three days later she handed over the £1800 worth of subscription tickets to Norman, and work on Carlisle House forged ahead. With only twenty-three days left before the new season was due to start, a veritable army of plasterers, carpenters and painters was brought in and made to work 'extraordinary hours' by the light of dozens of expensive candles to get the interior finished on time. Teresa watched over their every move with a perfectionist's eye. The chimneypiece in the concert room had to be painted five times before it met with her approval, and the walls received seven coats before she accepted them as 'dead white'.

Furniture and soft furnishings began to arrive from Norman's workshops. They included thirteen pairs of fine blue or yellow damask curtains and swathed valances; countless ornate rococo mirrors; mahogany sofas and matching stools covered in yellow damask; eight folding dining-room tables and circular tables designed to fit round the columns in the centre of the banqueting room; a further large mahogany table to seat ten people; a total of fifty-eight cushioned benches, 'all filled with curled hair', some with backs and some without; glass girandoles with cherubim heads; additional oval mirrors in glass-bordered frames; 'Scotch carpeting' for the stairs floor and a further huge fine carpet, measuring twenty-five feet by fourteen; a mahogany writing table 'with conveniences' costing £6 18s, with a matching India-back elbow chair upholstered in crimson. In addition, there was 'A very large Inkstand with four glasses' for Teresa's office; 'a mahogany bedstead and check furniture etc Bedding complete', presumably for her own bedroom; a large crimson door curtain to keep out cold draughts from the hallway; and an array of small items, which included butler's trays, candlesticks, mahogany side lanthorns, and even a lowly wooden ironing-board.

At last the house was finished. On 6 November Teresa placed a notice on the front page of the *Public Advertiser* informing the nobility and gentry that the first of the season's meetings of the Society in Soho-square would take place in six days' time. On 12 November, the freshly painted front doors of Carlisle House were thrown open, as were the doors of a new Ladies' entrance in Sutton Street, and the fashionable *ton* poured through them in full force.

Everyone was awestruck at the spacious, glittering 'fairy palace' Teresa had created in the heart of Soho. Carlisle House was truly magnificent in both scale and elegance. The somewhat tired old house had been transformed into an elegant and ultra-modern suite of rooms, and the new building at the back, designed by Jacob Leroux, eclipsed every other assembly and concert room in London, and threw many private mansions into the shade. With its no-expense-spared rococo plasterwork, its state-of-the-art furniture, its dozens of expensive mirrors, and its scores of chandeliers and wall-mounted candle sconces, Carlisle House set a new benchmark in interior design.

The first meeting could not have gone better. Dressed in their finest evening clothes and jewels, the crowd swarmed through the newly decorated rooms of the old house, drinking tea, wine, champagne and orgeat, a cooling drink made from orange-flower water and barley. After supper, which was served in the huge ground-floor banqueting hall, they poured upstairs to Teresa's breathtaking Concert Room. There, under the thirty-foot-high ceiling, hung with chandeliers, and with the rococo mirrors reflecting their own images, they listened to the orchestra play, and then, under Teresa's discreet direction, talked, danced and gambled for the remainder of the night.

Towards dawn, the final coach rattled loudly across the cobbles and out of Soho Square, taking home the last of Mrs Cornelys's exalted guests, and Teresa congratulated herself on the extraordinary success of her new rooms. But what should have been a day of triumph was soon to turn into a nightmare: while the glorious first-night party had been going on at Carlisle House, John Fermor had been sitting at home plotting his erstwhile lover's downfall. Though she had been lavishing money on Carlisle House, Teresa had not yet paid him what she had promised him at the end of October. Tired of waiting for it, he had resorted to the Court of Common Pleas to try to get it from her.

As Teresa's servants began the arduous task of clearing up the debris of the opening-night ball, Fermor's bailiffs arrived at Carlisle House with a writ for their mistress's arrest. Rather than resist them, Teresa took the dramatic step of surrendering herself. Locked in their cart like a common criminal, she was driven away through the streets of Covent Garden, into the City and across London Bridge to Southwark, where she was thrown into the King's Bench prison.

As a publicity stunt, the scandal could not have been bettered. It ensured that Teresa would be talked of incessantly over the next few days and that, in her dealings with Fermor, it was she who would appear as the wronged party.

Within days, Teresa had paid off her debt to Fermor, and was back in Soho. On a personal level, she was now more famous – or infamous – than ever, and with her brilliant flair for self-promotion she made the most of it. From that day onwards, London's newspapers shouted her name in capital letters: 'MRS CORNELYS acquaints the Nobility and Gentry, Subscribers to the Society in Soho-square, that the second meeting will be This Day the 26TH inst,' read the notice for the second meeting a fortnight later. The Prussian Count Friedrich von Kielmansegge recorded his visit to Carlisle House that night in his diary:

On the 26TH we went to Court, and in the evening to an assembly at Soho. This consists of a concert and a ball, which take place every fortnight in a fine room, which has been much improved this year. Several ladies have a book, in one of which every one signs his name, paying five guineas for twelve nights. In order that only those people may be subscribers who are known to one of the ladies, the subscription books are kept by the ladies only, and the power to admit or to exclude whom they like is confined to them, and is not given to the owner of the rooms, who is an Italian by the name of Cornelia [sic]. The rooms in which they play, as well as the large ballroom, are very fine and beautifully lighted, and exceedingly well-furnished. The vocal and instrumental music, by an orchestra at the end of the room, begins at 7 o'clock and lasts until nine; dancing afterwards goes on until one or two. Tea, lemonade, and cake are served in two rooms.

Although Teresa's first year in business had been a triumph, her second year dwarfed it. November 1761 was the start for her of twelve years of unprecedented success. The formula of her evenings – a serious concert performed in sumptuous surroundings by high-calibre musicians, followed by dancing, gambling and eating until the small hours – was a winning one, and during this period the Society in Soho-square had as many subscribers as the staff could handle, and often more. They included the Duke and Duchess of Devonshire, the Duke of Portland, the Earl of Carlisle, the Countess of Pomfret, the Countess of Harrington, Lady Spencer, the Duke and Duchess of Northumberland, the Duchess of Bolton, Sir Horace Walpole, the novelist Fanny Burney, the Earls of Huntingdon, Sandwich, Falmouth, and Cholmondley, Lord Palmerston, Lord Bolingbroke, the Prince of Monaco, the King of Denmark, and almost every foreign ambassador and envoy who came to London during that period. With the exception of the king and queen, every member of the British royal family frequented Carlisle

House, including the Duke and Duchess of Gloucester, the Duke and Duchess of Cumberland and, most notably, the young playboy Duke of York, who was so taken with Soho that he seldom missed a night at Carlisle House.

Teresa's concerts and meetings were usually attended by between three and eight hundred members of the nobility and gentry, but on gala nights numbers passed the thousand mark. The original rather sedate meetings centred on a concert soon escalated into balls, masquerades and full-scale drums – an eighteenth-century term used to describe 'a riotous assembly of fashionable people of both sexes at a private house; not unaptly styled a drum, from the noise and emptiness of the entertainment'. The drums – or drum-majors as they sometimes turned into – lasted at least until two or three o'clock in the morning, and on many occasions carried on until eight or nine. Teresa always presided personally over the events, and her vivacious presence infused the atmosphere with gaiety.

A large part of Carlisle House's attraction was the snob value of its membership scheme and its strict ticket-only admission policy. But while this was popular with those on the list, it was not always easy to enforce. Year in, year out, subscribers arrived for Society meetings without the relevant admission tickets. In order to simplify the system, Teresa had the tickets for each separate meeting engraved in different coloured inks and, with the help of her English secretary, a Mrs Brooks, she wrote detailed newspaper announcements reminding subscribers what colour ticket to bring on which particular night: 'Mrs Cornelys begs Leave to acquaint the Nobility and Gentry, Subscribers to the Society in Soho-square, that the *Ninth* Meeting will be on Thursday next, the 17TH Instant, and the Rooms lighted up precisely at Eight O'Clock. The Colour of the Ticket is *Crimson*, and printed in Front *Ninth Night*.'

To make the system even clearer, the tickets were adorned with elaborate and rather titillating designs, often showing bare-breasted women surrounded by cherubs, or being led astray by half-naked men. These were drawn and engraved for Teresa by the Italian artists Giovanni Cipriani and Francesco Bartolozzi, both of whom lived in Soho.

In practice, Teresa's supposedly foolproof admission system did not work. Ugly scenes occurred at the door of Carlisle House as the footmen struggled to keep out gatecrashers or those who had left their tickets at home.

Several ungenteel Attempts having been made to gain Admittance without Tickets, and sometimes with Success, which has afterwards been boasted of to Mrs Cornelys's Prejudice [she lectured in one of her newspaper notices], and as many Ladies and Gentlemen frequently lend or forget their Ticket, or bring the wrong One, and *nevertheless* make Application and *expect* to be admitted, thereby subjecting Mrs Cornelys to the painful Alternative of either breaking through the Rules of the Society, or of giving Umbrage by a refusal: She thinks it necessary, therefore, to give this Notice, that additional Persons are employed, and the utmost Vigilance will be used to prevent all future possibility of Succeeding.

Aristocrats used to pulling rank did not take kindly to being turned away from a place of commercial entertainment by these 'additional persons' – they were, in effect, London's first nightclub bouncers. So, in order not to lose people's favour, Teresa had to issue frequent public apologies in the newspapers, stating,

It was with the most inexpressible Concern she was obliged, on the last Meeting, to refuse Admittance to several who came without their Tickets; and that nothing but the firmest Belief of it's [sic] being a DUTY, in the strongest Sense, due from her to the Subscribers, in general, could have induced her to act in any Manner that could possibly give offence, or carry the most distant Appearance of a Want of Respect.

In other words, non-ticket-holders had been turned away from Carlisle House for the general good.

Teresa also stressed that it was not her fault if she occasionally had to refuse admission to non-ticket-holders. Rules were rules, and 'the Ladies who hold Books have *now* given Orders to her, and insist upon her Compliance therewith, that, on no Pretence whatever, any Person (Subscriber or not) shall be admitted *without* a Ticket, or with one for *any other night*'. Shifting the responsibility from herself to 'the Ladies who hold Books' – Miss Chudleigh, Lady Cowper, Lady Harrington and the Duchess of Ancaster – was a canny move that helped Teresa to distance herself from any unpleasantness over the admission policy. However, it did not stop gatecrashers from continually trying their luck at the door.

Before long there was a thriving black-market in Carlisle House admission tickets. With each flimsy piece of paper worth between one and two guineas, stealing them became a great temptation, particularly for servants whose monthly wages were but a fraction of that amount. On one occasion, a *valet de chambre* was instantly dismissed for selling his master's spare tickets to a Society assembly. On another, 300 counterfeit tickets to a Carlisle House ball were produced and sold, and Teresa had to issue a whole new set to her genuine subscribers.

A more legitimate way for non-subscribers to obtain tickets was to place an advertisement in the local papers, such as this one, which appeared in 1769:

SOHO. WANTED three Tickets for Mrs Cornelly's [*sic*] the fifth Night, being next Thursday. Whoever can spare them, and will leave them with Mr Wright at the Crown Coffee House, Charles-street, Covent Garden, shall receive Three Guineas, and this same proportion for a smaller Number. N.B: They are for three Foreign Gentlemen of Consequence, who will not be in England another Night, which is the only Apology that can be made for this Mode of Application.

Genuine subscribers would sometimes give away their spare tickets to their less well-connected friends. One such recipient was Miss Ann Dewes, the niece of the writer Mary Granville (better known as Mrs Delaney), who wrote home to her father during her stay in London in 1763:

Last Tuesday was sevennight I was at an assembly at Lady Hillborough's. Wednesday I was at the Oratorio; Thursday Mrs D., Mr G., and Miss

Chapone, and my brother, went to the play, I was to have gone, but the Duchess of Queensberry sent me a ticket to go to a ball in Soho Square, and I went with my Lady Cowper. It is a very fine room. The Duke of Y[ork] was there, and he began the ball; I danced but two dances; it was so hot; there was not any minuets. The French horn, fiddle, and other instruments, played till the ball began, which was about nine.

Giving away or even selling one's unwanted subscription tickets might have been common practice, but it was frowned upon by Miss Chudleigh and her friends, who ordered that under no circumstances were tickets to be given to the wrong kind of person. Teresa was forced to warn her customers that 'for the future, those Subscribers who shall again lend their Tickets in such like manner, shall be scratched off the List, and their Admittance refused'.

Neither the fear of being blackballed nor the embarrassment of being turned away put people off coming to Carlisle House. If anything, it made them keener. On assembly nights Soho Square was packed with onlookers who came to witness the arguments at the front door and watch the arrival of the hundreds of high-born guests whose coaches, horses and sedan chairs blocked the surrounding streets, sometimes for hours on end. Simply getting to the front or side doors of Carlisle House became so problematic, chaotic and even dangerous on assembly nights that Teresa had to ask her patrons

to order that their Coachmen and Chairmen will prudently bring them to the door, for fear of breaking either coach or chairs, as she takes as much care as is in her power to prevent any accident that may happen. Also that the Nobility and Gentry &c. Coaches and Hackney chairs, are to stay at the door in the Square, all towards the side of Greek Street, to let the passage be free for the Ladies Chairs to go to the door in Sutton Street; and she hopes that the Hackney Chairmen will make no disturbance.

Teresa also took it upon herself to initiate London's first one-way traffic system:

A Coach having been overturned the last Concert Night at the Door, owing to the Obstinacy of the Coachman, in insisting upon coming up the wrong Way, the Nobility and Gentry are again most earnestly solicited to be *peremptory* in their Commands to be set down and taken up with the Horses Heads towards Greek Street; by which all Danger to themselves, and Injury to their Cattle and Carriages, will be wholly prevented.

The overcrowding inside Carlisle House was as intense as it was out in Soho Square. By the middle of the evening, the reception rooms were often overpoweringly hot and sweaty. Constantly vigilant to her clients' complaints, Teresa did her best to deal with the problem, and promised on more than one occasion that 'Proper Ventilators will absolutely be erected in the Great Room; by which the present Complaints of excessive Heat will be obviated, without subjecting the Subscribers to the least Danger of catching Cold.'

Since no self-respecting aristocrat travelled anywhere without a retinue of servants (and, in Elizabeth Chudleigh's case, her black male slave) it was even more of a crush below-stairs than in the main rooms. Arguments frequently broke out between the scores of maids, chairmen and footmen waiting in attendance on their masters and mistresses, and occasionally these resulted in fights. Teresa understood the importance of servants, not only to their employers but also to her own success: on 12 February 1763 she even rewarded them by holding a special evening of card-playing and country dances for the 'upper servants of Persons of Fashion'. Yet she would not condone unruly behaviour in the entrance hall or servants' quarters. 'Mrs Cornelys therefore . . . humbly presumes to recommend it to those Ladies who have several Footmen attending them to the Society, to order a less Number of Servants to remain in waiting for them afterwards,' she begged in one newspaper notice, adding for good measure, 'And as the Glasses of many Chairs have been broken, and the Ladies thereby somewhat alarmed, Mrs Cornelys also begs to submit it to the Consideration of the Ladies whether some Contrivance of Blinds or Shutters, in the Manner of Chariots, would not be an useful addition, in order to be drawn up upon all such Occasions.'

The mayhem and noise from dusk until dawn in what had formerly been a quiet residential area infuriated many residents of Soho Square. Some, like Speaker Arthur Onslow, left the neighbourhood soon after Carlisle House opened. Others, such as the Spanish ambassador, the Conde de Fuentes, became Teresa's frequent guests.

Among the Conde de Fuentes's London suite was a Flemish mechanical genius named Joseph Merlin, whose inventions included a wheelchair, numerous clocks and watches of the finest quality, a barrel-organ, mathematical and musical instruments and a 'perpetual motion machine'. An exhibitionist at heart, Merlin loved demonstrating his inventions in public, and he frequently appeared with them at Mrs Cornelys's parties. On one occasion he came dressed as the goddess Fortune, propelling himself through the rooms in an especially made wheel-of-fortune pedal car, and on another he dressed up as a barmaid in a public house 'where he had a bar of his own fitting up, with all the appendages of glasses &c. &c.'.

However, Merlin's most spectacular appearance at Carlisle House was on the night he decided to make a grand entrance playing the violin while wearing his newest and most famous invention: roller-skates. With the metal-wheeled contraptions strapped to his shoes, the mechanic skidded into the room at top speed, and 'not having provided the means of retarding his velocity, or commanding its direction, he impelled himself against a mirror, of more than five hundred pounds value, dashed it to atoms, broke his instrument to pieces, and wounded himself most severely'. Far from being overly sympathetic to Merlin's injuries, it was rumoured that Teresa demanded immediate compensation for the damage he had caused.

By 1763 Teresa was giving twelve balls and twelve assemblies a year for the nobility and gentry, and throwing an equal number for the middle classes. She employed three dozen servants. She had her own carriage and six horses. She even rented a country house by the Thames at Hammersmith. A formerly destitute singer, a woman, a foreigner and a single mother, she had transformed herself from a pauper into the most successful impresario in London. Most important of all, she had found work that fulfilled her many talents. Her early mastery of the arts of flirtation and manipulation, her knowledge and appreciation of music, the entrepreneurial skills she had absorbed from her father, the feel for interior design she had learned from the margravine, the manners and taste she had acquired while singing in the courts of Europe, her education in the hard-knocks school of business studies, and her understanding of what made the aristocracy tick: all the things Teresa had learned during her eventful life, and her various gifts, came together in running Carlisle House.

The thousands of pounds she was taking every month were almost irrelevant to her. Carlisle House was her vocation, and she gloried in it. She was bringing the brightness of an Italian spring into the gloom of the English winter. She was distilling the spirit of Venice in London, and re-creating the magic of its Carnival within the walls of her house. Her presence in England's capital had transformed what had formerly been a dull and parochial social scene into something altogether more dynamic, exciting and international. Her taste and manners had influenced the most important people in the land.

This was the superficial picture that Teresa presented to the outside world. But those behind the scenes at Carlisle House had a very different view. Mrs Cornelys had a dangerously high opinion of herself. Though she was a brilliant impresario, she had no head for business. In purely financial terms, her phenomenal success was a flimsily disguised disaster-in-the-making. The doyenne of masked parties was living a masquerade of her own.

Eleven

By the spring of 1763, Teresa had been in business for almost three years. She appeared to be making a fortune. At a time when an unskilled labourer earned five shillings a week, and a domestic servant seven or eight pounds per annum, Carlisle House was bringing in the once-destitute singer an estimated £24,000 a year.

But, incredibly, Teresa had no savings. Even worse, rumour had it that she owed four times more than she earned. Her extravagant personal lifestyle, which included a governess and maid for Sophie, the country house and her carriage, was only partly to blame for the dire state of her finances. Extraordinarily successful though it was, Carlisle House lost rather than made money, for Teresa ran it to exacting standards, regardless of cost. The real purpose of business – to make a profit – was beyond her comprehension. Instead of thinking of her concerts, assemblies and balls as potentially money-making events she sought only to make each one as perfect as possible.

Perfectionism might have been the secret of Teresa's success but it was also her downfall. Though she took more than twelve hundred guineas on each assembly night, nearly all of this money was immediately paid out in expenses, and she never thought to cut her costs either to make a profit or even to balance the books. Not that there were any books to speak of. Her accounting methods were at best sloppy, at worst non-existent. Consequently, her thirty-five-strong team of servants never lost an opportunity to steal from her, and tradesmen habitually overcharged her.

In common with many small businesses of the modern age, cash-flow was a day-to-day problem. Her desk was piled high with unpaid invoices. Like the upper classes who frequented her assemblies, she survived on credit and deferred paying her debts for as long as she could. When she could defer no longer she borrowed money to pay off her creditors, and the people who lent it were seldom paid back.

This had led to a further drain on Teresa's resources: litigation and legal bills. She was already embroiled in three cases in the Court of Chancery, the civil court that settled financial disputes. Two involved John Fermor, and the third her builder Samuel Norman.

In October 1761, Teresa had promised Norman £1800 worth of assembly tickets in lieu of payment for his work on her building. Although she had given him the tickets so that he could sell them to society members, somehow he had never received any money for them. By June 1762, he was desperate to be paid and sent Teresa a new invoice. She retaliated by claiming that his workmanship on her new assembly rooms and the furniture he had supplied were substandard, and she told him that she had decided to dispute the bill.

In a typically dramatic gesture, one day over that summer Teresa got her servants to load some of Norman's furniture on to a cart and unceremoniously dump it in the street outside his workshops. She also appointed two surveyors to inspect her assembly rooms and the remaining furniture for faults. It was yet another sign of her extravagance that these men were two of the best known in their fields: the country-house architect James Paine, and furniture-maker Thomas Chippendale who, since the publication of his catalogue, *The Gentleman and Cabinet-maker's Director* in 1754, had been the most fashionable furniture designer in London.

At Teresa's request, Norman came round to Soho Square on the day Paine and Chippendale were inspecting the building, only to find that Teresa's servants would not let him in. As a result of the survey, Teresa declared that she owed Norman £400 less than the £1800 he was demanding. Although he subsequently appointed his own surveyors to inspect Carlisle House, it proved impossible to settle the matter because, as he later testified to his lawyer, 'he has never been able to get a meeting between her surveyors and his'. In despair of getting the matter sorted out by himself, Norman sold on his bill-notes from Teresa to a City businessman named Henry Bodycoate, who took the matter to the Court of Chancery on the builder's behalf.

Even more convoluted than her case with Norman and Body-coate was Teresa's legal battle with John Fermor. By the end of 1761, the lovers were so enmeshed financially and legally that it was virtually impossible for them to make a clean break from each other. On two occasions Teresa had promised to buy Fermor out of Carlisle House: the first time in October 1761, when they had argued in front of Samuel Norman; and again on 3 February 1762. However, on neither of these occasions had her money materialized. At the end of February 1762, Fermor issued a writ against her, and bailiffs were sent in to seize some of her furniture – furniture that, Teresa argued, did not belong to her but was only leased from Norman.

By the start of 1763, Teresa and Fermor were locked into a four-year-long battle in the Court of Chancery over the ownership of Carlisle House and the business that took place within its walls. Teresa's view of the matter was clear-cut: since she had paid the builders – albeit with Fermor's money – the house belonged to her; their business partnership did not exist, and it never had. It was she and Miss Chudleigh who had had the initial idea to open Carlisle House. It was she who ran it. It was she who did all the work and came up with all the ideas. It was she whose name was known to the public. Most important of all in the eyes of the law, it was she who was in possession of the building.

Fermor was a straightforward country gentleman, and his view of the matter was blunt. As Carlisle House had been set up with money he had given Teresa, he believed that he was entitled to at least a fifty per cent share of its profits. And since the lease was in his name and she had never paid him anything towards it, he considered the property his to dispose of.

In January 1763, Fermor duly sold the lease of Carlisle House to a Mrs Mary Brackstone, a wealthy widow from Southampton, for £1550. Mrs Brackstone and Teresa knew each other: back in 1761, Teresa had entertained the widow and her sister at Carlisle House, and in March 1762 she had even borrowed £210 from her.

When she heard that Fermor had sold the lease of Carlisle House to Mrs Brackstone, Teresa went straight to her lawyers, claiming that the house was in fact hers. Fermor appealed to the Court of Chancery in an attempt to show that, on the contrary, Carlisle House was technically his. It had been his idea to open up a London assembly rooms, he said, and he insisted that he and Teresa had agreed right from the start on having a fifty-fifty partnership in it. As evidence of this, his lawyer produced a copy of the agreement he had forced Teresa to sign in August 1760, which stated clearly that they were in partnership for a term of six years, and that any profits the business made would be divided between them 'Share and Share alike'.

However, Fermor claimed, Teresa now insisted that they had never had a partnership agreement. Furthermore, she also insisted that any agreement they *might* have made in August 1760 had been dissolved the following 21 January in a subsequent agreement made at Kingston House, Elizabeth Chudleigh's home. If Fermor *had* agreed to dissolve their partnership at Kingston House on 21 January, he had only done so because he had been 'compelled to sign the same by the Threats of the said Mrs [sic] Chudleigh that she would ruin the said undertaking if your orator should refuse to sign the same'. All this was irrelevant anyway, because the following June Teresa had signed yet another agreement with him, this one rendering null and void the disputed agreement of 21 January in return for Fermor's standing surety for Samuel Norman's furniture.

Fermor complained – not unjustly – that Teresa had often promised to pay him back the £1950 he had spent buying Carlisle House, just as she had promised to pay Saunders and later John Machin the rent for the house. But she had never paid back any money to anyone. Although she claimed that Fermor had given her 'but very small and inconsiderable sums' over the years, he swore he had given her, personally, more than five thousand pounds, and in addition that he had bailed out the business to the tune of another ten thousand. What had happened to all this cash, he wanted to know, and to the thousands of pounds Teresa must have received in subscription fees over the last two and a half years? Because she refused to produce any proper accounts, he was resorting to the Court of Chancery 'to the End therefore that the said Teresa Cornelys and her confederates may upon their corporeal oaths respectively full and true answers make to the several matters aforesaid'.

'The said Teresa Cornelys and her confederates'. The phrase made Elizabeth Chudleigh (to whom Fermor was no doubt referring) and Teresa sound like a couple of hardened criminals plotting to embezzle him out of money he was rightfully owed. These were serious allegations. And to anyone who had more than a passing acquaintance with either woman, they had an uncomfortable ring of truth.

Teresa and Elizabeth were both clever and ruthless, and neither was above using manipulative behaviour or blackmail to get her own way. Charming as she could be, Elizabeth was at heart a high-handed and selfish woman accustomed to using her looks, her powers of persuasion and her position in her own interest. Teresa, though brilliant at wheedling money out of her admirers when she needed it, was never conscientious about paying it back. She had no knowledge at all of bookkeeping, and could not – or perhaps deliberately would not – understand the finer points of the British legal system, except when it was in her interest to do so.

No sooner was Fermor's claim before the courts than Teresa made a counter-claim against him. If she *had* ever signed a partnership agreement with him in August 1760, she said, she had done so under threat, and had not understood what she was signing. When she had bought Carlisle House, Fermor had tricked her and put his own name on the head-lease. His recent sale of the house to Mary Brackstone was not so much a sale as a form of pawn, Teresa argued, because Fermor could redeem the lease whenever he wanted to. In Teresa's opinion, Fermor and Brackstone were in league with each other for the sole purpose of taking Carlisle House, her successful business, from her.

Whatever the truth behind the accusations and counter-accusations flying between Teresa and Fermor, the legal situation between them was a mess and, as in many legal cases today, the only people to profit from it were the lawyers. Fermor's motivation in bringing his case was simply to get his money back. Teresa's was desperation. To her, the situation was simple: Fermor was a wealthy man and, despite her lavish lifestyle, she was poor. If he lost his case, he would still be rich, but if she lost, she would be destitute, and so would Sophie. With no financial safety-net, no savings, and no wealthy admirer waiting in the wings to look after her if she failed to look after herself, only Teresa's tenacity stood between success and possible ruin. To give in to Fermor's demands would mean condemning herself to the grim conditions of a debtors' gaol.

By April 1763, Teresa was battling for her survival. The pressures on her were huge. Not only did she have to fight Fermor and Henry Bodycoate in the courts, she also had to run Carlisle House: deal with the servants; order the food; hire the musicians and choose what they would play; sweet-talk her suppliers, to whom she owed a fortune; and, on assembly nights, appear calm, collected and charming in front of her subscribers as she presided over the events. She had no time to relax, and no time for nine-year-old Sophie.

What Teresa needed, she decided, was a man to bring some order to her chaotic and stressful life. Not a man who would try to take charge of her but a man she could be in charge of. Someone who would take over the running of Carlisle House, without interfering in its direction. Someone she could trust not to run off with her money. Someone who could deal with the thieving servants, the bookkeeping and her angry creditors, and leave her free to concentrate on the creative side of the business.

Only a family member would be able to fulfil all these duties with the loyalty she demanded. And that meant her son, Giuseppe Pompeati, who was still living in Paris under Casanova's guardianship. By now the boy was sixteen, and the perfect age to become her apprentice.

Accordingly, in the spring of 1763 Teresa wrote to Casanova, asking him to give her son back to her.

Since they had parted in January 1759, Giacomo Casanova's life had been even more eventful than Teresa's. Accused of fraud after a business venture foundered, he had, like her, been imprisoned for a short spell in Paris's For-L'Évêque prison. Freed after the

Marquise d'Urfé interceded on his behalf, he was sent to the Dutch Republic by the French government on a second business mission. Unlike his first mission, this one failed, and in his absence a Parisian court convicted him of forging bills of exchange.

Since then, Casanova had ricocheted restlessly between France, Prussia, Switzerland and Italy, charming people with his prodigious and challenging intellect, leaving a trail of gambling debts behind him, and getting embroiled in countless love affairs. In Stuttgart, he fell prey to card sharps and was thrown into prison. In Switzerland, like many intellectuals of the time, he made a pilgrimage to Les Délices, a château just outside Geneva, to meet the French writer and satirist Voltaire, the man who, more than any other, embodied the spirit of the Enlightenment. In Naples the following year, Casanova unwittingly proposed marriage to his own seventeen-year-old daughter by Donna Lucrezia, a woman with whom he had had an affair in 1744: when he discovered his mistake, he made love to the mother while their daughter lay naked beside them in the same bed.

After visiting Rome, Florence, Parma and Turin, the increasingly amoral Casanova spent four months in Augsburg, where he represented Portugal at the Augsburg Congress, held to bring an end to the Seven Years War. At the end of 1762, he returned briefly to Paris, where he continued to sponge off the Marquise d'Urfé. Over the next seventeen months he strung the credulous widow along with talk of spiritual 'regeneration', and occult 'operations' intended to help her give birth to a baby. In this he was helped by three fellow swindlers: a woman named Marianne Corticelli, his own brother, Gaetano Casanova, and Gaetano's secretary, Giacomo Passano.

Casanova finally returned to Paris in May 1763 after a sixteen-month absence. Waiting for him were two letters from Teresa. In the first, she requested politely that he bring Giuseppe to London. In the second, written when he had failed to reply to the first, her tone was impertinent to say the least: if Casanova did not bring Giuseppe to her immediately, she snapped, she would be forced to come to Paris and fetch him.

Casanova saw trouble ahead. The last time Giuseppe had seen his mother had been in January 1759. He had been a fresh-faced twelve-year-old, full of spirit and on the point of puberty, and the hand-to-mouth existence he had led with Teresa had left scars on his nature, which remained. Left in pawn with her creditors, he had been 'redeemed' for money, then handed over to a stranger who had spirited him away from everything and everyone he had known. Giuseppe had done his best to act according to the precepts his mother had instilled in him – the most important being that it was often prudent to keep one's true feelings hidden – but nevertheless his new 'father' had been highly critical of his behaviour. In Casanova's opinion, the boy was sly, ignorant, incapable of honesty and unworthy of true friendship. The so-called discretion Teresa had taken such pains to instil in her son was a nauseating combination of dissimulation, distrust and false confidences.

Casanova wanted to re-educate Giuseppe according to his own precepts, but preferably not at his own expense. With this in mind, as soon as they arrived back in Paris, he left the boy at his apartment and went alone to visit the Marquise d'Urfé. He found the rich widow as obsessed with the occult as ever, and still hoping to achieve her spiritual rebirth through the body of a young boy. In a cool manner guaranteed to incite her interest, Casanova told her that he had brought a boy back from Holland with him, and added that he intended to enrol him in a local boarding-school. Presuming that this was the immortal infant she had been waiting for, the overjoyed marquise offered to place the child in the same boarding-school her nephews attended at her expense. What was the boy's name, she asked, and where was he? And why had Casanova not brought him straight to see her?

Knowing that she would not be able to contain her curiosity, Casanova assured the marquise that he would present the boy to her in a few days' time. The moment he left her, she impatiently jumped into her carriage, drove over to Casanova's *hôtel* and kidnapped Giuseppe. This was just what Casanova had wanted her to do. When he visited her mansion the following morning, he found the confused boy lying in the marquise's arms. Casanova told him that he must regard the old lady as his queen from now on, and always be honest with her. But far from being honest himself, Casanova did everything he could to encourage the marquise's belief that Giuseppe was not human but a spiritual being belonging to the Rosicrucian order who had been sent to her by an oracle, and that through him she would achieve the mystical rebirth she so much desired.

As it turned out, it was Giuseppe who achieved a kind of rebirth through the marquise. From then on she took charge of him. She bought him clothes, jewels and watches and, as she had promised Casanova, she enrolled him at Viard's, the best boarding-school in Paris. If the boy was confused by the sudden about-turn in his fortunes, it was more than understandable. Just weeks before, he had been living in poverty in tenement rooms with his penniless mother. Now, out of the blue, he had everything he could desire: money, respect, fine clothes, his own pony and the best teachers in France. Giuseppe even had a mistress, in the shape of Monsieur Viard's pretty teenage daughter, whose duty it was to look after him from the moment she brought him breakfast in the morning until she put him to bed in the evening and climbed in beside him.

Since he was thoroughly ashamed of his humble origins, Giuseppe told everyone, including the marquise, that he was connected to a noble Spanish family, and he insisted they call him the Count of Aranda. 'A prince could not have been better lodged, better treated, better dressed, nor more respected by everyone in the establishment,' Casanova later wrote of the new count's life at Viard's. No wonder Giuseppe was happy: he had been rescued from a life of destitution and transported straight to an earthly paradise.

By 1763 Giuseppe's early life was simply an unhappy shadow on his memory. Four years in Paris had turned him into a spoiled adolescent used to the indolent life of a wealthy French nobleman and thoroughly accustomed to getting his own way. He had grown to think of himself as an aristocrat entitled to a leisurely existence. Academically speaking, his expensive education had been wasted on him. Though he was bright, musical and well versed in French manners, he could scarcely read or write, his maths was appalling and his knowledge of the wider world as narrow as a Parisian back-street. By now, the marquise knew all about his real family. Over the years she had become like a mother to him, and Giuseppe had no desire to see Teresa again. However, Teresa had demanded that Casanova bring him to London, and even though he knew that the boy was ill-suited to a working life, the adventurer felt duty-bound to do so.

Besides, the Marquise d'Urfé had tired of her young charge. She had also tired of Casanova. It had been seven years since he had first promised to help her achieve the spiritual regeneration she desired, and she had now come to terms with the fact that it would never happen. Earlier that year, he claimed he had impregnated her in a mysterious ceremony in Marseille, and told her that when her baby was born she would die and her soul would be translated into it. When she had not conceived, the widow had lost faith in him. His years of sponging off her were at an end.

This was the perfect time for both the marquise and Casanova to shrug off their responsibilities towards sixteen-year-old Giuseppe. Together, they hatched a plan to lure him to England. In his memoirs, *Histoire de Ma Vie*, the adventurer laid bare their underhand tactics. Teresa was visiting France, he and the marquise told Giuseppe, and she naturally wished to see her son. Since Casanova was planning to go to England soon, he would ride with Giuseppe to Abbeville to meet Teresa in eight days' time, and then travel on to London with her while Giuseppe returned to Paris. But how would he get back to Paris, Giuseppe asked. '"By yourself," the marquise told him, "preceded by a postilion." "In the saddle. Ah, that'd be fun . . . I'll dress up as a courier." "Yes, I'll have a beautiful jacket and some chamois trousers made for you, and I'll give you a superb warrant bearing the French coat of arms."' Giuseppe was thrilled at the thought of riding back to Paris in such style. Anyone who saw him in his courier's outfit would take him for an envoy of the French government, and that was what he would pretend to be.

Had the youth but known it, neither the marquise nor Casanova had any intention of letting him return to Paris, either in the saddle or out of it. He was in the process of being duped both by his adoptive mother and by the man who always presented himself as a champion of truth.

At the beginning of June, dressed in the courier's outfit the marquise had promised him, complemented by a new pair of riding boots of which he was inordinately proud, Giuseppe left for Abbeville with Casanova and his valet Clairmont. When he saw that they were to travel in a hired coach, rather than on horseback, he was ashamed to be seen wearing the wrong clothes. After three days in the coach, the trio reached Abbeville only to find that Teresa was not at their hotel to greet them. Giuseppe smelt a rat. Casanova described what happened next:

I ordered something to eat, he asks me where his mother is, I answer that we'll find out and I ask him to come with me to see the van Robais cloth factory.

'But we can find out in a moment if my mother's here or not.'

'Well, if she isn't here, we'll carry on and meet her en route. We'll certainly run into her before we reach Boulogne.'

'You go and see the factory, and I'll sleep while I wait for you.'

'You're the boss.'

The moment Casanova left the hotel, Giuseppe borrowed a horse and fled. Casanova was furious with himself for having been so easily duped by the youth he himself had been in the process of duping. A postilion was dispatched to catch up with the escapee on the Paris road, and he promised to return Giuseppe to the hotel by six o'clock that night. True to his word, he caught up with him just before Amiens, and returned him to Abbeville 'looking like a corpse'. Too furious to speak to the boy, Casanova ordered that he be locked overnight in a room with a comfortable bed and a good meal. The following morning he asked Giuseppe whether he would prefer to travel to London of his own free will or bound hand and foot. Of his own free will, the young man said proudly, and only on condition that Casanova let him ride on horseback in front of the coach for '"I don't want anyone to be able to say that you had me pursued as if I were a thief."'

Having given his word of honour that he would not attempt to run away again, Giuseppe rode to the coast, proud to be able to show off his skill in the saddle and to have won this small victory over his guardian. But his moment of glory did not last long: waiting for him at a Calais inn was a trunk containing all of his possessions, which the marquise had forwarded from Paris. Not only had Giuseppe been betrayed by the man he regarded as his father, he had also been betrayed by the woman he now thought of as a mother.

A gale was blowing when the three travellers set out from Calais, and with the wind behind them the Channel crossing took only two and a half hours. Exhausted and hungry, they finally arrived in London on the late afternoon of 13 June and, following the detailed instructions Teresa had sent him, Casanova directed their carriage to take them to Soho Square. Familiar as he was with life's changing vicissitudes, he must have been impressed by the extraordinary improvement in his friend's circumstances. When he had last seen her, she had been living in a tenement in Rotterdam. Now his carriage drew up before a grand mansion in one of London's smartest squares.

Casanova left Giuseppe in the carriage and entered Carlisle House expecting that Teresa herself would run and greet him. Instead, he was left to wait alone in an impressive hall while a footman went upstairs and announced his arrival. Two minutes later, another servant brought down a note, informing him that Mrs Cornelys was busy and asking him to go to a nearby lodging-house, where she promised to join him for supper later that night. Though he felt slighted and disappointed, Casanova supposed she must have her reasons for keeping him waiting.

Years later, when he was writing *Histoire de Ma Vie*, the memory of what happened next still smarted keenly, as his vivid prose reveals. When his coach drew up outside the house where Teresa had arranged for them to lodge, a plump Frenchwoman named Madame Raucour came rushing out of the house accompanied by two servants. Instead of greeting Casanova in the obsequious manner he expected, she ignored him, threw her arms round Giuseppe, kissed him and expressed her joy at his happy arrival. Inside Madame Raucour's house, Casanova's possessions were placed in an inferior back room suitable only for a subordinate while his charge's trunk was put into a grand three-room apartment next to it. To compound the insult, the landlady told the astonished youth that her two footmen were at his disposal and she was his most humble servant.

Casanova was a proud man who guarded the position he had attained in life with all the feistiness of a choleric terrier. Although outraged at being treated as Giuseppe's inferior, he nevertheless managed to keep his temper (this was 'a very rare occurrence', he admitted) even when he found out that he had suffered a further mark of disrespect: his trusted valet Clairmont had been allotted a bed in the room where Madame Raucour's servants slept. Barely controlling his anger, he went into Giuseppe's room where he found Madame Raucour seated next to the boy, deep in conversation with him.

Without bothering to glance up at Casanova, Madame Raucour carried on talking about Mrs Cornelys's 'magnificent position, her huge business, her immense credit, the superb mansion she'd had built, the thirty-three servants she employed, two secretaries, six horses, country house and I know not what'. Unaware that Casanova was Sophie's father, the landlady also prattled on about Mrs Cornelys's daughter who, she said, was known as Miss Cornelys, never as Sophie. Miss Cornelys, it seemed, was a beauty and an infant prodigy. She sang, danced, played countless musical instruments by sight, spoke three languages and had her own governess and maid. Exhausted by this litany of praise for the sister he scarcely remembered, Giuseppe asked weakly when they would be eating. Not before ten o'clock that evening, Madame Raucour replied, because Mrs Cornelys was tied up with her lawyer until then, discussing her legal case against Mr Fermor.

Casanova had heard more than enough about the famous Mrs Cornelys. Shocked to the core by the way Teresa had – or, rather, had not – received him, he grabbed his hat and cane, stomped out of the house and wandered down through Soho towards St James's. In a coffee-house in the Haymarket he encountered an Italian writer named Vincenzo Martinelli, with whose help he quickly found superior lodgings in Pall Mall. Having arranged to move in the following day, he reluctantly returned to Soho. While his charge dozed, Casanova awaited Teresa's arrival with growing impatience, determined not to betray how angry he felt.

At ten o'clock that night, when her meeting with her lawyer was over, Teresa took a sedan chair the short distance from Soho Square to Madame Raucour's house. She arrived just as the bells of nearby St Anne's Church sounded the hour and hurried upstairs. Casanova looked on, somewhat sourly, as she embraced Giuseppe with real emotion:

I hear her hurrying upstairs, she comes in, she's joyful and very happy to see me, but she doesn't throw herself at my neck; she doesn't remember how she parted from me in The Hague; she hurls herself at her son, she hugs him and covers him in kisses which he accepts sleepily and returns coldly, saying, 'My dear Mama, my dear Mama.'

Something of his old desire for Teresa must have stirred in Casanova for her genuine pleasure at seeing her son made him unaccountably annoyed. The boy was tired, he snapped, and for people who she knew must be in need of rest, Teresa had kept them waiting for a very long time.

During the next few hours, Casanova witnessed at first hand the extent to which success had changed Teresa from the playful, flirtatious Venetian girl he had once known. In his memoirs, he creates a unique portrait of her at this, the most successful period of her life. She had always been proud; now she seemed downright self-important. Her egotism bordered on narcissism, and she seemed truly to believe that everything she did or said was right. Her manners, even towards him, were as stiff as those of the English aristocrats she now lived among.

Eager to play the gracious hostess, Teresa offered Casanova her arm so that he might take her in to dine. Four places were laid at the table, but she ordered that one be taken away. It was to have been for Sophie, she said, but she had left her at home for misbehaving: when she had heard that the travellers had arrived, Sophie had immediately asked if Casanova was in good health. Had she punished her daughter for that, the adventurer asked. 'Of course,' Teresa answered, 'because in my opinion she should have enquired about her brother's health first, and yours second. Don't you think, I'm right?' Poor Sophie, Casanova remarked. Obedience had more power over her than blood ties. Teresa disagreed: 'It's not a question of feeling,' she told him, 'but of teaching young people to speak as they should.'

Teresa's opinions on educating children annoyed Casanova as much as they had in the Dutch Republic four years earlier. In fact, everything she said that night annoyed him. She told Giuseppe that she was working hard to leave him rich when she died, and that she needed him in London because he was now old enough to share her work:

'I give,' she said, 'twelve suppers and balls a year to the nobility, and twelve to the middle classes at two guineas a head, and I often have five to six hundred people; the outlay is immense, and being on my own I'm certainly robbed, because since I can't be everywhere at once I have to put my trust in people who perhaps abuse it, but now that you're here you can oversee everything, my dear son, keep everything under lock and key, do my correspondence, keep hold of the cash, pay out, collect the receipts, and go around the house making sure that the ladies and gentlemen are well looked after, in short, take on the duties of the master in a house where, as my son, you will effectively be so, and be looked upon as such.'

Appalled by the idea of having to take on all this work, Giuseppe answered his mother guardedly, his eyes downcast and with no affection in his voice. He said that he doubted he would be able to do everything she wanted him to. Since she had never enjoyed the luxury of not working hard, as he had, Teresa was not overly sympathetic. He would soon learn how to do everything, she insisted, for one of her secretaries would move into Madame Raucour's house with him and show him the ropes. During his first year in London all he would have to do was to study English and attend her assemblies so that she could introduce him to the people who mattered. Gradually he would become an Englishman, and everyone would talk about Mr Cornelys. Cornelys? Giuseppe repeated curiously. Teresa assured him that that was indeed his name. 'I'll have to write it down so that I don't forget it,' he said.

Teresa seemed surprised by her son's slow wits, and she suggested that he go to bed. Once he had left the room, she complained that he seemed to have been badly brought up. What had he been learning in Paris during the last four years? Since Giuseppe had been at the best school in the city he should have learned everything, Casanova answered. However, the boy had only studied the things that interested him, such as playing the flute, horse-riding, fencing, dancing minuets, telling a story prettily and dressing elegantly. Because he had never bothered to apply himself to his studies he did not have a clue about literature, he could not write, he was no good with figures and he was unconcerned with geography.

Giuseppe had wasted his time in Paris, Teresa remarked drily. Sophie was so much better educated than her brother that she would laugh at him, she said, adding pointedly, 'But then it's I who have brought her up.' The aristocratic women who attended her assemblies all fought over Sophie, who was well versed in history, geography, languages and music, and could argue with an infinite intelligence. Teresa finished her eulogy about her daughter by inviting Casanova to dinner on the following Sunday, when Sophie ate with her and he could see the girl for himself. Since it was only Monday at the time, Casanova felt even more insulted. Did Teresa not think he might want to see his own daughter before then?

Although Teresa and Casanova sat up talking until two in the morning, he complained that 'She never asked me if I was comfortable in the lodgings, she wasn't curious to know if I was thinking of spending some time in London and what I might do there, and she offered me neither her services nor her credit, except to say with a laugh that she never had a cent.' Since she showed no curiosity at all about his life, he amused himself by volunteering no information on the subject. And as he was only wearing a simple watch and none of his diamonds, she had no idea that he was extremely wealthy.

Teresa did not notice his silence. As on their first evening together in The Hague, she was fully occupied in talking about herself, and she gave him a first-hand account of the legal case she was currently embroiled in with John Fermor:

He claimed that the house which she had built at a cost of ten thousand guineas belonged to him, because he had given her money for it; but he was wrong according to the law she was citing, because it was she who had paid the workers and she to whom they had made out their bills; so the house belonged to her; 'But that money didn't belong to you,' Fermor had told her. She had challenged him to prove this, to produce a single receipt. 'It's true that on several occasions you gave me more than a thousand guineas at one time,' the honest woman had told him, 'but that was generosity on your part, and not at all unusual in a rich Englishman, since we loved each other and were living together.'

This case, which in two years she had won four times and which would not end because of the strength of the squabble which Fermor was employing to contest her victory, had cost La Cornelys dearly, and as we were speaking it was being called before Equity where, *beati possidentes*, they might have to wait thirteen or fourteen years for the ruling. She tells me that the case dishonoured M. Fermor, and I could see that; but I couldn't conceive how it would show her in a good light; yet that's what she believed in good faith.

(*Beati possidentes* – 'Blessed are those that are in possession' – refers to the privilege by which someone in possession of a house or object was not obliged to prove that he was rightfully in possession of it.)

The last meeting of the Society in Soho-square that season was to be held at the end of the month. Teresa told Casanova that she could not sell him a ticket because she was only allowed to give them to the nobility. However, if he wished he could come along in the capacity of her friend, and by sticking close to her all evening he would see everything. If anyone asked her who he was, she would tell them that he was the man who had taken care of her son in Paris and that he had come to London to bring the boy back to her. 'I'm very grateful to you,' Casanova answered, but his sarcasm was lost on her.

Teresa had been anxious to impress Casanova, but she had succeeded only in doing the opposite. When she left, he congratulated himself on having discovered what he called her 'bad character'. London had changed her, but not, it seemed, for the better. Nothing she could do during the rest of his stay could make up to him for the slights he felt he had received at her hand. Eager as he was to see his daughter again, he determined not to visit Carlisle House before the following Sunday, when Teresa had asked him to dine with her. The stage was set for a show-down between them.

Twelve

Teresa's high-handed behaviour was nothing but a front. The last time she and Casanova had met, he had been the one in a superior position. Then he had acted with extreme generosity towards her by giving her enough money to pay off her debts and taking Giuseppe off her hands. But now it was Teresa who, as the driving force behind London's most fashionable assembly rooms, had the whip hand. She also had a position to defend. It had taken her three years to establish herself as London's leading impresario. She had become respectable and, for professional reasons, she needed to remain so. Carlisle House was the favourite haunt of upper-class women, and if they were to continue to attend its balls, concerts and meetings, Teresa had to maintain her own reputation, as well as that of the Society in Soho-square.

Her fear of being discovered for what she was – a wanted debtor and a failed opera singer who was little better than a high-class courtesan – took precedence over the gratitude she felt towards Casanova, and she was anxious to distance herself. To the English, he might appear to be a well-connected French aristocrat, but she knew him for what he was: the son of two Italian actors, a gambler, a schemer and an adventurer who survived by the skin of his teeth. As she was herself.

The strain of running a business, dealing with law suits and being, in effect, a single parent was telling on her. All her time and energy was invested in keeping Carlisle House up and running, and she had none to spare for thinking of other people's sensibilities. Nine-year-old Sophie bore the brunt of her mother's preoccupation with business. Teresa might have doted on her daughter, but she had no understanding whatsoever of her emotional needs. Sophie lacked nothing except her mother's attention. In common with the children of the English nobility Teresa sought to emulate, she spent much of her life in her nursery with only her governess and maid for company. There, and at a nearby art school where she studied drawing, she was taught intensively by a variety of private tutors. Then, on special occasions such as assembly nights, she was trotted out in front of her mother's guests and expected to display the skills she had so expensively acquired.

Sophie's relationship with the mother she seldom saw was uneasy. She was both in awe and frightened of Teresa. Starved of ordinary maternal affection, and with no father in sight, she craved her mother's praise; and she had learned that the only way to get it was by doing exactly as she was told.

The girl had been over-schooled in 'good' behaviour, as Casanova observed when he eventually dined at Carlisle House the following Sunday. He had spent the morning at St James's Palace where he was presented to the king and queen. Afterwards, still in his court clothes, he took a sedan chair to Soho. Anyone dressed as smartly as he was dared not walk through London in case he was attacked or mugged:

Some porter, or idler, or scapegrace from the dregs of society would pelt him with mud, laugh in his face, or push him around in order to get him to say something disagreeable so that the fellow had an excuse to start a fight. The spirit of democracy exists in the English even more than it does in the French; but the strength of the constitution keeps them down. The spirit of rebellion thus exists in every large town, and the great task of a wise government is to keep it dormant, for if it awoke it would be a torrent which no barrier could hold back.

No such spirit of democracy existed inside Carlisle House where he found Teresa holding court with all the gravity of an empress. Although she greeted Casanova politely, she did not introduce him to her four other guests and carried on talking to them in English, a language he neither spoke nor understood. When her major-domo announced that dinner was served, she ordered that her children be brought in. Casanova leaped up to kiss Sophie, but at a signal from Teresa the little girl pulled back, curtsied deeply, and muttered some trite compliment that she had obviously learned by heart.

Teresa was determined to behave as correctly as possible in front of the English. She presented Giuseppe – or Joseph Cornelys, as she called him – to them and, switching into French and referring to Casanova as the Chevalier de Seingalt, the name he now went by, she introduced him as the man who had taken care of her son in Paris. At the table Teresa placed herself between her two children, and although Casanova was seated opposite her she all but ignored him. So did Sophie.

Enraged by what appeared to be a conspiracy to slight him, Casanova nursed his grievances quietly by entertaining the other guests with a string of harmless anecdotes on English manners while pointedly ignoring his hostess. However, when the conversation turned to his visit to court that morning, and Teresa started to interfere in her children's conversation, he could not stop his anger breaking out in several terse exchanges, which he later recorded verbatim in *Histoire de Ma Vie*:

'Did you see the king?' Sir Joseph Cornelys asks me.

'My son,' his mother tells him, 'one never asks questions like that.'

'Why not, dear mamma?'

'Because this question could displease Monsieur.'

'On the contrary,' I tell her, 'it gives me pleasure. I taught him six years ago that he must always ask questions. A boy who never asks anything always remains in ignorance.'

When Giuseppe asked Casanova who had presented him at court, Teresa interrupted him again. The question was too impertinent, she insisted. 'Asked of someone else, but not of I who am his friend,' Casanova replied. 'You see that the answer he obliges me to give does me honour. If I hadn't wanted anyone to know that I'd been at court I wouldn't have come to dinner at your house dressed like this.'

The other guests watched warily as the tension between their hostess and her foreign guest mounted by degrees. By the end of the meal, it was embarrassingly obvious to everyone that Sophie had been warned not to address a single word to the Chevalier. Realizing that she had perhaps gone too far with her instructions, Teresa now urged the child to speak to him:

'I don't know what to say, dearest mamma. Make him say something to me and I'll answer him as well as I can.'

'Well!' I say to her, 'my beautiful child, tell me what you are studying at the moment.'

'Drawing, and I'll show you my work if you like.'

'I'd love to see it. But tell me how you think you've offended me, for you look guilty.'

'Me! I don't think I've done anything to you.'

'You're talking to me without looking at me. Are you ashamed to have such beautiful eyes? And now you're blushing. So what crime have you committed?'

'You're embarrassing her,' her mother tells me. 'Tell him that you haven't committed any crime, but that it's out of respect and modesty that you don't stare at the people to whom you are speaking.'

That Sophie stayed silent was a clear implication in Casanova's eyes that Teresa had indeed instructed her not to look at him. It seemed to him that the impulsive, outspoken girl he had grown up with in Venice had become as stiff-backed and conventional as the English with whom she sought to ingratiate herself, and that she was raising Sophie under an emotionally repressive regime. Later that evening, he tried to break through his daughter's reserve by refusing to look at her drawings unless she looked directly at him first:

'Go on,' says her mother, 'look at Monsieur.'

'Oh, *now* I recognize you,' I say to her. 'And do you remember having seen me before?'

'Even though it was six [*sic*] years ago, I recognized you the moment you walked in.'

'How could you have recognized me when you didn't ever looked at me? My angel, if you only knew what unforgivable bad manners it is not to look at the person you're talking to! Who could have taught you such a bad precept?'

The little one looked at her mother, who'd gone over to the window. When I saw that I'd exacted my revenge, and that the English people had understood everything, I began to look at her drawings and to praise everything in detail, congratulating her on her talent, and complimenting her mother for providing her with such an excellent education.

Once he had exacted his revenge on Teresa for slighting him, Casanova changed his tactics and began to praise her. The tension between them suddenly eased, and even Sophie relaxed. Urged on by Teresa, the pretty child performed her party tricks. She sang in Italian. She played the harpsichord and the guitar. Accompanied first by her somewhat awkward brother and then by Casanova, she danced perfect minuets. Casanova was charmed by her precocious talents. He sat her on his knees and gave her 'all the kisses she deserved, which she returned with all the affection I could ask for. Her mother simply laughed, and also kissed her tenderly when, after leaving me, Sophie went to ask her if she was annoyed.'

By the end of the uneasy dinner party, the deep affection Teresa felt for her old lover had gone some way to overcoming her suspicion of him. Before he left, she took him aside and showed him her new building, and he was easily convinced 'that there was no assembly room in London so vast'. Teresa confided that she employed more than twenty maidservants and twelve footmen: 'From what she said, all this rabble robbed her, but they were essential to her; that's how it had to be.'

Casanova left Carlisle House that night admiring Teresa's achievement and courage and wishing her good fortune. But even so, he refused to be beholden to her again. Although she had invited him to her last ball of the season in the capacity of her friend, he instead purchased his own ticket from Lady Harrington, to whom he had been given a letter of introduction by the Venetian ambassador in Lyon. His pride meant more to him than money. Although he would see Teresa many times during the rest of his stay in London, he never quite forgave her for slighting her as she had done.

The ball Casanova attended was magnificent. Lady Harrington had assured him that he would see all the nobility at Carlisle House, and he was not disappointed. The six hundred guests who turned up at Soho that evening included most of the aristocracy and all the royal family, with the exception of the king, the queen and Princess Augusta. Teresa was much in evidence in a role that was part major-domo and part celebrity hostess. She greeted people when they arrived, mingled with the crowd, paid court to the nobility and orchestrated events with a light and charming touch.

Lady Harrington arrived soon after Casanova. She told Teresa that she had a great deal of ticket money to give her and, turning to Casanova, said that she had guessed when she sold him the ticket that he and Mrs Cornelys knew each other, but had not dared to mention it: '"Why, milady? I've had the honour of knowing Mrs Cornelys for a long time." "I can believe that," she laughed, "and I compliment you on it. You surely know this charming girl too."' Lady Harrington was referring to Sophie, whom she now picked up like a doll and kissed. If Casanova loved himself, he must love the child too, she said playfully, because they looked exactly alike.

Although Teresa had wanted to keep the truth about Sophie's paternity a secret, it proved impossible. The likeness between father and daughter had grown even more pronounced over the past four years than it had been in the United Provinces. Lady Harrington was intrigued, and decided to have some fun at Casanova's expense. With one arm linked through his, she took Sophie's hand and walked mischievously through the crowded assembly, attracting everyone's attention and provoking countless comments from curious bystanders. Although the mysterious Mrs Cornelys was thought by everyone to be a widow, word went around that her 'husband' had arrived. Despite Lady Harrington's half-hearted protests that this was not the case, it was continually remarked that no child had ever resembled its father as much as Miss Sophie Cornelys resembled the Chevalier de Seingalt.

After a while, Teresa came over to Lady Harrington and Casanova, 'and having to answer all the questions about my being her husband, she handles it by saying that I am only her very old friend, and that people were right to be surprised at the resemblance between her daughter and I. Everyone laughs and says that there is nothing surprising in that.' Discreetly changing the subject, Teresa boasted that Sophie had learned to dance the minuet to perfection, and at Lady Harrington's request a fiddler was brought into the side room where they were seated. 'Wishing the little one to do herself honour', Casanova partnered her in the dance.

To all outward appearances, Sophie relished the attention she received that night. Not so 'Joseph Cornelys'. Although Teresa made sure to introduce him to everyone, the youth appeared tongue-tied and uncomfortable. Since he spoke no English, he made deep bows to everyone, which, though appropriate behaviour in Paris, was not the done thing in London.

Giuseppe was deeply upset by the unhappy reversal in his fortunes. He wanted nothing more than to return to Paris, and his life with the Marquise d'Urfé. Casanova had already demolished this fantasy by warning him that he might never be welcome at her home again. It was a cruel blow. In his early teens, the boy had been dropped into a life of riches he had grown to love. Now, just as suddenly, he had been plucked from this idyllic existence and recast in a role he hated and to which he was ill-suited: that of a subordinate to the nobility. Despite his mother's efforts to make him feel at ease, he cut a pitiful figure all evening and appeared to Casanova to be 'the most embarrassed boy on earth'.

After the ball, the London season ended. As the sun fought its way through the stifling blanket of London smog and the open drains in streets began to reek of rotting sewage, the aristocracy fled to spend the summer in the fresh air of their country estates. Left behind in Soho with the artisans, the middle classes and the slum dwellers of nearby St Giles, Teresa closed her new assembly building and retired to the upper floors of Carlisle House with her children to sit out the quiet months.

It was touch-and-go whether she would survive them. She would have no more income until Carlisle House reopened the following November. In the meantime, she had to pay her lawyers' bills, feed herself, Sophie and Giuseppe, and keep on the essential members of her staff. Her creditors were plaguing her to pay them the hundreds of pounds she owed them, and although she pawned some of her belongings over the summer to do so, she could not raise enough cash to clear her debts.

On Sundays Teresa, like all English debtors, could go out in the streets without fear of being arrested, but from Monday through Saturday, bailiffs hovered on the margins of Soho Square like persistent Venetian mosquitoes, waiting for an opportunity to attack her. As long as she stayed inside and kept her doors and windows shut, they could not get at her, for by law an Englishman's home was quite literally his castle, and no bailiff could break into it to make an arrest. However, they could legally gain access to the building by slipping in through an open window or door. And if a bailiff waited long enough, or tipped a servant generously enough, the front door of any house was bound to open a crack.

Teresa knew in her heart that it was not so much a question of if she would be arrested, as when. One morning in mid-August, she was horrified to find herself face to face with a bailiff inside Carlisle House. Before she could run away or call for a servant to oust him, he presented her with a writ for two hundred guineas, forced her ignominiously into a cart, drove her to his house and locked her up.

The following morning, desperate to get out of the ruffian's clutches before she was taken to prison, Teresa cast aside her pride and appealed to the only man in London she felt she could rely on to help her – Casanova. He later recorded her letter to him in his memoirs:

'Yesterday a bailiff waited for the moment when my front door was open, came into my home and arrested me. I was forced to go with him, and I'm imprisoned in his house; but if I don't raise security today, he'll take me tonight to the real King's Bench prison. The bail is 200 guineas which I owe for a bill of exchange which has fallen due and I can't pay. Get me out of here at once, my generous friend, because otherwise tomorrow I might have the misfortune to see other creditors who'll lock me up, and if that happens the abyss will be inevitable. Prevent my ruin and that of my innocent family.'

Teresa was in serious trouble. Her high-handed behaviour towards Casanova had been nothing but empty posturing, an attempt to convince him – and perhaps also herself – that she had somehow made it in England. The reality was that she was surviving by the skin of her teeth. A thin line of credit had been separating her from possible destitution, and that line had now been breached by the bailiff. With her aristocratic friends all in the country, Teresa had no choice but to ask for Casanova's practical help, and although the beginning of her letter was genuinely heart-rending, it ended on a far more prosaic note as she explained exactly how he could get her out of the bailiff's clutches:

'Because you're a foreigner you can't stand bail for me; but you only have to say a word to some householder, and you'll find him ready to help. If you have the time to come and see me, come and you will learn that if I hadn't signed the bill of exchange I wouldn't have been able to hold the ball, because I had pawned all the crockery and the porcelain. My son has the address of the house in which I am being detained.'

Using Giuseppe as a go-between, Teresa sent this letter to Casanova's Pall Mall lodgings. Not surprisingly, the adventurer was with a woman. Eschewing the dubious pleasure of calling at Soho Square to visit his daughter, Casanova had spent the month of June socializing in London's taverns and coffee-shops, picking up whores at the Covent Garden bagnios and visiting the Vauxhall and Ranelagh pleasure gardens. Pleasant as this rather vacuous existence had been, he soon became bored with it. Something was missing from his life: 'My house was perfect for keeping a mistress discreetly,' he later wrote. 'I needed only that to keep me happy. But how to find in London this woman made for me, whose character resembled one of the women I had loved so much in the past?'

Finding a lover to keep him company over the summer became

Casanova's obsession. In common with many single city dwellers today, he decided to help matters along by advertising in one of the local papers. On 5 July, he placed a notice in the *Daily Advertiser*, asking for a flatmate, preferably female, whom he would put up in rooms in the house where he lodged at a reduced rent in return for unspecified 'companionship'. The lucky recipient of the subsidized apartment, which Casanova sub-leased from his landlady for the purpose, was a beautiful, refined and emotionally vulnerable Portuguese woman on the run from her family. Her name was Pauline and, in time-honoured tradition, Casanova soon fell deeply in love with her.

He was, however, taking his time to seduce her, and on the day Giuseppe turned up with Teresa's letter, Casanova had invited Pauline to dine with him for the first time. This was one occasion when he was not inclined to bail out his old friend. He told Giuseppe that as far as he was concerned Teresa could rot where she was, and he did not even want to know where she was being kept. He wrote Teresa a curt note saying that although he pitied her he did not have time to visit her, and that he himself would be ashamed to beg his friends to stand surety for a bill of exchange that had fallen due and which in all honesty ought to be paid. Then he sent Giuseppe packing.

That was not the end of the matter. Later that day, as Casanova was dining with Pauline, Sophie burst into his room, accompanied by Giuseppe's obese French landlady Madame Raucour, threw herself on to her knees in front of her father and burst into such pitiful tears that she was unable to speak. Though he had easily held out against Giuseppe's rather cool pleading on his mother's behalf, Casanova crumbled in the face of his daughter's distress.

Were Sophie's tears heartfelt or put on? She was already a mistress of the arts of manipulation and hypocrisy. As soon as she realized that Casanova was going to help her, she cheered up and stayed on to eat a hearty dinner, during which her precocious conversation in turn astonished and enchanted Casanova and the new woman in his life. The subject of their discussion was Teresa, and Sophie's seemingly disingenuous answers to her father's probing questions were exactly what he wanted to hear:

Reasoning like a twenty-year-old, she could only condemn her mother's conduct and call herself unfortunate to be obliged to depend on her and do her bidding blindly.

'So you don't love her then?'

'How could I love her when she frightens me all the time? I'm afraid of her.'

'So where did those tears come from before dinner?'

'From the pity which I feel for all our family. From her words that it was only I who could move you, that I was her only hope.'

Sophie had not appealed to Casanova of her own free will, and she wanted him to know it. Her suppressed feelings of resentment towards her preoccupied and often absent mother spilled out in an unstoppable torrent. Teresa, she said, lied about her age. It was Teresa who had ordered her not to look at Casanova the first time he had dined at Carlisle House. Everybody else said that the Chevalier de Seingalt was surely her father – and in Holland Teresa had said as much herself – 'but here she tells me that I'm the daughter of Monsieur de Montpernis'. If this was news to Casanova, he did not show it. Instead, he attempted to assure Sophie that she was actually the legitimate child of Angelo Pompeati, her mother's husband. 'Then how come I look so much like you?' the girl persisted. By chance, he answered.

Sophie had Casanova wrapped round her little finger, and her winning performance did not stop there. When Casanova jokingly told her that Pauline was his wife, Sophie threw her arms around the Portuguese woman and called her 'her dear mamma'. She knew exactly how to play to an audience, and her performance earned her the enormous sum of £200. Although this was enough for Teresa's bail, Casanova stressed that he was giving the money to Sophie. If the girl wished to pay her mother's debts with it, she could.

'In return for that sum, my dear Sophie, your mother will be able to sleep in her own bed tonight.'

'Write to her that you have given the money to me, for I wouldn't dare tell her myself.'

'My dear child, I couldn't write that, for I would be insulting her. Do you understand that?'

'Yes, very well.'

'You can tell her that she'll be giving me great pleasure every time she sends you to dine or sup with me.'

Sophie would not give up. Appealing to Pauline she begged her 'dear papa' to write this down in a note to Teresa; and once again she got her way. Teresa had instructed her daughter well in the art of manipulating men.

There was something that Casanova wanted from Sophie, too. His feelings for her were much more complicated, and much murkier, than they at first appeared. His ulterior motive emerged on the first Sunday after Teresa had used Sophie's money to buy her way out of the bailiff's clutches. In order to thank Casanova, she brought Sophie over to dine with him. At the child's request, Teresa left her to spend the night with Pauline, in the upstairs room. When Casanova accompanied his daughter and his lover to bed that evening, he promised he would join them for breakfast on one condition – that Sophie did not get up before he arrived for, as he admitted, 'I wanted to see if she was as pretty in bed as she was dressed.'

As he candidly confessed in his memoirs, what happened the following morning revealed a side of Casanova that even he knew was best kept hidden: 'Sophie laughingly hides herself under the blanket when she sees me appear, but before I throw myself on the bed beside her and begin to tickle her, she sticks out her face which I cover with kisses, and I use my paternal rights to see how she is made all over, and to praise everything she has, which is still very immature. She was very small, but made to be ravished.' This intimate examination was prompted by a predatory sexual interest in his daughter, rather than a paternal one: 'Pauline sees me giving her these caresses without attributing a shade of malice to them, but she was mistaken. If she hadn't been there the charming Sophie would in one way or another have put out the fire that her tiny charms had lit in her father.'

Even in old age, Casanova's interest in women was matched only by his interest in young girls. Though attitudes to adult–child sex were more relaxed in the eighteenth century than they are today, the incest taboo was strong. Casanova had already shared a bed with one of his daughters in Naples – albeit with her mother lying between them. But whereas Leonilda had been seventeen years old and a willing participant in what had turned into an incestuous orgy, Sophie was only nine, and already disturbed enough without being sexually abused by her father.

Poor Sophie's childhood had been anything but stable. She had lived with her dominating mother in at least four countries, under conditions that had ranged from dire poverty to lavish wealth. Since moving to London, her life had been marred by emotional neglect and the pressure of an education she was force-fed from dawn till dusk. Though she had only a vague idea of who her real father was, she had seen her mother work her way through countless men, including John Fermor, whose stormy relationship with Teresa had resulted in bitter quarrels and, lately, open warfare. To make matters worse Teresa, who was the only real point of stability in Sophie's life, was herself living in constant fear of bankruptcy.

It was understandable that all this left Sophie unsettled and depressed. During that summer of 1763, a time when her mother scarcely dared leave the house and the man she suspected was her real father expressed an unhealthy interest in her, she exercised control over the only area of her life she was able to: what she ate. By mid-autumn she was skeletally thin and gravely ill with a constant fever. The cause might well have been anorexia nervosa.

Teresa had been somewhat humbled by her arrest that summer. She was worried sick about how she was going to live from day to day. But as she watched her daughter decline, she became frantic. Yet again she turned to Casanova, who was shocked to find Sophie lying in bed in her room in Carlisle House, 'looking at me with eyes that said that she was dying of grief. Her mother was in despair, for she loved her madly; I thought she was going to hit me when I told her in the presence of the invalid that if the girl died it would be she who had killed her.' With an extraordinarily modern perception straight out of twentieth-century Freudian psycho-analysis, Casanova attributed Sophie's physical and emotional state to bad mothering. The child's sickness, he said, was all Teresa's fault: Sophie was dying because her mother did not understand her, frightened her and, moreover, oppressed her like a tyrant.

Although Casanova's analysis of the relationship was painful and shocking, Teresa was strong and brave enough to accept what he said. She might have been an emotionally clumsy woman, but in her own way she loved Sophie dearly. Certainly the child's health and happiness mattered far more to her than her own pride and self-worth. When Casanova went on to say that Sophie needed to get away from her, Teresa accepted that he was right, and when he offered to pay for their daughter to attend a boarding-school for the next year or so, she was overcome with gratitude. What she lacked in insight, she made up for with genuine affection for her children. She only ever wanted the best for them. If she was not able to provide it, it was because she was as much a victim of her own upbringing and circumstances as they were of theirs.

In the end, Sophie's illness brought Teresa and Casanova closer together. When Teresa next wrote to Casanova, asking him to come with her to view a boarding-school in the Thames-side village of Hammersmith, near her country house, she referred to Sophie as *their* child. For the first time since Casanova had arrived in England, she was prepared to acknowledge that her daughter was also his, and her symbolic gesture of apology and recognition was not lost on him.

Thirteen

Boarding-school turned out to be just what Sophie needed. Even the promise of being removed from her cloistered existence on the upper floors of Carlisle House revived her. Within weeks she was well enough to travel with her parents to Hammersmith to visit a select school recommended by Lady Harrington.

Run by the Institute of Mary under the direction of a charming and spirited sixty-year-old mother superior, the Nunnery, as it was popularly known, had sixteen or so pupils under the age of fourteen, who welcomed their young visitor with hugs and kisses. Casanova had already expressed an unhealthy interest in his young daughter, and now he fixed his desires on her schoolfriends, whom he declared to be 'angels incarnate'. Once Sophie had moved to Hammersmith, he visited her frequently, though the attraction was not so much her as the other girls' 'brief dresses with an English whalebone corset that exposed all their breasts', which sent him into ecstasies. One thirteen-year-old, Nancy Stein, so inflamed him that he invited her to dine with him and Sophie at his Pall Mall lodgings, when he smothered her in kisses. The rest of the company erroneously attributed this to his professed paternal interest in her.

Casanova's other guests that day included a destitute woman and her four daughters, all of whom he had recently pressganged into becoming his lovers in return for his financial help. Also present were Teresa and Giuseppe, who had been invited at Sophie's request. While Teresa watched Sophie show off the new fur-lined coat Casanova had bought her, she congratulated her ex-lover on his new conquests. She had often thought of having her own male seraglio, she joked, but felt that the problems of doing so would be insurmountable.

In reality, finding a lover was the lowest of Teresa's priorities. She had learned to her cost that even a wealthy and generous man could quickly turn into an expensive liability rather than an asset, and at the age of forty she was revelling in a new-found sense of freedom. With Sophie now away at school, and Giuseppe lined up to take over as her right-hand man, she could devote herself to running her assemblies with more peace of mind, as her light-hearted behaviour at Casanova's lunch party illustrated.

Although it was still unprofitable, the Society in Soho-square was more popular and influential than ever. By the start of 1764 Carlisle House had become the favoured venue for royal events. When the Dukes of Devonshire and Grafton decided to hold a subscription ball on 21 January to celebrate the marriage of George III's sister Augusta to the Hereditary Prince of Brunswick, Soho Square was the obvious place to hold it. 'The ball, last night, at Carlisle House, Soho, was most magnificent,' Horace Walpole wrote of the occasion to the Earl of Hertford. 'One hundred and fifty men subscribed, at five guineas each, and had each three tickets. All the beauties in town were there, that is, of rank, for there was no bad company. The Duke of Cumberland was there too, and the Hereditary Prince so pleased, and in such spirits, that he stayed till five in the morning.'

Teresa's short spell of imprisonment during the previous summer had not dampened her spirits. As she confided to Casanova, she had emerged from the bailiff's house bursting with 'several fanciful ideas which would make her rich in no time at all'. The first of these was to start a subscription concert series on Wednesday afternoons, to make use of her premises at a time when they would otherwise have been closed.

These 'Grand Concerts of Vocal and Instrumental Music' would become an annual institution at Carlisle House and have a trans-forming effect on the musical life of the capital. Teresa's pro-grammes, which combined the latest German symphonic music with Italian operatic arias, coupled with her policy of social exclu-sivity, made going to concerts extremely fashionable. During the first season, she herself directed them in collaboration with Gioacchino Cocchi, an Italian composer and the former music director of the King's Theatre. Three years older than she was,

Cocchi would have been well acquainted with Teresa's father, for one of his many operas, *Siroe, re di Persia*, had been premiered at Venice's San Giovanni Cristostomo Theatre during the 1750 Carnival, a time when Giuseppe Imer had been its manager. And since another of his operas, *Rosmira Fedele*, had been premiered at the San Samuele on Ascension Day 1753, Teresa, who had been in Venice at the time visiting her parents, might have met him then.

While working with Teresa at Carlisle House in the spring of 1764, Cocchi was contacted by another musician, Leopold Mozart, who had recently arrived in London from Salzburg with his infant prodigies, his twelve-year-old daughter Maria Anna (or Nannerl as she was called) and his even more brilliant eight-year-old son, Wolfgang Amadeus. Since the previous summer, the Mozart family had been on a Grand Tour of Europe. Their musical circus – in which the younger child was often forced to accompany at sight, to name any note that was played and to play the harpsichord with a cloth covering the keys – had so far taken them to Bavaria, Paris and Brussels, where they had played for Teresa's one-time lover, Prince Charles Alexander of Lorraine.

In London, the Mozarts were living in modest rooms above a hairdresser's shop in Cecil Court, St Martin's Lane, on the fringes of Soho. Unlike Teresa, Leopold always had an eye for economy, and his prime motive in taking his children travelling was to make money, which he did by playing at the royal courts and giving private concerts at commercial music venues. After his children had performed for the king and queen at St James's Palace on 19 May they were awarded a double payment of twenty-four guineas, prompting him to write home gleefully, 'If this happens every three or four weeks, we can put up with it!' Later that month, Wolfgang and Nannerl gave their first public concert in London, in Hickford's Rooms, Brewer Street. 'I have had another shock, that is the shock of taking in one hundred guineas in three hours,' their father wrote drily to a friend afterwards. 'Fortunately it is now over.'

The Mozarts' stay in London got off to a good start, but after a summer of ill-health and poor audiences, their fortunes declined. Leopold saw only one way to recover them, and that was to perform at Carlisle House. 'It is therefore a question of recovering this winter the losses sustained during the summer,' wrote his Parisian patron, Baron Friedrich Melchior von Grimm, to Ernst Ludwig of Saxe-Coburg on 13 December 1764, 'and the father's plan is to give a subscription concert at each assembly at Mrs Cornelys's in Soho Square. Now the Duke of York, the King's father [in fact his brother] is one of the chief members of this assembly, and if his Royal Highness were to patronize these children, whose name is Mozart, their concert would doubtless be welcomed by the whole assembly and their fortune would be made.'

Tragically for Teresa, and perhaps also for the Mozarts, this never happened. Wolfgang and Nannerl might have visited Carlisle House, but Teresa's concert programme was already too full to accommodate a performance by them. Though Teresa was often in the vanguard of change and innovation, on this occasion she missed out on the one musical coup that would have assured her a prominent place in history. Her next afternoon concert series was due to start in February 1765, and she had already handed over the management of it to two well-known musicians: Carl Friedrich Abel, who had worked for her in 1761; and the German composer Johann Christian Bach.

The eleventh son of the genius Johann Sebastian Bach, still thought by many people to be the greatest composer in the history of Western music, Johann Christian Bach had studied under his father until the latter's death in 1750. After a spell in Italy, he emigrated to London in 1762 where he quickly took over Handel's position as the most famous London musician of the age. In 1764 he was made music master to the queen, and he remained in the city for the rest of his life, earning himself the name 'the London Bach'.

Bach and Abel shared a house in Carlisle Street, on the west side of Soho Square, where the Mozart family doubtless visited them (Bach got to know them well during their London stay, and became the young prodigy's mentor). The two composers were not only room-mates but also working colleagues and close friends. Their 1765 concert series for Teresa, which they both starred in and directed, was the start of a lengthy and acclaimed collaboration between them. It turned them both into the darlings of the upper classes and put attending a concert at Carlisle House on a social par with going to the opera at the King's Theatre. For a one-off fee of five guineas, subscribers could attend 'seven of Bach's, seven of Cocchi's, and seven of Abel's' concerts at Carlisle House, according to Mrs Harris, wife of the MP and future Earl of Malmesbury, James Harris, who insisted in a letter to her son that 'We approve of the place so much that both your father and I have subscribed.'

With all the bills she had to pay, Teresa could not afford to rest on her laurels. At the same time as she was hosting her balls, assemblies and the Bach and Abel afternoon subscription concerts, she was also trying to re-establish herself as a soloist. On 15 February, she starred at the King's Theatre in a production of Thomas Arne's oratorio *Judith* (the Mozart family's own concert, planned to take place at the Little Theatre that same night, had to be postponed because of it). The oratorio was repeated at the old Lock Hospital in Southwark at the end of the month. Contemporary music was not to everyone's taste: 'some parts of it were exceedingly fine,' John Wesley, the father of Methodism, noted in his journal, after watching Teresa in the second performance, 'but there are two things in all modern music which I could never reconcile to common sense. One is singing the same word ten times over; the other, singing different words by different persons, at one and the same time. And this in the most solemn addresses to God, whether by way of prayer or thanksgiving. This can never be defended by all the musicians in Europe, till reason is quite out of date.'

The pressure on Teresa that year was relentless. With Carlisle House doing so well, it was only to be expected that someone would try to open a rival establishment. Sure enough, the previous spring a Scotsman named William Almack had announced his intention to build a set of assembly rooms in King Street, St James's. Almack was an ex-servant of the Duke of Hamilton. He already owned a gaming club in Pall Mall, famed for the recklessness of its gamblers. The young *maccaroni*s – dandies who loved French and Italian culture – who frequented his tables turned their coats inside-out for good luck, slipped on leather cuffs to save their shirt-ruffles from being spoiled, and wore wide-brimmed straw hats to keep their long hair out of their eyes and hide their emotions while playing quinze. It was not unusual for Almack's members to lose five, ten, or even twenty thousand pounds at a single sitting. ('Lord Stavordale, not one-and-twenty, lost 11,000*l* there last Tuesday,' Horace Walpole once reported to Sir Horace Mann, 'but recovered it by one great hand at Hazard.')

Not content with taking his cut of the huge stakes being lost and won at his tables, Almack, inspired by Teresa's success, had now decided to branch out, and since many of his members were also subscribers to the Society in Soho-square his plans posed a potentially serious threat to her. 'Almack is going to build some most magnificent rooms behind his house, one much larger than that at Carlisle House,' Mrs Harris wrote to her son on 5 April 1764. 'The subscription is 10 guineas for a gentleman, and the same for a lady, to have only one ticket each; the ladies may lend theirs, but the gentlemen cannot; there are to be between three and four hundred subscribers; a ball and concert, the same as Mrs Cornelys. As there is already so commodious a place, it seems an unnecessary piece of extravagance.'

No doubt Teresa heartily agreed with this sentiment when she got wind of Almack's plans, which included a scheme to poach her best female clients and set them up as a rival committee to the women who vetted the membership list of the Society in Soho-square. When a newspaper story on 8 May announced that work-men had begun building a grand concert room in St James's that would 'be the grandest thing of the kind in town', Teresa launched into a bitter tirade against Almack and those who had threatened to defect to him. Later that month, she was forced to publish a veiled apology for her outspokenness in the newspapers:

And where it has been industriously reported, to the disadvantage of Mrs Cornelys, that she had expressed herself dissatisfied with a subscription now on foot to build a large Room in opposition to hers, she esteems it in her duty in this public manner to declare, that she never once entertained a thought so unjust and unreasonable. She let her house with the greatest willingness and pleasure, for the accommodation of the Nobility and Gentry, for the Wednesday Night's Concert; and so far from presuming to make any complaint, she humbly begs leave to return thanks for the honour done her already. Her house and best services are at their command, until they have completed their own. – She humbly hopes she has not been wanting in duty and gratitude to her protectors, and cannot sufficiently be thankful for the comforts she enjoys in this happy country, which she hopes never to leave.

If Teresa was conducting a dirty-tricks campaign, she was not the only one. That same month, a rumour spread through town that Mrs Cornelys had secretly been selling cut-price tickets to her assemblies to people who were not *bona fide* subscribers of the Society, and its author was probably Almack. Teresa crushed the rumour by writing another letter to the newspapers, this one assuring her clients that 'Such aspersion is entirely false; and as a further proof of my innocence, give it now under my hand, that I will oblige myself to pay 50*l.* for every ticket that any person can prove my having sold in so mean a manner.'

Next, a paper was circulated among the fashionable *ton* claiming that Carlisle House was little more than a high-class brothel. Scandalized – and at the same time conscious of the marketing opportunity this afforded her – Teresa once again hit back indignantly in the press:

Mrs Cornelys is so truly conscious that her deportment, from the first establishment of her house . . . to this time, has been diametrically and invariably opposite to the slanderous reports of it in the public papers, that she cannot but humbly hope and trust, that it will more than ordinarily engage her past and present Subscribers to support her (by generous exertion of their interest on her annual Subscription night) in expensively combating the machinations and malevolence of her enemies.

The war between Soho and King Street had started in earnest. In November 1764, with the winter season at Carlisle House already successfully under way and the builders still in his unfinished premises, Almack published the 'principal Rules' of his assembly rooms, which showed that it was to be run on uncannily similar lines to the Society of Soho-square:

1. Seven Ladies have each of them opened a Subscription Book.
2. Each Book to contain the Names of 60 Subscribers.
3. Subscription for one Season Ten Guineas.
4. Subscription Money to be paid at the first Ball of each Season.
5. Subscription binding for one Season only.
6. Twelve Balls to be given in one Season.
7. The Entertainment of each Night to consist of a Ball, in a Room 90 feet long, 40 feet broad, and 30 feet high; Tea and Cards in separate Rooms; and Supper in a Room 65 Feet long, 40 Feet broad, and 20 Feet high, with a Concert of Music from a separate Orchestra.

Almack also sent a rather nervous letter to the newspapers, reassuring his subscribers that

The Building already erected, and now finishing for the Purposes of your Meeting, is in such Forwardness, that every Thing will be done by the Time proposed; and that at any Rate there will be sufficient Time for the number of Balls, which are to be given in the latter end of this Winter. Conscious of this Truth, I also beg Leave to mention, that the Work in Point of Strength, Convenience, and Elegance, is, and shall be executed in the best, most neat, and richest Manner: And being sensible that such large Undertakings draw the Attention of the uninformed Public, and that Opinions are formed and Falsehoods propagated, which may have reached your Ears, it would be no less necessary to say that there has not been the smallest Alteration from the original Intention.

Teresa had been spreading rumours again. Whenever she was under threat her instinct was to fight back rather than cave in, and it did not desert her now. As the opening of Almack's loomed ever closer she began the extensive and almost constant programme of redecoration and refurbishment that would eventually lead to her bankruptcy.

'Mrs Cornelys, apprehending the future assembly at Almack's, has enlarged her vast room, and hung it with blue satin, and another with yellow satin,' Horace Walpole wrote to George Montagu on 16 December 1764, 'but Almack's room, which is to be ninety feet long, proposes to swallow up both hers, as easily as Moses's rod gobbled down those of the magicians.' Walpole's letter went on to list some of the rival assemblies that were taking place that season: 'Well; but there are more joys, a dinner and assembly every Tuesday at the Austrian minister's; ditto on Thursdays at the Spaniard's; ditto on Wednesdays and Sundays at the French ambassador's; besides Madame de Welderren's on Wednesdays, Lady Harrington's Sundays, and occasional private mobs at my Lady Northumberland's. Then for the mornings, there are levees and drawing-rooms, without end.'

With the paint still wet on its walls, Almack's assembly rooms finally opened on 13 February 1765. Despite the promised social fireworks, the first night was something of a damp squib. The Duke of Cumberland, hero of Culloden and himself a Carlisle House regular, was one of only a handful of people present at the opening ball. The place was 'very magnificent, but it was empty', Horace Walpole wrote two days later, for 'half the town is ill with colds. And many were afraid to go, as the house is scarcely built yet. Almack advertised that it was built with hot bricks and boiling water – think what a rage there must be for public places, if this notice, instead of terrifying, could draw anybody thither. They tell me the ceilings were dropping with wet . . .'

Once people had recovered from their ailments and the building was finished, Almack's new premises soon caught on, and by March they had become extremely successful. Writing to the Earl of Hertford on Easter Sunday 1765, Walpole noted that, while waiting for supper to be served at Northumberland House the previous evening, the company 'wore out the wind and the weather, the opera and the play, Mrs Cornelys's and Almacks, and every topic that would do in a formal circle'. The ballroom in King Street could hold up to seventeen hundred people, but although it was beautifully decorated with gilt columns, pilasters and classical medallions, its style was far more restrained than Soho, which by now dripped with rococo opulence.

Like Elizabeth Chudleigh and the Duchess of Northumberland at Carlisle House, Almack's female patronesses could ruthlessly use their power of veto to strike off the admission list anyone who did not meet their approval. And they did. It was soon being reported that 'The Duchess of Bedford was first blackballed, but is now since admitted; the Duchesses of Grafton and of Marlborough are also chosen. Also Lady Holderness, Lady Rochford are blackballed as is Lord March.' The writer and MP Henry Luttrell mentioned the tyranny of Almack's list in his satirical poem 'Advice to Julia':

> *All on that magic list depends;*
> *Fame, fortune, fashion, lovers, friends,*
> *'Tis that which gratifies or vexes*
> *All ranks, all ages, all sexes.*
> *If once to Almack's you belong,*
> *Like monarchs, you can do no wrong;*
> *But banished thence on Wednesday night,*
> *By Jove you can do nothing right.*

Although Almack's quickly established itself as part of the London social scene, the proprietor and his wife lacked Teresa's charm and sense of style ('Almack's Scotch face, in a bag-wig, waiting at supper, would divert you, as would his lady, in a sack, making tea and curtseying to duchesses,' wrote one patron). Teresa proved herself an admirable competitor. Determined that Almack would not destroy her, she conducted a relentless and brilliant public-relations campaign in the columns of the London newspapers, single-handedly devising what is still the advertising world's most effective weapon: the art of hype.

From this point on, her newspaper notices overflowed with superlatives and hyperbole as they described the improvements that were being made to her premises: the provision of ventilators 'by which the present Complaints of excessive Heat will be obviated, without subjecting the Subscribers to the least Danger of catching Cold'; the 'very considerable, additional and ornamental Improvements' costing 'little less than £2000', which would turn Carlisle House into 'by far the most magnificent place of public entertainment in Europe'; the building of a second entrance door on Soho Square 'by which she flatters herself the coming and going of the Nobility and Gentry, will not only be rendered more easy, but the usual Confusion attending on both, greatly prevented, if not wholly removed'; and the addition of 'the most curious, singular and superb ceiling to one of the rooms that was ever executed or even thought of'. Perhaps this was a claim too far. In case the curious ceiling was not curious enough, it was later said that she added ceiling panels in the Banqueting Hall painted by the fashionable Swiss artist Angelica Kauffman.

In the end Teresa's constant improvements at Carlisle House, coupled with her hard-hitting advertising campaign, won the day. Although Almack's would outlast Carlisle House by more than a century, the assemblies there never reached the celestial heights of those in Soho Square. As one 1766 newspaper report put it, 'A lady of fashion who subscribes both to Mrs Cornelys's and to Mr Almack's, and who is remarkable for what the French call the *Jeu d'Esprit*, being asked the other day, by a great personage, her opinion of each place, readily replied, "Going to Almack's, Sir, is only like going to church, but going to Mrs Cornelys's is going to Heaven at once."'

Fourteen

Attending an assembly or ball at Carlisle House might have seemed close to heaven, but running the place was ruinous. 'Not being acquainted with accounts nor keeping any books of account', as she had once admitted to her lawyer, Teresa had learned nothing about efficiency during the past five years. Her bills were still paid in a slapdash and haphazard fashion, she never asked for receipts, she did not pay her staff on a regular basis and yet she often entrusted them with large quantities of cash. All this laid her open to theft on all sides, particularly by her servants who, while publicly complaining that their employer did not pay them regularly, continually helped themselves to the subscription money and even ordered goods from her suppliers for their own personal use.

Corruption among the servants did not stop there. In 1765 Teresa took on a live-in helper by the name of John Francis Berger, who persuaded her to buy all her wines from his vintner brother, Albert. Year in, year out, from then on Albert supplied Carlisle House with wine and champagne without once sending Teresa a proper invoice. John Berger simply told his employer what she owed his brother, and Teresa credulously handed over wads of cash to him, which the brothers secretly stashed away.

If Giuseppe had only applied himself to learning mathematics while at Viard's in Paris, the dire situation at Carlisle House might have improved. But despite his presence, the fatal concoction of extravagance, non-existent accounting and lax security that had begun under Teresa's direction remained unchanged, and the business continued to haemorrhage its potential profits.

Meanwhile Teresa's legal bills grew ever larger as her case against John Fermor, and his against her, dragged on through the Court of Chancery, the complexity of their arguments reflected in the scratchy handwriting of the lawyers' clerks whose job it was to transcribe their conflicting 'Complaints' and 'Answers' upon the thick parchment testimonies submitted to the judges. Roll after roll of written evidence attempted to unravel the web of broken promises, false pledges, unpaid IOUs and disappointed expectations, but no conclusions were ever reached. The interminable legal wrangling always boiled down to the same two simple questions: who actually owned Carlisle House, and who was entitled to the profits of the activities conducted inside it?

Though the case was costing him dearly, Fermor would not give up his fight to get his hands on what he naturally presumed to be a highly profitable business. At the beginning of 1765 he tried another gambit, and accused Teresa of 'gross fraud and imposition', saying that she had erased his name from the original lease of Carlisle House in April 1760 and inserted her own in its place. With the imminent opening of Almack's very much on her mind, Teresa was forced to spend the afternoon of 7 February 1765 in the bankruptcy courts with her lawyer John Hodgson, answering this new complaint. She admitted that her own name had 'been wrote upon an Erasure' in the original contract, but pleaded that 'how such Erasure happened this defendant sayeth she does not know or can form any belief'.

Fermor, Teresa counter-claimed, was the real villain of the piece. Having 'pretended friendship' with her and offered to help her rent Carlisle House and its contents from Samuel Norman 'for her sole benefit', he had subsequently forced her by 'Menaces and Threats to sign different times several paper writings without being permitted to read the same over or being at the time she signed the same acquainted with the contents thereof'. His estimates of how much money she now owed him were grossly exaggerated, as were his estimates of the profit she had made between 1760 and 1763, which was £22,000 by his reckoning, and less than £6500 by hers. While agreeing that she had not been 'so particular in keeping accounts as she otherwise could have been', Teresa insisted that 'her costs have outweighed any more she might have been given'.

Carlisle House was a loss-making enterprise. It had never made a profit because she had never had enough money in the kitty to discharge her debts.

By May 1765, these debts included the ground rent of Carlisle House, which was seriously in arrears, and Teresa saw no option other than to throw herself on the mercy of her twenty-seven-year-old landlord, William Cavendish Bentinck, the third Duke of Portland. 'My Lord Duke,' she wrote to him on 7 May:

> I am not insensible that an application of this sort must carry with it all the appearance of intrusive temerity; because, it is breaking into your Grace's time with a subject too unimportant for your Notice. I am, however, my Lord Duke, so disagreeably situated, that there are no means remaining that promise the most distant hopes of Success but the having resource to the Fountain Head. The Case, my Lord Duke, is this. I am unavoidably somewhat in Arrears with your Grace; in respect to the Ground Rent of Carlisle House; and though your Grace's Steward has given me all the Indulgence he consistently can yet I fear, at last, his Duty will prompt him to make a Distress upon me, unless your Grace shall be induced to interpose in my behalf; and, by a timely exertion of the generosity of your Disposition, prevent it. You have beheld, my Lord Duke, with Eyes of Reflection, and, I believe, of Approbation, the very extraordinary expences [sic] I have been at this year, for the better Accommodation of the Subscribers; and as this extraordinary Expence [sic] was indispensibly [sic] necessary, as well in point of Duty and Gratitude as Accommodation, I am led to hope and request, that, not withstanding I have been so much indulged already, your Grace will compassionately grant me a further Indulgence to a few weeks after the commencement of the ensuing Winter's Assemblies; and your Grace may absolutely rely, that I will then make a final Settlement with your Steward up to Christmas next; as well as that I shall ever retain the most grateful Sense of your Grace's goodness so kindly and serviceably extended to my Lord Duke, Yr Grace's most obedient and devoted Hmble Srvt Teresa Cornelys.

Could forty-two-year-old Teresa possibly have been the duke's lover? It seemed she had only to ask a favour of him for it to be immediately granted, for within four days he had done what she had asked. And when she wrote to him again, on 6 September that year, begging for 'an Audience, for a few Minutes, any time to morrow (if possible) on an affair of a Public Nature, and of the utmost Importance to herself', Portland agreed to see her the very next day.

This 'affair of a Public Nature' was none other than Teresa's proposed purchase of the King's Theatre, London's only opera house and perhaps the most prestigious theatre in the country. Its lease – along with its coveted licence to stage Italian opera – had suddenly come on the market, and Teresa was desperate to buy it. She was already the ruling empress of London's night-life. Owning the city's opera house would be the jewel in her crown.

For many years the lease had been the property of the Swiss impresario Johann Heidegger. When he had died in 1749 he had left his theatre to Miss Elizabeth Pappet, his natural daughter by the theatre's bookkeeper. In March 1750, the Lord Chamberlain had granted Miss Pappet a renewable licence to perform operas at the King's, as her father had done before her. However, shortly afterwards Miss Pappet had married a naval officer named Sir Peter Denis, and instead of running the theatre herself she had sublet it.

By the mid-1760s, Captain Denis was well known in Court circles: in 1761 he had been entrusted with commanding the royal yacht when it sailed to Germany with the Duchesses of Ancaster and Hamilton on board to bring George III's bride Princess Charlotte of Mecklenburg-Strelitz to England; and he had stayed in charge of the *Royal Charlotte*, as the yacht was called, ever since. Though neither he nor his wife had any intention of running the King's Theatre themselves, in September 1761 they reacquired a seven-year lease on it from its then owner, Edward Vanbrugh.

During the spring of 1765 the erstwhile Miss Pappet died, and the widowed Denis decided to sell on his interest in his late wife's theatre. There was already one prospective purchaser in the pipeline: Peter Crawford, who had been treasurer of the King's for the past eleven or twelve years and, as such, its acting manager.

Crawford was not the most sparkling of impresarios, and under his direction, which he shared with two colleagues, John Gordon and Thomas Vincent, the opera house had become dilapidated and its productions desultory. Though the three men claimed that they had spent £26,000 renovating the building that year, the Duchess of Northumberland, writing in her diary in November, said this was 'incredible. The House is newly painted and the Boxes are newlined but the Dresses Scenes &c. are all shamefully Old & Dirty. Elsi the first Singer has lost his Voice & is grown as fat as a porpoise . . . The Spagnoletti was as ugly as the Devil, half her Face being burnt away, she supplies it by Pasteboard, has a Glass Eye, dresses like a Gorgon & is as hoarse as a Raven. Visconti is tolerably pretty but has not the least Idea of Music.'

Teresa, too, had performed as a principal singer at the King's Theatre that season, and when she heard that Crawford, Gordon and Vincent had formed a consortium to buy its lease from Captain Denis for £14,000, she immediately decided to match their bid. She was convinced that she could run London's opera house better than they could. And owning the building in the Haymarket would provide the perfect venue for her to stage galas and masquerade balls on an unprecedented scale. With this in mind, she marshalled all her contacts, raised promises of financial support and set off to see the Duke of Portland who, as luck would have it, had recently been appointed Lord Chamberlain by Lord Rockingham's newly elected Whig government.

As the effective head and chief financial officer of the royal household, the duke had acquired numerous powers with his new job, including the appointment of royal staff, the arrangement of royal ceremonial occasions, the censoring of plays and, most conveniently for Teresa, the licensing of all the theatres and opera houses in England. Portland granted Teresa an audience on 7 September. The meeting was a testament to her powers of manipulation. Although she was still in arrears with her rent, she managed to persuade him that she was the right person to run the King's Theatre, and that she could raise the money to purchase it. She had £7000 in Drummond's Bank, she told him, and an equal amount elsewhere. As a result of their meeting, the duke agreed to put her case to Captain Denis, and to press him to accept Teresa's offer for his late wife's theatre. Almost ill with excitement, Teresa wrote to Portland as soon as she returned to Carlisle House:

I find, my Lord Duke, that the Dutchesses [*sic*] of Ancaster and Hamilton have some knowledge of Captain Denis (through his commanding the Yacht which brought over her Majesty). If, therefore, your Grace should have the opportunity of speaking to either, or both, of those Ladies at Court tomorrow, I most earnestly request you would recommend my affair of the Opera House to a protection so powerful as an Interposition of such a kind, in my favor [*sic*], must inevitably be with Capt. Denis – I should not presume to be so intrusively pressing, but that the time allotted me for making this application to Capt. Denis is, unluckily, so very short; nor would I take the Liberty of requesting such an Application to be made to him if I was not professed of every moral certainty, that if it meets with success, I shall thereby be enabled to bring the Matter to a very happy conclusion.

Again, Portland did not hesitate to do what Teresa had asked him to. But the Duchesses of Ancaster and Hamilton were not pleased with his interference – perhaps they disliked feeling manipulated – even though they were both staunch patronesses of Carlisle House. They turned on the duke furiously. Teresa had pushed her case a little too far. On 27 September she wrote to Portland again, this time in a tone that managed to be apologetic, obsequious, grateful, flattering and melodramatic all at once. Only the 'strong and irresistible Temptations of Gratitude' had allowed her to bother him again, she said:

I am the more, too, my Lord Duke, induced to this Intrusion (though I hope your Grace's goodness will give it a softer Appellation) as it was necessary that some Opportunity should be snatched to declare with what unfeigned Regret I look back on that precipitate Step I took, in inconsiderately desiring your Grace to intercede for me through the means of the Dutchesses [sic] of Ancaster and Hamilton. The then critical state of the Matter had put me in the situation of an indigent sick Person, who labouring under a dangerous Disorder apparently curable only by the most skilful and celebrated Physician of the age, desperately makes the Application, without averting to the humbleness of his Station, and his consequent inability to command the Attendance and Assistance of a Practitioner of such superior knowledge, and such distinguished Rank: And thus sensible of my Rashness, your Grace cannot but be persuaded (I hope) that your Interposing with Commodore Denis in my favour, subsequent to my being guilty of such a Fault, must impress me with a sense of Gratitude too deep to be ever lessened or removed.

There is a saying that 'No good deed shall go unpunished'. Portland had got himself into hot water for taking Teresa's side in the affair. And it was to get even hotter. Far from taking the duke's word that Teresa had £14,000 at her disposal, Captain Denis decided to check the matter for himself. Discreet inquiries were made at Drummond's Bank, where it was found that Mrs Cornelys's account contained only £1000, and not the £7000 she had claimed. The inference was that Teresa had lied about the money. Caught out, she wrote yet again to the duke on 30 October in a last-ditch attempt to explain the situation and resolve it in her favour:

My Lord Duke – when I consider how very troublesome I have already been I can scarcely form to myself the possibility of finding even the Shadow of an Excuse for my yet becoming more so; but, on the other hand, when I reflect in how contemptuous a light I must stand with your Grace till a particular Circumstance is cleared up, I can not only reconcile to myself the present application as pardonable, but absolutely incumbent.

When I had sometime since the honour of an Interview with your Grace; I said that I had a thousand Pounds in Mr Drummond's Hands and six more ready to produce, if Commodore Denis would accept of that sum (one half of his Demand) and security for the remainder. By my not (as I must suppose) clearly explaining myself, your Grace apprehended that I said I had the whole £7000 at Mr Drummond's, and to that Apprehension (in consequence of my inaccuracy of Expression) I am, my Lord Duke, to attribute your acquainting the Commodore (when you did me the very great favor [*sic*] of speaking to him on my behalf) that I had actually that sum in the Banker's Hands. This, I hear, led Commodore Denis to make an Enquiry; &, that finding I had only a single thousand there, he wrote to your Grace the Intelligence he had received. A communication of this sort must, very naturally, induce you to believe I had been guilty of advancing a Falsehood, but I do, most solemnly, aver to your Grace that I related, or meant to relate, to you, the circumstance just as I have stated it above, and therefore flatter myself, my Lord Duke, that your Candour will do me the justice to believe, that I did not in that, nor ever shall in any point, attempt to attain the patronage of your Grace at the Expense of my Veracity.

Teresa's verbal squirming did not work. Portland had lost faith in her, and Captain Denis did not trust her to produce the £14,000. On 25 November he went ahead and assigned the lease of the King's Theatre to Peter Crawford's consortium. Teresa's attempt to take over London's opera house had foundered on the rocks of her own financial incompetence. She closed down her account at Drummond's, and put her ambition to stage opera in London on hold for another five years.

In the meantime, her expansionist plans to corner more of London's entertainment market continued to simmer, and by the spring of 1766, she was negotiating to build new premises in the City. Outraged by the very idea, one local businessman wrote to the editor of the *Public Advertiser* on 14 March 1766:

Sir – Being at one of the Coffee-houses near the Royal Exchange, this morning, according to custom, I could not help observing two young fellows, both attorneys clerks, that sat near me, expatiating upon the elegance, magnificence and politeness of *Mrs Cornelys Assembly in Soho Square*, and at the same time said she was coming into the City, and they would subscribe, at which declaration, I own I was greatly alarmed; but could get no further intelligence of it, than that she had taken a place in Bishopsgate Street, whither I immediately posted to learn if there was any truth in it, and to my great amazement found it strictly true, that a court within Bishopsgate, and some houses adjoining, were purchased to pull down, and be rebuilt for Assembly Rooms by Mrs Cornelys. O Monstrous absurdity! in a Street! In the situation of *that* Street! that has been hitherto a place of as much trade and commerce as any in the City of London; and to be appropriated to idleness and extravagance. What an age of depravity and corruption do we live in; how opposite are we getting to that industry, uprightness and proper management of business, for which this Metropolis has ever been so famous. But, I am sorry to say, it must be lost, lost in reputation, both at home and abroad, from such degeneracy and compliances as these; and in a few ages trade must be totally ruined, – a foundation from the king to the peasant which all must stand on. I plead a cause that every man of business must acknowledge is just; but as it is confined intirely [*sic*] to the worthy Aldermen and Common Council, whether a licence is granted, I am induced to think it will not take place and revive at the reflection, that upon their maturely weighing and considering this affair in its true light and circumstances, they will intirely put a stop to such injurious proceedings. You will very much oblige a daily customer to your paper, Mr Woodfall, if you will give this a place as soon as possible; not that I am interested in the affair, but a well-wisher to the prosperity of the City in general, and hope through the channel of your page, to see some able penman handle this subject more properly. I am, Sir, your humble Servant, A CITIZEN.

Like the thousands of other foreign immigrants who inhabited London's West End, Teresa was seen by the staunchly xenophobic City as a dissipated foreign menace intent on polluting English soil. The Corporation did not take kindly to the thought of her opening a suite of assembly rooms in their midst, and her plan was immediately crushed.

To John Fermor, the rumours that Teresa had tried to buy the King's Theatre for £14,000 and now planned to expand into the City shockingly confirmed what he had suspected all along: that she had secretly amassed a fortune at his expense. Although she claimed to be broke, she continued to throw money around. As he watched the decorators move in for yet another seemingly unnecessary refurbishment of the Soho mansion he had bought for her six years earlier, Fermor grew increasingly infuriated by Teresa's slippery 'answers' to his 'complaints' against her in the Court of Chancery. Backed by his large inheritance, he pursued his case against her with renewed vigour.

By May 1766 the situation had reached deadlock, with both parties deeply entrenched behind their own differing versions of the truth. But which version was the more accurate? Had Teresa willingly agreed to a fifty-fifty partnership with her ex-lover, or had he tricked and threatened her into it? Had the penniless foreigner fallen victim to a wicked rich Englishman, or was she an evil woman trying to cheat him out of his just dues?

There was one person who could help Teresa to answer the complaints against her, and that was Elizabeth Chudleigh. Elizabeth had helped her to set up Carlisle House, and she had been present at many of her meetings with Fermor. Both as observer and participant, she had witnessed the lovers' discussions and rows. If anyone could throw light on the matter, and support Teresa in her fight to hang on to Carlisle House, it was she.

Hopeful of enlisting her as a defence witness, in June Teresa's lawyers dispatched a commissioner for oaths and a clerk to Chalmington in Dorset, where Elizabeth was recovering from the excesses of a European tour. She had left England to demonstrate to the Duke of Kingston how much he would miss her if she was not around, and in this she had succeeded. Her hard drinking and often uninhibited behaviour while abroad had also enhanced her reputation as a wild and infamous woman: at one party in Berlin, Frederick II had seen her staggering across a dance floor, having just drunk two whole bottles of wine.

George Cooper and Nicholas Stickland, the commissioner and

his clerk, arrived in Chalmington on 20 June and tentatively approached the haughty and notorious aristocrat at her home. But Elizabeth (whom the embarrassed clerk, at a loss how to define her marital state, variously described in the report as both a 'widow' and a 'spinster') simply refused to be drawn into the case, and her answers were as carefully framed as their questions. When asked whether she knew the defendant and the complainant she said vaguely that she had known them both 'for two years last past or upwards'. Questioned as to whether she had ever heard Fermor talk about being a partner in Teresa's enterprise, she grudgingly admitted that 'she hath often heard disputes between the Complainant and the Defendant relating to the undertakings at Carlisle House . . . but, according to the best of her Knowledge, Remembrance or Belief cannot set forth any particular circumstance relating thereto'. When shown agreements between the two parties, which she herself had signed, Elizabeth agreed that the signature was hers but refused to comment further, and when asked if she knew of any further evidence that might be of use to Teresa she declared coldly that 'she cannot set forth or depose any Matter or Thing material of use for the Defendant in this course according to the best of her Knowledge, Remembrance or Belief other than what she has already done'.

For the last six years Elizabeth had basked in the reflected glory of being in charge of Carlisle House's list of subscribers, but she was making it plain that, when it came to any legal case, Teresa was on her own. Her own reputation was already shaky enough without risking it any further. Her clandestine marriage to Hervey was a wide-open secret and her affair with the Duke of Kingston, which had been going on for more than ten years, was a matter of public knowledge among the *ton*. Now in her forty-seventh year, the last thing Elizabeth needed was to be drawn into another scandal before achieving her goal, which was to marry Kingston and secure her position before her own protectress, the ageing Princess Augusta, died.

Teresa had been naïve and presumptuous in thinking that her former patroness might support her. Increasingly isolated, she struggled to keep Carlisle House going through the quiet summer months. Meanwhile, her enemies and rivals plotted against her. Soon another rumour about her expansionist plans – this one false – spread through the town: that, having failed to get into the City, 'Mrs Cornelys of Soho-square had purchased Mr Tyer's rights and title to Vauxhall Gardens for a considerable sum of money'. In December, a pernicious report was published in the papers that she had fled to France with thousands of pounds 'to the total ruin of several of her creditors'. Outraged by the constant personal attacks on her, Teresa struck back through the pages of the *Public Advertiser* on 8 December at the 'many false reports that had been industriously though (praise be to Justice!) ineffectually propagated, at times, for these six years past', all of them with the iniquitous design of accomplishing her ruin:

Conscious (let her say) of her own integrity, AND HAPPILY ABLE, AND FROM PRINCIPLE WILLING, (having, as she is ready to prove, paid upwards of ELEVEN THOUSAND POUNDS within these thirteen months) TO DISCHARGE EVERY JUST CHARGE UPON HER; the *story*, to her, had something in it so singularly cruel and absurd, that she could never have been persuaded of its finding such a general belief, if the intelligence she received from various quarters, and the particular assurances of persons of the highest rank and honour, of the actual existence of such an extensive rumour, had not placed the circumstances beyond the possibility of a doubt. – Upon recollection, however, Mrs Cornelys cannot but think, that the worthy inventor of this *very probable* tale (whoever the party may be) has *inadvertently* over-shot the intended mark; for, as she had the favourable opportunity, on Thursday last, to convince, BY HER PRESENCE, a numerous assembly of the Nobility and Gentry of the utter falsehood and consummate malice of the report, (and who did her the honour to express the strongest satisfaction thereat) she cannot but reasonably entertain the warmest hopes that every future effort to prejudice her with the world, will, in consequence thereof, meet with all the detestation, and all the contempt, which such unmerited treatment loudly and justly calls for.

Teresa went on to offer a reward of a hundred pounds 'for the discovery of the author of this calumny', and another of fifty if anyone was convicted of spreading it. It was not reported at the time whether anyone did come forward to denounce the scandal-monger and claim the reward money. But if they did, it is highly unlikely that Teresa ever paid them.

Fifteen

'Besides Ranelagh and Vauxhall, I have been at Mrs Cornelys's assembly, which, for the rooms, the company, the dresses, and decorations, surpasses all description.'

Tobias Smollett, *Humphrey Clinker*, 1771

The perennial problem of cash–flow never stopped Teresa maintaining Carlisle House to the highest standards. Between 1767 and 1772, she spent well over five thousand pounds on refurbishing the house, and had several rooms completely redecorated by furniture-maker Thomas Chippendale. Teresa had known Chippendale since 1762, when she had employed him to survey the standard of Samuel Norman's carpentry. His own work at Carlisle House included a ground-floor 'China Room', completely done out in the chinoiserie style, which he had popularized through his 1754 trade catalogue, *The Gentleman and Cabinet-maker's Director*. Chippendale's mahogany open armchairs with pierced backs in pagoda-like lattices, japanned cabinets decorated with gilded Chinese scenes, carved gilt wood overmantel mirrors and intricate lattices, many emulating bamboo, turned Carlisle House into London's most fashionable residence. In addition to the furniture, he installed an extraordinary fretwork lattice 'Chinese Bridge' three feet high and twenty-five feet long, which began in the original part of the house and led directly into the Concert Room.

As a showcase, Chippendale's work at Carlisle House could not have been better placed, for it guaranteed him exposure to his ideal market – the richest and most fashionable members of society, people who had a keen desire to ape Teresa's inimitable trend-setting style. Hopefully it led to him getting many new commissions for, of course, Teresa never paid him in full.

Carlisle House now looked more sumptuous than ever. Yet there was no stopping Teresa. Other novelties she introduced in the late 1760s and early 1770s included an indoor grotto room planted with shrubs and evergreens, a well containing a mineral spring, a petrified cave painted with Egyptian hieroglyphics, and several rooms in the Gothic style popularized by Sir Horace Walpole in his Twickenham 'castle', Strawberry Hill.

The new-look Carlisle House with its themed rooms was not to everyone's liking. In 1768, Bach and Abel, the music directors of what had become Teresa's annual spring subscription concert series, defected to the more conventional décor of Almack's in St James's to run concerts in competition to Soho's. Teresa shrugged off their loss. Carlisle House was still incredibly popular with the English nobility and gentry, and by now it had become an obligatory stop on every foreign tourist's itinerary. When the Milanese Enlightenment intellectual Alessandro Verri visited London in 1767 he wrote of having attended 'il ballo di Giovedi ad una magnifica sala di una Italiana, La Signora Pompeati', and when Honoré III, the Prince of Monaco, came to London the following April it was Carlisle House, not Almack's, that he visited.

On the night of Honoré III's visit, Teresa gave 'a remarkably brilliant assembly'. Nearly every member of the British royal family was in attendance, along with a bevy of foreign ambassadors and most of the first nobility. 'The Prince seemed astonished at the profusion of taste, elegance and expence [sic] displayed throughout the house,' the *Public Advertiser* reported glowingly, 'and declared his perfect approbation of the assembly, as by far exceeding the highest of his expectations, or what he could have possibly conceived of any place of entertainment of that nature.'

On 4 September that year, Carlisle House received an impromptu visit from Christian VII, the eighteen-year-old Danish king, who arrived at a masquerade ball late one night after a visit to the opera. There was no one in London more fitting than Teresa to entertain the young monarch: as a member of the Mingotti company, she had sung to his parents in Denmark, and she had even been present in Charlottenborg on the day of his birth.

However, the long-awaited Danish heir had not lived up to his country's expectations. By January 1766, when he acceded to the throne at the age of sixteen, he was physically stunted, debauched, frequently drunk, riddled with venereal disease and already displaying signs of the mental derangement – probably schizophrenia – that would haunt him for the rest of his life. These character defects, however, had not prevented his cousin, England's George III, sanctioning Christian's marriage to his own sister, Princess Caroline Matilda, a sheltered fifteen-year-old who had been packed off to Denmark like a lamb to slaughter in October 1766.

Not surprisingly, the marriage had proved a disaster. By 1768 the couple were practically estranged, and Christian forbade his wife to accompany him to England, even though Caroline was desperate to see her brothers and sisters and her mother again. Despite the royal princess's absence, Christian was received in London with due pomp and circumstance. Among his train on the night of his visit to Carlisle House were the Polish Prince and Princess Czartoryski, the Spanish ambassador Prince Masserano, the Venetian Princess Barbarigo, the Prussian, Danish, Swedish and Venetian ambassadors, the Duke and Duchess of Ancaster, Lady Grosvenor, the Earl of Huntingdon, the Earl of March, and Teresa's patroness the Countess of Harrington. 'All the most beautiful and richest ladies in England were there in fancy dress of singular taste and magnificence,' noted one French gentleman, who was present. 'Several ladies, and among them Lady Spencer, one of our acquaintances, wore more than one hundred pounds sterling worth of diamonds.'

Carlisle House was lit by more than two thousand candles on the occasion of his visit, and the orchestra was instructed to start playing the moment Christian entered the ballroom. As the newspapers later reported, the young king 'opened the ball with the Duchess of Ancaster, & danced the second minuet with the Countess of Harrington'. Later he retired to a private room to take tea from Teresa's best Dresden china, 'the whole being so judiciously arranged and so happily dispersed, as to produce a very pleasing effect; and procure Mrs Cornelys repeated encomiums from the

Nobility on her peculiar taste for elegance'. The lunatic Christian was charmed by Teresa. Before he left Carlisle House at one o'clock the following morning he 'graciously condescended to do Mrs Cornelys the honour of personally assuring her of his most perfect satisfaction at his night's entertainment'.

Teresa was unstoppable. The atmosphere of Venetian gaiety she created in her home made it a magnet for the fun-loving English aristocracy and the younger members of the royal family. The Duke of York had been an almost permanent presence at her balls and assemblies until his untimely death in Monaco in September 1767. On 8 March that year, shortly before his twenty-eighth birthday, Lady Mary Coke had noted him slipping out of a dull concert at St James's Palace to go to a Carlisle House masquerade, and when he overtook her in the park the following day 'he told me he had stay'd at the Ridotta till five that morning, that there were nearly two thousand people'.

Even with thousands patronizing her premises, Teresa was still so short of money that she was prepared to deal with her old enemy, John Fermor. In February 1768 she signed an indenture reassigning Carlisle House to him for the sum of £2517. Despite everything that had passed between them and their ongoing legal wrangles, her old lover was as much under her thumb as ever: along with his partners in the deal, the widow Mary Brackstone, Edward Aylett and Thomas Middleton, he promised Teresa she could stay on as the manager of her business, even if she did not pay them back as arranged.

Teresa was shameless about using Fermor and his contacts. Carlisle House was bursting at the seams and she was desperate to expand. That year, she entered into a partnership with an upholsterer named James Cullen, who held the lease on three adjoining properties in neighbouring Greek Street. Number eleven Greek Street, formerly the King's Square Coffee-house, now became known as Teresa's Little House, while numbers twelve and thirteen, once the home of the third Viscount Chetwynd, became known as her Great House, and later as Portland House. For the next three years the three properties were used as an overflow for Carlisle House, and occasionally for separate assemblies.

With a business empire now consisting of three properties, and with up to two thousand guests a night attending her assemblies, each paying between one and five guineas for their tickets, Teresa was raking money in and, as usual, spending it just as fast. Her next project was to turn the cellars beneath Carlisle House into a new dancing gallery. In terms of popularity, it seemed that she could not have been more successful. But against all odds, her situation was about to get even better. Elizabeth Chudleigh, her patroness ever since she had arrived in London, was on the point of achieving the respectability she had dreamed of.

After seventeen or so years as the Duke of Kingston's lover, Elizabeth's position was an anomalous one. She was still a close confidante of the royal family and accepted in the highest social milieus, yet her 'secret' marriage to Augustus Hervey was gossiped about incessantly, and she was often ridiculed in private. Although she was in effect a married woman living in sin with a man who was not her husband, she had realized long ago that silence was her best defence, and with remarkable *sangfroid* – or perhaps self-deception – she admitted to nothing and ignored the scandal.

That was now to change. In the spring of 1768, Hervey decided to divorce Elizabeth. He wanted to marry again – this time to a spouse who was prepared to acknowledge him – and he sent Elizabeth a message to this effect. But there was a catch: before he could obtain a divorce, he first had to prove that he was married to her. And although she was as anxious to be free of him as he was to be of her, Elizabeth wanted to avoid the shame that a public disclosure of her marriage would bring – so much so that, in the past, she had once made a special trip to Lainston church, where the marriage had taken place, rifled the parish register, and torn out the page upon which the details were entered.

With remarkable short-sightedness, Elizabeth stubbornly refused to admit that she had ever married Hervey, and in her high-handed manner she threatened him with ruin if he persisted with his suit.

As the vituperative Lady Mary Coke noted in her diary on 7 August 1768, Hervey was 'going to prove his marriage, as the first step for being unmarried, and he has sent the Lady who goes by the Name of Miss Chudleigh a letter to signify his intention; to which She has return'd this answer: that if he proves the marriage, he will have some sixteen thousand pounds to pay, as she owes that sum of money.'

Strangely, neither her profligate spending, her liaison with Kingston, nor her murky past seemed to have any effect on Elizabeth's popularity at court. By the end of September, Lady Mary was lamenting that although the so-called Miss Chudleigh had retained lawyers to advise her about the divorce, 'yet she had the honour of attending Her Royal Highness the Princess to the Queen's Ball, and danced in company with their Majesties: such are the times'.

In the end, Elizabeth and Hervey reached a compromise. Elizabeth instituted a suit of jactitation against him in the ecclesiastical court, which prevented him claiming he was married to her; and Hervey made such a poor answer to it that it was widely presumed that they had colluded with each other to make sure that the suit succeeded. With great trepidation, Elizabeth swore on oath before the clerical judges that she had never married Hervey, and on 11 February 1769 she was duly declared a spinster.

At long last, Elizabeth was a free woman. She did not remain so for long. On 8 March she married the Duke of Kingston at the society church of St George's, Hanover Square. He was fifty-eight, she was forty-nine. Her conscience must have weighed heavily on her, for, according to Mrs Harris, she was 'so hurried and confused the day she was married that she fainted after supper'. Thomas Whitehead, Kingston's servant, called the wedding 'the worst ceremony I ever saw in my life' – but, then, he had always detested his new mistress and his opinion of her did not improve now. On the morning after the long-awaited wedding night, he observed that the duke came down from his room a crushed man and thereafter 'felt the matrimonial chains gall him severely'.

Perhaps Casanova's view that marriage was 'the tomb of love' was right in the Kingstons' case, or maybe the disgruntled

Whitehead was simply jealous that Elizabeth now had a legitimate place in his beloved master's life. From now on, he would record her every misdeed, angry word and temper tantrum for *Original Anecdotes of the Late Duke of Kingston and Miss Chudleigh*, a venomous book he published after the duke's death. These ranged from the way Elizabeth sold the spare vegetables grown in her kitchen garden rather than give them to her servants, to the fury with which she once threw her husband's trunks off their carriage, simply because they had been loaded on to it before her own.

Never one to watch her behaviour, the new Duchess of Kingston did not care a fig what she did now. Having waited so long to become a peeress, she intended to milk her new position for all it was worth. On 17 March, Mrs Harris wrote to her son that 'The Duke and Duchess of Kingston are to be presented Sunday . . . Gertrude and I go to court Sunday, on purpose to see her finery.' The two women were not disappointed: Elizabeth was 'so loaded with jewels, pearls, etc. that she could scarcely move; indeed it was thought that no bride ever appeared at St James's so richly dressed'.

When Teresa opened a dancing gallery and apartments in the cellars of Carlisle House on 11 April 1769, the bejewelled duchess and her equally profligate if put-upon husband were present. And over the next few years they continued to make frequent and spectacular appearances at the Soho balls and assemblies. As the decade drew to a close, the duchess's power went from strength to strength, and Teresa's position as the unofficial ruler of the fashionable set still remained unrivalled. It seemed that she had reached the apotheosis of success when, on 6 June and 'with the Patronage, and at the Insistence of several Persons of great Distinction; and under the particular Sanction of the Protectresses of the Society', she hosted a sumptuous festival at 'exceedingly great' expense to celebrate George III's birthday.

As Teresa's newspaper notices boasted, Carlisle House was transformed for the occasion with 'numerous and Extraordinary' wax illuminations all over the house. The refreshments, and in particular the dessert, were a special feature, served 'in the English and Foreign modes . . . disposed of in different Places and Apartments; several considerable temporary Erections and Accommodations are being now prepared, for that particular purpose'. Tickets were a guinea each. The gala began with a grand concert of coronation anthems and concertos directed by the famous violinist, composer and conductor Felice de Giardini, and to add a further touch of magic, the orchestra was dressed 'in rich Venetian Dominos, without Masques'.

The following January Teresa hosted yet another royal gala, this one to celebrate the queen's birthday. The newspapers reported that the number of tickets was 'limited to one thousand, though the house will easily accommodate several hundred persons more', and that costs for the evening were estimated at about a thousand pounds, 'which must certainly place the *Gala* amongst the most magnificent sights and most sumptuous entertainments that this country has produced'. This level of expenditure would also have wiped out any potential profit Teresa might have made. So sure was she of the demand for tickets that she boasted that they would only be sold to 'Peers and Peeresses in general, the Foreign Minister, and past and present Subscribers to the Assemblies, and such of their Friends as they shall accommodate with written orders for that Purpose'. It was she, not her aristocratic customers, who called the tune now.

Her fame had already spread as far afield as the American colonies where, on 17 August 1769, the *Virginia Gazette* had reported, in a scandalized tone, that tickets to Mrs Cornelys's Soho assemblies were now a guinea each. Notwithstanding this exorbitant price, people were still desperate to get hold of them. A newspaper article published in London in 1770 talked of the Society in Soho-square as being 'the first assembly of the kind in the Kingdom, both for the figure of the company, and the taste and elegance of the rooms'. The writer described his visit to Carlisle House in minute detail, starting when the doors were thrown open at nine o'clock to let the first guests into the suite of six ground-floor rooms, 'each superior to the other'. Few fashionable people arrived before ten o'clock, the journalist said, 'and those who profess themselves of the genteelest order, not until eleven, where they will walk about and amuse themselves with accosting their acquaintance, and forming themselves into select parties for the evening, then regaling [themselves] with jellies, syllabubs, cakes, orgeat, lemonade, fruits &c, prepared in a kind of arched shelving, all round the hangings of the tea-room'.

At ten o'clock, the huge crowd crushed upstairs and spilled through the two large reception rooms into the great Concert Room or Ballroom. This was 'furnished and hung in the most superb taste, with an exceedingly good band of music, in an orchestra erected at the upper end, and rows of benches down the sides, placed one above the other'. After country dances, there was a pause for tea, which was taken at small round tables. At midnight, everyone descended into the basement 'cotillion gallery' in the house's huge cellars 'which, from the vast variety of furniture and ornaments, the grandeur and magnificence of some, the elegant simplicity of others, together with the amazing beauty of the lights, one of the principal excellencies throughout the whole, form a view on descending a perpendicular flight of stairs, most sumptuous and pleasingly striking'. Here they danced until four in the morning. The journalist concluded by praising 'the profuse soul of Mrs Cornelly [sic], the conductress' who was 'not more justly praiseworthy for any part of the entertainment than for the good order of the whole'.

'The good order of the whole'. Strictly speaking, this phrase was not true. Teresa's assemblies were becoming wilder and more licentious every week. Her costume balls had fired the *ton* with a craze for masquerades that had lain dormant since the 1720s when Heidegger had introduced them at the King's Theatre. Then, the Church had railed against 'this grand Enemy to Liberal Sciences' and lamented 'the decay of *Wit*' that such superficial entertainment as a masquerade brought in its wake. In his 'Letter to the Bishop of London', written in verse and published in 1724, Heidegger had fought back against the Church's anti-masquerade stance:

My Lord,
Your sermon, preach'd at Bow
Came to my Hands some Weeks ago.
By which I find you seem afraid
That harmless Pastime, MASQUERADE,
May spoil the Reformation Trade.

Poking fun at his own hideous face, Heidegger had even suggested that masquerades could be of benefit to ugly people:

'Tis Prudence to supply with Art
Where Nature fails to do her Part:
When Borrow'd Looks give less Offence,
To use one's own is Impudence.

With the King's Theatre now firmly in the hands of the dull Peter Crawford and his colleagues, there was no one in England more fitting to take on the late Heidegger's role as London's masquerade supremo than Teresa, who had grown up in Venice, the home of intrigue where the wearing of disguises was almost the norm, and from 1769 onwards, masquerade balls became the staple form of entertainment at Carlisle House. They provided the perfect opportunity for the nobility to flaunt their wealth and display their imaginations by commissioning elaborate, bejewelled costumes from their tailors and dressmakers, which would often take weeks to make. At the balls, their disguises and masks allowed them the freedom to make countless secret assignations, and even to slip away and make love in the mansion's many private salons and bedrooms.

To the Church and the moral majority – or, rather, minority, as it was then – the Society of Soho-square began to seem like Sodom and Gomorrah. In January 1770 a long satirical article, 'Something After the Manner of Le Sage', appeared in the *Gentleman's Magazine* in which the character of Didius held a conversation with the Devil who told him:

'*Madrid* is not the only city for a devil to amuse himself in; *London* will do as well; and one house alone in this metropolis will exhibit some *hellish* high scenes. I frequently step into this house to reconnoitre the company there, and always find curious personages, who make a spirited figure of the true diabolical style . . . The devil turned him away to Soho Square, stopped at Carl– H, and finding the doors open, sidled in with the easy careless air of a man of the first fashion.'

But with royalty on Teresa's side, not even the protests of Church leaders could stop her masquerades. Although the Bishop of London pleaded with George III to prevent a huge masked ball being held at Carlisle House on the night of 27 February 1770, the bishop's own wife, and those of three other high clerics, were among Teresa's aristocratic guests.

This infamous masquerade was sponsored by sixteen noblemen, members of the Tuesday Night Club, each of whom had paid Teresa a hundred guineas for an allotment of fifty tickets each. Throughout February, the *ton* talked of little else, and the streets around Covent Garden were blocked from morning to night with the carriages of those attending costume fittings. London's theatre managers even allowed their tailors and dressmakers time off work so that they could make the outfits.

The costumes were indeed sumptuous and extraordinary. The Duke of Cumberland had ordered a Henry VIII disguise, and the Duchess of Buccleuch was to be dressed dramatically as the Witch of Endor. The actor-manager David Garrick would appear 'in the character of a celebrated Doctor at the Maccaroni' and his wife, the admired German dancer Eva-Maria Veigel, as a shepherdess. But no outfit was more spectacular than that made for Lord Gallway's daughter, Miss Monckton, the 'Indian sultana': it consisted of a rich veil, a robe made out of cloth-of-gold with seams embroidered with precious stones, and a head-dress adorned with 'a magnificent cluster of diamonds'.

Liberty reigned in Soho on the night of the twenty-seventh, and not only inside Carlisle House, where preparations for the masquerade had been taking place for many days, even weeks. As so often before one of Teresa's grand parties, thousands of spectators gathered in Soho Square and the surrounding streets to see the guests arrive. However, that night the mob had an additional agenda: they were calling for the release from prison of the radical politician John Wilkes.

Wilkes has the reputation of being England's answer to Casanova. Almost as hideous as Heidegger – Dr Samuel Johnson declared he was one of the ugliest men he had ever met – he was nevertheless a notorious womanizer and, at the same time, a brilliant wit. When Lord Sandwich commented that Wilkes would die 'either of the pox or on the gallows', Wilkes retorted, 'That will depend on whether I embrace your lordship's mistress or your lordship's principles.'

The son of a malt distiller, in 1747 Wilkes married an heiress from the Buckinghamshire town of Aylesbury and subsequently became a noted rake. As a member of Sir Francis Dashwood's infamous Hell Fire Club (their motto was 'Fay ce que voudres' or 'Do what you will') he participated in wild orgies in Medmenham Abbey in Berkshire, and in caves in nearby Wycombe. Eventually his dissipated lifestyle palled, and Wilkes separated from his wife and entered politics. Elected as the Member of Parliament for Aylesbury in 1757, he became an outspoken critic of the Earl of Bute's government, and to counter the influence of the Establishment mouthpiece the *Briton*, he established a weekly opposition newspaper called the *North Briton*.

Through the pages of this irreverent journal, Wilkes savagely attacked both the Prime Minister and the king. In 1763, in his forty-fifth issue, he denounced the Peace of Paris, and was arrested for seditious libel. Imprisoned for a spell in the Tower of London, Wilkes claimed the privilege of his position as an MP to avoid being brought to trial. The move turned him into a champion of liberty. His expulsion from the House of Commons the following year, his subsequent flight to Paris, his conviction on two further charges of seditious, obscene and impious libels and the declaration that he was a *bona fide* outlaw only added to his popular appeal.

By the time he returned to England early in 1768, Wilkes had

19. A Soho concert ticket to J. C. Bach and Carl Abel's subscription concert series at Carlisle House.

20. Regatta ticket. An elaborate admission ticket to the fabled 1775 Venetian Regatta Ball at Ranelagh Gardens that Teresa organized.

21. *The World in Masquerade*, engraving by I. Cole. A masquerade ball at Carlisle House, *c.* 1771.

22. Girandoles and chairs (*opposite left and above*), designed by Thomas Chippendale and showing his mastery of the rococo and chinoiserie styles, which Teresa favoured at Carlisle House.

23. *The Harmoniac Meeting.* A satire showing Teresa's opera. All the participants are depicted with animal heads. Guadagni is at the lectern, and Teresa is on the far right, with a mob-cap and whiskers.

24. *Trial of the Sovereign Empress of the Vast Regions of Taste.* Teresa's trial for staging an unlicensed opera satirized in the *Oxford Magazine*. Declaiming 'You shall pay dearly for your insolence', an unrepentant Teresa is carried before Sir John Fielding on the shoulders of the Duchess of Northumberland and her counsel. Guadagni throws up his hands in horror on the far left.

25. *The Macaroni – A Real Character at the Late Masquerade.* A masquerader poses in front of his toilet table.

26. The Pantheon, Oxford Street. James Wyatt's magnificent hall, shown during a demonstration of Vincenzo Lunardi's hydrogen balloon in 1784.

27. *Cupid Beating up for Volunteers.* Cupid drums up support for the auction of Carlisle House outside St James's Palace. Teresa, holding the flag of 'Folly', is followed by the Duchess of Northumberland.

28. *Cupid Turn'd Auctioneer, or, Cornelys' Sale at Carlisle House.* Teresa fans herself in the foreground while Cupid auctions off an aristocratic gentleman perched on a stool.

29. Casanova, aged sixty-three. A gaunt Casanova, pictured in Prague in 1788, three years after he had moved to Dux Castle.

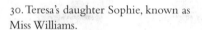

30. Teresa's daughter Sophie, known as Miss Williams.

31. Carlisle House. A side view of Teresa's assembly rooms after their conversion to a Roman Catholic chapel. The protruding doorways were the ladies' entrances installed by Teresa to ease congestion at the front door.

become a public hero on both sides of the Atlantic. The American revolutionary group, the Sons of Liberty, which included John Adams and John Hancock, took its name from a comment he made to Parliament ('Do not underestimate the sons of liberty'), and they asserted that 'the fate of Wilkes and America must stand or fall together'. Although he was elected as a Member of Parliament again that year, this time for Middlesex, the government arrested Wilkes in April and declared the election null and void because the candidate had been imprisoned.

A re-election was held, with the government lackey Henry Lawes Luttrell standing against him, but once again Wilkes emerged as the clear winner. This political fiasco was repeated twice more. On the fourth occasion Luttrell was declared the victor even though he had polled fewer votes. Meanwhile, crowds of Wilkes's supporters kept a constant vigil outside the King's Bench prison where their hero was being held. On 10 May 1768, a mob of around fifteen thousand gathered there, chanting, 'Wilkes and Liberty!' and 'No Liberty, No King!' Troops opened fire on them, killing seven people and prompting disturbances throughout London. Three weeks after what became known as the Massacre of St George's Fields, Wilkes was sentenced to a further twenty-two months in prison, and a radical committee named the Bill of Rights Society was formed to attempt to secure his release.

In January 1770, when the Whig politician Lord North was appointed as George III's seventh prime minister in the space of ten years, there were renewed calls for Wilkes to be freed. Only the thought of the approaching Carlisle House masquerade distracted people from the matter. The ball was to be *the* event of the season, and the two-guinea entrance tickets were so much in demand that even an offer of fifty pounds could not procure one on the black-market.

On the afternoon of 27 February, parliament adjourned early so that Members had time to go home and dress for Teresa's masquerade. Meanwhile, thousands of Wilkes's supporters began to gather outside Carlisle House, along with the regular sightseers who were there simply to see the costumes. From nine o'clock that night until midnight, as the masqueraders' coaches and sedan chairs struggled through the densely packed side-streets into an equally packed Soho Square, the mob went wild, chalking the sides of carriages with the words 'Wilkes and Liberty', yelling for the MP for Middlesex to be freed, and demanding that the aristocratic passengers let down their windows so their disguises could be better seen. Horace Walpole reported the riot in a letter to Sir Horace Mann:

> Our Civil war has been lulled to sleep by a subscription masquerade, for which the House of Commons literally adjourned yesterday. Instead of Fairfaxes and Cromwells, we have had a crowd of Henrys the Eighth, Wolseys, Vandykes [*sic*], and Harlequins; and because Wilkes was not mask enough, we had a man dressed like him, with a visor, in imitation of his squint, and a cap of liberty on a pole. In short, sixteen or eighteen young lords have given the town a masquerade; and politics, for the last fortnight, were forced to give way to habit makers. The ball was last night at Soho; and, if possible, was more magnificent than the King of Denmark's. The bishops opposed: he of London formally remonstrated to the King, who did not approve it, but could not help him. The consequence was, that four divine vessels belonging to the holy fathers, alias their wives, were at this masquerade. Monkey again! . . . The mob was beyond all belief: they held flambeaux to the windows of every coach, and demanded to have the masks pulled off and put on at their pleasure, but with extreme good humour and civility. I was with my Lady Hertford and two of her daughters, in their coach: the mob took me for Lord Hertford, and huzzaed and blessed me! One fellow cried out, 'Are you for Wilkes?' another said, 'Damn you, you fool, what has Wilkes to do with a masquerade?'

It was almost as crowded and wild inside Carlisle House that night as it was in Soho Square, as Walpole discovered once he and his companions had squeezed through the crush at the door. For the first few hours the eight hundred guests were crammed into the smaller rooms, talking loudly, sweating profusely, flirting wildly, their wit fuelled by gallons of wine and champagne. Only at midnight were the large banqueting hall and Concert Room opened. Then the orchestra struck up, dancing began, and a cold buffet supper was served. 'The feast of the night was calculated rather to gratify the eye than the stomach,' reported one newspaper of the rather meagre portions served to the inebriated masqueraders, 'and seemed to satisfy the conductor's sense of its being prepared almost on the eve of Ash Wednesday.'

However, the carping journalist conceded that the 'richness and brilliancy of the dresses were almost beyond imagination', and went on to list the masqueraders and their costumes. They included William Cavendish, the Duke of Devonshire; Lady Waldegrave, Lady Pembroke, the Duchess of Hamilton and Lady Almeria Carpenter; the Duke of Gloucester 'in the old English habit'; Miss Monckton in her bejewelled Indian sultana's outfit; the Dowager Countess of Waldegrave; the Duchess of Ancaster, who 'claimed the attention of all the company in the dress of Mandane'; the Countess of Pomfret, dressed as a Greek sultana, making a complete group with 'the two Miss Fredericks, who accompanied her as Greek Slaves'; the Duchess of Bolton, captivating as the goddess Diana; Lady Stanhope, as Melpomene; Lady Augusta and Lady Caroline Stuart, dressed simply but elegantly as a vestal virgin and 'a Fille de Patmos'; and the Earl of Carlisle, 'very richly dressed' as a running footman with diamonds in his cap spelling out the name of the Tuesday Night Club, which had sponsored the event. The Duke of Grafton was disguised as a jockey, the new Prime Minister, Lord North, as a harlequin. Representing the opposition was a 'Political Bedlamite, run mad for Wilkes and Liberty'.

John Wilkes was finally released in April, having served the entire twenty-two months of his sentence. As soon as he had scrubbed the stench of prison off his skin he dressed himself up in a domino and attended a Carlisle House masquerade. His long incarceration had certainly not crushed his rebellious spirit: when a gentleman dressed as a Scottish Highlander came up to him during the evening and proceeded to play the bagpipes to him two or three times, Wilkes 'told him, if he played to all eternity, he should never dance to the Bagpipe. The Highlander asked, to what music he would dance? Mr Wilkes answered, to any but the Bagpipe and the German Flute' – a reference to the Hanoverian king.

From January 1770 onwards, masquerade followed hard on the heels of masquerade at Carlisle House, despite the continual protests of the Church, and almost every such event was followed by a lengthy write-up, either in the press or in someone's diary: the mingling of smells, good and bad, the crush of the aristocratic crowd, the sumptuousness of the costumes, the delights of the music, the beauty of the décor – approve of them or not, these things were unforgettable. 'The magnificence of the rooms, splendour of the illuminations and embellishments, and the brilliant appearance of the company exceeded anything I ever saw before,' the eighteen-year-old Fanny Burney noted in her diary, after a visit to Carlisle House that April:

The apartments were so crowded we scarce had room to move, which was quite disagreeable, nevertheless the flight of apartments both upstairs and on the ground floor seemed endless . . . The Rooms were so full and so hot that nobody attempted to dance . . . I must own this evening's entertainment more disappointed my expectations than any I ever spent, for I had imagined it would have been the most charming in the world.

The young Miss Burney might have felt disappointed, but it was said of Teresa's masquerades in May that year that 'Mrs Cornelys' taste never appeared to greater éclat than in the arrangement of the lights, and the oeconomy [sic] of the supper and dessert, where plenty and elegance went hand in hand.' Even the combined protests of Church leaders were powerless to stop them. 'The Bishop of London persuaded that good soul the Archbishop to remonstrate against them,' Walpole wrote to George Montagu, 'but happily the age prefers silly follies to serious ones, and dominoes, comme de raison, carry it against lawn sleeves.'

Teresa's subscribers seemed determined to outdo each other in conspicuous display, decadence and sheer excess. On 6 May a 'lady of high quality' appeared as an Indian princess, 'most superbly dressed, and decorated with jewels and pearls to upwards of 100,000*l.* in value. Her suite is to consist of three young black female slaves, of different heights and ages, holding up her train; and two young black male slaves, supporting a canopy over her head.'

That month everybody who was anybody came to Carlisle House. On the night of 14 May, those present included the Dukes of Grafton, Roxburghe, Kingston, Beaufort, Ancaster and Manchester; the Earls of Hardwick, Winchilsea, Northampton, Corke, Peterborough and Barrymore; Lords Abergavenny, Barrington, Aynher, Bateman, Pigot, Dartry, Dunkellan, Irnham, Palmerston, Sutton, Beauchamp, Molyneaux, Stavordale and Burghersh; and at least ten knights. Of all those present that evening it was said that 'The Duke and Duchess of Kingston were the Persons of the greatest Distinction, none of the Royal Family being present.'

London's intelligentsia were also represented. They included John Wilkes, fresh out of prison, and Angelica Kauffman. It was later reported that 'the cleverest thing that was uttered was probably that by the D— of G—n [Duke of Grafton] to Mrs K— [Kauffman], who, envious of the praise Miss G— received in the character of Leonora, could not refrain saying, "Bless me, what business has she for a mask – an inch thick of paint is surely a good vizor." Indeed, replied the d—ke, I should not have thought Miss G— painted had not so great a judge of the matter as Mrs K— peremptorily determined it.'

Carlisle House was at its most successful. Yet, incredibly, Teresa was still in debt. It was rumoured after the ball on 14 May that she was 'some hundred pounds out of pocket by this masquerade; owing chiefly to the ladies being admitted so cheap, and their swallowing with their mouths and pockets such uncommon quantities of sweet-meats'. Her extravagance, her perfectionism and her sloppy business practices were all equally to blame.

Nevertheless, by the end of the 1769/70 season, her influence over London's *beau monde* was stronger than ever. And, despite her precarious financial position, so was her self-confidence. Her phenomenal success in her tenth year in business gave Teresa the sense that she was invulnerable and that, like her patroness the Duchess of Kingston, she was beyond the reach of the law.

She was wrong. Elizabeth's close friendship with the king's mother and her marriage to Kingston gave her an unprecedented degree of freedom – at least for the time being – but as a working woman Teresa did not enjoy the same degree of protection. Her Church critics and her rivals wanted nothing more than to see her brought down. A poem published that year dubbed her 'the Circe of Soho' and likened her to a

> Sweet sorceress, whose powerful chains enslave
> Wise men and fools, the coward and the brave;
> Within thy magic will the frozen prude
> Feel her cold blood unchill'd, her fears subdued.
> And wanton dames, who to the nuptial bed
> Reluctant by some mitred prelate led
> Long were sad victims to his ghostly care,
> Condemn'd to shaded parts and days of pray'r.
> Far different here the midnight hours employ
> And melt in visions of unholy joy.

Far more vicious was the letter published in the *Public Advertiser* on 31 May, which likened Carlisle House to a 'Shrine of Luxury' and a 'great *Shew Box*' peopled by crowds of foolish, lewd puppets 'which appeared in Variety of Dresses, and by the Art of the *Shew-woman*, who directs the whole, to speak, or rather *squeak* in several characters, to the Admiration of all beholders'. Calling himself Old Noll, the anonymous writer scathingly attacked Carlisle House's 'grand Babel Rout, which would exceed all belief of the little Vulgar, since it amazes even the *Great* themselves', and went on to lambast 'the *Heat* and *Smell* arising from a Hogshead of flaming Spermaceti, and Tons of Meat and Drink. The Effluvia of essence Bottles, perfumed Heads and handkerchiefs, together with all the *natural and acquired odours* issuing in warm Weather and a great Croud [*sic*] from *fine Ladies* and Gentlemen who fare sumptuously every day.'

Stinking, vulgar, immoral, decadent, debauched. With a dangerous disregard for middle-class social mores, Teresa ignored Old Noll's complaints, just as she ignored all her critics. But this time it was at her peril. Jealous of her position as reigning monarch of the *ton*'s social life and eager to usurp her throne, a host of enemies, rivals and would-be competitors were growing impatient for the opportunity to depose London's Empress of Pleasure. Ironically, she would help to bring about her own downfall. Teresa was about to become a victim of her own success.

Sixteen

A serious rival to Carlisle House was in the offing. And unlike Almack's, which was over in St James's, this one was going to be just round the corner from Soho Square.

Oxford Street formed the northern boundary of Soho. Over the last hundred years it had been transformed from a narrow rutted country track into a broad metropolitan shopping Mecca lit by necklaces of lamps and thronged day and night by wealthy visitors. Here and there, between the expensive sweet shops, drapers' stores and coffee-houses, there still remained a handful of undeveloped plots of land. One such lay behind two old dwellings on the south side of Oxford Street, two hundred yards east of Soho Square. It consisted of a large shrub- and tree-filled garden some fifty-six feet wide and eighty-three feet deep, backing on to Poland Street, and it belonged to a small-time property speculator and businessman, Philip Elias Turst.

Turst lived with his wife in Percy Street, a minute's walk north of Oxford Street and a short stroll from Soho Square. As his wife had a close friend who had in the last year or so become one of Teresa's ardent supporters, it seems likely that the couple often visited Carlisle House. Mrs Turst's friend, a spinster named Margaretta Ellice, was 'a person of fortune'. Her family hailed from Edinburgh, owned large tracts of land in Scotland and held substantial business interests in New York and Canada, where they were involved in import and export and provided the pioneer stock of the large fur-trading companies; one of the clan, Alexander Ellice, was managing director of the Hudson's Bay Company.

Wealthy, independent, well connected and with plenty of spare time on her hands, Miss Ellice was a useful woman for an impresario to cultivate. Rather unwisely, as it later turned out, Teresa appears to have allowed her to get involved in the running of Carlisle

House to an unusual degree: Miss Ellice would later claim that she had 'had a principle [*sic*] share in Planning and Conducting the Entertainments of the Nobility at Mrs Cornelys's in Soho Square, in which she had met with the highest approbation'. But when Mrs Turst died in July 1768, Miss Ellice shifted her interest from Soho Square to Percy Street, where she provided a willing shoulder for her late friend's husband to cry on. As often happens, the bereaved husband and his late wife's confidante quickly developed what was delicately described as 'a great Intimacy and friendship'.

Before long, Turst was looking for a new project to distract him from his grief. Along with Miss Ellice, he came up with the idea of turning his empty site on Oxford Street into a central London indoor 'winter Ranelagh'. He had no intention of going into competition with Carlisle House: on the contrary, both he and Miss Ellice considered the famous Mrs Cornelys to be 'the most proper person' to run the proposed assembly rooms. Towards the tail end of 1768 Turst approached Teresa with the idea that she join him in the venture.

Although she had recently gone into partnership with James Cullen in Greek Street, Teresa was taken with Turst's idea that her business might expand even further, this time into brand new premises on fashionable Oxford Street. Turst sent a written proposal to Carlisle House, and negotiations between the two began. But by May 1769, their proposed collaboration had been called off. Turst, it seems, had wanted Teresa to invest a substantial sum of money in his speculative venture, and when he realized he was not going to get it from her he turned instead to his wealthy lover and pressed her into becoming a major shareholder. In return for a substantial investment (she was to buy thirty of the fifty £300 shares that Turst proposed to sell) Miss Ellice was to receive a major share of any profits, and also to run the Pantheon, as his 'winter Ranelagh' was to be called.

This was unwelcome news to Teresa. Instead of expanding her empire, she had acquired a rival just round the corner. A rival, moreover, situated in purpose-built premises that were to be managed by a woman with an insider's knowledge of running Carlisle

House. When, against the wishes of his other shareholders, Turst engaged a completely inexperienced architect named James Wyatt, Teresa might have anticipated gleefully that the new building would be a disaster, but her smile must have frozen when she saw the plans.

Twenty-two-year-old James Wyatt came from a family of architects: his father and four of his brothers were all either architects or builders, and in his teens James, who was obviously headed down the same path, was sent to Italy to study classical and Renaissance architecture. After spending four years in Rome and a further two in Venice, where he came to the attention of Richard Dalton, librarian and antiquarian to George III, the young Wyatt returned to England steeped in classical ideas. Within a matter of months, and having not yet constructed so much as a lowly cowshed, the architectural *wünderkind* landed himself the job of building Turst's Pantheon, the largest private building to be constructed in London for years and one of the most prestigious commissions then on offer in England.

Just how Wyatt pulled off this coup is something of a mystery. It might have had something to do with his friendship with Richard Dalton, or the fact that two of his brothers were closely involved in getting Turst's scheme off the ground: John Wyatt, a surgeon, was one of Turst's original investors; and Samuel Wyatt was the builder in charge of construction. William, a third Wyatt brother, later joined the Pantheon's board as treasurer of the enterprise.

Of course, Teresa had faced competition before in the shape of Almack's and seen it off without so much as a scratch. But when in June 1769 Samuel Wyatt and his labourers began to clear the Oxford Street site of its trees, dwellings and shrubs, she was apprehensive. For the time being, however, the completion of the project lay a long way off and, as with any speculative venture, there was a good chance that it would founder before it was completed. Turst was already squabbling with Miss Ellice and his other shareholders, who felt that they had not been properly consulted over his choice of architect.

While relations between the Pantheon speculators soured, and the costs of Wyatt's elaborate and ornate Byzantine design, first estimated at £15,000, escalated by the week, Teresa put her head down and carried on working. Since 1770 was her most dizzyingly successful season yet, it seemed she had little to worry about. But as the walls of the Pantheon rose higher on their foundations, the possible threat it might pose to her became increasingly tangible. As a Carlisle House regular, Miss Ellice was in a good position to poach its subscribers who, loyal as they had been to Teresa so far, might desert her in pursuit of novelty.

If she was not to be put out of business when the Pantheon opened, Teresa had to devise a plan to keep her customers. As always when she was under pressure, she came up with what at first appeared to be a brilliant idea: she would turn Carlisle House into an Italian opera venue to rival the King's Theatre.

More than four years had passed since Teresa had failed to buy the lease of the opera house over the head of its then manager, Peter Crawford. Under his direction the theatre's reputation had sunk to an all-time low. In 1769, desperate to revive its fortunes, Crawford had gone into partnership with the Hon. George Hobart, the future third Earl of Buckingham, with whose help he had begun to phase out the light-hearted *opera buffa* that had proved so unsuccessful during the past season, and to reintroduce *opera seria*. Since the operas were considered as vehicles for stars rather than as works worthy of notice in their own right, Hobart's first job was to attract well-known performers for his opening season. On a trip to Europe that year he recruited a soprano named Anna Zamperini, whom he took as his mistress, and an extremely famous Italian *alto castrato* named Gaetano Guadagni.

Guadagni had first appeared in London in 1749, performing in Handel's oratorios at the King's Theatre, and he later worked at Drury Lane, where the actor-manager David Garrick instructed him in the art of naturalistic acting. When he returned to Europe afterwards, his new skills earned him a reputation as a great performer. 'As an actor he had no equal on any stage in Europe,' Dr Charles Burney wrote of him. 'His figure was uncommonly elegant and noble; his countenance replete with beauty, intelligence, and dignity; and his attitudes and gestures were so full of grace and propriety, that they would have been excellent studies for a statuary.' However, Guadagni's angelic, somewhat feminine appearance belied a true diva's personality: vain and temperamental, he held 'strong resentments and high notions of his own importance' and rarely fulfilled his contractual obligations. In other words, Hobart's new *primo uomo* was also a *prima donna*.

When Guadagni returned to the King's Theatre in 1769, he was accompanied by his sister, a well-known soprano in her own right. He received a star billing matched by the size of his salary, which amounted to £1150 for the season. But relations with his manager got off on a bad footing right from the start when Hobart stupidly promoted his own mistress over the head of the castrato's sister. Guadagni was livid, and the London audience divided over the resulting fracas. La Zamperini was jeered by the gallery whenever she appeared, and on several occasions the audience erupted into near-riots, causing Hobart to call in the troops. Eager to score popularity points against each other, the rival sopranos each sang so many encores during their performances that, according to Horace Walpole, 'the operas last to almost midnight'.

Perversely, Guadagni refused to perform any encores at all, or to stop and bow when he was applauded mid-scene, as was the custom at the time. True to his training under Garrick, he aimed to stay in character until the bitter end of every opera, which antagonized the audience even more. Infuriated by their constant interruptions and calls for encores, the castrato would stomp angrily off-stage or pause between arias to lecture the audience about the integrity of the performance. This haughty behaviour led to him being hissed and booed, even by his employer. When challenged, George Hobart retorted that he paid the castrato to sing, not talk.

The season at the King's limped to an end in the spring of 1770 with audiences attracted more by the outrageous behaviour of the star performers than by any real interest in *opera seria*. Still at loggerheads, Guadagni and Hobart unwisely began to negotiate the singer's contract for the following year. Guadagni demanded a rise of £450 on his previous year's earnings, with £1000 to be paid that

July and the remainder to be paid as his salary at fifty pounds per month. Hobart refused to hand over such a large lump sum. Tired of his star's histrionics, he named Ferdinando Tenducci, the second man at the opera house, as Guadagni's successor. Guadagni, one of the most famous castratos in Europe, was out of work.

Society was shocked. Under the title 'Musical Dissention', the *London Magazine* published a report criticizing the 'obnoxious' Hobart for treating his star singers as 'miserable menials', and Guadagni swore that he would never work for him again. Relishing the scandal, the Duchess of Northumberland and Lady Harrington appealed to Teresa to save the situation by starting an opera of her own.

Teresa knew it would be a risky venture to stage an opera without first obtaining the necessary licence from the Lord Chamberlain. She also knew that he would not grant her one. Nevertheless, she did not hesitate. Relishing what seemed like a golden opportunity to get back at Crawford, establish a new niche for Carlisle House and challenge the King's Theatre's monopoly on Italian opera into the bargain, she signed up Guadagni as her lead singer. Acting as a producer, she assembled a team of top musicians and singers, including the composer Matteo Vento and the musical director Felice de Giardini, with whom she was now running her subscription concerts. She also enlisted the help of a ballet dancer named Simon Slingsby, who promised to guarantee the money for the costumes, scenery and dancers' salaries in return for a share of any profits.

As Teresa's new company began rehearsals of *Artaserse*, she attempted to legitimize her venture by applying to the Lord Chamberlain's office for permission to stage opera at Carlisle House. Unfortunately for her, her landlord and former ally the Duke of Portland was no longer employed by the royal household, and the current post-holder refused to grant her a licence until Hobart had been informed of her plan and given the opportunity to rectify the dismal situation at the King's Theatre, which, of course, Hobart did. The last thing he wanted was competition from Teresa. If she succeeded he would face ruin, for London's opera audience was not large enough to support a second opera house.

It looked for a while as if Teresa's plan had been scuppered. But with a stubbornness that was almost suicidal, London's Empress of Pleasure refused to give up. With her aristocratic supporters staunchly behind her, she defiantly decided to go ahead and stage *Artaserse* without a licence. In order to circumvent the law, she would not call it an opera but, euphemistically, an 'Harmonick Assembly'. And instead of selling tickets to a fully staged opera on the open market, she would claim to be putting on a private platform performance, rather than a public show.

Word of Teresa's plan soon spread through London, exciting the *ton*'s interest. As Mrs Delaney wrote to Viscountess Andover on 27 December, though the opera at the King's had been dismal that year, 'a spirit of opposition has arisen which may mend matters, and a new opera planned by the supporters of Mrs Cornelly [*sic*], which, as it is *lawless* (and you know that gives it zest) is to be called the *Harmonick Assembly*!'.

The first of Teresa's Harmonick Assemblies was scheduled to take place on the night of 24 January. Was it really to be a platform performance taking place in front of a select audience of private subscribers or, as Hobart suspected, a fully dramatized commercial opera performed without a licence and in contravention of the law? He was deeply worried, and with good reason: few of his usual subscribers were buying advance tickets for the King's Theatre that season, but by the first week in January more than six hundred subscribers had signed up for the Harmonick Assemblies, each promising to pay twelve guineas for a series of eleven performances; and the Duchess of Northumberland was said to be recruiting new subscribers at the rate of sixty a week.

With the prospect of ruin looming over him, Hobart swallowed his pride and approached Teresa with the idea of going into partnership with her. On 12 January Horace Walpole wrote to Lady Mary Coke describing the 'desperate wars between the opera in the Haymarket and that of Mrs Cornelys. There was a negotiation yesterday for a union, but I do not know what answer the definitive courier has brought. All I know is that Guadagni is much more haughty than the King of Castille, Aragon, Leon, Granada, etc. In the mean time King Hobart is starving, and if the junction takes place his children must starve, for he must pay the expenses of both theatres.' Having heard news of the Harmonick Assembly's dress rehearsal that same day, Mrs Harris declared that 'Giardini's opera at Mrs Cornelly's [sic] really fills, and undoubtedly will greatly injure that of Mr Hobart in the Haymarket'.

In the end, the proposed union between Carlisle House and the King's Theatre did not take place. With so many subscribers already won over to the idea of her Harmonick Assemblies, Teresa did not need Hobart – or so she thought. As London ground to a halt that month in the coldest weather for years, she threw open the doors of Carlisle House for her annual Grand Gala in honour of the queen's birthday. Although their carriages and sedan chairs had to struggle to Soho through deep snowdrifts, the nobility and gentry turned up in force.

An opportunist to the core, Teresa used the dreadful weather to garner publicity for her Harmonick Assemblies, and also to help herself circumvent the Licensing Act. On the morning of 24 January, with the first performance of *Artaserse* due to take place that evening, she published a defiant notice on the front page of the *Public Advertiser*. The sole intention of her Harmonick Assemblies, it said, was 'to produce a Specimen of a more elegant Amusement for the Nobility and Gentry than has hitherto been exhibited'. It was also to be a charitable venture: any surplus money left over after the expenses had been paid off 'shall be applied to such humane and good purposes as the Patronesses of the Harmonical Meetings shall think proper to direct'.

'On account of the peculiar Severity of the Season,' the notice continued, Teresa had already decided to give away free coal to the poor of the parish of St Anne's, Soho. Anyone wishing to claim this was invited to apply for a certificate at Carlisle House, where 'Regard will be particularly had to those who are indigent through a Largeness of Family, sickness, or other peculiar Distress.'

This was a shameless ploy by Teresa to get the mob on her side. And it succeeded brilliantly. But her declaration that 'Mrs Cornelys is to receive no Profits or Advantages therefrom, and no person is to perform thereat for Gain, Hire, or Reward' – that is to say, the Harmonick Assembly was not a commercial enterprise – was clearly a sop to appease the Lord Chamberlain.

Hobart was not fooled. In opposition to Teresa's *Artaserse*, he staged a performance of *Gios, Re de Giuda* at the King's Theatre that same evening, set to a score by Johann Christian Bach. Only a handful of people turned up to see it. The others were all at Carlisle House.

Like all of Teresa's ventures, her Harmonick Assembly was an instant hit with the *ton*. Inspired by the fact that he was revenging himself against Hobart, Guadagni was on top form that evening; and, thrilled by the event's dubious legal status, the audience were in the mood to be won over by what turned out to be an electric occasion. As Mrs Harris wrote to her son, people talked afterwards 'of nothing but the charms of the Harmoniac [*sic*] meeting; the Anti-Harmoniacs will allow no merit at all to it, save the fine drop-curtain, so I must wait for an opportunity of seeing and hearing before I can determine'.

There were not to be many such opportunities. Unknown to Teresa, Hobart immediately started his own undercover investigation to prove that she was breaking the law by selling tickets on the open market. On 30 January, he dispatched his servant Matthew Simpson to Soho armed with a wad of money and a letter written under a false name, requesting tickets for the remaining Harmonick Assemblies. When Simpson arrived at Carlisle House, he was let in by a footman and directed to an office where he handed his letter to a clerk. The man read it, then left the room, saying that he would show it to 'Mistress Cornelys'. A few minutes later he returned carrying a stack of engraved tickets to the Harmonick Assemblies, each signed by Teresa herself.

The second Harmonick Assembly took place the following evening. Using one of the tickets Simpson had obtained for him, Hobart slipped into Carlisle House incognito, and joined the six-hundred-plus crowd seated in the Concert Room. As he had suspected, this was no platform performance. A huge orchestra had been assembled, a proscenium arch and curtain had been erected in the apse at the end of the room, and when the curtain was drawn back it revealed painted scenery and costumed performers. *Artaserse* was being performed just as it would have been in his own theatre – but to a higher standard. Hobart scurried home and prepared an 'information' against Teresa.

Unaware of the gathering stormclouds, a few days later Teresa threw a lavish masquerade ball for her supporters. The candelabra and wall sconces burned with four thousand wax candles, and a hundred musicians were spread about the house. Though tickets to the event cost a hefty two and a half guineas each, hundreds of costumed revellers once again fought their way through the snow to Soho. According to the *London Chronicle* they included 'their Royal Highnesses the Dukes of Gloucester and Cumberland, the Dukes of Buccleugh [*sic*], Bolton, Manchester &c., the Earls of Huntingdon, Sandwich, Carlisle, Falmouth, Berkeley, Cholmondley, Spencer, Barrymore, Corke, March, Sussex &c; Lord Bateman, Bolingbroke, Palmerston, Molyneaux, Aylmer, Grantham, Stavendale [*sic*], Pigot, Craven &c.; Countesses of Effingham, Berkeley, Aylesbury, Spencer, Corke &c. &c.; Lady Archer, Lady Craven, Lady Charlotte Dundas, Lady Bridget Lane &c. &c.; the Imperial, Danish, Hanoverian, & Several Foreign Ministers'.

The costumes that night were as imaginative as they were magnificent, and included a duke dressed as an old woman, several lords disguised as glorified country farmers, a Savoyard leading a man disguised as a bear, and the goddess Diana 'who did more execution with her eyes than the bow which she held in her hand'. To the consternation of the Church, two beautiful young women came in novice nuns' habits with plunging necklines, several rakes were dressed up as devils and 'a friar whose face was the picture of luxury and voluptuousness, was incessantly preaching up penitence and abstinence'. The more religious people's costumes, the more they seemed to drink: the *London Chronicle* reported that 'Two pretty Quakers did great execution, but they followed the scripture rule, for all their conversation was *yea* and *nay*: they never felt the spirit till the champaign [*sic*] was pushed about.'

But of all the hundreds of costumes worn that night, the most controversial was that of a walking corpse in an upright coffin, upon whose lid was pinned this warning verse:

> Know Passenger! This Mortal here inshrin'd
> Some good old Christian virtues left behind;
> Which to a sinful town were thus bequeath'd
> Ere its last orisons the spirits breath'd.
> My Honesty – I give the Bill of Rights,
> My Godliness – I give it all to White's;
> 'Twixt Hayes Harem and the Coterie
> I give, in equal shares, my Modesty;
> Item – I give to Rakes and reigning Beauties
> A strict regard for chaste domestic duties.
> Accept ye hot-brain'd Statesmen, I beseech,
> An artless zeal for truth in decent speech.
> I leave to L– and H–'s dancing wife
> A sense of what befits each stage of life.
> Now deckt in virgin white my flesh and bones
> With fringes, flounces, nosegays and pompoons;
> That plac'd at Dame Cornely's [*sic*] Masquerade
> I therefore warn the giddy hectic maid
> To shun harmonic routs and midnight revel,
> Lest she and I should soon be on a level.

The identity of the walking corpse was never discovered – he was either John Wilkes's old parliamentary rival Colonel Henry Lawes Luttrell or his brother – but his message was clear: unless Teresa cleaned up her act and renounced her illegal opera she would be destroyed. According to the *Gentleman's Magazine*, not content with his stark visual message the corpse

began at first to exhort the company to reform in a puritanical stile [*sic*], but being told it was out of character for a dead man to speak, he remained silent the rest of the night. The agreeable Mrs D addressed herself to the shroud, saying, 'I cannot help seriously telling you (and to shew you I am in earnest I unmask) that you must be an ill-natured, spiteful wretch, that can neither enjoy the amusement this place affords yourself, nor let us partake of it, without casting a gloom upon our spirits, by your horrid appearance, which is not only indecent, but illiberal and uncharitable; if you are dead, as you seem to be to all sense of pleasure, you have no business here; if you are alive, and capable of enjoying the past-time of the place, throw off that shocking covering and assume the dress of mirth and festivity.'

This arrogant diatribe typified the devil-may-care attitude of London's fashionable élite. Far from being alarmed by the coffin's message they derided it. Furthermore, they all turned up in force again on 11 February when Teresa held another masquerade. 'Mr Charles Fox has offered to supply us with tickets,' Mrs Harris wrote to her son. 'Your sisters and I mean to go; tis the only masquerade I wish them to go to. I shall try my utmost to persuade Mr Harris to accompany us. One difficulty is in the way; that is, no gentlemen are admitted in dominos.' Afterwards Mrs Harris reported, 'We were greatly entertained, for it was the first masked ball I ever saw. We supped soon after one, and then everybody unmasked, and a number of acquaintance we found, though we had among us found out many before. We got home soon after five, and, old as I may be, I never left a public place with more regret.' However, the *Middlesex Journal* declared that many women were disappointed by the lack of dancing that night, the 'Gentlemen chusing [*sic*] to prefer the pleasures of Burgundy and Champaigne after the supper, to the solicitations of the amiable sex'.

More alarming to Teresa than people's reluctance to dance was the rumour that was being spread around London by Hobart and one of her own disaffected maids. As the *Middlesex Journal* put it, 'Some very extraordinary secrets have transpired relative to a certain fashionable house in Soho. It is said there were actually found to be no less than forty beds made and unmade every day.' There was at least a kernel of truth in the rumour. By now, Carlisle House had become a pleasure palace in the widest sense. Its upper floors contained bedrooms as discreetly hidden as the secret *casini* to which the Venetian patrician classes stole away with their lovers, and subscribers to the Society in Soho-square doubtless made good use of them during masquerades. But if the behaviour of some revellers was as unlicensed as Teresa's opera, where was the harm in it? Extramarital sex was a perfectly acceptable pastime in the eighteenth century, at least for gentlemen; what made Carlisle House's masquerades unacceptable was that they provided ample opportunity for 'respectable' women to take part in the sport, too.

Hobart and Crawford were determined to destroy Teresa before she destroyed them. As the servants cleared away the debris of the 11 February masquerade and rebuilt her stage in preparation for a third performance of *Artaserse*, which was to take place that night, the two men sprang into action and presented their information about the Carlisle House operas to the Justices of the Peace at Bow Street. In a move that had both the *ton* and the popular mob up in arms, Teresa and Guadagni were immediately arrested. She was charged with holding an unlicensed opera 'for hire, gain or reward, without proper authority, contrary to the Statute 10 Geo II, c.28', and Guadagni was charged with taking part in it.

Two sensational trials followed. That very morning, and with the third performance of *Artaserse* due to take place in the evening, Guadagni appeared in the dock of the Rotation Office in Bow Street before a bench of magistrates led by Sir John Fielding. Though the castrato claimed that he was not being paid for performing in Teresa's opera, two celebrity witnesses were called in to testify that he was. They were none other than Teresa's former *protégés*, Carl Abel and Johann Christian Bach.

Guadagni was not famed for his discretion, and Bach swore on oath that the singer had recently said within his hearing 'that he must sing where he was asked and that he must get his Bread', which implied that he was indeed being paid to perform at Carlisle House. This evidence was corroborated by Carl Abel, who testified that Guadagni had also boasted that he must look after his own financial interest and 'do something for himself'.

Acting for Guadagni, Teresa's attorney Mr Kenyon cited three reasons why neither Bach nor Abel were disinterested parties in the case. First, the pair were currently running a concert series at

Almack's in opposition to Teresa's. Second, the ill-attended *Gios, Re de Giuda*, which had taken place at the King's Theatre on the night of the first Carlisle House Harmonick Assembly, was set to Bach's score. Third, along with Hobart, the two composers both stood to lose financially by the success of Teresa's Harmonick Assemblies.

Despite Kenyon's feisty defence, Guadagni was found guilty, fined fifty pounds and threatened with higher fines, a whipping and even a spell in Bridewell prison if he should ever again perform at an unlicensed opera. Understandably, the singer was so shaken by the experience that he refused to appear in *Artaserse* that night. 'The Harmoniac met last night, but there was no performance,' Mrs Harris wrote the following day. 'When they asked Mrs Cornelly [*sic*] the reason, she said Sconi was taken ill, but the truth is Mr Hobart has informed against them; they have paid 50*l*. but the penalty grows higher as they persist, so they must at last submit to the law.'

Teresa's own trial took place at Bow Street on 20 February, when the bench of ten magistrates was led by William Kelynge and Sir John Fielding. For once Teresa's courage deserted her. Although the public benches were crowded with her supporters she failed to turn up at the court, frightened perhaps that she would be immediately sent to prison or arrested on bankruptcy charges if she were to leave her safe haven in Carlisle House. In her place she sent her attorneys Mr Kenyon and Charles Lawrence, whose fees were being paid for her by the Duchess of Northumberland.

The charge against Teresa was that she 'did without Authority by virtue of Letters Patent from his Majesty or any of his Predecessors and without licence from the Lord Chamberlain of his Majesty's Household for the time being cause to be Acted Represented and performed for hire gain and reward a certain Opera and Entertainment of the Stage in the Italian language called Artaserse contrary to the form of the Statute in such case Made and Provided'.

Kenyon and Lawrence pleaded not guilty on Teresa's behalf. But as the full extent of Hobart's secret investigations was revealed, it became clear that his information against her was damning. First,

Hobart's servant Simpson recounted how he had bought tickets for the Harmonick Assembly from the clerk at Carlisle House. Next, a second witness, Edward Aylett, was called in to verify that it was indeed Teresa's signature on the back of the tickets. Third, a costumier named Thomas Suppino was forced to admit that he had made costumes for Guadagni and several other performers to wear during *Artaserse*, for which work Teresa had paid him sixty pounds.

The most damning evidence of all, however, came from Hobart himself, who told of his secret visit to the Harmonick Assembly on the night of 31 January:

where he saw an Italian Opera called Artaserse acted represented and performed, that the persons acting representing and performing the respective parts in the said Opera were dressed and habited in Dresses proper to represent their respective characters, that there was a Stage with Scenery built at the said Dwelling House of the said Teresa Cornelys whereon the said Opera was performed, that there were Musicians with different Instruments of Music, and that the whole of the said Opera was acted represented and performed in like manner as it is usually acted represented and performed at the Kings Theatre in the Haymarket.

Having listened to the prosecution evidence, the magistrates then asked Charles Lawrence if he had anything to say in Teresa's defence. The lawyer's answer was lame. He merely said that Mrs Cornelys had only been the manager of the Harmonick Assembly, which had been given by private subscription, and not an interested party in it.

The bench of magistrates considered the evidence before them, and Sir John Fielding summed up the case. As a close friend of the Duchess of Kingston, he was under heavy pressure to side with Teresa and her aristocratic supporters. But he struck fear into their hearts when he began in a defiantly legalistic vein: 'We are well apprized that the complaint before us relates to the amusement of many of the first nobility in this kingdom; but rank, when it shall be opposed to law, will never convey any ideas of fear to this bench, but on the contrary it ought and will animate the magistrates to discharge their public trust with the greater exactness, fidelity and attention.'

In a reference to the Duchess of Northumberland's financial support for Teresa in the shape of her lawyers, Fielding said that although people of fashion could procure themselves 'the ablest assistance of the Bar', it was the duty of the bench to treat the case impartially. While recognizing that none of the prosecution witnesses was a disinterested party, Fielding ruled that in this case the prosecution was 'founded on a real and substantial injury, and carried on to support a private right founded on a grant from the Crown which has been confirmed by Act of Parliament'. He concluded that 'the sages of the law . . . all agree in one circumstance, that you ought first to consider the spirit and reason of the law, and secondly the letter, by which means you at once see the mischief and the remedy, and that these laws should be construed strictly agreeable to the intention of the Legislature, and upon these principles it is I do adjudge Mrs Cornelys to be guilty of the offence mentioned in the aforesaid Act, and that she hath thereby forfeited the sum of fifty pounds.'

The case and its outcome received blanket coverage in the press. One article read,

At the trial of Mrs Cornelys on Wednesday, before the bench of Justices in Bow Street, Messrs Hobart, Simpson, Aylett and Rupini [Suppino] were examined on the part of the Informer . . . It was urged by Mr Kenyon, council [sic] for Mrs Cornelys, that the proofs alleged against her were only presumptive, consequently inadmissable [sic]. Sir John Fielding dwelt long on the number of Public Places of Amusement, and said there were already sufficient. The arguments were strong and nervous on both sides; but on summing up the evidence, Sir John declared the Defendant guilty of the facts laid to her charge. Her council agreed to stop any further performance of Dramatic Entertainments of what kind soever till an appeal can be made to a higher Court, provided the Plaintiffs would not lay any fresh information against her. This was assented to, and Mrs Cornelys was pronounced guilty, and liable to the penalty which, we are informed, was 50l.

So determined was Fielding that the judgement should not be misrepresented by the press that he sent a verbatim copy of his summing up to the *Gentleman's Magazine*, to which he added a long addendum assuring the readers that the decision of the bench had been 'unanimously concurred'. While recognizing the importance of entertainments and diversions, he reminded the public of the great number of places of entertainment that already existed in the metropolis: the Theatres Royal of Drury Lane and Covent Garden, the opera house, Ranelagh, Sadler's Wells and the Marylebone Gardens. Given all these, he concluded,

What honest Englishman can say he wants amusement? Surely it is evident that luxury has been taking such gigantic strides as ought to make the magistrates jealous of her dangerous progress. And before I conclude, I cannot help observing that what the magistrates said on Wednesday the 20TH of February, as well as what none of them said, has been published in a newspaper; and though I again repeat, that I wish all my actions, not as a magistrate only, but as a man, might be known through the whole world, and though I am content that everyone who heard me should have a shorthand-writer, and publish everything I have said; yet I do desire that nothing may be published but the truth, for I fear not truth, but misrepresentation.

Articles and cartoons for and against Teresa and her opera peppered the newspapers and magazines for weeks afterwards. One anti-Harmonick letter to the *Town and Country Magazine* that month, written in the form of a conversation, satirized Guadagni as a 'squeaker' and a eunuch who 'like capons, should be confined in cages, and properly dieted'. It also dragged up Teresa's affair with John Fermor and gave her the soubriquet of the 'Empress of the Vast Regions of Taste, Elegance, and Magnificence':

C.G. Who is this empress?
T.G. Bless me, are you so ignorant! I thought her fame was spread over the whole globe; but I will tell you. This lady was an opera figure dancer, and having made a connexion with a gentleman of fortune, she took C–

house in Soho-square, furnished it in a most brilliant manner, raised subscriptions for concerts, balls, and masquerades; and having a scribbling Cicisbeo to puff for her, the papers are every day filled with nauseous elogiums upon her *uncommon taste* and *astonishing elegance*, in decorating her apartments, and displaying a sideboard. By these means she has gained very considerable sums, though she protracts her payments as long as she can . . .

The *Oxford Magazine* carried an open letter dedicated 'To the Duchess of N–R–D' criticizing Carlisle House, along with a caricature of the proceedings at Bow Street entitled 'Trial of the sovereign Empress of the vast Regions of Taste'. Wearing a lace-trimmed mob-cap, an unrepentant Teresa was shown being carried shoulder-high by her counsel Mr Kenyon and his pay-mistress the Duchess of Northumberland, who was assuring the attorney that 'Money shall not be wanting, Councellor [*sic*]: You and I must defend her against the blind boy's insolence.' 'Not so blind but I can hit the right place for intrigue,' warns the blindfolded Sir John Fielding, who was seated on a raised platform holding the sword and scales of justice in his hands. Looking plump and rather feminine, Guadagni was in the background, his hands raised in horror at the proceedings, exclaiming, 'Madame la Duchesse do make him repent taking Guadagni so – den you will Piercy mine Art wid your Goodness' – 'Piercy' being a pun on the Duchess's surname, Percy.

Along with Lady Ancaster, the Duchess of Northumberland was also ridiculed by the *Middlesex Journal*, which reported on the day after the trial that 'A certain D–s who is a principle [*sic*] promoter of the new opera-house declared lately she would persist in supporting of Mrs C. whatever was the consequence; for, said she, I hate the thought of mixing with any body, merely because they have half a guinea in their pocket; and that such scum should sit on the same bench and think themselves on a level with the first nobility. – "I agree with you, (says Lady A–) and I am aggrieved to think, that we are one day or other to mix in Heaven with the dregs of the people." – "God forbid (says the D–s) I should ever be in such company."'

If, on the whole, the newspapers took Hobart's side in the affair, the opposite was true of the *ton*. 'The Harmoniac is over,' a crestfallen Mrs Harris wrote to her son that week, 'and what is worse they threaten hard to indict Mrs Cornelly's [*sic*] as a house of ill-fame, and say that forty beds are made and unmade every day, which is hard, for a friend of ours says it is never more than *twenty*; but (joking apart) if they choose to demolish Mrs Cornelly all elegance and spectacle will end in this town, for she never yet had her equal in those things, and I believe got but little, as all she undertakes is clever to a degree.'

Horace Walpole was more dispassionate when he reported the 'serious war' between Teresa and the opera house to Sir Horace Mann on 22 February. Calling Teresa 'the Heidegger of the age', he went on to praise her assemblies: 'Her taste and invention in pleasures and decorations are singular. She took Carlisle House in Soho Square, enlarged it, and established assemblies and balls by subscription. At first they scandalized, but soon drew in both righteous and ungodly. She went on building, and made her house a fairy palace, for balls, concerts and masquerades.' Teresa's Harmonick Assemblies had been

splendid and charming. Mr Hobart began to starve, and the managers of the theatres were alarmed. To avoid the Act, she pretended to take no money, and had the assurance to advertise that the subscription was to provide coals for the poor, for she has vehemently courted the mob, and succeeded in gaining their princely favour. She then declared her masquerades were for the benefit of commerce. I concluded she would open a bawdy house next for the interests of the Foundling Hospital, and I was not quite mistaken, for they say one of her maids, gained by Mr Hobart, affirms that she could not undergo the fatigue of making the beds so often.

Now her opera had been quashed by the courts, and in Walpole's opinion one good thing had come out of it: Guadagni 'is not only fined but was threatened to be sent to Bridewell, which chilled the blood of all the Caesars and Alexanders he had ever represented;

nor could any promises of his lady-patronesses rehabilitate his courage – so for once an Act of Parliament goes for something'.

With the threat of rearrest hanging over her, Teresa put an end to her Harmonick Assemblies. Guadagni was out of work, and the costumes, scenery and decorations paid for by Simon Slingsby were thrown away. Slingsby had invested every penny he had in the production in the hope of making a large profit. Now he was forced to pay off the performers he had hired, and was ruined.

Teresa retreated to the inner sanctum of Carlisle House to lick her wounds, but her troubles were just beginning. There was to be no respite from the assaults on her that month. As Mrs Harris and Walpole had both hinted, there had already been another 'information' brought against her accusing her of keeping and maintaining a 'common disorderly and ill-governed house' and of suffering 'loose, idle, and disorderly persons, as well men as women, to be and remain, for and during the whole night, rioting, and otherwise misbehaving themselves, to the great noise and disturbance of all the quiet and liege subjects of our said Lord the King inhabiting thereabouts' at her masquerade of 6 February.

At a meeting of the General Session of the Peace at Hick's Hall, St John Street, on Thursday, 25 February, it was represented to twelve Middlesex magistrates that 'there have been many disorders and disturbances of the peace occasioned by the Publick Meetings and diversions at the House of Mrs Theresa Cornellys [sic] . . . tending greatly to Promote Riots and Tumults as well as Imorality [sic] and Profligacy'. Furthermore, the informants accused Teresa of causing 'certain common Nuisances in the Keeping and Maintaining a common disorderly and ill-governed house, and likewise for suffering disorderly persons in Masques to make a great noise and Tumult there'. While recommending that Teresa ought to be prosecuted for these crimes, the session came to the conclusion that unless the king's attorney general chose to pursue the case 'the said presentment however well founded and intended may lye unprosecuted'.

Although two of the magistrates were ordered to bring the matter to the attention of the attorney general, they had little success. The moral middle classes, the Church and the City might have wished to drum Teresa out of town, but the *ton*, the mob, the court and even the government were firmly on her side. One night that May, when the secretary at war diverted a contingent of seventy guards destined to keep order at the King's Theatre to 'a noted *unlicensed* house in Soho-square kept by a foreign papist where a Masquerade was intended for that night', it was not to break up the riotous occasion but to participate in it. Much the worse for drink, the guards were spotted lurching out of Carlisle House's back door the following morning 'on a par with many joyous guests who sallied forth from the *celebrated temple*'.

For the time being 'the Sovereign Empress of the Vast Regions of Taste' was safe from being toppled. But she was hanging on to power by a fraying thread.

Seventeen

'I hear a great deal of the magnificence and elegance of the Pantheon in Oxford Road, which is now finishing with all expedition,' the Hon. Mrs Boscawen wrote to Mrs Delaney in November 1771. 'I suppose Almack's and Soho must *hide their diminished heads.*'

Two and a half years after construction work had begun, Turst's 'winter Ranelagh' was nearing completion, and to those who ventured behind the mountain of wooden scaffolding it was clear that it was going to eclipse both Carlisle House and Almack's in scale, splendour and extravagance. 'It amazed me myself,' wrote Horace Walpole, after visiting the building site. 'Imagine Balbec in all its glory! The pillars are of artificial *giallo antico*. The ceilings, even of the passages, are of the most beautiful stuccos in the best taste of grotesque. The ceilings of the ball-rooms and the panels painted like Raphael's *loggias* in the Vatican. A dome like the Pantheon, glazed . . . Monsieur de Guines said to me, "*Ce n'est qu'à Londres qu'on peut faire tout cela.*"'

After countless delays, the grand opening was set for 27 January 1772. As the scaffolding was taken down, Teresa had good reason to be anxious. Since she had opened Carlisle House in 1760, she had enjoyed a near monopoly over the upper end of London's entertainment market. Even Almack's had been unable to compete with either her musical entertainment or her premises. But the Pantheon was a rival worthy of her fear. On 16 January the *Public Advertiser* reported an anonymous gentleman saying that it 'would certainly be of infinite prejudice to the entertainments at Soho'. The gentleman's friend, 'a lady of quality', apparently scolded him for having 'but little idea of the spirit, ability, and industry of Mrs Cornelys to entertain such an opinion; I will venture to differ from you greatly: opposition, so far from damping, will serve but as a spur to her active genius; and take my word for the event, whilst there is any matter left to work upon, her courage, talents, and assiduity, will ever be producing something beyond the reach of her competitors'.

Teresa certainly had no intention of going down without a fight. On Thursday, 23 January she held her annual gala and concert to celebrate King George III's birthday, with principal singers hired from the opera house and a choir consisting of gentlemen and children from the Chapel Royal, St James's. Newspaper notices claimed that she expected 'a very numerous and brilliant company' to turn up for it, but Teresa's confident boast belied her underlying apprehension. Her patronesses were already playing her up, possibly with a view to defecting to the Pantheon in the pursuit of fashion and novelty, and they now forced her to discontinue her usual practice of allowing people into Carlisle House to view the gala preparations. A newspaper announcement cancelling the preview stated simply that 'various inconveniences have been found to attend these visits: complaints have been made of the confusion and irregularity they occasioned in the house; and Mrs Cornelys has, through an impossibility of paying an equal attention to all the persons who have been present on these occasions, frequently (though inadvertently) offended several of her best friends'.

When the Pantheon opened its doors to the public five days later, Teresa's so-called best friends were all present in Oxford Street, unwilling to miss out on a major social event. The opening night was a sensation. According to the *Gazetteer and New Daily Advertiser*, there were more than seventeen hundred 'of the first people of this kingdom' present, including all the foreign ambassadors, the Lord Chancellor, the Prime Minister and eight dukes and duchesses. The *Public Advertiser* estimated the crowd at between fifteen hundred and two thousand.

Wyatt's architectural début was a sensation. People tripped over their own superlatives in their attempts to do justice to his building. To one foreigner, it 'brought to his mind the enchanted Palaces described in the French Romances, which are said to have been raised by the potent wand of some Fairy; and that, indeed, so much were his senses captivated he could scarcely persuade himself but that he trod on fairy ground'. In the opinion of Edward Gibbon, the great historian of the fall of the Roman Empire, the Pantheon was 'the most beautiful edifice in England' and 'the wonder of the XVIII Century and the British Empire'. Horace Walpole's friend, William Mason, called it the 'most astonishing and perfect piece of architecture that can possibly be conceived'. To the *Gentleman's Magazine*, the Pantheon afforded 'a striking instance of the splendour and profusion of modern times'. 'Imagination cannot well surpass the Elegance and Magnificence of the Apartments, the Boldness of the Paintings, or the Disposition of the Lights, which last are reflected from gilt Vases, suspended by gilt Chains,' eulogized the *Public Advertiser*.

All of this praise was a vindication of Turst's belief in the project and in his young and hitherto untested architect. The construction of the Pantheon had taken far longer than expected, and its cost, originally estimated at a hefty £15,000, had risen week by week: by midsummer 1769 it was said to have reached £25,000; and some put the final bill as high as £60,000. As the sums had spiralled upwards, so Turst's relationship with his investors had correspondingly plummeted. He and Miss Ellice had fallen out almost as soon as her signature on their original agreement was dry, and in the autumn of 1770 she had begged him to release her from her contractual obligations. 'Principally out of friendship' he had done so. His other shareholders had not been so lucky, and they ended up fighting him all the way to the law courts.

The final bill for the Pantheon was probably in the region of £37,000, but despite being £22,000 over budget Wyatt had exceeded the confidence placed in him by Turst. Behind its plain classical façade, the building was vast and ornate beyond belief. Its fourteen card rooms and reception rooms, countless halls and galleries and endless passages linking the multitude of different areas were all decorated in exquisite taste, and larded with stuccos in the grotesque style. Wyatt's *pièce de résistance*, however, was the huge central rotunda modelled on the Cathedral of Santa Sophia in Constantinople. Tiers of Corinthian and Ionic columns, the lower ones imitating red porphyry, the upper range Sienna marble, lined the walls, with statues of 'heathen deities' nestling in niches between them. The structure was roofed in by a vast dome sixty feet in diameter, in the centre of which was a glazed oculus in imitation of the ancient Pantheon at Rome.

To some people, however, the Pantheon was altogether too large, too lofty and too formal. Its assemblies certainly lacked the intimacy and charm of those at Carlisle House. Though she declared that it was 'grand beyond conception', Mrs Harris criticized it too: 'So many rooms, no communication with the galleries, the staircase inconvenient, all rather contribute to lose the company than show them to advantage.' The eponymous heroine of Fanny Burney's novel *Evelina* (1778) noted in her diary that the Pantheon had 'more the appearance of a chapel than of a place of diversion; and, though I was quite charmed with the magnificence of the room, I felt that I could not be as gay and thoughtless there as at Ranelagh, for there is something in it which rather inspires awe and solemnity than mirth and pleasure'.

To the more snobbish members of the *ton*, the Pantheon's strength — that it was open to everyone, like the pleasure gardens that had inspired it — was also its weakness. The *Public Advertiser* noted that it was frequented by 'an Olio of all sorts; Peers, Peeresses, Honourables and Right-Honourables, Jew-brokers, Demireps, Lottery Insurers, and Quack Doctors' (the 'Jew-brokers' included Sir Jacob Wolf and Isaac Alvarez, two of the original shareholders in the scheme). But the cosmopolitan nature of its customers, drawn from a broad spectrum of society, and its awe-inspiring architectural style immediately caught the public's imagination, and the infatuation did not wear off. Within days it had become *de rigueur* to see the Pantheon. When Boswell commented to Dr Johnson that there was not half a guinea's pleasure in the sight, Johnson shrewdly replied, 'But, Sir, there is half a guinea's worth of inferiority to other people in not having seen it.'

By 7 February even the doubting Mrs Harris, who for so many years had been loyal to Teresa's assemblies, had been won over by Turst's Oxford Street building and its concerts and assemblies, which directly competed with those in Soho Square. 'It is undoubtedly the finest and most complete thing ever seen in England,' she wrote to her son in Berlin. 'Such mixture of company never assembled before under the same roof. Lord Mansfield, Mrs Baddeley, Lord Chief Baron Parker, Mrs Abbington, Sir James Porter, Mademoiselle Heinell, Lords Hyde and Camden, with many other serious men, and most of the *gay* ladies in town, and ladies of the best rank and character; and by appearance some very low people.'

Soho simply could not compete with the Pantheon. The *ton* deserted Carlisle House by the score. Teresa had invested twelve years of her life in her business. Now she watched helplessly as it was wiped out overnight. For once it was beyond her ability to outwit the competition. Her Chinese Room and Bridge, created for her by Thomas Chippendale and once considered the height of fashionable taste, looked insignificant next to Wyatt's Roman-style halls; her grotto and Egyptian caves appeared cheap, and her magnificent Concert Room felt poky in comparison to the vast, lofty rotunda. Even the calibre of the entertainment she offered seemed second-rate, for she did not have the money to pay her singers and musicians the high fees they were soon being offered by Turst.

With no choice but to carry on regardless, Teresa threw her efforts into publicizing a masked ball that was to take place in mid-February. There was 'general joy visible on every countenance that is in the most distant measure interested by the ensuing masquerade at Soho,' claimed one newspaper's puff, which she no doubt paid for and wrote herself. Another such 'report' claimed:

The house in Soho-square, in which the Masquerade will be held on the 13TH instant, is perhaps one of the best-disposed buildings for that purpose that ever was erected; so many rooms are opened on the occasion, that an opportunity of displaying a variety of elegance and brilliancy is afforded the conductor of the entertainment, while so perpetual a change of scene and place is given to the masques, that the dullness arising from an unvaried spectacle in any one room, however elegant, splendid, or replete with diversity of figure is totally prevented.

Teresa was hoping to win back her customers. But fate was against her. On 8 February, only a fortnight after the opening of the Pantheon, the king's mother Princess Augusta died at Carlton House at the age of fifty-two and the court, which had just finished grieving for the king's aunt, the Landgravine of Hesse Cassel, was plunged into mourning yet again. Through Elizabeth Chudleigh, Princess Augusta had been Teresa's strongest link to the royal family since the death in 1767 of the Duke of York. Coming so soon after the opening of the Pantheon, her death was an unexpected and, as it turned out, fatal blow.

The old order under which Teresa had flourished for so long had gone. As the columns in the London newspapers filled with drapers' notices advertising stocks of black mourning crape, she notified her subscribers that she was to hold a grand public elegy or *Threnodia Augustali* in honour of the late princess on 20 February. In a final burst of extravagance, she draped her premises in hundreds of yards of black material, and commissioned composer Matteo Vento and Oliver Goldsmith, author of the best-selling *The Vicar of Wakefield*, to write a musical elegy. Goldsmith scribbled down 262 lines of verse, and Vento cobbled together a score, but neither put much effort into it, and they were both so ashamed of the resulting work that they insisted on taking their names off it. A pamphlet containing Goldsmith's poem – or, rather, his 'compilation', as he chose to call it – sold at the door on the day, carried an apologia for the words and music, which, it said, were more 'an industrious effort of gratitude than of genius'.

The elegy was not the worst part of the occasion. For once Teresa's sense of the dramatic badly misfired. Even in the eyes of Mrs Harris the *Threnodia Augustali* was melodramatic to the point of being bizarre: 'A large kind of frame was made round the glasses and in various parts of the room with lamps stuck in it, and black crape strained over the lamps to make the light solemn,' she wrote. 'At the upper end of the room was a black canopy, under which was a white tomb with "Augusta" writ on it; on one side stood a man, the other side a woman, who sang forth the praises of the Princess; a most ridiculous whim of the woman's. Window curtains all black &c.'

Was the hitherto indestructible Mrs Cornelys crumbling at last? It was almost as if Teresa was lamenting the death of Carlisle House. Although she held a masked ball in early March, and an annual subscription assembly on 2 April (for which she announced Carlisle House was undergoing 'several Alterations, Additions and Improvements which have been sometime in Agitation and which will be no less considerable in their Extent than splendid in their Effect'), London's Empress of Pleasure had effectively been deposed. Market forces were against her. As she fought to compete with Turst, her expenses shot up and her income declined. Teresa was under intolerable pressure from all sides. Scenting blood, her creditors encircled her, like hounds around a fox, and prepared to move in for the kill.

Teresa took refuge in her house, the one place where the bailiffs could not touch her. On 14 April a vitriolic and xenophobic article appeared in the newspapers, prophesying the imminent downfall of 'a certain *polite* lady near *Soho*' who was availing herself 'of that defence which the law wisely intended to be the security of our personal liberty and property against arbitrary encroachment – not to be the asylum of fraud and injustice. Like an eastern Sultana, she is inaccessible to all comers; and immured within her castle, bids defiance to every approach of justice.' Furthermore, the piece also mysteriously reported that 'an unlucky prank that was played on her sometime since has not little increased her native *bashfulness* and *modesty*' – hinting, perhaps, that forty-nine-year-old Teresa was either pregnant or suffering from a venereal disease.

The day after this article appeared, Teresa fought back one last time from inside her castle walls by advertising a 'Grand Masked Ball (the last of the season)' on 28 April, which was 'to be on a totally and strikingly different plan of any Entertainment of the kind hitherto held'. For the first time ever, supper was to be served in the first-floor Concert Room where 'the whole floor is to be raised by a gradual yet almost imperceptible ascent, from the entrance quite up to the orchestra; the tables are to be picturesquely arranged on a very novel mode, and to accommodate ten persons each; there is to be room for some hundred persons to sup at one time; and the whole of the masks and tables, by this contrived ascent and arrangement, will be comprehended at a single view'. The notice ended by asking the readers, 'Can imagination extend to the forming [of] a more strikingly beautiful appearance than this?' The truthful answer to this rhetorical question was a resounding *yes*. It would take more than a raked floor and a few picturesquely arranged dinner tables for Carlisle House to outclass the Pantheon.

As Teresa prepared for the masked ball, two new blows fell in quick succession. On 26 April, two days before the event, she was arrested and held to bail in the King's Bench prison at the request of her former servant John Berger and his vintner brother Albert. The Bergers had been fleecing Teresa for years. Now they claimed she owed them a total of £375 'and upwards' in unpaid wages and wine bills. And on the following day, as Teresa attempted to secure her release from prison, the managers of the Pantheon paid a newspaper to reprint verbatim the 1771 indictment against her for keeping 'a common disorderly and ill-governed house'.

In a last-ditch attempt to avoid bankruptcy, Teresa mortgaged Carlisle House to a man named Arthur Jones. The wealthy Mr Jones had admired her for a long time: since, in her own words, he had 'always acted with great Indulgence and kindness' towards her, it is probable that he was her lover. Not only did he now pay her a massive £6000 for the lease of her property, he made a somewhat foolhardy promise to let her remain in her home, come what may.

Unfortunately, the £6000 did not clear Teresa's debts or pave the way to a more solvent future. Still in dire straits, she had one very small hope left: that the king might grant her the licence to stage Italian operas at Carlisle House that she had been denied up till now, and so allow her to compete legally with the King's Theatre and the Pantheon.

In a petition that was a *tour de force* of emotional blackmail as well as a brilliant summing up of her career, Teresa applied to George III for a licence to stage operas. Her written memorial (erroneously attributed to the year 1770, but from its content obviously written in 1772) 'humbly' told the story of how she had come to England and set up Carlisle House 'under the most dignified Patronage and the most unexceptionable regulations' and then went on to explain her present situation:

That although she has been in the receipt of very considerable sums of Money, yet the ardent desire of producing something worthy of the distinguished Company that resorted to her House, has always induced her to make such expensive Alterations and Embellishments, from Year to Year as have constantly obliged her to dispurse with one hand, what the liberality of the Nobility and Gentry, her Subscribers, have paid her in the other. That after carrying this stupendious [sic] Undertaking through (great indeed, for a Woman, a widow and a Mother, fortuneless and a stranger) with severe and unremitted labour, to the present time; and after struggling with a Siege of Troubles during a longer Period than the Siege of Troy; your Majesty's memorialist is, at last, in hourly jeopardy of falling a Prey to her Assailants, and of being driven from a Country many Years and Sufferings have given her a kind of natural love for, and entitled her, as it were, to all its natural Benefits. That your Majesty's memorialist has not only to stand against the oppressive rivalship of powerful Imitators; but merely for producing last year to the Nobility and Gentry a species of a more elegant and dramatic musical Amusement than any they had ever seen before, has already been harassed with vexations and expensive Prosecutions, as interestedly litigious, as innocently incurred!

That under these affecting Circumstances her dernier resort is in the benevolence and compassion of Your Majesty; before whom she prostrates herself, and with all humility, fervently implores Your Royal protection, in granting her a Patent for the Exhibition of musical dramatic Entertainments, by Private Subscription of the Nobility and Gentry; as the only means of saving her from destruction; and of giving her, at last such Recompense as she may reasonably hope for, from the uncommon intenseness of her Labours.

The king turned down Teresa's petition. With no hope now of diversifying to attract new customers, she clung on tenaciously at Carlisle House. She still had a few friends left in the government. William Shute, second Viscount Barrington and the secretary for war, sent a contingent of fifty foot-soldiers to swell the depleted numbers at a Soho ball on 7 May, and although he was later denounced for doing so, he repeated the kindness on 8 June.

Shute's guards were among only 250 people present that night. As if sensing that this was going to be the last masquerade at Carlisle House, the revellers drank the cellar dry, danced and cavorted licentiously and, to the joy of the mob waiting outside in Soho Square, flung bottles of wine, whole meat pies and 'temples of pastry' out of the windows.

Their wild partying, which continued until six o'clock the following morning, had something of the desperation of an all-night wake. Which in a way it was. Teresa had reached the end. Even though her admirer Arthur Jones had promised to let her stay on in Carlisle House, he now turned against her, dismissed her servants and threw her out.

On 17 June, Teresa was arrested by a bailiff at the orders of a group of her creditors. Apart from John and Albert Berger, they included Patrick Sinclair, Lewis Smith, George Ridge, Gaetano Colzi, Francis Glossop, John Tubman, John Parker, William Grantham, Richard Robinson, William Smith, Patrick Gillicord and James Ross. Two days later, she was committed to the King's Bench prison in Southwark by an avalanche of writs.

The relatively modern King's Bench, which had been rebuilt in the 1750s, was by no means the worst of London's prisons. Used mainly for debtors and those convicted of libel – the MP John Wilkes had been imprisoned there in 1768 – it was, like most gaols, a profit-making institution. Prisoners had to pay for everything from their bed and board to commitment and discharge fees, and even for being transported there in the first place. Those who could afford to would pay the marshal an extra eight to ten guineas, plus a high weekly rent, to stay in the best building, which was known as the 'State House', or for the privilege of living in specially designated houses within a short radius of the prison known as the 'Rules'. Fair as conditions were – there was a plentiful supply of water, and windows to let in fresh air – the place was so overcrowded that prisoners frequently had to share beds, the rooms were overrun with vermin, and diseases such as smallpox were endemic.

However superior her conditions at the King's Bench were by the standards of the time, they made a grim contrast to the luxury Teresa had enjoyed at Carlisle House. Worst of all, she had lost her liberty. While she languished in gaol over the summer, her creditors were informed that they were 'most earnestly requested to deliver forthwith a particular Account of their several and respective Demands' to Mr Hickey in St Alban's Street. Over the next few weeks countless creditors came forward, including Turst's ex-partner Miss Margaretta Ellice, the cabinet-maker Thomas Chippendale, James Cullen, Teresa's partner in her Greek Street premises, Samuel Spencer, a 'Gentleman' of St Giles, and Augustus Lesage, a jeweller and goldsmith from Suffolk Street, Pall Mall.

By autumn, Teresa was still locked up. Her spirit seemed crushed. Although she was occasionally allowed out overnight to run assemblies at Carlisle House for the benefit of her creditors, the tone of her newspaper notices was uncharacteristically humble. On one occasion she regretted that she could not apply to her past subscribers in person, and cited as her reason 'the well-known present unhappy State of Mrs Cornelys's health'.

Running assemblies on the shoestring budget her creditors allowed her was anathema to Teresa. Despite the publication that autumn of a poem about London's entertainment centres, which claimed that 'The place of all places is Madam Cornelly's [sic]' she could not begin to match the Pantheon's standards. Besides, the nobility and gentry who had patronized her for years no longer wanted to be associated with what was clearly a failing enterprise run by a debtor, and they did not show up for her events.

The winter was fast approaching, and with it Teresa's last chance of earning enough money to pay off her debts and secure her release from prison. If she did not avoid bankruptcy now, ruin lay ahead. On 28 October, as her creditors plied the marshal's offices at the King's Bench with applications for her continuing confinement, she made a last-ditch attempt to fight back against them through the Court of Chancery by applying for an injunction to prevent them selling her house from under her feet.

Teresa's application, compiled in her prison cell with the help of her lawyer, shows just how convoluted her financial affairs had become. Though in February 1768 she had signed an indenture assigning the house to John Fermor, Mary Brackstone, Edward Aylett and Thomas Middleton for the sum of £2517, she had also recently mortgaged it to Arthur Jones for £6000. Teresa swore that she had already paid back her creditors a total of £4300, but that some of this money had not been passed on to them. Although Mr Jones had 'always acted with great Indulgence and kindness' towards her and had assured her that he would let her stay on in Soho Square come what may, he was now conspiring with her other creditors to ruin her by making sure she remained locked up in prison while they bought her business at a low price and sold off fifty shares in it at £500 each.

Teresa claimed that this amounted to nothing less than a conspiracy against her. Her creditors were trying to ruin her in three ways: by charging her for goods she had never received; by not taking account of money she had paid them back; and by employing 'every method to gain themselves the absolute management' of Carlisle House. 'All of which actings doings and pretences of the said confederates are contrary to Equity and good conscience and tend to the manifest wrong injury and oppression of your oratrix.'

This desperate attempt to stop the sale of Carlisle House came to nothing. An abyss had opened up before Teresa, and it was inexorably sucking her in. She had wriggled out of many similar situations in the past but this time there was to be no reprieve. On Tuesday, 3 November her name appeared in the Bankrupts List of the *London Gazette* where she was described simply as 'Teresa Cornelys, a widow, dealer and chapwoman'. The notice ordered her to surrender herself to the bankruptcy commissioners 'on the 14TH and 15TH day of November, instant, at five of the clock in the Afternoon, and on the 29TH day of December next, at Ten of the clock in the Forenoon, at Guildhall, London, and make a full Disclosure of her estate and Effects; when and where the creditors are to come, prepared to prove their Debts, and at the second sitting to choose Assignees; and at the last sitting the said Bankrupt is required to finish her Examination'. Furthermore, anyone owing Teresa money or holding any of her personal effects or belongings was instructed 'not to pay or deliver the same but to whom the Commissioners shall appoint, but give notice to Messrs Hickeys, Attorneys at law, in St Albans Street'.

Teresa's assets were assigned to her four main creditors: Samuel Spencer, Thomas Chippendale, James Cullen and Augustus Lesage. Along with nine other creditors, they decided to auction Carlisle House and its contents as one single cut-price lot. At the beginning of December, they advertised the sale in the newspapers:

CARLISLE HOUSE, SOHO – At Twelve o'clock, on Monday 14TH instant, by order of the assignees, Mr Marshall will sell by auction on the premises, in one lot, All that extensive, commodious and magnificent House in Soho Square, lately occupied by Mrs Cornelys, and used for Public Assemblies of the Nobility and Gentry. Together with all the rich and elegant Furniture, Decorations, china, &c., thereunto belonging, too well known and universally admired for their aptness and taste to require here any public and extraordinary description thereof.

Anyone wanting to attend the auction was invited to apply to the auctioneer's office in St Martin's Lane where they could buy a catalogue for five shillings, which would admit them to the sale.

Teresa had not been wrong about her creditors' intentions. Twelve of them, including Margaretta Ellice, Chippendale, Cullen and Joseph Hickey, the attorney in charge of the sale, were trying to get their hands on Carlisle House and its contents as cheaply as possible with the intention of running it themselves. This was not only at Teresa's expense, but also at the expense of her forty-odd other creditors. The auction, originally to have taken place on 14 December, was postponed while the conspirators organized a joint bid: Chippendale contributed £2500 to the kitty, Cullen £2000, and most of the others £1000 each.

The sale of Carlisle House eventually took place on 22 December. As Teresa had suspected, the building and its contents were sold off as a single lot to the Chippendale consortium for the knock-down price of £15,000. This was a much lower sum than would have been raised if the contents had been auctioned separately, and her other creditors were up in arms about it.

Teresa was allowed out of prison to see the teetering 'fairy palace' she had constructed with her blood, sweat and sheer ingenuity sold for a pittance. Her female patronesses, who had stood by her for years only to desert her after the opening of the Pantheon, came along to the auction and sobbed uncontrollably, but Teresa maintained an extraordinary and stoical dignity. The press, which had lauded her for years as a celebrity, now turned tail and put the boot in. A satirical eleven-page report of the auction appeared under the headline 'Cupid turned Auctioneer; or Mrs Cornelys's Sale at Carlisle House' in the next two issues of the *Westminster Magazine*:

The Empress of the Regions of Taste, being dashed from the pinnacle of feminine monarchical grandeur, all the impliments [*sic*] of luxury, the regalia of taste and dissipation, – together with those rich coverings of silken folly, which fashion, with a hand of snowy elegance, had collected to indulge the rapturous ease of lulling, lolling, lewd, lascivious Courtiers, – have been seized upon by the cold iron hand of merciless creditors, who have abandoned and exposed them to the eyes of the vulgar.

I beheld this gay Queen of Extravagance, who has so long dictated from her satin throne of mode and magnificence; – I saw this slipshod Empress of Velvet venery walk fearless and majestic, supported by the meanest of ceremonious masters, – a tip-staff – to a greasy hackney coach! O what a falling off is there! To behold the person of the elegant leader of foppery and folly seized – her goods confiscated – her throne stripped – and all her properties condemned to the voluble tongue of an auctioneer – to be exposed to the slow finger of scorn – to be purchased by the dull and impotent, and whirled the gods know where. No horror ever equalled this!

After twelve years of ruling the roost in London, the Empress had at last been deposed. Her competitors rejoiced in their good luck. Her enemies gloried in her downfall. Chippendale and his cronies congratulated themselves on the bargain they had snapped up. Everyone from John Fermor to Teresa's former patronesses the Duchesses of Kingston and Northumberland presumed that the notorious impresario of Carlisle House would now bow her shamed head and disappear from public life for ever.

Eighteen

In the winter of 1772, Sophie Cornelys was nineteen years old. After two years of boarding at the Nunnery in Hammersmith at Casanova's expense, she had moved back to Carlisle House, and she had been there ever since. Rather than improving the relationship between mother and daughter, her temporary break at school had made it worse. Sophie was more resentful of Teresa than ever. Far from admiring her mother's achievements, she despised them. Teresa's dominating and at times overwhelming personality had cast a permanent shadow over her life, and her imprisonment came as a liberation to Sophie. Though homeless and without an income, she was at long last free of Teresa. She could make her own decisions for the first time in her life.

Her instinct was to get away. Until now she had been forced to share all of her mother's vicissitudes, good and bad, but Teresa's bankruptcy, and the shame it brought on herself, proved the last straw for Sophie. Scandal followed her as she fled from Soho Square. She had only to say who she was to provoke curious stares and awkward questions.

Miss Cornelys. The name was like a brand on her forehead. John Taylor, a writer at whose parents' home Sophie occasionally took refuge following Teresa's arrest, explained in his memoir, *Records of My Life*, how

. . . one night, when a knock was heard at our street door, to quiet her fears lest a stranger should hear her name, she begged that I would go to the door myself and prevent intrusion. The person who knocked, happened to be an inquisitive little friend, who was too intimate with the family to be excluded; and asking who was in the parlour, a common name occurred to me, and I told him a Miss Williams. From that time she adopted this name, and retained it amidst all her vicissitudes till her death.

A more logical explanation than Taylor's self-aggrandizing one would be that Sophie chose the surname Williams by anglicizing her middle name, Wilhelmine.

How was the newly created Miss Williams to live? She had never had to trouble herself with earning a living until now; Teresa had always taken care of that side of life. Going into business on her own account was out of the question – she had witnessed too many of Teresa's difficulties to want to follow in her footsteps. Besides, like some children of ambitious, self-motivated and successful parents today, she lacked direction and drive. What Sophie yearned for was a kind of boring respectability, which was the antithesis of her daring and unscrupulous parents. Since she was young, pretty and highly educated, there was only one reputable opening that would help her to achieve her goal, and that was to become a governess to an aristocratic family. As Casanova had observed during his stay in London, Sophie had always been a favourite with Lady Harrington. Shortly after Teresa's imprisonment, Lady Harrington asked Sophie to become a paid companion to her daughters. Sophie immediately said yes and moved to Stable Yard, St James's.

Giuseppe, too, changed his name and went into service following Teresa's bankruptcy. He had once led the Marquise d'Urfé to think that he was part of the Spanish family of Aranda, and now he took the surname of Altorf, from a town outside Strasbourg. Although the spoiled youth who had been snatched away from his idyllic existence in Paris nine years earlier had never brought order to the chaotic finances of Carlisle House, he had matured into a fine, thoughtful and educated young man who had reconciled himself to his lowly position. Now in his twenty-seventh year, Joseph Altorf was taken on as a tutor to the Earl of Pomfret, from whose Northamptonshire seat of Easton Neston he sent an allowance to his mother.

This regular but modest amount was a pittance compared to what Teresa had been used to, but it was enough to keep her from starvation. Released from prison once her debts had been paid off with the £15,000 raised from the sale of Carlisle House, she immediately began to look for a new money-making venture. During the early months of 1773 one fell into her lap through the auspices of Jacob Leroux, the architect of her assembly rooms.

Like most architects and builders of the time, Leroux was also a small-time developer, and in the late 1760s he had drawn up plans to build a speculative up-market housing estate on the fringes of the relatively quiet south-coast town of Southampton. The Polygon, as it was to be called, was to be a twenty-two-acre twelve-sided development whose situation 'commanded a most delightful prospect of Southampton Water as far as Calshot Castle, with fine views of the New Forest and the town of Southampton . . . and a distant view of the isle of Wight'. Each side of the Polygon was to consist of three mansions with gardens at the rear backing on to a pool or basin of water, which, when the estate was completed, would form the hub of a vast wheel; the whole area was to be surrounded by a long curtain wall reminiscent of today's secure gated developments.

Leroux's innovative scheme also included plans for a shopping-and-leisure centre to consist of boutiques run by London companies, a colonnaded tavern and assembly rooms, and a grand hotel. The project was being backed by two local men: a speculator named Isaac Mallortie; and General John Carnac, a wealthy retired officer of the East India Company's army, whose country house – Cams Hall, near Fareham – Leroux had remodelled in 1767.

Building of the Polygon had begun in August 1768 when local MPs Viscount Palmerston and Hans Stanley had laid the foundation stone. But due to Carnac's difficulty in getting his money sent from India the project was slow to get off the ground. By early 1773 only the hotel and a handful of houses had been built, and the venture looked like foundering.

What Leroux desperately needed was publicity to draw potential clients to Southampton. Who better to attract it than the erstwhile Empress of Pleasure? With this in mind, he approached Teresa and offered her the lease of his hotel. It was a godsend to her. As Carlisle House had once done, the Polygon Hotel would provide her with a home, a form of income and, above all, a challenge for her creative skills. She would make the building a magnet for the English nobility and turn the sleepy seaside town of Southampton into a fashionable resort that would rival the spa town of Bath!

Perhaps Teresa was unaware of the dark financial clouds hanging over the Polygon's future. Alternatively, she might have ignored them. Beggars could not be choosy. Early in 1773 she signed a thirty-year lease on the hotel at a rent of £300 and somehow scrounged enough money to fit it out. No matter that her new premises were isolated on a building site on the edge of town, by the summer the Polygon Hotel had been furnished with 'superb, elegant and valuable household furniture' and decorated in Teresa's inimitable style.

All she needed to make the venture a success were some guests. But only a scant handful arrived. To make matters worse, Isaac Mallortie, one of the Polygon's two financiers, went bankrupt, and his partner, General Carnac, had to return to India to track down his money. Leroux's unpaid builders downed tools on the scattering of half-completed houses, and Teresa found herself marooned in a state-of-the-art hotel in the middle of nowhere. Instead of a glittering future to match her glittering past, she faced ruin yet again. Fearful of being arrested, she put the Polygon Hotel and its contents up for auction. Though it was 'most elegantly fitted up . . . very large and spacious, and fit for the immediate Reception of Company', nobody wanted it.

Teresa returned to London. She had seen more than enough of provincial life to have realized that there was only one place where she belonged: in bustling cosmopolitan Soho. She was determined to get back into Carlisle House somehow, and by January 1774 she had succeeded, this time managing assemblies there on behalf of her creditors while they squabbled with each other over the ownership and value of the property. That month she advertised her annual Grand Gala in honour of the king's birthday with her usual promises that 'every Power of genius and Expence [sic] will be exacted to render this Entertainment not only the most novel but also the most agreeable of any that have been in this House'. 'Mrs Cornelys seems to be coming into play again,' noted one newspaper gleefully. 'She is once more got into Carlisle House;

and is to superintend the Masquerade next Wednesday; though the price of Tickets being low, will not admit of the exertion of that Lady's abilities in regard to taste and elegance, yet it is expected to be a night of high festivity.'

For a brief moment it seemed just like the old days. But the tradesmen with whom Teresa was dealing now knew better than to let her run up enormous credit, and they demanded to be paid on the nail. By March, she was bankrupt once more, and out of Carlisle House. The following winter, the public were notified that assemblies there were to take place under a new manager chosen by the subscribers.

It was Teresa's third business disaster in two years. Once again, the fashionable world presumed that she would hang her head in shame and disappear for good. They were underestimating her irrepressible determination. Nothing, but nothing, could keep her down for long.

In June 1775 she resurfaced at the Ranelagh Gardens in Chelsea, where she helped to organize a Venetian regatta on behalf of the Savoir Vivre Club, a group of young bloods who included Charles James Fox and Lord Lyttleton. The regatta, which took place on 24 June, was the social event of the season, and it had all the hallmarks of a Carlisle House masquerade right down to the tickets, which were designed and engraved by Teresa's favourite artists, Cipriani and Bartolozzi.

Everyone from Georgiana, Duchess of Devonshire, to Sir Joshua Reynolds, Lord North, David Garrick and the Dukes of Gloucester and Richmond took part in the regatta. By noon, the Thames between London Bridge and Millbank was crammed with so many boats, barges and Venetian-style gondolas that there was only a slim channel left down the centre of the river in which the rowing races could take place. Temporary seating stands had been constructed along the riverbanks and even on the roof of Westminster Hall, and gambling tables had been set up on the approaches to Westminster Bridge. By five o'clock in the afternoon, the bridge itself was so crowded that people even squeezed into the iron lamp-holders affixed to its sides.

The number of spectators watching the races was estimated at between two hundred thousand and a rather exaggerated three million. What was certain was that the rest of London was a ghost town that day. As Mrs Hester Thrale, the close friend and future biographer of Dr Johnson, wrote to him, 'Every shop was shut; every street deserted; and the tops of all such houses as had any catch of the river swarmed with people like bees settling on a branch.'

Towards evening, the Lord Mayor sailed up from the City in a sumptuous barge, followed by Lord Edward Bentinck whose own barge was fitted up to resemble a huge gondola. Twenty oarsmen pulled it along the tidal river, and two small boats preceded it, each filled with musicians dressed in blue and white uniforms.

Soon after six o'clock, a cannon was fired to herald the start of the regatta, and at seven o'clock the races began. A dozen rowing-boats, each crewed by two young watermen who had recently finished their apprenticeships, scudded down the narrow channel in the middle of the river to Blackfriars, where they rounded a vessel moored off Waterman's Hall and raced back up to Westminster. Just at this moment, the British weather conspired to try to ruin the occasion: the sky darkened, a gale blew up, torrential rain poured down and the river became so rough that two boats overturned, one a racing vessel and the other a spectator's boat containing several women; luckily everyone was saved.

After the prize-giving ceremony – the first prize was ten guineas and a new boatman's coat and badges – the thousands of flag-bedecked boats, large and small, sailed 'in a picturesque irregularity', upriver towards Chelsea, where there was to be a masked ball at Ranelagh for some thirteen hundred guests. Ticket-holders landed at the gardens at nine o'clock, and although the organizers had requested that their boats be moored in a crescent shape around the main landing steps so that the company could disembark in an orderly fashion to the sounds of three military bands, chaos ensued as another gale blew up, drenching the women in their obligatory white dresses. 'As to the musick,' Mrs Thrale noted, as she watched their arrival from the riverbank, 'we heard none but the screams of the frightened company as they were tossed about at the moment of getting to shore.'

Notices for the masquerade had boasted that 'The supper and its decorations are to be conducted under the immediate inspection of Mrs Cornelys, so justly celebrated for her elegance and taste.' Everything was indeed indelibly stamped with Teresa's personal style. A temporary 'Temple of Neptune', lined with linen striped in the British naval colours, had been set up for dancing, and the rotunda was filled with circular tables 'in such a manner as to form a magnificent amphitheatre (pyramidically rising towards the center [*sic*] and terminating in an orchestra) where the whole company of 1300 persons may be commodiously seated at once'. While an orchestra of 120 musicians played under the direction of that old Carlisle House regular, Felice de Giardini, the revellers sat down to dine. But although Teresa had been allowed a budget of seven hundred guineas to pay for the refreshments, there was not enough wine to go round and the food was afterwards described as 'indifferent' and even 'execrable'.

Despite the appalling weather and the disappointing food, London's first Venetian regatta became one of the most celebrated events in the history of Ranelagh, thanks to Teresa, who had proved that, although she was now fifty-two, she had lost none of her touch when it came to organizing parties. When Carlisle House was advertised as for sale again that August, this time by private contract rather than auction, she was the perfect choice to be its new manager.

By the following winter the irrepressible Teresa was back in Soho yet again, and busy publicizing her return. A rash of letters and articles supporting her appeared in the *Morning Post*. One letter, purportedly written by a man who had been absent from England for some time, expressed horror at the sale of Carlisle House ('that magnificent and unrivalled assemblage of taste and splendour'), criticized the 'vile artifices' of Mrs Cornelys's enemies and 'sincerely wished that she may still long direct and continue with as certain success and emolument to herself, as she is sure of giving the utmost satisfaction to the Nobility and gentry, whom I cannot suffer myself to doubt, will, in justice to her uncommon taste and genius, and in gratitude for the many days and nights she has laboured for their pleasure and amusements, amply bestow their most noble and generous support'. Another correspondent insisted that even Teresa's enemies 'must allow that none ever arrived at higher perfection in the elegant art of managing entertainments of this nature'. A letter apparently written by a shopkeeper stressed 'how much in particular she is intitled [*sic*] to the gratitude and utmost friendship of all ranks of tradespeople, amongst whom she has been the cause of the circulation of a most incredible sum, for every year for these fifteen or sixteen years past'. The writers of these puffs signed themselves by names like 'A Lover of Masquerades' or 'Veritas', but it did not take a genius to tell that the Empress of Pleasure herself had penned them.

Against all the odds, Teresa made a spectacular comeback that winter at Carlisle House. If her clientele were not as exalted as they had once been, they made up for it with the gusto and licentiousness with which they enjoyed themselves. There had always been a sexual undercurrent to her assemblies, and now it took over. If the Pantheon had garnered the market in elegance, Teresa would aim, shamelessly, for people's baser instincts. 'This was a night of harlotry,' wrote one man of a Soho masquerade. 'There was not a brothel in town, but what had emptied its meretricious contents in this house; and as the wine mantled, the ladies grew more riotous.' Still, the writer praised Carlisle House's manager for conducting the wild evening 'with pleasantry and elegance'.

Teresa no longer cared who came to her assemblies or what they did there. She was making money for the first time in three years. By January 1776 she was running Carlisle House 'on her own account' again, and the newspapers were wishing 'Mrs Cornelys (the Mother of Masquerades, Taste and Elegance) that success at her ensuing Bal Masqué, which her great merit and perseverance in the public cause deserve'. Bored by the awe-inspiring classicism of James Wyatt's rotunda, many of her old subscribers now flocked back to Soho, attracted both by its intimacy and by its increasingly risqué atmosphere.

Now it was the proprietors of the Pantheon who were running scared. Terrified by Teresa's sudden resurgence in popularity, they deliberately and ruthlessly tried to put her out of business by holding masquerades on the same nights as hers. Outraged, Teresa struck out at them through the press:

I am myself unequal to the task of combating with so powerful a body as these proprietors. I envy them not in their successes – cruel then it is that they should attempt to prevent mine. If they should not succeed in their advertised Masquerade their property cannot feel the loss; but if I fail, irreparable ruin is the consequence. – This they too well know. My distresses have been too public to be unknown to anyone; I did not think they would have attempted to take the advantage of them. – I shall, with a never-disappointed confidence, throw myself into the arms of a people whose characteristic is a detestation of oppression, and an exalted benevolence to the oppressed.

A letter to the *Morning Chronicle*, signed simply Benevolus but obviously written by Teresa or one of her new backers, expressed disbelief 'that so large a set of men of fortune could be guilty of such unmanliness as to oppose the fair attempts of a weak, defenceless woman! Am I to think that men like these have *deliberately* joined to sink down an emerging woman and plunge her a second time into the deepest distresses, from which, a second time, it were next to impossibility that she should ever arise? – Virtue – Heaven – forbid!' If the misogynist Pantheon board persisted in its plans to hold masquerades in opposition to hers, 'it must indisputably be with the most unmanly design of overwhelming a female with ruin – overwhelming, too, not a little ungratefully the very person to whom, as proprietors of the Pantheon, you owe even your present being. Had her yet unequalled talents in elegant entertainment never appeared in this kingdom, ye, in your proprietary capacity, had never been known.'

To everyone's astonishment, Teresa won the propaganda battle. During the spring and summer of 1776 her unexpected success excelled even her most optimistic expectations. This was not so much a second wind as a veritable hurricane. While other proprietors struggled to fill their premises once a month in high season, she entertained a full house every ten days at least, even during the quiet summer months.

Teresa's determination not to go bankrupt once more swept aside all obstacles. Having glimpsed the abyss, she was desperate not to fall into it again, and consequently she never stopped working. To the horror of the Church she even introduced special 'Lent Assemblies' during March, ostensibly as charitable events for the good of the children of the Marylebone and Westminster Lace Manufactories but in reality to line her own purse. With between eight and fifteen hundred subscribers a night regularly attending her balls and masquerades, each paying up to two and a half guineas for their tickets, her substantial income allowed her party-planning skills to reach hitherto uncharted heights.

These culminated in a series of stunning and vastly expensive 'Rural Masquerades', which began in February and continued well into the summer months. On one occasion Teresa landscaped the Chinese Room as a garden filled with perfumed flowers and surrounded by thickets, and the Supper Room was carpeted with fresh turf. On either side of the dance-floor she created elegant walkways bordered by green hedges. Behind these, she built raised platforms where dinner was served on large round tables 'enriched with trees, under whose embowering shade the masks will sup, as if they were *en pleine campagne* with the pleasure of seeing the rustic Swains and their Lasses mix in the gay Dance on the green turf beneath them'.

So enamoured was the *ton* with 'the Arcadian felicity in this *Paradis Terreste*' that rural masquerades became the biggest draw at Carlisle House. Teresa's imagination ran riot. 'The Bridge-room was converted into an elegant garden,' enthused one newspaper of a rural masquerade she designed that April, 'the sides were full of shrubs and odoriferous flowers, at the extremity was a kind of Arbour filled with green-house plants and pots of flowers, and in the centre stood an elegant pavilion hung with festoons of silk; on the top (to which the company ascended by a temporary stair-case,) was spread a table for a dozen persons, in the middle of which was a fountain of water, and a reservoir, with gold and silver fish swimming about in it.' Teresa's *pièce de résistance* that evening was her stunning transformation of the Concert Room where 'lofty pines stood at equal distances along the sides, and branched to each other at the top', hot fowls, crayfish, asparagus, strawberries, oranges and syllabubs were laid out under 'an elegant erection of Gothick-arches' decorated with festoons and coloured lanterns, and the orchestra apse was surrounded by orange trees lit by 'a moving spiral pillar of lights, which terminated in a brilliant sun'.

Where Teresa found all these out-of-season flowers, fruits, trees and plants is a mystery. As for the food, so many chickens and turkeys were served at Carlisle House that season that the public were soon complaining that there were none left in town and Teresa was accused of being 'a Monopolist, (of all characters the most injurious to society)' for taking them all. The *Morning Post* even published a poem on the subject:

> What! Think us all such pamper'd sinners,
> That thus you cheat us of our dinners?
> So priests forbid good Christians meat,
> That, cheaper they themselves may eat;
> For ev'ry bird that wings the air,
> It's [*sic*] flight directs to *Soho-square*;
> Condemn'd, alas! To be devour'd
> Midst groves where once, perhaps, they pour'd
> Their dulcet notes, e'er birds and shades
> Were doomed to grace your masquerades.
> So now's proclaim'd the general fast
> And we must make some coarse repast;
> 'We're all engag'd' – the poult'rers tell us,
> Nor fowl can they afford to sell us.

Unlike the poor dead fowl served at her tables, Teresa was flying. At the age of fifty-three, she had reached the zenith of her capabilities. Once again she had transformed the social life of the *ton*.

As one journalist said of her that year, 'The credit of masquerades set with her evening sun and again rises with her second dawn.'

But as the Empress's sun rose again over the streets of Soho, that of her friend and patroness the Duchess of Kingston was on the wane. Elizabeth's scandalous past had at last caught up with her. On 15 April she was put on trial for bigamy in Westminster Hall.

Nineteen

On 23 September 1773, Evelyn Pierrepont, Duke of Kingston, died in Bath where he and his wife had gone to take the waters. As was customary, for one day his entire household was plunged into deepest mourning. Two professional mourners stood outside the front door carrying black poles decorated with black plumes. The windows were draped with black crape. The horses were rubbed down with black cloths. Even the kitchenmaid in the scullery scoured the pans with a black rag.

Upstairs, in a darkened chamber lit by a single candle, the distraught Duchess received visitors sitting in her sumptuous bed. The following day, between fainting fits and in hysterical tears, she left Bath with her husband's coffin and headed for Holme Pierrepont, her late husband's Nottinghamshire seat. No one had ever seen anything like Kingston's long, dramatic cortège. The procession was led by thirty-two torch-bearers, six mutes and a coach containing four clergymen. Two gentlemen on horseback followed, carrying the duke's cushion and coronet. Behind them travelled the hearse, followed by numerous bearers on horseback. Then came three more coaches containing Kingston's servants and tenants, who in turn were followed by thirty-six tradesmen on horseback (no doubt they were mourning the loss of business that the death of the spendthrift duke would mean).

As the procession rolled slowly from village to village, the duchess, dressed in black and wearing an extremely long and heavy veil, sat in her own coach weeping uncontrollably. When the cortège stopped overnight at coaching inns, she made sure that the duke's coffin was placed in the best room, and the corridors echoed with her terrible wails. In London, Elizabeth's 'extravagant' mourning was taken with more than a pinch of salt. 'Everybody gaping for the Duke of Kingston's will,' wrote Mrs Delaney. '£4000 a year he settled on her at his marriage (if such it may be allowed). Her widow'd grace fell into fits at *every turn* on the road from Bath; true affection and gratitude surely cannot inhabit such a breast?'

When the duke's will was finally read, the gossips were not disappointed. Evelyn Meadows, Kingston's nephew and presumed heir, had been cut off with only £500, and the duke had bequeathed everything he owned to Elizabeth, with the single proviso that she never marry again. On her death, the estate was to pass to his nephew Charles Meadows, Evelyn's younger brother. 'The Duchess of Kingston is a miracle of moderation!' Horace Walpole wrote soon after the reading. 'She has only taken the whole real estate for her own life, and the personal estate for ever. Evelyn Meadows is totally disinherited.'

Conscious, perhaps, of the things being said about her, Elizabeth did not remain in England for long. As soon as she got her hands on her late husband's legacy she commissioned a sumptuous yacht to be built, hired a captain, loaded the vessel with her clothes, her best jewellery and the finest paintings from the duke's collection, and sailed for Italy. In Rome, the Pope showered honours on her and offered her the use of a cardinal's palace for the duration of her stay. In return for his hospitality, Elizabeth ordered her captain to sail her yacht up the river Tiber into the city, where thousands of citizens cheered her as she waved regally from the deck.

From that moment on, Rome was at Elizabeth's feet. She threw lavish balls, and on one occasion paid for the entire Colosseum to be illuminated for a party. She travelled around in the finest coaches. She bought herself anything and everything she wanted, including, it was said, a theatre. Her vibrant personality, regal manner and reckless spending endeared her to everyone from the highest official in the Vatican to the humblest tradesman.

Yet there was something almost pathological in her sociability. Underneath it, the duchess seemed to be genuinely grieving for her husband – or so she intimated in a letter to the Duke of Portland on 27 April 1774: 'As you do me the honour to interest yourself in my regard, I shall add that my sorrow knows no end, but at Rome I have found Rest, Sleep has restored me to a better state of health than when I left England, but happiness is not for me on this side of the grave.'

While Elizabeth was soaking up adulation in Italy, a small event took place in England that was to have enormous repercussions for her. Ann Craddock, Elizabeth's aunt Mrs Hanmer's now elderly servant from Winchester, went to see Elizabeth's lawyer, Mr Field, and told him that she had been a witness to the former Miss Chudleigh's marriage to Augustus Hervey thirty years earlier. Craddock had kept quiet about this for many years, but she was now very hard up and wanted money for her continuing silence. Field stubbornly refused to give her anything: Elizabeth's status as a spinster had been certified by an ecclesiastical court before her marriage to Kingston, and he would not on principle succumb to blackmail, even when Craddock hinted that if he did not pay her for her information she would take it to Evelyn Meadows, who certainly would.

And he did. Armed with Craddock's testimony, Meadows began his own investigations into his aunt-by-marriage's murky past. Before long he presented the courts with a bill of indictment for bigamy against Elizabeth. A grand jury found the bill true, motions for a trial were set in train and Mr Field was informed that if his client did not return to England to answer the charges against her she would be declared an outlaw.

Field dispatched a letter to Rome, and the moment it reached her Elizabeth ordered her 'maids-of-honour' (as she had always called her female servants) to pack up her clothes and jewellery. While they were doing so, she went to the house of her Roman banker, Mr Jenkins, to get money from him for her journey home. To her dismay, Jenkins's servants insisted that he was out. The Machiavellian Meadows had already been in touch with the banker and had asked him to delay the duchess for as long as he could. When Jenkins did not answer her letters and was continually absent from home, Elizabeth guessed what had happened. Furious, she sat waiting for him on his doorstep, a pair of pistols clutched in her hands. When the banker finally appeared she threatened to shoot him if he did not hand over her money right away. Since she was known to be a good shot (all that hunting she had done with Kingston had not gone to waste), Jenkins caved in.

Leaving her cardinal's palace in the charge of one of her servants, Elizabeth hurried back to England as fast as she could. Ill with anxiety at what she might face, she was carried across the Alps in a litter and forced to take to her bed for a few days in Calais. In London she found an attachment, or writ, waiting for her at Kingston House, Knightsbridge, which prevented her leaving the country again. Terrified by the prospect of imprisonment, she fled. 'Weakened by sickness, as well as sorrow, I have not philosophy enough to support me,' she wrote to the Duke of Portland on 11 July. 'I was obliged to submit, after twenty-four hours being in my house, to be put into my coach, once more to embark for Calais.'

Back in France, Elizabeth took to her bed, convinced that Kingston's disappointed heir was trying to kill her with anxiety. 'Mr Meadows has broke the braised reed and Nature yields to my great affliction; my life is all my enemys [sic] desire' she wrote to Portland at the end of July. By September she had recovered sufficiently to ask him to send her pineapples from his hothouse, her own having failed that year, and she was well enough to instruct him that the fruits 'should but be just turning yellow, and cut with a long stem'.

It was not until the following summer that Elizabeth finally returned to England. By then her story had taken another bizarre twist: Augustus Hervey's elder brother had died without issue in March, and her detested first husband had become the third Earl of Bristol. Elizabeth now had the choice of two titles: if the court found that she was not the Duchess of Kingston, she would become by default the Countess of Bristol.

Assured by Lord Mansfield that she would be granted bail if she returned home, Elizabeth wrote to the Duke of Portland on 14 May, claiming that she was preparing to return home 'arm'd with innocence' and asking him to stand bail for her along with another of her supporters, the Duke of Newcastle. Towards the end of the month, she appeared in the court of King's Bench before her friend

Lord Mansfield, who ordered her to stand trial before her peers at Westminster Hall on an indictment for bigamy. Bailed on sureties of £8000, she started to prepare her case and to educate herself in the law.

Soon Elizabeth had to face yet another scandal when she heard that Samuel Foote, a well-known playwright, had written a comedy rumoured to be based on her story. Lady Kitty Crocodile, the central character of *A Trip to Calais*, was a foul-mouthed harridan who cried crocodile tears over her late husband and badly mistreated her female companions whom, like Elizabeth, she called her 'maids-of-honour'. Mention was made in the play of 'two husbands', private yachts and 'Iphigenia', the masquerade character as whom the young Miss Chudleigh had appeared in a transparent dress back in the 1740s.

As imperious as ever, Elizabeth summoned Foote to Kingston House to read her his play, which included among other incriminating scenes this dialogue:

O'DONOVAN: She couldn't bear to stay in England after the death of her husband, everything there put her so much in mind of her loss. Why, if she met by accident with one of his boots it always set her a-crying. Indeed, the poor gentlewoman was a perfect Niobe.

CLACK: Indeed, I found her Ladyship in a very uncontionable [*sic*] way when I waited on her upon the mournful occasion. Indeed, she was rather more cheerful when she tried on her weeds; and no wonder, for it is a dress vastly becoming, especially to people inclined to be fat.

Half-way through Foote's reading Elizabeth jumped to her feet and told him that the insult was too much to bear. Though he disingenuously insisted that the play had nothing to do with her, Elizabeth offered to buy it from him for £1400. When he demanded £2000, she upped her offer to £1600, but Foote turned her down.

Infuriated, Elizabeth attempted to get the slanderous play banned. If she did, Foote said, he would publish it in book form. A public slanging match followed. Threatened with a whipping by the Duke of Newcastle, Foote was eventually forced to back down. 'I really,

Madam, wish you no ill, and should be sorry to do you an injury,' he wrote to her on 13 August 1775. 'I thereby give up to that consideration, what neither your Grace's offers, nor the threats of your agents could obtain; the scenes shall not be published, nor shall anything appear at my theatre, or from me, that can hurt you. Provided the attacks made on me in the newspapers does not make it necessary for me to act in defence of myself.'

In high dudgeon and seemingly oblivious to the fact that Foote had capitulated, Elizabeth dashed off an angry reply to his 'ill-judged' letter that same evening:

> I know too well what is due to my own dignity, to enter into a compromise with an extortionable assassin of private reputation. If before I abhorred you for your slander, I now despise you for your concessions . . . You first had the cowardly baseness to draw the sword, and if I sheath it, until I make you crouch like the subservient vassal as you are, then there is no spirit in an injured woman, nor meanness in a slanderous buffoon.

Foote replied to this letter with renewed, if controlled, vitriol, referring to her approaching trial for bigamy:

> In those scenes which you so unaccountably apply to yourself, you must observe, that there is not the slightest hint at the little incidents of your life, which have excited the curiosity of the Grand Inquest for the county of Middlesex. I am happy, madam, however, to hear that your robe of innocence is in such perfect repair. I was afraid it might have been a little the worse for the wearing: may it hold out to keep you warm the next winter.

After a good deal of bad publicity, position triumphed over freedom of speech and *A Trip to Calais* was suppressed. Elizabeth did not remain out of the public eye for long: in April 1776, news of the revolution taking place in the American colonies was slashed from the newspapers to make way for reports of her bigamy trial. London was feverish with excitement as the first day of the hearing approached, and tickets to Westminster Hall, where it was to take place, were even more in demand than those for the rural masquerades at Carlisle House. 'All the world, great and *small*, are gone to Westminster *Hall*!' Mrs Delaney wrote to Mary Dewes on the morning of 15 April. 'The solicitude for tickets, the distress of rising early to be time enough for a place, the anxiety about the hairdressers, (poor souls hurried out of their lives), mortifications that feathers and flying lappets should be laid aside for that day, as they would obstruct the view of those who sit behind; – all these important matters were discussed in my little circle last night.'

A huge mob assembled outside Westminster to watch the five thousand peers, peeresses and wealthy spectators arrive. The women were dressed up as if for a ball, and since they would have to remain in their seats for hours on end most carried picnics in their workbags. At half past ten the queen, the Prince of Wales and the Princess Royal entered and took their seats in the royal box, and three-quarters of an hour later a long procession of peers, masters in chancery, judges, barons, bishops, viscounts, earls, marquesses and dukes marched in, followed by the Lord High Steward, the Lord Privy Seal and Black Rod.

Dressed in deep mourning, with a black hood, black gloves and a gown ruffled in black crape, Elizabeth entered Westminster Hall in great style, accompanied by three female attendants, a chaplain, a physician and an apothecary. As she approached the bar she bowed three times then dropped dramatically to her knees, prompting the Lord High Steward to tell her to rise. The charge against her was read out: she was 'indicted of polygamy, and feloniously marrying Evelyn Pierrepont, late Duke of Kingston, she being then married, and the wife of the said Augustus Hervey'. As the Lord High Steward put it, this was 'a crime so destructive of the peace and happiness of private families, and so injurious in its consequences to the welfare and good order of society, that by the statute law of this kingdom it was for many years (in your sex) punishable by death'.

In the months between her return to England and the trial Elizabeth had boned up on the legalities of her case. With great self-possession, she now read out a prepared statement saying that she could not be tried on the present indictment because she had already been found a spinster by the ecclesiastical court in 1769 and had therefore married Kingston in good faith. Told that she must answer the charge, she pleaded not guilty and said that she wished to be tried 'by God and my peers'.

The hearing began. Over the next five days, every sordid piece of dirty linen that Elizabeth had tried to hide over the last thirty years was aired in front of the very people she had sought to keep it from. These ranged from her secret marriage to Hervey in Lainston to the subsequent birth and death of their child. Witnesses for the prosecution included her aunt's old servant Ann Craddock, who had been at the wedding and who had subsequently seen her lying in bed with Hervey, and also Caesar Hawkins, the surgeon who had delivered her son and had later acted as a go-between in their jactitation suit.

Not every witness came willingly to the bar: Lord Barrington, for one, staunchly refused to betray his friend Elizabeth by repeating their confidential conversations; and although the surgeon Caesar Hawkins tried to hide behind his Hippocratic oath of confidentiality, the prosecution pressed him into admitting that he had delivered Elizabeth of a child and that she had talked of Hervey being her husband.

Elizabeth retained a remarkable composure in the face of this all too public humiliation. Her behaviour at the trial was so impeccable that it even impressed her old enemy Horace Walpole. 'Instead of her usual ostentatious folly and clumsy pretensions to cunning, all her conduct was decent, even seemed natural,' he wrote. Yet beneath her calm surface, the duchess was deeply shaken: during cross-examination on the third day of the trial she broke down dramatically and was taken away to be bled by her physician – a sight that Mrs Delaney declared was '*awfull* [*sic*] and *splendid* beyond imagination'.

After a day's adjournment the trial resumed on the eighteenth. The decision of the ecclesiastical court that Elizabeth had been a spinster when she married was set aside, and against the wishes of her lawyers the duchess took the stand to assure her peers of her honest intentions in marrying Kingston, if not her innocence:

'My Lords, with tenderness consider how difficult is the task of myself to speak, nor say too little nor too much; degraded as I am by adversaries, my family despised, the honourable title on which I set an inestimable value, as received from my noble and late dear husband, attempted to be torn from me . . . I appeal now to the feelings of your own hearts, whether it is not cruel that I should be brought as a criminal to a public trial for an act committed upon the sanction of the laws. An act that was honoured by his Majesty's most gracious approbation, and previously known and approved by my Royal mistress, the late Princess Dowager of Wales; and likewise authorised by the Ecclesiastical jurisdiction . . . If therefore I have offended against the law . . . I have so offended without criminal intention, where such intention does not exist your lordships' justice and humanity will tell you there can be no crime, and your lordships looking at my distressed situation with an indulgent eye, will pity me as an unfortunate woman deceived and misled by erroneous opinions of law, of the propriety of which it was impossible for me to judge.'

The lords were moved – but not moved enough to find Elizabeth innocent. As her friend the Duke of Newcastle put it when asked to give his verdict, she was guilty 'erroneously, but not intentionally, upon my honour'. Brought in to hear the verdict, Elizabeth had the cheek to claim the privilege of the peerage – if not as the Duchess of Kingston, then as the Countess of Bristol, the title she now assumed by default – to avoid the barbaric punishment for bigamy that ordinary felons had to suffer, which was to be branded on the hand. The attorney general argued that this was a privilege enjoyed only by male peers, but it was decided in the end that their spouses shared this right with them, and the new Countess of Bristol left the court a free if 'unduchessed' woman (as Mrs Delaney put it) discharged after paying her fees.

Evelyn Meadows was also free – free to pursue Elizabeth through the courts for the return of his uncle's estate and capital. Without wasting a moment, he organized a writ demanding the new

Countess of Bristol's arrest. Elizabeth knew what was coming, and she decided to go out in style. She invited several friends to dine with her the following evening, and made her way back to Kingston House. That night her carriage was seen driving through the streets of London, and it looked to everyone as if she was sitting inside it. But the woman was a stand-in. Elizabeth had already fled to Dover where, rather than wait for the packet boat to leave the next morning, she persuaded her captain to commandeer a small open fishing-boat and sail her straight to Calais, beyond the reach of Meadows's grasping hand.

As the luminous white cliffs receded behind her and bled into the rainy black night, the usually fearless Elizabeth might have experienced a tremor of apprehension about her future. From now on, she would always be an exile. Although she would live for another twelve years, she would never stand on English soil again.

If there was one person who shed tears over her departure, it was Teresa. Since she had arrived in London in 1759, Elizabeth Chudleigh had been her friend, her patroness and her staunch supporter. Being taken up by her had been the making of Teresa. Elizabeth's brilliant social connections and loyal patronage had proved invaluable, and her departure under such a cloud left Teresa in an extremely vulnerable position. For if the notorious and hitherto invulnerable Miss Chudleigh could fall from grace, so Teresa, too, might finally be dashed from the high pinnacle of success she had achieved.

Twenty

Welcome, welcome, Brother Debtor,
To this poor but merry Place,
Where no Bayliff, Dun or Setter
Dare to shew their frightful face.
But, kind Sir, as you're a Stranger,
Down your Garnish you must lay,
Or your Coat will be in Danger, –
You must either strip or pay.

'The Humours of the Fleet' – Poem, An Humorous, descriptive, poem. Written by a Gentleman of the College. 1749

In June 1776 the *ton* toasted Teresa as 'the Mother of Masquerades, Taste and Elegance'. Four months later, abruptly, they abandoned her. An impromptu ball held at Carlisle House in early December might have let people know that Mrs Cornelys was 'still in the land of the living', as one newspaper report put it, but most of her old subscribers did not attend it, and the evening was a dull and somewhat desultory affair. The low price of the tickets had deterred the *beau monde*, who disdained 'to come to any entertainment within reach of the vulgar'. Instead of the eight hundred people Teresa had been expecting, only half that number turned up for it, and most of them were middle-class bank clerks, office workers, journalists, 'filles de Joie and Demireps'.

By the following spring, the quality of Teresa's subscribers had deteriorated even further. 'Composed of persons of every order, and many of them without order', they still included several members of the fashionable set – Georgiana, Duchess of Devonshire, and Lady Grosvenor among them – but although on some occasions the crowd at Carlisle House was a thousand strong, standards of behaviour were low. Evenings at Soho Square now often ended in angry gambling sessions or drunken brawls with the women being insulted by lechers and the men chanting, 'Champagne, Champagne, or no Cornelys!' until Teresa was forced to open another dozen bottles.

Teresa soldiered on. Her sole object now was to stay in business at any cost. If she was forced to lower the high standards she had always prided herself on, that was how it had to be. During the summer break she renovated Carlisle House as best she could on a shoestring budget, and in November reopened her doors to anyone who would pay for tickets. The famous lists of subscribers kept by the Duchesses of Kingston and Northumberland were a thing of the distant past.

To the middle classes who had hitherto been denied access to the famous Soho institution, this presented an unparalleled opportunity to see how the other half lived. 'The night I came to town there was to be a masquerade at Mrs Cornelys's rooms in Soho Square, and Emily said I must go to it with her,' wrote the lawyer William Hickey, of an evening he spent in Carlisle House's 'truly magnificent suite of apartments' that September with his friend's mistress, Emily Warren:

> I therefore sent for a domino, etc, and at ten o'clock she and I drove there . . . She promised me to go home early as I was tired by my journey and little sleep the preceding night, and said that to avoid being importuned to stay by any of her acquaintances. Vanity, however, prevailed over her inclination to oblige me, for, finding herself followed and admired in every direction, she did not resist taking off her mask to let the delighted beholders see that the face corresponded with the figure they had been pursuing from room to room. One mask in particular persevered in following her, and whenever opportunity offered by my talking to any friend, poured abundance of fulsome compliments into her ears. I suspected from her manner she knew who it was, though for some time she assured me she did not.

In the long term, the decline in the quality of Teresa's clientele did not augur well for her. The masquerades and assemblies she was so good at arranging were going out of fashion, and without rich subscribers to bankroll her business she was faced with countless new cash-flow crises. By March 1778 she was broke and Carlisle House was up for sale again. Still she clung on desperately, returning to Soho for a short spell in May 1779. But by the end of November she was back in prison, committed to the King's Bench by a group of creditors who included her old foes Thomas Chippendale and the jeweller Augustus Lesage, a man to whom she now owed £900.

By the following summer, Teresa was still inside, and might safely have predicted she would remain there for ever. However, she was about to be freed in a most unexpected and dramatic way – by the anti-Catholic lobby, the very people who had sought to ruin her first visit to London in 1746. In 1778, the Whig politician Sir George Savile had successfully introduced the first Catholic Relief Act in Parliament, which absolved Roman Catholics who wished to join the army from having to take an oath of allegiance to the Church of England. Passed by Lord North's ministry, the Act had enraged hard-nosed Protestants such as the eccentric and extremist Lord George Gordon, the third son of the third Duke of Gordon.

Gordon founded the Protestant Association, an extremist organization dedicated to repealing Savile's act. On 2 June 1780, he marshalled a huge anti-Catholic demonstration in London. It consisted of more than twenty thousand people, many wearing blue cockades and carrying blue flags bearing the legend 'No Popery'. The demonstrators marched on the House of Commons to present a petition bearing the signatures of between thirty and forty thousand men. In the aftermath, a huge mob assembled in London and would not disperse.

During the next few days Catholic targets, such as chapels and private homes, were attacked, ransacked and burned down, and both Catholics and Protestants were harassed and robbed in the streets. By Tuesday, 6 June, the unrest had turned into a full-blown riot on a scale London had never experienced before. Chaos and anarchy took over the streets, and 'uproar, confusion, and terror reigned in every part'. Lord North was attacked as he left Parliament, the homes of the pro-Catholic Lords Rockingham, Devonshire, Mansfield and Savile were attacked and set on fire, and the increasingly wild and anarchic mob turned its anger on London's prisons. First Newgate prison was set alight and destroyed, and the mob 'dragged out the prisoners, many of them, by the hair of the head, by the legs or arms, or whatever part they could lay hold of'. They helped them escape down ladders, and ambushed a hundred-strong contingent of policemen sent in to save the gaol. Later, the rioters broke open the doors of the Fleet prison and set fire to it, and crossed the river to Southwark where they set upon London's main debtors' gaol, the King's Bench.

Locked in her cell, Teresa could hear the baying of the anti-Catholic mob outside the walls and the splintering of the wooden gates as they were prised open with crow-bars. She could hear the pounding of feet as the rioters ran wild in the corridors, and smell the smoke. When the anti-Catholics broke open her cell door, she did not stand around waiting for explanations but took her chance and fled down the smoke-filled corridors, out into the yard, through the open gates and out into the surrounding streets.

Where did she hide, and to whom did she turn for help? Unlike many of the other 1600 prisoners freed in London that night, who could successfully melt away in the crowd, Teresa was a foreigner and a celebrity, as well known to the mob as she was to tradesmen and society people. Yet even though her face and accent were instantly recognizable, she managed to evade the authorities for nearly three months. By the end of August, she was living in rooms in Cartwright Street, Westminster. There, on the thirty-first, she was picked up, arrested and dragged back to the King's Bench where, like all recaptured prisoners, she was forced to sign an acknowledgement of surrender: 'I do acknowledge myself to have been in the Custody of the Marshall [sic] of the King's Bench prison but set at Large by the Fire of the 7 of June, and came this Day to surrender myself again as Witness my hand this 31 Day of August

1780.' Her signature – a brief T. Cornelys – lacked its usual flourish. Instead, it bore the signs of tiredness and defeat.

Teresa remained in the King's Bench prison until 23 February 1782, when she was discharged at the orders of Lord Chief Justice Lord Mansfield. While she languished in her cell, unable to earn money to pay off her debts and so secure her freedom, the social events at Carlisle House were organized by a variety of managers: a Mr Fierville, Messrs Fisher and Piquais, and a Mr Hoffman of Bishopsgate Street, who had been one of Teresa's creditors when she was arrested in 1779. None of them seemed able to make a success of it. Teresa's past reputation eclipsed them all. When Horace Walpole wrote to the Reverend William Mason on 19 February 1781 that 'Mrs Cornelys, Almack and Dr Graham are forced to advertise diversions by public sale, and everybody goes indolently and mechanically to them all, without choice or preference,' he was referring to Carlisle House, not to Teresa herself. Although the Soho mansion was then under the management of William Wade, the ex-Master of Ceremonies in the city of Bath, to society people it would always be synonymous with Teresa's name.

Throughout most of 1784, Carlisle House was unoccupied. No one wanted it. Teresa's splendid curtains gathered dust at the windows. Chandeliers that had once burned brightly grew tarnished inside their dust-sheets. As shabby and neglected as it had been before Teresa took it over in 1760, the Soho Square mansion was auctioned off yet again in June 1785 when it was advertised as 'late the property of Teresa Cornelys'.

With this sale, Teresa's association with the house that had been the focus of her life for so many years finally ended. At the age of sixty-two, she disappeared from the public stage. She might have lost the business that had given her such a strong sense of identity but she had not quite lost her charms, for sometime during the next five or six years she unexpectedly married again. Nothing is known about her new husband, with the exception of his name, Frederick Smith. By her marriage to him, as if she was playing a joke on history, Anna Maria Teresa Imer Pompeati de Trenti Cornelys became plain Mrs Smith, and as such she slipped neatly into obscurity.

She resurfaced in the cruel glare of publicity in May 1792 when she was referred to in a short article in the *Morning Herald*, under the headline 'Masquerade Intelligence': 'The regular Vauxhall season is this year to be preceded by a Masquerade – the most splendid preparations are in the making, and if we give credit to the general report, the ensuing Fête will as far surpass that of last year, as that exceeded every thing of that kind known in this country since the time of Mrs Carnavelli.' Incensed by this ironic reference to her name, Teresa proudly dashed off an angry letter to *The Times* under the pseudonym Amicus:

Sir, finding the name of a person whom I much esteem mis-represented in the Herald of the 4TH inst., I beg you will insert the following in your excellent Paper as early possible [*sic*]. The day of the above date, in a paragraph entitled *Vauxhall Masquerade*, the Editor of the Herald alludes to Mrs CORNELYS under the appellation of Carnavelli. This same Editor has never failed to write Mrs Cornelys' name properly, when he was pleased to calumniate and take from her the good character she brought into this country, and which she still retains. Mrs Cornelys can produce ample proof to substantiate the truth of both these assertions. It is necessary therefore to inform the Editor of the Herald, as well as you, Sir, (Mrs Cornelys being a constant reader of both your papers) that if you have any occasion in future to make mention of her name, do it in that respectful manner which her great genius and strict probity demands. Her name was Cornelys, is now, and has been for some time past, SMITH, – widow of the late Frederick Smith Esquire. I am Sir, your most obedient humble Servant, AMICUS.

Widowed for the second time – Angelo Pompeati had died back in 1768 – Teresa was by now 'slightly subdued by adversity'. Yet, despite her advanced years – she was sixty-nine – she was still desperate to return to the business she loved and had not yet given up hope of making a comeback. With that in mind, she rented a house in Knightsbridge, which, though barely half a mile from built-up Mayfair, still retained the character of a country village 'quite out of London'. Knightsbridge Grove, as the property was called, was a stone's throw from Elizabeth Chudleigh's old villa, Kingston House. The building dated back to 1670 when a man named Henry Swindell had opened a pleasure garden on the site. By 1711, Swindell's Spring Gardens were being used, among other purposes, to graze a flock of asses; it was advertised in the *Post Boy* that the beasts' milk was 'to be had at Richard Stout's, at the sign of the Ass, at Knightsbridge, for three shillings and sixpence per quart, the ass to be brought to the buyer's door'. When Teresa took over the Grove, the asses were still being dispatched daily to various parts of London. Not only did she continue this practice, she also tended the flock herself.

To her old critics, it seemed like poetic justice that the notorious foreign soprano who had once dictated fashionable mores to the frivolous fast set should be tending asses. The newspapers had a field day: 'The once celebrated Mrs CORNELLYS [*sic*] has taken the house at Knightsbridge, lately occupied by the dealer in *asses milk*. And the grounds are now about to be laid out in a very superior stile, as a *female archery*,' sneered one rag.

It was not, of course, the asses that had aroused Teresa's interest, but Swindell's large if old-fashioned house. Named variously Grove House, the Rural Retreat and the Rural Castle, it stood at the end of a stately avenue of trees surrounded by extensive gardens. In Teresa's opinion, it was the perfect place to introduce the urban English to the kind of 'simple' rural pleasures enjoyed until the French Revolution by Queen Marie Antoinette at Le Petit Trianon in Versailles. Hopeful of attracting a young, aristocratic clientele, who would enjoy picnics, archery, music and simply meandering beneath the trees reciting poetry, Teresa laid out the Grove's gardens with pretty walkways and filled the house with books and musical instruments. Unable to curb her extravagance, she purchased silk-upholstered furniture for the interior and, although the days were long gone when she could afford grand rococo mirrors, she decorated the walls and ceiling of her largest reception room with small pieces of coloured looking-glass.

With the spring sunlight playing off these fragments of tinted mirror like sunlight refracting off an oil-slicked Venetian canal, Teresa sat and waited for the *ton* to arrive. They never came. The pages of the books she had bought remained uncut, and the musical instruments were seldom played. Still hopeful that the venture would take off, she planned to hold a public *fête champêtre* under the patronage of the then Prince of Wales, and when the writer John Taylor dropped in to see 'Mrs Smith' on his way to Hammersmith one day she asked him to persuade the Prince to patronize it.

In the end, her *fête champêtre* never took place. The effort of running the Grove and tending the asses proved too much even for Teresa, and her strength began to give out. But it was her extravagant silk furniture that proved her final downfall. Demanding payment of the £60 14s. she still owed them, the men from whom she had purchased her sofas and chairs sent the bailiffs to Knightsbridge to arrest her. As the brutes manhandled Teresa into their cart she tried bravely to fight them off and received a painful blow to her chest. Although she was injured, the bailiffs hauled her off to Newgate.

Even by the standards of the time, this prison in the City of London was notorious for its dreadful conditions. Burned down during the Gordon Riots, it had been rebuilt to so-called modern standards, but it was still a terrifying place. Prisoners were confined behind four-inch-thick doors in damp plank-lined cells where typhus fever was as rife as the vermin. The only light and air came from small double-gratings set high in the walls. 'I was told by those who attended them,' wrote the prison reformer John Howard, 'that criminals who had affected an air of boldness during their trial, and appeared quite unconcerned at the pronouncing sentence upon them, were struck with horror, and shed tears, when brought to these darksome solitary abodes.' Visiting Newgate during the year before Teresa's incarceration, Dr J. C. Lettsom observed that inmates of both sexes were 'poor, depraved, half-clothed objects', whose dirty garments barely afforded them any modesty, and that even in the women's infirmary the patients were 'in a very distressful state of clothing and filth'. Two hundred women, many of them awaiting transportation to Botany Bay, were crowded together in one ward on the felons' side, and conditions in the female debtors' ward were not much better.

Old, sick and forgotten by her friends, Teresa remained locked up in Newgate for many months, 'reduced to abject misery, and want,' as one newspaper journalist put it, 'immured within the walls of a prison, without any companions to comfort her, but those who are indebted themselves to the humane and benevolent for sustenance'. Worst of all, she had no hope of ever being freed. The conditions in which she was kept and the cruelty with which she was treated by the female warder in charge of her were scandalous: and although the injury to her breast turned into an open, bleeding, cancerous sore, she was denied bandages and water with which to cleanse the wound.

No one visited her, not even her children. Sophie had built a new identity for herself and wanted nothing to do with her mother. Giuseppe had gone abroad. At first he sent Teresa a small allowance. Then she heard he had died. She had lost not only a son but also one of her few remaining sources of income. It would later be claimed that Teresa received a small annuity from one of her old patronesses, Lady Cowper, but there is no evidence to substantiate this. She had been effectively abandoned by society, and her plight scandalized the foreign tourists to London who had once patronized her house. As the Prussian travel writer Johann Wilhelm von Archenholz commented in his guidebook, *A Picture of England*, 'One may with great justice affirm that this person has in an eminent degree contributed to the progress of luxury in England; and it is not a little remarkable that a woman who has occasioned such an extraordinary revolution in the manners and pleasures of a nation be at this moment languishing amidst all the horrors of wretchedness.'

In the autumn of 1796, an old admirer took pity on Teresa and persuaded the authorities to move her from the foetid cells of Newgate to the less harsh confines of the Fleet prison, where she was detained on 9 November, 'committed for want of bail', to answer writs brought by three men: George Clarke, Abraham Porter and William Nicholls.

Though marginally better than Newgate, the Fleet was still a grim place. Sour with the stench of rotting meat from the nearby slaughterhouses of Smithfield market, any breeze that blew over the prison's twenty-five-foot high curtain wall somehow failed to penetrate to the building's heart. The smell inside was nauseating, as it was inside all such English institutions. When compiling his comprehensive report *The State of the Prisons in England and Ireland* John Howard had been unable to sit inside his coach when travelling from prison to prison because the smell that clung to his clothes literally made him sick. Before he could even read through his note-book he first had to fumigate the pages in front of a fire. 'Air which has been breathed,' he wrote, 'is made poisonous to a more intense degree, by the effluvia from the sick, and what else in prisons is offensive.'

The Fleet was no exception. Like Newgate, it had been destroyed in the Gordon Riots of 1780 and rebuilt the following year, but the new building was not much cleaner than its predecessor. The long narrow galleries that ran down the centre of each floor did not lend themselves to the circulation of fresh air, being sixty-six yards long and only seven feet wide with just a small window at either end. Twenty-seven small rooms led off each gallery, each containing a chimney, a window and, for inmates who could afford one, a bed.

As in the outside world, money ruled inside the Fleet. Everything had to be paid for in hard cash, from the chairs one sat on to the leg-irons one might be clapped into. When prisoners arrived they had to pay a £1 6s. 8d. commitment fee, the weekly rent for beds and bedding was half a crown, the best rooms cost up to eight shillings a week, being allowed out for an appearance in court cost 7s. 6d., and discharge fees were twopence less. Then there was 'chummage' – the 'strip-or-pay' practice whereby existing prisoners divested newcomers of their money, valuables and, if there was nothing else to take, their clothes.

If prisoners had money, they lodged on the superior Master's Side of the Fleet where they enjoyed privileges, even luxuries if they could afford them. Their spouses, children and dogs could live with them, they ate decent food and drowned their sorrows in the first-floor tavern, which was run by tapster John Cartright. As well as providing food and drink at a price to the prisoners, Cartright hosted a Wine Club on Mondays and a Beer Club on Thursdays, drinking sessions that went on until 2 a.m. and were enjoyed by the local community as well as by the wealthier inmates.

Not everyone was as lucky. Prisoners with less than five pounds to their name – and that meant many of the debtors – lodged on the Common Side of the gaol, a wing reserved for the destitute. Here, maltreatment and neglect were the norm. As one female inmate of the Fleet that year put it, on the Common Side 'You are considered by the world as a *pauper*, and avoided as if in a lazaretto for the plague; while the *felon*'s side, on the contrary, is the resort of friends.'

Instead of having their own cells, those on the Common Side were crowded into twenty-four-feet-square wards, containing seven sleeping closets or cabins a side. Since there was no such thing as a prisoner's right to eat or a daily ration of bread, they lived off charitable donations made to the prison by wealthy individuals, or off money they had begged from passing pedestrians through a grating in the prison wall. The Common Side was, as one contemporary put it, 'much more unhealthy and not much cleaner than a pig's sty'. Dressed in dirty rags, half starved and suffering from diarrhoea, gaol fever and a variety of illnesses, its inmates literally rotted in their own filth.

It was to the Common Side of the Fleet that seventy-four-year-old Teresa was taken to die. As she drifted in and out of consciousness a dog's bark, a raucous cackle along the gallery, the distant clank of drinking glasses or snatch of a drunken song would take her back to her Soho mansion. Only when she opened her eyes would she have seen that the walls surrounding her were of bare brick and not chinoiserie wallpaper, that the floorboards were rough planks and not a Turkish carpet, and that the hard wooden cot on which her pain-racked body lay was not made up with fine linen pillows and a silk counterpane but, on the contrary, covered with filthy lice-ridden rags. The woman 'who had set the fashions to the most capricious and phlegmatic nation in Europe' had fallen among the lowest of the low.

Then, one day, Sophie deigned to visit her. Though now forty-four, she was still nursing a bitter grudge against her mother. She told her that she believed she was not her daughter at all, but the illegitimate offspring of 'a lady of quality' and Prince Charles Alexander of Lorraine. By this master-stroke of fantasy, designed as much to hurt Teresa as to delude herself, the self-styled Miss Williams disowned both her parents: the most famous lover of all time, and the pioneering businesswoman and impresario who had turned Soho into the centre of London's night-life.

Thereafter, out of form rather than affection, Sophie sent Teresa 'the trifling pittance of half-a-guinea a week', but since this was not enough to pay for a room and food Teresa remained on the Common Side of the prison, living off charity. Word soon spread among her fellow inmates that the famous *Mrs Cornelys* who had once ruled over 'the Vast Regions of Taste' was the same elderly white-haired Mrs Smith, who was now dying of cancer in their midst; and they came to gawp at her out of sheer curiosity.

Among them was Joseph Sumbel, a handsome Sephardic Jew from Morocco. A sometime secretary to the Moroccan ambassador, Sumbel had been detained in the Fleet two days after Teresa had been moved there, when a quarrel with his brother had resulted in him being arrested for contempt of court. Dressed in his colourful and exotic robes, he sat beside Teresa's bed for hours, deeply impressed by her pleasing address, her affable manners and her up-to-date general knowledge, which ranged from the latest news from Westminster to the smallest village gossip. Though she was in her mid-seventies and racked with pain, Teresa had not retreated into bitterness or self-pity. On the contrary, she had retained her exquisite manners, her charm, and her interest in the outside world.

Sumbel was more moved by Teresa's dreadful state of health than her own daughter had been, and thereafter he sent her a pint of wine every day to help relieve her pain. He also told his fiancée Mrs Wells all about her. Mary Wells was a beautiful and famous

English actress who had been detained in the Fleet the previous September for debt after guaranteeing some six hundred pounds' worth of bills on behalf of her feckless brother-in-law. Here she had met Sumbel and had fallen so in love with him that she had changed her name to Leah and was converting to Judaism to marry him (she had broken off relations with her common-law husband, Edward Topham, years before).

Despite the gap in their ages, Teresa and Mrs Wells found they had much in common, for they both knew what it was to be abandoned by the outside world. 'The friends I had in the sunshine of my prosperity had dropped off one by one, and I was left almost destitute,' Mrs Wells would later write in her autobiography, *The Life of Mrs Sumbel, late Wells*. Disgusted as much by her liaison with the Jewish Moroccan as by her conviction for debt, her daughters by Edward Topham were 'altogether lost to the feelings of nature', just like Sophie. They neither came to see her nor sent her money.

Mrs Wells was as impressed by Teresa as Sumbel had been. 'I have known many remarkable characters since my *entré* [*sic*] in life,' she wrote, 'but none deserves to be noticed more than the *once* great Mrs Cornells [*sic*].' Having herself had first-hand experience of the laws governing the treatment of debtors, the actress was contemptuous of them. In her opinion, Teresa's case seemed to typify their worst aspects:

She was removed to Newgate, the county-gaol, for *offending* the bailiff who arrested her, and thus, by those laws which might justly be called *penal*, we see a woman dragged into misery, wretchedness, and want, by the person appointed to execute them – through the vile, villainous *feelings* of a sheriff's officer – a woman, who had the honour of ranking among those who frequented her house the late king of Denmark when in this country, and the first nobility of Europe.

It had been Teresa's misfortune, like her own, to be sent to the Common Side of the prison, and Mrs Wells was at a loss to account for the better treatment meted out by the justice system to real criminals 'unless it be that a highwayman, a housebreaker, or a pickpocket, has a *right* to more lenity from the laws of his country than a debtor'.

Although she was suffering terribly, Teresa still managed to charm Mrs Wells; the skills of seduction she had learned all those years ago in Senator Malipiero's salon overlooking the Grand Canal had never deserted her. Determined to do something to help her, Mrs Wells summoned one of the most famous doctors in London. The Chevalier Bartholomew Ruspini of St Alban's Street was surgeon-dentist to King George III. He was also something of a philanthropist: he did frequent 'good works' for the poor, he was deeply involved in Freemasonry and in 1788 he had founded a charity school called the Royal Cumberland Free Mason School for Little Children (this later became known as the Royal Masonic Institution for Girls).

As well as being an expert in false teeth – he had studied dentistry in Paris – Ruspini had invented an opium-based styptic, which he applied to Teresa's cancerous breast. The abscess dried up, but her pain did not lessen. Without charging her for his services, Ruspini repeatedly returned to attend the elderly Mrs Smith. He did not have to visit her many times. Cancer was single-handedly accomplishing what the combined force of the English courts, her creditors and the vicissitudes of life had failed to do: it was bleeding her dry.

Death was rushing towards her, and Teresa, who had never been scared of anything before, feared it with a vengeance. She had wriggled out of countless tight corners during her lifetime, but this coming confrontation with her Maker was one she could not avoid. Haunted by thoughts of what might await her in the afterlife, she fought against death as forcefully as she had once fought to stay in business.

It was a losing battle. During the third week of August Teresa deteriorated fast. With no relative to call on, the prison governor summoned Mary Wells to her deathbed. The actress found her sitting bolt upright with a large crucifix clutched tightly in her hands. 'In a voice that denoted the most dreadful horror', Teresa cried out repeatedly, 'The devil is dragging me down! The devil is dragging me down!'

Terrified of what was to come, and racked with agonizing pain, Teresa Cornelys, Soho's Empress of Pleasure, died in the Fleet prison on 19 August 1797. She was seventy-four years old.

Epilogue

Teresa Cornelys's Obituary, *Gentleman's Magazine*, 1797

In the Fleet prison, at a very advanced age, Mrs Cornelly [*sic*], a distinguished priestess of fashion, who once made much noise in the world of gaiety . . . She came to this country between thirty and forty years ago; and being of an enterprising spirit, possessing a good understanding, great knowledge of mankind, and specious manners, she contrived to raise herself into notice, and obtained the patronage of the fashionable world to all the amusements her taste and fancy suggested. For many years her large mansion (Carlisle-house) in Soho-square was the favourite region of amusement among the nobility and gentry; and it was so well contrived for diversified amusement, that no other public entertainments could pretend to rival its attractions . . . She remained in obscurity many years, under the name of Mrs Smith; but, a year or two ago, she came forward again; and here the reader will no doubt learn with surprize [*sic*], not unmixed with risibility, the strange transition in her fate; for she, who was once a leader of fashion, became, literally, the superintendent of asses, for she kept a house at Knightbridge [*sic*], and was a vendor of asses' milk. In this situation, however, she still retained a desire of resuming her former pursuits, and for this purpose ornamented a suite of rooms, in order to have, occasionally, a public déjeuné [*sic*] for people of fashion. The manners of the times, however, were changed, and her taste had not adapted itself to the variations of fashion; and, after much expence [*sic*], employed in gaudy and frivolous embellishments, she was obliged to abandon the scheme, and seek an asylum from her creditors . . . Such was the fate of the once-celebrated Mrs Cornelly, whose melancholy end holds forth a warning to the imprudent; for, with common discretion, she might have closed her life in affluence . . . She had a liberal allowance from a lady related to the family of Earl Cowper, who would have increased that allowance, and have settled it on her for life, if she would have renounced her projecting turn, which flattered her with the hope of reviving all her influence in the fashionable world. This visionary prospect, however, she would not resign, and, while she was dreaming of a palace, she died in a gaol!

At the time of Teresa's death, Sophie Williams was still a spinster. When told that her mother was to be buried at the expense of the local parish, she sent back a message that this 'was a burial good enough for a woman who had led such an improper life'. So, on 22 August 1797, three days after her death, Teresa was given a pauper's funeral at the Church of St Sepulchre-without-Newgate, close to the Fleet prison. Her married name, Teresa Smith, was entered into the parish record book, and her age was recorded – inaccurately – as eighty-two.

'An improper life'. It was a damning indictment of a pioneering businesswoman who had realized in the eighteenth century what two hundred years later would become the staple of popular fiction – the rags-to-riches-to-rags story. But Sophie, the daughter on whom Teresa had always doted, despised her mother, and she wanted everyone to know it. Her expensive formal education had taught her to look down on Teresa, not only for being a bankrupt but for being in such a *déclassé* trade as entertainment. Too much rubbing shoulders with the aristocracy had turned Sophie into a snob of the worst kind.

She was also, I suspect, deeply jealous of Teresa. She resented her successes as bitterly as she lamented her failures. And, to Sophie, her mother's worst fault was that she had failed her. Had Teresa really been such a terrible mother? Certainly, she always put her career before her children's happiness, unavoidable in the competitive, cut-throat entertainment business. Likewise, her desire to mould her children's characters in her own image, however misguided, was born out of the desire to equip them to survive in the real world. If Teresa was insensitive to Sophie and Giuseppe's emotional needs, she shared this in common with most eighteenth-century parents. Casanova had rare flashes of insight into the workings of his daughter's mind, but the concept of family dynamics and nurturing psychology had yet to be invented.

Though she did not begin to understand Giuseppe and Sophie, Teresa was scrupulous about providing for them, at no matter what cost to herself. She might have demanded obedience from them, but she also indulged them, and she certainly never expected more from them than she did from herself.

Casanova once suspected that Teresa intended to turn their pretty daughter into a high-class courtesan as an insurance policy for her own old age but, as it turned out, nothing could have been further from the truth. Though *Town and Country Magazine* carried a portrait entitled 'Peeking Tom of Coventry and Miss W . . . ms' in its 'Tête-a-tête' series in 1775, linking Sophie to Lord Coventry, and on one occasion she accused her mother of trying to push her into bed with Lord Pigott, Sophie never married and almost certainly remained a virgin until she died – a marked difference between her and the parents from whom she made such efforts to distance herself.

Teresa always lived life bravely and to the full. Sophie, by contrast, was constantly on the run from the gritty cut-and-thrust of existence. She eventually found refuge in Catholicism, and followed it with rigid dogmatism. Was she content with the loveless, celibate half-life she created for herself? She might have taken great pride in her irreproachable, unblemished reputation but there was a nasty side to her character shown in her attitude to Teresa, and also witnessed by John Taylor, the author of the memoir *Story of My Life*.

Taylor first met Sophie in the early 1770s, when she was fleeing from the scandal of Teresa's bankruptcy and took refuge in his parents' house in Hatton Garden. Captivated by her musical skills and soft, calm, plaintive singing voice, he at first thought her 'a very agreeable companion'. However, underneath the sweetness, he found her hypocritical and 'totally devoid of sensibility'. Though she lacked any real feeling for others – a trait she had perhaps inherited from Teresa – Sophie often pretended to be empathetic in order to please the people she was with.

Poor Sophie had changed her name but she could never escape her childhood. Being brought up in the shadow of her notorious celebrity mother had left her bitter, confused and insecure. Even in her old age, when she was working as a private almoner for George III's daughter, Princess Augusta, she was so suspicious and unforgiving that, as John Taylor recorded, 'a lady who was also patronized by the same Princess for her talents as an artist . . . assured me she was obliged to pay the most cautious homage to Miss Williams, lest she should deprive her of the royal patronage'.

In case his readers might think he was being too harsh on Sophie, Taylor defended himself by claiming that he had 'a moral duty not to suffer artifice, hypocrisy, and ingratitude, to put themselves forward as virtuous qualities'. He had been too young when he had met Sophie 'to be able to pierce through the veil of practised subtlety and dissimulation which she assumed. Far from regretting that I have thus unmasked an artful hypocrite, who has not left any relations to lament her death, I conceive it but just that I should undeceive those whom her cunning might have ensnared into friendship, and hold out a warning to amiable credulity.'

Throughout her adult life Sophie was beholden to the nobility and gentry she so much wanted to be a part of but never could. Instead of going into business on her own account as Teresa had done, she settled for the humble life of a governess. The situation was one of the few respectable options open to her, but that did not stop it being 'considered in the light of a degradation', according to Mary Wollstonecraft, in *Vindication of the Rights of Woman* (1792).

When Sophie first left Soho Square, Lady Harrington employed her as a paid companion to her daughter. After this she worked for Lady Cowper, the Duchess of Newcastle, the Duchess of Beaufort, Lord Newhaven, Lord Dormer, the Marchioness of Tweeddale and the Dowager Lady Spencer. On behalf of Princess Augusta, Sophie later helped to set up the Adult Orphan Institution and the Cheltenham Female Orphan Asylum. What better way to reject one's own parents than by championing the cause of those who have none?

Sophie died on 25 June 1823 at the Mayfair home of the Dowager Viscountess Sidney. She was sixty-nine. Until the end of her life, she remained something of a curiosity, for though she was quick to deny her origins other people never forgot them. Ironically, the obituaries written about her were mostly filled with stories about her infamous mother. Despite her good works on behalf of the orphans whose parentless state she secretly envied, Sophie's relationship to Teresa remained her only real claim to fame.

Giuseppe also went into service after Teresa's downfall. As Joseph Altorf, he took a job as tutor to Thomas William Fermor, the future fourth Earl of Pomfret. One can only presume that the lazy seventeen-year-old ignoramus, who had arrived in London in 1763 scarcely knowing how to hold a pen, had received a better education under his mother's guidance than he had at the best school in Paris, for his charge later praised his old teacher's 'talents, attainments, and moral character'.

Some time between leaving Lord Pomfret's service and Teresa's final imprisonment, Giuseppe went abroad, and his name disappears from the records. As Teresa told the actress Mary Wells, he continued to send her an allowance until his own death, which was some years before hers.

Angelo Pompeati, Giuseppe's nominal father, enjoyed a long and successful career as a choreographer, opera director and set designer at the Habsburg court in Vienna. He was rewarded for his work with gold snuffboxes and an annual salary of three hundred florins. But in his late fifties or early sixties, Pompeati developed a serious intestinal disease. Unable to stand the pain, he killed himself on 21 March 1768 by cutting open his stomach with a razor and 'tearing at his entrails'. Since he was buried in Vienna's St Stephan's Cathedral, where he and Teresa had been married twenty-four years earlier, his death must have been considered an accident rather than suicide.

The Pantheon, which had put Teresa out of business, burned down in 1792, and although it was rebuilt soon afterwards it was never quite as popular again. As for Carlisle House, no one but the remarkable Mrs Cornelys could make a success of running it. Without her, its balls and assemblies were lacklustre. As one journalist wrote in 1780, 'The genius of these rooms, which formerly animated this species of diversion, seems entirely to have deserted them.'

That same year, the house briefly became the headquarters of the School of Eloquence, a debating society run by the grandly named Academy of Sciences and Belle Lettres of Meard Street, Soho. A library of improving books and periodicals was installed, lectures were held on the English language and English customs, and on Thursday nights there were debates on morally uplifting topics such as 'Is Pride in the Class of the Virtues, or of the Vices?' and 'Is not the hope of reclaiming a Libertine a principle [*sic*] cause of conjugal unhappiness?' According to the 'Oratorical Intelligence' column in the *Public Advertiser* which had now replaced the gossipy 'Masquerade Intelligence', these debates promised to provide a 'rational evening's amusement, where hilarity, improvement and decency go hand in hand'.

At the same time, Carlisle House's new owners held thrice-weekly promenades. They attempted to keep up standards of decorum ('No Gentleman will insist on being admitted in Boots' ruled one notice; and another, 'No Gentleman can be permitted to speak in a Mask'), but the evenings lacked the excitement, informality and glamour of Teresa's assemblies. Samuel Curwen, the American loyalist, attended a promenade on the night of 12 November 1780 and found much of Teresa's decorations still intact: her grotto with its ferns; her Egyptian room with its painted hieroglyphics; the Chinese Room and Bridge with their Chippendale furniture and screens; the Concert Room's silk sofas and glass chandeliers. But, as Curwen noted, there was not much life in the place: 'The employment of the company is simply walking through the rooms; being allowed tea, coffee, chocolate, lemonade, orgeat, negus, milk, etc.; admission by ticket, cost, three shillings; dress, decent, full not required; some in boots . . . The ladies were rigged out in gaudy attire, attended by bucks, bloods, and maccaronies, though it is also resorted to by persons of irreproachable character: among the wheat will be tares.' The crowd was seven hundred strong that night, but there were so few staff that it took Curwen a full two hours to get a dish of tea, 'and when served, it was in a slovenly manner on a dirty tea stand. I never saw a place of public resort where the company was treated with so little respect by servants.' These slapdash standards would never have been tolerated in Teresa's day.

The badly run promenades soon petered out, the School of Eloquence closed down, and in January 1782 a series of scientific lectures was held in Carlisle House. This ended in disaster one night when the speaker's apparatus broke down and a drunk pushed his way in 'and not only insulted the Lecturer but the whole Company, who to their discredit had not Spirit enough to give him due chastisement at the rude attack of his unmannerly assailant, and left the Room evidently afraid of personal Injury'.

The life-span of the building was all but over. Later that year, Count Boruwlaski, a thirty-nine-inch tall musician known as 'The Polish Dwarf', performed in Carlisle House's Concert Room during the London lap of his world tour. After that, the mansion was advertised as vacant and to let. By the summer of 1789, it had grown so dilapidated that the *European Magazine* published a long, rambling poem about it entitled 'An Elegy written in Soho Square, on seeing Mrs Cornelys' House in Ruins':

> The fallen fragments of this pile survey,
> Then yield to Memory's toils the residue of day.
> Here Civil phrenzy was approv'd and known;
> Here fashion's tainted stream was bade to flow;
> Here Reason left her elevated throne . . .
> These walls which echo'd with a lover's sighs,
> And gave responsive many an idiot's tale,
> Those gaudy shades which dazzl'd magic eyes
> Those pregnant sounds which harmonized the gale;
> Are all dismember'd, driven, crush'd and torn,
> Like worthless, weightless chaff . . .
>
> The rout is o'er, the revelry is done,
> And irresistless Fate has cloud'd Folly's fun.

Carlisle House was demolished in 1791 and replaced by two smaller buildings fronting on to Soho Square. However, Jacob Leroux's assembly rooms, which Teresa had added on in 1761, were left standing. A committee of Roman Catholic subscribers purchased them, removed the upper floor and consecrated the lower part as a chapel for use by the poor, uneducated Irish Catholics living in the neighbouring parish of St Giles. Thus Teresa's banqueting room, where four hundred of Britain's wealthiest aristocrats had often feasted together at one great horseshoe-shaped table, became in 1792 the religious refuge of undernourished slum-dwellers and a place of solemn sermons.

> To consecrate a Scene to Heaven
> Where thousands knelt at *Beauty's shrine*,
> On High must surely be forgiven;
> Since it but makes it *more divine*

read an epigram published that year 'On a Report that Mrs Cornellys's [*sic*] once celebrated Ball-room is to be converted into a chapel'. The ecclesiastical future of the site, where thousands had once joyously and blasphemously revelled, was set to last. In 1866, the freehold of the entire plot was acquired by 'a very numerous and respectable body of Catholics' and in 1891 all the buildings on the plot, new and old, were pulled down to make way for the present-day St Patrick's Church and its presbytery. As the labourers dug up the foundations of the old assembly rooms, one uncovered a small engraved copper plaque fixed to a wall. 'Not Vain but Grateful,' read the inscription, 'In Honour of the Society and my first Protectress Ye Honble Mrs Elizabeth Chudleigh is Laid the First Stone of this edifice June 19 1761 by me Teresa Cornelys.' What did he make of it? By the late nineteenth century Carlisle House's glittering past had been forgotten, and Soho itself had changed beyond recognition from the days when Teresa had lived there. No longer the haunt of the nobility, it was described variously as 'one of the worst, and hence the cheapest quarters of London', 'a reeking home of filthy vice', and 'a focus of every danger which can menace the health and social order of a city'.

Soho's healthy air, which two hundred years earlier had attracted citizens of the plague-ridden City, was a thing of the past. In 1854, the parish had had its own plague, when more than six hundred of its residents died in 'the most terrible outbreak of cholera which ever occurred in the kingdom', which broke out around the Broad Street pump. Houses once occupied by duchesses, Members of Parliament and the wealthy middle classes were now subdivided into vermin-infested multi-occupancy tenements rented out to poverty-stricken English families, penniless foreign exiles such as Karl Marx, desperate prostitutes and drug addicts (Thomas de Quincey wrote 'The Confessions of an Opium Eater' after sleeping rough in a rat-ridden house in Greek Street). In short, the area had become a festering sore and an embarrassment to the upper classes who, if they ventured into Soho at all, entered with great trepidation and only to undertake charitable works.

Teresa's 'Protectress', whose name had been erroneously inscribed on the copper plaque as 'the Honble *Mrs* Elizabeth Chudleigh' (my italics), was, like Teresa, dead and forgotten. After her final flight from England, the disgraced Duchess of Kingston – or Countess of Bristol as Elizabeth then officially was – settled in Calais for two years while her late husband's disinherited nephew, Evelyn Meadows, pursued her through the English courts in an attempt to get his uncle's will overturned. He failed. The Kingstons' marriage might have been bigamous, but the Nottinghamshire estate, the money and all the possessions the duke had left Elizabeth were ruled to be indisputably hers.

Elizabeth proceeded to do her best to fritter them away. In 1777, she built herself a new yacht and, having obtained permission to fly the French colours from its mast, she sailed it from Calais to St Petersburg, where Catherine the Great plied her with gifts of land and expensive jewellery. Eager to put down new roots, Elizabeth splashed out £12,000 on a vast estate near the city. She called it 'Chudleigh', and set up a brandy distillery there. When she grew bored with Russia she returned to Rome, and later to Paris where she bought a grand house for £9000 and a magnificent mansion, said to have three hundred bedrooms, in St Assise. This huge estate, which had formerly belonged to the French king's brother, was on the market for £55,000, but somehow, in the grand tradition she and Teresa had perfected, Elizabeth managed to get away with paying only £15,000 for it. When it was discovered that the land was overrun with rabbits, she had them shot and sold in the Paris markets, netting herself a handsome income of three hundred guineas a week.

Even in old age, Elizabeth kept the Midas touch, her regal air and her looks. At the age of sixty 'she still retained traces of more than ordinary beauty, and her deportment was the most dignified I ever remarked,' wrote the Baroness d'Oberkirch, Comtesse de Montbrisson, who met her at this time. 'She moved with all the grace and majesty of a goddess . . . Her great knowledge of society, her wit, and brilliant imagination, which reflected as a mirror all that passed before it, gave a brilliancy to her conversation that I have seldom seen equalled.' However, the baroness could not help remarking on Elizabeth's intolerant attitude towards other people: she found her 'proud and self-willed, opposed to almost all received maxims, and variable and inconstant in her fancies and opinions'.

Haughty, charming and still bewitchingly attractive, Elizabeth made two new conquests during her old age. The first was a penniless Albanian adventurer, the second a wealthy Polish aristocrat, Prince Radziwill, who spent the equivalent of £250,000 on wooing her. Although she turned him down, Elizabeth was not without her soft side – or, at least, some sort of a conscience. On hearing that her old enemy Evelyn Meadows was to be arrested for debt at Metz, she hurried from Calais to Versailles and begged the French king for clemency. Then, in an uncharacteristically generous mood, she hired a house for Meadows near Paris, and settled on him the pension that had been destined by the Duke of Kingston's will to go to his younger brother Charles on her death. 'I will only ask whether you have heard that the Duchess of

Kingston has adopted the eldest Meadows, paid his debts, given him £600 a year, and intends to make him her heir?' commented her old foe Horace Walpole, in a letter to Lady Ossory on 6 September 1787. 'Methinks this is robbing Peter to pay *Peter*.'

On 26 August 1788, a year after her reconciliation with Meadows, Elizabeth died unexpectedly at the Hôtel de Parlement d'Angleterre in Paris. She was sixty-eight. Back in England it was rumoured that she had been poisoned 'for she was not one hour dead, till she smelled, and turned black, even to her fingernails! The perpetrator is not known.' Even in death she remained a spendthrift: her corpse was kept at the hotel at a cost of thirty *louis d'or* for a month. Her principal heir was named by the French government as her distant relative, Colonel Glover, but by the time he arrived in France to claim her fortune, Elizabeth's jewels and plate had disappeared into Evelyn Meadows's hands.

Forced to give them back, Meadows once again found himself disinherited. He was missing out on a tidy sum. Elizabeth's Calais palace – 'In splendour it vies with Hampton Court in the days of Wolsey,' claimed the *Star and Evening Advertiser* of 12 May 1789 – was valued at £60,000 and its furniture at a further £8000. Her French fortune was valued at £94,000, her Russian fortune at £100,000 and her English fortune at £20,000. Her cache of jewellery was sensational. It included gifts from the Duchess of Gotha, the Electress of Saxony and Catherine the Great as well as from her late husband, and consisted of diamond rings, diamond combs, diamond buckles, diamond earrings, diamond lockets, diamond necklaces, diamond bracelets, diamond snuff boxes, diamond pins and diamond sprigs for her hair. Then there were her rubies, her emeralds, her pink pearls and her amethysts . . . No wonder a contemporary wag wrote this epitaph for her:

> Here's plac'd at length the rich Maid of Honor.
> How's this! A Single stone upon her?
> 'Tis known to many, nor said by a few,
> Her Title she gain'd, by playing with two.

Teresa outlasted Elizabeth Chudleigh by nine years. Giacomo Casanova outlived Teresa by nine months. After fleeing London in 1754 (like Teresa he was wanted for debt), his peripatetic wanderings took him to Russia, Poland, Austria, Spain, France and back to Italy. It was as much his insatiable intellectual curiosity as his sexual appetite that made it impossible for him to settle anywhere for long. He lived in Venice between 1774 and 1783, supposedly as a secret agent of the Inquisitors, but then he was off again, back to Holland and later to Austria, where in 1784 he entered the service of Sebastian Foscarini, the Venetian ambassador in Vienna.

It was while working as Foscarini's secretary that Casanova first met a young Bohemian nobleman, Count Joseph Charles de Waldstein, seigneur of the castle at Dux. Despite the difference in their ages, Waldstein and Casanova had many things in common, including a love of gambling, Freemasonry and the occult. Waldstein was so taken with Casanova that he asked him to return to Dux with him, and offered him a post cataloguing his vast library, said to consist of some forty thousand books. Initially, Casanova turned him down. But when Foscarini died the following year and he suddenly found himself in need of work, he accepted the count's renewed offer and moved to Bohemia.

Isolated from the society that had been his life-blood, Casanova remained at Dux Castle for the rest of his life. He was not happy. The Prince de Ligne, Waldstein's uncle, met him there when the adventurer was sixty-five, and wrote of him:

He'd be very handsome, if he wasn't ugly. He's tall, of Herculean proportions; but an African complexion, lively eyes full of truth, but which always hint of touchiness, anxiety or rancour, making him seem rather ferocious, easier to anger than to please . . . His spirited turn of phrase and his witticisms are like an extract of Attic salt. He is sensitive and grateful; but if one happens to displease him, he's nasty, aggressive and odious. Giving him a million would not atone for one small joke at his expense.

Although he was still obsessed with women and young girls, Casanova could now only fantasize about them, and took out his frustration on food. As the prince put it, 'No longer able to be a god in the gardens or a satyr in the forests, he's a wolf at the table.'

Frustrated, increasingly peevish and cynical, demanding respect although not necessarily meriting it, Casanova continued to roam the world restlessly, but now his travels were only in his head. In 1788 he published *Icosameron*, a novel about a journey to the centre of the earth. Then, bored almost to the point of madness, he time-travelled into his past and relived his exploits, adventures, friendships and love affairs in vivid detail and recorded them with disarming honesty, in French, in what is today one of the most notorious memoirs ever published, his twelve-volume *Histoire de Ma Vie*.

Despite what he himself called their outrageous cynicism, Casanova predicted that his memoirs would be translated into every language in the world and make him famous. He was right, but it took time. Although he finished the first draft in 1792, the first edited extracts from his memoirs were not published until 1822, a year after his heirs had sold the manuscript to the German publisher F. A. Brockhaus. Not only was Brockhaus's version translated into German, it was also heavily adapted from the original. When parts of this adaptation appeared in France, translated back into French, Brockhaus decided to publish a French edition of his own, and he handed Casanova's original manuscript over to Jean Laforgue, a French professor at Dresden.

Laforgue took what he himself described as the 'indispensable' liberty of rewriting and adapting Casanova's prose to fit the morals of the times. Not only did he remove some of the most 'voluptuous images', he also added many florid passages of his own.

Incredibly, Casanova's original unexpurgated French text did not appear in print until as late as 1960. By then, despite Laforgue's efforts to clean up the memoirs, his name had long become an international byword for a seducer and ladies' man, and the infant once dismissed as an imbecile had spawned a huge and insatiable industry of books, plays, films, exhibitions and academic theses.

The British Library's catalogue currently lists 168 books either by Casanova or about him. They include his own works, his collected letters, biographies and countless eclectic titles scrutinizing every aspect of his life: Casanova the European, Casanova the scientist, Casanova and dissipation, Casanova and the occult, Casanova and the art of happiness. There is a book entitled *The Medical Interest of Casanova's Memoirs* (John Rolleston, 1917), another about his imaginary meeting with the Italian film director Federico Fellini, who made a film about him in 1976 starring Donald Sutherland (*Casanova Rendez-vous con Federico Fellini*, by Liliana Betti, 1975) and the unforgettably titled *The Casanova Sexicon: a manual for liberated men* (Eric Nicol, 2001). Although his memoirs offer readers an unparalleled window into all aspects of eighteenth-century life, including philosophy, it is of course Casanova's countless sexual exploits that are an obsession with the modern world.

Bitter, unhappy, alone but for a relative by marriage and his dog Finette, the man destined to become the most famous lover of all time died at Dux Castle on 4 June 1798, just nine and a half months after Teresa had died in the Fleet prison. The two had certainly been friends and lovers. But might they have been even closer?

Towards the end of Casanova's life, he published a pamphlet entitled *Ne'Amore, Ne'Donne* in which he claimed that his real father was not Gaetano Casanova but Michele Grimani, the owner of the San Samuele theatre. I have another theory, and Teresa is its author. In June 1763, shortly after Casanova brought Giuseppe to London, Teresa received two letters from Giacomo Passano, a Genoese adventurer and sometime employee of Gaetano, Casanova's brother. Both Gaetano and Passano had been party to one of Casanova's attempts to 'impregnate' mystically the gullible Marquise d'Urfé. Now Passano was attempting to blacken the adventurer's name with her. In his letter to Teresa, he asked her to corroborate his view of Casanova's bad character. This was her reply:

Monsieur, I have received two letters from you addressed to Mrs Cornelys, one dated 6TH June and the other the 15TH, both of which merit silence rather than a reply, but I like to see the aim of people who are at either end of the scale, that is to say extremely good or extremely bad. So, with your permission, I would like to find out which one of those qualities is in you. It's certain that you have been very badly informed about Mrs Cornelys's position, monsieur, as you certainly don't know her, for if you did you would not mention a marriage between her and M. de Seingalt. Consequently, as you have promised me a detailed account of his character, I'll tell you everything I know of him. You should therefore know that M. de Casanova was known to my family before I came into this world, and held very dear by it; his birth was also very well known to my father. At four or five years old I was insensible of knowing him, at the age of ten or 11 I lost sight of him, having started to travel. In the year '45 I married in Vienna, in the church of St Stephans. In '54, I saw him again at my father's house, where I had returned to show off my children, who were then in their most tender youth. In '59, I met up with him again in Holland, where he honoured me with a thousand offers of friendship and service. I was on the point of sending my son to Paris, and on discovering that was so he had the kindness to take him there with him to enrol him in the school that I had chosen for him, begging him to send me news from time to time of how he was doing, which M. de Casanova very graciously did according to my wishes and his generous promise.

My son not writing to me as often as I would have liked, I perceived that he was losing the fondness he owed to his mother, consequently I believed it was time that he came to know her and pay her his rightful respect. For this reason, I asked M. de Seingalt, since he was coming to London, to bring him over to me. Having left him in his care, I felt it was right that he brought him back to me as he received him, which he did with great kindness, and I was pleased to be still in time to cure my son's worst faults and to show him everything that belonged to him, here as well as elsewhere.

So you see, Monsieur, that I know nothing of M. de Casanova other than kindness, polite gestures and friendship, and I repeat that I know nothing of him other than honour and integrity, and towards me (as I do not doubt towards everybody) the actions of an honest man.

It's true that all men do thoughtless things during their life, and those who do not do them in their youth do them in their old age, with the unhappy result that when one is old one takes their foolishness with malice, but when one is young one thinks them a dice cast in accordance with their age.

I thank you for all the warnings you have chosen to give me, but believe that I have not taken them as addressed to me.

It remains for me to tell you that the letter which you wrote to my son gives me authentic proof that the author is a man who is unfortunate to have a spirit full of malice and to be the common enemy of good sense.

N.B. This is where to reply to me. My home is still Carlisle House.

This letter speaks volumes about Teresa's loyalty to Casanova. It also hints that something deeper than friendship ties them together. It is the fifth sentence which is so intriguing: 'You should therefore know that M. de Casanova was known to my family before I came into this world, and held very dear by it; his birth was also very well known to my father'.

Although Teresa's assertion that Casanova was known to her family before she was born was untrue (she was two years older than he was) we can attribute this lie to the endearing vanity of a forty-year-old woman anxious not to reveal her real age. However, she goes on to say, 'his birth was also very well known to my father'. Not *very well known* to her entire family, or to both her parents, but *very well known to her father* in particular. What did Teresa mean by this? Perhaps she had discovered something since Sophie's birth that neither she nor Casanova had known before.

Although Casanova writes in his memoirs that his mother first trod the boards under the stage name La Buranella in London, it is extremely likely that Zanetta Casanova joined Giuseppe Imer's San Samuele theatre company immediately after her marriage to her husband Gaetano. We know from Goldoni that Giuseppe was in love with Zanetta, and that they were lovers between 1733 and 1735. Could they, I wonder, have been lovers much earlier than that?

Like most actresses of the time, Zanetta was unfaithful to her husband: her second son, conceived in London, was rumoured to be the child of the then Prince of Wales. Since providing sexual favours to the theatre owners or managers was common behaviour for an actress, Zanetta's affair with Imer might well have begun in 1724 when she first joined the San Samuele troupe. If this was the case, Casanova might have been Giuseppe Imer's natural son and Teresa's half-brother. This would explain what Teresa was hinting at when she wrote that Casanova's birth was 'very well known to my father'.

In many ways, Teresa and Casanova led parallel lives. They were born in the same Venetian parish within yards of each other's homes and within two years of each other. They were baptized in the same church. They played in the same streets and their parents worked in the same theatre. During their teens they were both taken under the wing of the same wealthy benefactor, Senator Malipiero, who loved them both, if in different ways. Though their physiques could not have been more different – Casanova was dark, tall and muscular, Teresa small, voluptuous and fair – their faces were remarkably similar: they shared the same high forehead, the same thick eyebrows, and the same proud hooked nose.

Casanova and Teresa grew up into two restless spirits who travelled widely throughout Europe in search of fame and fortune. Both became infamous and resourceful adventurers, and both took countless lovers – though here Casanova outclassed Teresa by a long way. Like the relationship between many a rivalrous sister and brother, their friendship survived squabbles, harsh criticism of each other and years spent far apart. Having lived equally full lives, they died within nine and a half months of each other.

If Teresa and Casanova were indeed half-siblings, this would make Sophie the child of an unwittingly incestuous love affair. Only Zanetta Casanova or Giuseppe Imer would have been able to confirm this; and perhaps not even they. Casanova scholars prefer the adventurer's own theory – written in a moment of spite – that he was Michele Grimani's son. But what angry child has not at some point wanted to believe that he is not the offspring of ordinary people but of some wealthy nobleman or princess?

The mystery of Casanova's paternity is hidden in the unchanging stones of Venice. The Venetian Republic dissolved itself on 12 May 1797, just three months and a week before Teresa's death, but in the twenty-first century the city of her and Casanova's birth remains uncannily similar to how it was in their day. The cafés in the Piazza San Marco still serve overpriced coffee to tourists, gondoliers still tout for business on the quays of the Piazzetta, and over in the church of San Samuele a priest still celebrates Mass before the same altar where Teresa once said her prayers.

Across the *campo* from the church, the Palazzo Malipiero stands on the banks of the Grand Canal like a dignified elderly gentleman with a yellow pallor. Though it is now more than nine hundred years old, it stubbornly refuses to topple into the waves. Its top floor has been converted into rather grand time-share apartments. Those who can afford to can now sleep in the building where Teresa first embraced Casanova for around two thousand euros a week. Downstairs on the *piano nobile*, the vast salon where she tormented Alvise Malipiero in front of his fifteen-year-old *protégé* is frozen in time. One can almost see Teresa in the corner shadows, exchanging conspiratorial glances with Casanova, and hear her giggle as, egged on by her mother, she refuses the senator the kiss he so craves . . .

Along the back of the palazzo runs the narrow Calle Malipiero. A sign on the corner notifies the casual passer-by that it was once called the Calle della Commedia, and that Giacomo Casanova was born in a house in the street. Off to the left is the Calle del Teatro where the San Samuele once stood. Giuseppe Imer died in poverty in 1758, alienated from the profession he loved, and the site of his beloved theatre is now occupied by a school.

Just round the corner, a gap between two houses leads into a pretty cobbled courtyard called the Corte del Duca Sforza. A large tree towering up in the centre casts a shadow over the colour-washed houses, and at the far end is a small opening under-neath the buildings that leads directly on to a small wooden landing-stage on the Grand Canal. Here Teresa played as a child, and she lived here in one of the houses on the right. The rear windows back on to the Palazzo Malipiero's garden, and through them Malipiero first glimpsed the extraordinary young woman who would come to obsess him. Here, Casanova found Teresa in her bedroom with her admirer, Leonardo Doro. Thirteen years later, he made love to her here, and Sophie was conceived.

From this hidden parochial corner of Venice, Teresa started the long and eventful journey that led her, via Austria, Denmark, Prussia and Paris to the Austrian Netherlands and the United Provinces, and so to England in the hope of finding fame, fortune and an outlet for her prodigious talents. Did she succeed? The answer is, most definitely, yes. Teresa might have died in desperate poverty and she might have failed as a mother, but those are by no means the only criteria for measuring success.

Teresa's achievements were legion. She was a pioneering career businesswoman, an indomitable fighter who refused to bow before the limitations imposed on her by society. Although she was a woman, a Roman Catholic, a foreigner and a single parent, when it came to the world of pleasure she ruled the xenophobic English aristocracy, and clung to power for sixteen years using only her wits. Her subscription concerts, run by Carl Abel and Johann Christian Bach, had a lasting influence on London's musical life, and her balls, masquerades and assemblies gave pleasure to countless thousands. As a party-organizer, her creative skills were second to none. One only has to think of those rural masquerades she masterminded, when her concert room was filled with silk-festooned pavilions and landscaped as an elegant '*Paradis Terreste*', its floor carpeted with fresh turf and shaded by fully grown pine trees, its walls lined with shrubs, its tabletops decorated with odorif-erous hot-house flowers and fountains of water 'with gold and silver fish swimming about in it'.

To this day Teresa Cornelys remains one of England's most significant impresarios. Yet there is no monument to her, either in

Venice or in London. No plaque marks the site of her birth, and she does not have a grave. The London church where she was buried, St Sepulchre-without-Newgate, still stands on the corner of Ludgate and Giltspur Street in the City of London, but most of its graveyard was dug up in 1868 during the construction of a bridge, the Holborn Viaduct. Between 1 and 20 March that year, countless coffins and twenty-seven cases of human remains were disinterred and reburied in the City of London's new cemetery in Ilford, Essex. Teresa's bones were probably among them. But just as her spirit still haunts the Palazzo Malipiero, something of her inhabits St Sepulchre's today. The church has always been famous for its music: the original organ, installed after the Great Fire of 1666, was said to be one of the finest in London. In the late nineteenth century a gifted boy learned to play on it; at the age of fourteen he was subsequently appointed assistant organist at St Sepulchre's. His name was Henry Wood, and he went on to become a world-famous conductor, earn himself a knighthood and found the Promenade Concerts, which have now become an annual British institution at London's Albert Hall. When he died in 1944, it was to St Sepulchre's that Sir Henry Wood's ashes were brought. Teresa is not the only music impresario to have been buried here.

It is in Soho, however, that one senses her lasting presence. More than two hundred years after her death, the area is again the most fashionable corner of central London, and it is still world-famous for its restaurants and night-life. The vice industry that colonized it during the latter half of the twentieth century is now firmly under control, but Soho still reeks of wild nights, fun and illicit sex. There are traces of Teresa everywhere. The liveried footmen who once guarded the doors of Carlisle House might have disappeared long ago, but in their place outside the restaurants and bars one finds stocky bouncers uniformly dressed in sober black coats, whose job it is still to keep out the riff-raff. And although the subscribers list started by Elizabeth Chudleigh belongs to a bygone era, such things have not altogether disappeared. Those wishing to join Soho's fashionable Groucho Club today must still be proposed by two existing members and vetted by a committee of up to fifteen, although nowadays the applicant's eligibility to join is more likely to be a matter of their success rating, rather than a mere accident of birth. The *hoi-polloi* must be kept out somehow, the trendy separated from the unfashionable, the rich from the poor, those-in-the-know from the out-of-touch.

But these are more egalitarian times. In the spirit of the Venetian masquerade, all were equal under the mask of night. And to this day Soho casts a magic cloak over everyone who enters it, no matter how young, old, rich or poor they are. From dusk till dawn, seven days a week, the streets throb with the heartbeat of people who have one thing in common: they are hell-bent on enjoying themselves. You can see them every evening, drinking in groups outside Soho's pubs or sitting at crowded al-fresco café tables sipping cappuccino or a glass of wine. You can glimpse them through the windows of the private clubs and the public bars, the peep-show parlours and the burger joints, the cheap cafés and the luxury shops, the Chinese restaurants and the swanky eateries that, regardless of recessions, are booked solid night after night, week after week. You can brush past them as they spill out of Soho's theatres in the late evening and swarm boisterously along the pavements, talking, laughing, walking arm in arm.

And just as the nobility's coaches and sedan chairs once blocked the routes out of Soho Square on their way back to Mayfair or St James's in the early hours of the morning, so cars, taxis and minicabs begin their journeys home to the suburbs by negotiating Soho's maze of one-way systems, first introduced by Teresa, all crawling in one direction like so many horses 'with their heads towards Greek Street'.

The very breath of Soho's name is still synonymous with a night on the tiles. It conjures up images of seedy dives and elegant restaurants, trendy clubs and drunken midnight binges, late-night celebrations and hung-over mornings. Soho's spirit is one hundred per cent proof enjoyment and, more than any other person, Teresa Cornelys, the Empress of Pleasure, is responsible for creating it. It is the legacy she has left us.

Where Carlisle House attracts the light and gay,
And countless tapers emulate the day.
There youth and beauty chase the hours along,
And aid Time's flight by revelry and song;
There masques and dancers bound on footsteps light
To jocund strains that echo through the night,
Till morning's rosy beam darts full on all
Who leave, tho' loath, this gorgeous festival;
Then worn with pleasure, forth the revellers stray,
And hail with languid looks the new-born day: –
They seek their homes; – there, weary with ennui,
Joyless and dull, is all they hear and see;
Spiritless and void, of every charm bereft,
Unlike that scene of magic they have left,
They chide the lingering hours that move so slow,
Till the night comes, when they again can go
And mingle in the enchantments of Soho.

Bibliography

Four books, more than any others, proved indispensable when writing Teresa Cornelys's biography. The first was the *GLC Survey of London, Vol: 33, the Parish of St Anne Soho*. Pages 73–9 deal with Teresa's career at Carlisle House, and the corresponding endnotes proved invaluable. The second was Giacomo Casanova's *Histoire de Ma Vie*, for which I used the 1960–62 Édition Intégrale published by F. A. Brockhaus, Wiesbaden, and the Bouqins/Robert Laffont edition, edited by Francis Lacassin and published in Paris, 1993. Casanova's text contains many vivid portraits of Teresa and the worlds she inhabited, as well as reported conversations with her, which I have included where relevant.

In the British Library there is an eight-volume *Collection of Cuttings from newspapers, advertisements, playbills etc. formed by Fillinham* (hereafter referred to as Fillinham Collection). Volume II deals with Carlisle House, and contains dozens of contemporary articles about Carlisle House, as well as notices for Teresa's assemblies. The British Library also holds a small, privately published volume entitled *Mrs Cornely's [sic] Entertainments at Carlisle House, Soho Square*, Thomas Mackinlay, Bradford, *circa* 1840, which contains a potted history of Teresa's London career. Other newspaper cuttings about Carlisle House came from D. Foster's *Inns, Taverns, Ale Houses, Coffee Houses, etc. in and around London*, compiled *circa* 1900, and held by the City of Westminster Archives, and from the British Library's Burney Collection of eighteenth-century English newspapers.

Miraculously the Public Records Office in Kew (hereafter referred to as the PRO) still holds details of many of the court cases in which Teresa was embroiled. These are mostly filed under division C12: *Records created, acquired, and inherited by Chancery, and also of the Wardrobe, Royal Household, Exchequer and various commissions, Records of Equity Side, Courts of Chancery, the Six Clerks Office, pleadings 1758–1800*. In order of date, they are: C107/149 Cornelys v. Fermor; C12/1289/16 Cornelys v. Bodycoate;

C12/1585/16 Fermor v. Cornelys; C12/1471/1 Cornelys v. Fermor; C12/1592/3 Fermor v. Cornelys; C12/1485/15 Fermor v. Cornelys; C12/1518/16 Cornelys v. Chamberlain; C12/392/28 Cornelys v. Burger [*sic*]. These provided detailed records of Teresa's legal and financial affairs, her relationships with John Fermor, her *modus operandi* at Carlisle House and her day-to-day whereabouts. The Public Records Office also holds the Fleet Prison Commitment Books in which the details of all prisoners committed to the Fleet were recorded, as well as other records relating to the King's Bench prison and the Gordon Riots (PRIS10/136).

For Horace Walpole's letters I used: W. S. Lewis (ed.), *Horace Walpole's Correspondence*, Yale University Press, New Haven, 1937–61. For the letters of Mrs Delaney: Mary Granville, *The Autobiography and Correspondence of Mary Granville, Mrs Delaney, Edited by Right Honourable Lady Llanover*, Richard Bentley, London, 1862. For Lady Mary Coke's letters: *Letters and Journals of Lady Mary Coke*, Edinburgh, 1889–96. Mrs Harris's letters were taken from James Harris, *A series of Letters of the 1st Earl of Malmesbury, his family and friends from 1745 to 1820*, Richard Bentley, London, 1870.

Detailed information on opera and theatre in London during the eighteenth century came from: P. H. Highfill, K. A. Burnim and E. A. Langhans, *A Biographical Dictionary of Actors, Actresses, Musicians, dancers, managers & Other Stage Personnel in London, 1660–1800*, vol. 3, Southern Illinois University Press, Carbondale, 1975; and A. H. Scouten (ed.), *The London Stage 1660–1800*, Southern Illinois University Press, Carbondale, 1960–68.

Other sources of general information on musicians and composers I used were: Stanley Sadie and Ian Jacobs (eds), *The New Grove Dictionary of Music and Musicians*, Macmillan, London, 1995; Stanley Sadie (ed.), *New Grove Dictionary of Opera*, Macmillan, London, 1992; Sir Leslie Stephen and Sir Sidney Lee, *The Dictionary of National Biography*, Oxford University Press, Oxford, 1949–50.

One

Descriptions of Giuseppe Imer, Zanetta Casanova, the San Samuele Theatre Company's stay in Verona, and Carlo Goldoni's relationship with them, were drawn from Chapters 34 to 36 of Carlo Goldoni, *Mémoires de M. Goldoni*, Paris, 1787. Goldoni's memoirs also provided information on contemporary Venice, in particular the description of the city at night. Also for Giuseppe Imer: Francesco Bartoli, *Notizie istoriche de Comici Italiani*, Padova, 1782. For Teresa Imer as a child, her mother Paolina, and Casanova's early life: Giacomo Casanova's *Histoire de Ma Vie*, *op. cit.* For Marianna Imer: Aldo Ravà, *Lettere di donne a Giacomo Casanova*, Milan, 1912.

For details of Casanova's life, in this chapter and throughout the book, I used: his own *Histoire de Ma Vie*, *op. cit.*; J. Rives Childs, *Casanova*, George Allen and Unwin, London, 1961; Edouard Maynial, *Casanova et son temps*, Chapman & Hall, London, 1911; Charles Samaran, *Jacques Casanova, Vénitien, Une Vie d'Aventure au XVIIIème Siècle*, Calman-Lévy, Paris, 1914.

For the general history of Venice: Maurice Andrieux, *Daily Life in Venice at the time of Casanova*, translated by Mary Fitton, George Allen and Unwin, London, 1972; Christopher Hibbert, *Venice, the Biography of a City*, Grafton Books, London, 1988; Alfonso Lowe, *La Serenissima, The Last Flowering of the Venetian Republic*, Cassell, London, 1974; James Morris, *Venice*, Faber and Faber, London, 1960.

For descriptions of the English in Venice and the letters of Lady Mary Wortley Montagu: *The Letters and Works of Lady Mary Wortley Montagu*, George Bell and Sons, London, 1898; and Isobel Grundy (ed.), *Lady Mary Wortley Montagu, Selected Letters*, Penguin, London, 1997; Clare Honsby (ed.), *The Impact of Italy: the Grand Tour and beyond*, British School at Rome, London, 2000.

For theatrical life in Venice: Charles de Brosses, *Lettres écrites d'Italie à quelques amis en 1739 et 1741*, Paris, 1836; Marvin Carlson, *The Italian Stage from Goldoni to D'Annunzio*, McFarland, London, 1981; Carlo Gozzi, *The Useless Memoires of Carlo Gozzi*, translated by John Symonds, J. C. Nimmo, London, 1890; Taddeo Weil, *l Teatri Musicali Veneziani del settecento*, Venice, 1897.

The Goldoni Museum in Venice supplied further archive information, including original opera libretti. For Senator Malipiero and his relationship with Teresa, Casanova's *Histoire de Ma Vie*, *op. cit.*

Two

For information on Ascension Day in Venice, see books on the general history of Venice, cited on page 307. For Christoph Willibald Gluck, in this and subsequent chapters: Alfred Einstein, *Gluck*, translated by Eric Blom, J. M. Dent & Son, London, 1936; Patricia Howard, *Gluck, an eighteenth century portrait in letters and documents*, Clarendon Press, Oxford, 1995; Hedwig and E. H. Muller von Asow (eds), *The Collected Correspondence and Papers of Christoph Willibald Gluck*, translated by Stewart Thomson, Barrie and Rockliff, London, 1962.

For biographical details of Angelo Pompeati: Riki Raab, *Biographischer Index des Wiener Opernballets von 1631*, Hollinek, Vienna, 1994. For theatrical life in Vienna: Mary Kathleen Hunter, *The Culture of Opera Buffa in Mozart's Vienna, a poetics of entertainment*, Yale University Press, New Haven, 1999.

On the Jacobite rebellion: Roy Porter, *English Society in the 18th Century*, Allen Lane, London, 1982; Simon Schama, *History of Britain*, BBC, London, 2000. For the Duke of Cumberland: Sir Leslie Stephen and Sir Sidney Lee, *The Dictionary of National Biography*, Oxford University Press, Oxford, 1949–50. For details of what was going on in London when Teresa arrived there: contemporary editions of the *Daily Advertiser*, in the British Library's Burney collection.

Information on daily life in London in this chapter came from many sources including: Roy Porter, *London – A Social History*, Hamish Hamilton, London, 1994; contemporary newspapers in the British Library's Burney Collection. On smog: Pierre Jean Grosley, *A tour to London, or new observations on England and its Inhabitants*, translated from the French by T. Nugent, London, 1772.

For Johann Heidegger: Anon., *A Critical Discourse upon Opera's in England*, 1709; *Dictionary of National Biography*; P. H. Highfill, K. A. Burnim, E. A. Langhans, *A Biographical Dictionary of Actors, Actresses,*

Musicians, dancers, managers & Other Stage Personnel in London, 1660–1800, vol. 3, Southern Illinois University Press, Carbondale, 1975–93.

For information on London's musical scene in general: H. Diack Johnstone and Roger Fiske (eds), *History of Music in Britain: vol. 4: The 18th Century*, Blackwell, Oxford, 1990; Heinz Gartner, *John Christian Bach – Mozart's friend and mentor*, translated by Reinhard G. Pauly, Amadeus Press, Portland, Oregon, 1994; Ian Jacobs (ed.), *Grove's Dictionary of Music*, Macmillan, London, 1977; Ian Woodfield, *Opera and Drama in 18th Century London: the King's Theatre, Garrick and the business of performance*, Cambridge University Press, Cambridge, 2001. For general musical life: H. W. Pedicord, *'By Their Majesties' Command': The House of Hanover at the London Theatres*, Society for Theatre Research, London, 1991.

For details of anti-Catholic feeling in London in 1745/6, Gluck's fears, and review of *La Caduta*: Charles Burney, *A General History of Music, from the earliest ages to the present period*, London, 1776–89. For the libretto of *La Caduta dei Giganti*: Christoph Willibald Gluck, *La Caduta dei Giganti, The favorite Songs in the opera call'd La Caduta de' Giganti*, London, 1746.

For information on specific performances at the King's and other London theatres: A. H. Scouten (ed.), *The London Stage 1660–1800*, vol. 3, 1729–47, Southern Illinois University Press, Carbondale, 1960–68.

Three

For information on the Viennese opera and Teresa's labour, including excerpts from Count Khevenhüller-Metsch's diary: Elisabeth Grossegger, *Vienna: Theater, Feste und Feiern zur Zeit Maria Theresias 1742–1776*, Verlag des Österreichischen Akademie der Wissenschaften, Vienna, 1987; Gustav Zechmeister, *Die Wiener Theater Nächst der Burg und Näschst dem Kärntnerthor von 1747 bis 1776*, Vienna, 1971. For biographical details of Angelo Pompeati: *Biographischer Index des Wiener Opernballets von 1631*, Wien, 1994.

Information on the Mingotti company, including their performances and members, and the letters of Marianna Pirker came from: E. H. Mueller von Asow, *Angelo und Pietro Mingotti*, Dresden, 1917, and *Die Mingottischen Opernunternehmungen 1732–1756*, Dresden, 1915. Marianna

Pirker's letters to her husband, held by the Hauptstaatsarchiv in Stuttgart, ref: A.202 Bü: 2839–2842.

For the history of Bayreuth and life under the margrave and margravine: Edith C. Cuthell, *Wilhelmina, Margravine of Baireuth*, Chapman and Hall, London, 1905; Gérard Doscot (ed.), *Mémoires de Frédérique Sophie Wilhelmine, margrave de Bayreuth, soeur de Frédéric le Grand, depuis l'année 1706 jusqu'à 1742, écrits par sa main*, Paris, 1967; Hon. Mrs Mary Willoughby Burrell, *Thoughts for Enthusiasts at Bayreuth*, Pickering & Chatto, London, 1888–91; Constance C. Wright, *A Royal Affinity. The lives of Frederick the Great and Wilhelmina of Bayreuth*, Frederick Muller, London, 1967.

For information on the musical world of Europe: Charles Burney, *The Present State of Music in Germany, the Netherlands, and the United Provinces. Or, the Journal of a tour through those countries, undertaken to collect materials for a General History of Music*, London, 1773.

Four

Details of Teresa's return to Venice and her meeting with Casanova from Casanova's *Histoire de Ma Vie, op. cit*. For Casanova's life since leaving Venice: J. Rives Childs, *Casanova*, George Allen and Unwin, London, 1961; Edouard Maynial, *Casanova et son temps*, Chapman & Hall, London, 1911; Charles Samaran, *Jacques Casanova, Vénitien, Une Vie d'Aventure au XVIIIème Siècle*, Calman-Lévy, Paris, 1914.

I obtained details of Teresa's life and movements in Paris from *Archives de la Bastille*, 10242.f.445–6, held by the Bibliothèque de L'Arsenale, Paris. Also for Paris: Barbara G. Mittman, *Spectators of the Paris Stage in the 17th and 18th Centuries*, Ann Arbor, Michigan, 1984.

For Prince Charles of Lorraine: Jo Gerard, *Charles de Lorraine, ou La Joie de Vivre*, Luconti, Brussels, 1973; J. Schouteden-Wery, *Charles de Lorraine et son temps*, Charles Dessart, Brussels, 1943. For the Austrian Netherlands: Charles Butler, *Travels through France & Italy, and part of Austrian, French and Dutch Netherlands, during the years 1745 & 1746*, London, 1803; Frédéric Faber, *Histoire du Théâtre Français en Belgique depuis son origine jusqu'à nos jours, d'après des documents inédits*, Brussels, 1878–80; Maurice Heins, *Les Etapes de l'histoire sociale de la Belgique, Bruxelles,*

Anvers, Gand, Liège, Brussels, 1895; Albert Jacquot, *Documents sur le Théâtre en Belgique sous le Gouvernement du Prince Charles-Alexandre de Lorraine*, Paris, 1911; John Macky, *A Journey Through the Austrian Netherlands*, London, 1732; James Shaw, *Sketches of the history of the Austrian Netherlands; with remarks on the constitution, commerce, arts, and general state of these Provinces*, London, 1786.

For Teresa's stay in Gand: Prosper Claeys, *Histoire du Théâtre à Gand*, Gand, 1892; A. Neuville, *Revue Historique, chronologique et anecdotique du Théâtre de Gand de l'année 1750 à 1828*, Gand, 1828. For her stay in Liège: Jules Martiny, *Histoire du Théâtre de Liège depuis son origine jusqu'à nos jours*, Liège, 1887; *Journal Encyclopédique*, Gand, April 1758.

Five

Much of the information in this chapter is drawn directly from Giacomo Casanova, *Histoire de Ma Vie, op. cit.* The Bouquins edition contains countless useful footnotes with added information about Teresa's lovers in the Dutch Republic. Also: Charles Burney, *The present State of Music in Germany, the Netherlands, and the United Provinces*, London, 1773; Michael North, *Art and Commerce in the Dutch Golden Age*, translated by Catherine Hill, Yale University Press, New Haven, 1997.

Six

For details of Sir Henry Fermor: John Burke, *Burkes Extinct and Dormant Baronetcies of 1844*, J. Russell Smith, London, 1964. For details of the Fermor family: John Hackwork, *Sir Henry Fermor Church of England School 1744–1994, A History*, Sir Henry Fermor School, Crowborough, 1994. For Sir Henry Fermor's obituary: *Gentleman's Magazine*, June 1734. For details of Sir Henry Fermor's will probate of 1732: 01000/7/T89, and the title deeds to Fermor property ul1815/T2, held by Sevenoaks Public Library, Sevenoaks, Kent. Newspaper cutting on the Fermor Charity from *The Courier*, 11/05/1734. For information on the village of Crayford: Edward Hasted, *Historical and Topographical Survey of the county of Kent*,

1797–1801, vol. II. Information about John Fermor's relationship with Teresa in this and subsequent chapters is drawn from records of litigation between them held at the PRO, and listed above (pages 305–6).

Seven

For information on Elizabeth Chudleigh, the Duchess of Kingston, in this and subsequent chapters: Beatrice Curtis Brown, *Elizabeth Chudleigh, Duchess of Kingston*, Gerald Howe, London, 1927; Elizabeth Hervey, *The Life and Memoirs of Elizabeth Chudleigh . . . commonly called Duchess of Kingston*, London, 1788; Doris Leslie, *The Incredible Duchess: the life and times of Elizabeth Chudleigh*, Heinemann, London, 1974; Elizabeth Osborn Mavor, *The Virgin Mistress – A Study in Survival*, Chatto and Windus, London, 1964; Charles E. Pearce, *The Amazing Duchess: being the romantic history of Elizabeth Chudleigh*, Stanley Paul and Co., London, 1911; Sir Leslie Stephen and Sir Sidney Lee, *Dictionary of National Biography*, Oxford University Press, Oxford, 1949–50; Marchioness de la Touche, *Les Aventures trop amoureuses, ou Elisabeth Chudleigh . . . et la Marquise de la Touche sur la scène du Monde, etc.*, London, 1776; Thomas Whitehead, *Original Anecdotes of the late Duke of Kingston and Miss Chudleigh by Thomas Whitehead, Many years a servant to the duke of Kingston*, London, 1792; *An Authentic Detail of particulars relative to the Duchess of Kingston*, London, 1788. For Lady Mary Chudleigh's poetry: *Poems by Eminent ladies*, R. Baldwin, London, 1755; Eugenia (Lady Mary Chudleigh), *The Female Advocate; or, a plea for the just liberty of the tender sex, and particularly of married women*, Andrew Bell, London, 1700; Lady Mary Chudleigh, *The Ladies Defence: or, the Bride-Woman's Counsellor answered: a poem etc.*, London, 1709.

For descriptions of Kingston House: *GLC Survey of London*, vol. 45. For Elizabeth's circle of friends: Erroll Sherson, *The Lively Lady Townsend and her Friends*, William Heinemann, London, 1926. Details of the Duke of Kingston's profligacy and debts: J. V. Beckett, *The Aristocracy in England 1660–1914*, Basil Blackwell, Oxford, 1986.

Dates and details of the benefit concert held on Teresa's behalf, and her début concert at the Little Theatre came from contemporary newspapers for 1759/60 held in the Burney Collection of the British Library.

Eight

For life at the Hanoverian Court: Alan Lloyd, *The Wickedest Age: The Life and Times of George III*, David and Charles, Newton Abbot 1971; Roy Porter, *London – A Social History*, Hamish Hamilton, London, 1994. For Oliver Goldsmith's quote on the aristocracy: Oliver Goldsmith, *The Citizen of the World*, London, 1762.

For London's pleasure gardens: Giacomo Casanova, *Histoire de Ma Vie*, op. cit.; Friedrich von Kielmansegge, *The Diary of a Journey to England in the years 1761–1762 . . . translated by his wife*, Longmans and Co., London, 1902; Robert Lathan and Lillian Matthews (eds), *The Diary of Samuel Pepys*, Harper Collins, London, 1995; Mollie Sands, *The Eighteenth-century Pleasure Gardens of Marylebone 1737–1777*, Society for Theatre Research, London, 1987; W. W. and A. E. Wroth, *A Description of Ranelagh Rotundo, and Gardens etc.*, Richard Owen Cambridge, London, 1762, and *The London Pleasure Gardens of the 18th century*, Macmillan, London, 1896.

For musical and theatrical life in London: Thomas Bauman and Marita Petzoldt, *Opera and the Enlightenment*, Cambridge University Press, Cambridge, 1995; P. H. Highfill, K. A. Burnim, E. A. Langhans, *A Biographical Dictionary of Actors, Actresses, Musicians, dancers, managers & Other Stage Personnel in London, 1660–1800*, Southern Illinois University Press, Carbondale, 1975–93; Simon McVeigh, *Concert Life in London from Mozart to Haydn*, Cambridge University Press, Cambridge, 1993; F. Petty, *Italian Opera in London 1760–1800*, Ann Arbor, Michigan, 1980; Curtis Price, Judith Milhous and Robert D. Hume, *Italian Opera in Late 18th Century London*, vol. I, Clarendon, Oxford, 1995 and *The Impresario's Ten Commandments: Continental Recruitment for Italian Opera in London 1763–1764*, Royal Musical Association, London, 1992; A. H. Scouten (ed.), *The London Stage 1660–1800*, vol. 3, 1729–47, Southern Illinois University Press, Carbondale, 1960–68; Ian Woodfield, *Opera and Drama in 18th Century London: the King's Theatre, Garrick and the business of performance*, Cambridge University Press, Cambridge, 2001; *The Theatrical Monitor*, London, 1768.

For descriptions of contemporary London in this and subsequent chapters: Johann Wilhelm von Archenholz, *A Picture of England*, London, 1797; Mary Coke, *The Letters and Journals of Lady Mary Coke*, ed. J. A. Home, Kingsmead Bookshops, Bath, 1970; Henry Chamberlain, *A New and Compleat History and Survey of the Cities of London and Westminster*, London, 1770; John Entick, *A new and accurate History and Survey of London, Westminster, Southwark and Places adjacent etc.*, London, 1766; J. P. Grosley, *Londres (An account of the City and suburbs, with a map of the same)*, Paris, 1788; William Hickey, *Memoirs of William Hickey*, ed. Peter Quennell, Routledge and Kegan Paul, London, 1975; Sophie de la Roche, *Sophie in London, 1786: being the diary of Sophie V. de la Roche*, translated by Clare Williams, Jonathan Cape, London, 1933; *The Autobiography and Correspondence of Mary Granville, Mrs Delaney, Edited by Right Honourable Lady Llanover*, Richard Bentley, London, 1862.

For information on the general history of Soho, Soho Square and Carlisle House I used my own book, *Soho, A History of London's Most Colourful Neighbourhood*, Bloomsbury, London, 1989. Information on the lease of Carlisle House, its previous tenants and its dimensions was drawn from the Papers of the Third Duke of Portland, University of Nottingham archive (PL E10/2/1/2). Additional information on Soho and Carlisle House from the *GLC Survey of London*, vol. 33.

Nine

For further information on John Fermor: John Hackwork, *Sir Henry Fermor Church of England School 1744–1994, A History*, Sir Henry Fermor School, Crowborough, 1994. For Fermor's partnership agreement with Teresa, details of their meetings and their IOUs, and the early financial accounts of Carlisle House, I used Records held by Chancery at the PRO, as listed on pages 305–6, but in particular *Cornelys v. Fermor, Papers of Anna Maria Teresa Pompeati Cornelys* (C107/149) and C12/1471/1. Teresa's newspaper advertisements and announcements were placed in the *Public Advertiser*, 1760/61, available on microfilm as part of the British Library's Burney Collection.

Ten

For Teresa's contract with Samuel Norman, which contained details of the interior of Carlisle House: Records held by Chancery at the PRO in particular *Cornelys v. Fermor* (1763/4) C12/1471/1. For details of the IOUs written out between Teresa and Fermor, Records held by Chancery, *Cornelys v. Fermor*, Papers of Anna Maria Teresa Pompeati Cornelys, C107/149 (1760–61). For details of the meeting in October between Teresa, Norman and Fermor: *Fermor v. Cornelys* (1763) PRO C12/1585/16. For inventory of the furniture and building works at Carlisle House: *Cornelys v. Bodycoate* (1762) PRO C12/1289/16. For the inscription on the brass plaque: Westminster Public Library cutting in A.132.1.

Count Friedrich von Kielmansegge's description of a night at Carlisle House came from his *The Diary of a Journey to England in the years 1761–1762, by Count Friedrich von Kielmansegge, translated by his wife*, Longmans and Co., London, 1902.

For Joseph Merlin and his visits to Carlisle House I used: *GLC Survey of London*, vol. 33; *John Joseph Merlin*, catalogue of an exhibition published by the Iveagh Bequest, London, 1985; Thomas Busby, *Concert Room and Orchestra Anecdotes*, London, 1825.

For list of residents in Soho Square: *GLC Survey of London*, vol. 33; ratebooks for the parish of St Anne, Soho, Westminster Public Libraries.

For Miss Dewes's letter: *The Autobiography and Correspondence of Mary Granville, Mrs Delaney, Edited by Right Honourable Lady Llanover*, Richard Bentley, London, 1862.

Eleven and Twelve

For Teresa's business dealings with Samuel Norman, and John Fermor, Records held by Chancery at the PRO, in particular *Cornelys v. Fermor* (1763/4) C12/1471/1 and *Cornelys v. Bodycoate* (1762) PRO C12/1289/16.

Most of the information on Casanova's relationship with Giuseppe Pompeati; Giuseppe's sojourn in Paris; his relationship with the Marquise d'Urfé; Casanova and Giuseppe's journey to London; and Casanova's stay in London, including reported conversations with Teresa, Giacomo Casanova, *Histoire de Ma Vie, op. cit.* In addition: Horace Bleakley, *Casanova in England,* Bodley Head, London, 1923; A. Compigne, *Casanova et la Marquise d'Urfé,* Paris, 1922.

The scenes and reported conversations between Teresa, Casanova and her children in Chapter Twelve are drawn from Casanova's *Histoire de Ma Vie.*

Thirteen

For Sophie's boarding-school: Giacomo Casanova, *Histoire de Ma Vie, op. cit.*; *GLC Survey of London,* vol. 6, Parish of Hammersmith; Denis Evinson, *Pope's Corner, an historical survey of the Roman Catholic Institutions in the London Borough of Hammersmith and Fulham,* Fulham and Hammersmith Historical Society, London, 1980.

Sophie's obituary was in the *Gentleman's Magazine,* 1823; *Notes and Queries,* 7 July 1894 (p. 3); Horace Bleakley, *Casanova in England,* Bodley Head, London, 1923. For Mozart's connection to Carlisle House, and for the Bach/Abel subscription concerts: Emily Anderson, *Mozart, A documentary biography,* Macmillan, London, 1966; Emily Anderson (ed.), *The Letters of Mozart and His Family,* Macmillan, London, 1938; Heinz Gartner, *J. C. Bach, Mozart's Friend and Mentor,* translated by Reinhard Pauly, Amadeus, Portland, Oregon, 1994.

For information on Mrs Cornelys's concert series and London's musical scene in general: H. Diack Johnstone and Roger Fiske, *History of Music in Britain, vol. 4: the 18th Century,* Blackwell, Oxford, 1990; Ian Jacobs (ed.), *Grove's Dictionary of Music,* Macmillan, London, 1977; Ian Woodfield, *Opera and Drama in 18th Century London: the King's Theatre, Garrick and the business of performance,* Cambridge University Press, Cambridge, 2001. For general musical life: H. W. Pedicord, *'By Their Majesties' Command': The House of Hanover at the London Theatres,* Society for Theatre Research, London, 1991.

For information on Almack's Assembly Rooms: Edwin Beresford Chancellor, *Memorials of St James's Street, together with the annals of Almack's,*

Grant Richards, London, 1922; Robert Elkin, *The Old Concert Rooms of London*, Edward Arnold, London, 1955; Anthony Lejeune and Malcolm Lewis, *The Gentlemen's Clubs of London*, Macdonald and Jane's, London, 1979. For the poem: Henry Luttrell, *Advice to Julia*, London, 1820. For the letters of Mrs Harris in this and subsequent chapters: James Harris, Earl of Malmesbury, *A Series of letters of the First Earl of Malmesbury, his family and friends from 1745 to 1820*, Richard Bentley, London, 1870.

Fourteen

For Teresa's relationship with her servant John Berger: records held by the PRO as listed above but in particular: *Cornelys v. Burger* (1772) PRO C12/392/28. For the diaries of the Duchess of Northumberland: Elizabeth Percy, *Diaries of a Duchess, Extracts from the Diaries of the First Duchess of Northumberland, 1716–1776, edited by James Grieg*, Hodder & Stoughton, London, 1926. Teresa's debts and her attempt to buy the opera house are detailed in: *Catalogue of Papers of Third Duke of Portland*, PWF 3088-PW F 3095, held by the University of Nottingham, and are reproduced with their permission. For Elizabeth Pappet: P. H. Highfill, K. A. Burnim, E. A. Langhans, *A Biographical Dictionary of Actors, Actresses, Musicians, dancers, managers and other stage personnel in London 1660–1800*, Southern Illinois University Press, Carbondale, 1975. For Captain Peter Denis: Sir Leslie Stephen and Sir Sidney Lee, *Dictionary of National Biography*, Oxford University Press, Oxford, 1949–50. Details of leases of the King's Theatre: *Chancery Masters Exhibit*, C107/65, PRO. Details of Teresa's bank account at Drummond's are held by the Archives of Drummond's Bank in the Royal Bank of Scotland. For details of Teresa's lawyers' visit to Miss Chudleigh in Devon: Records held by Chancery, C12/1485/15, PRO.

Fifteen

Information on the money spent refitting Carlisle House comes from PRO, B1, vol. 59. For the quote from Alessandro Verri: C. Casati, *Lettere e scritti inediti di Pietro e di Alessandro Verri, annotati e pubblicati dal Dottore C. Casati*, Milan, 1879. For information about the Prince of Monaco's and King of Denmark's visits, cuttings held by Westminster Public Library; *Daily Advertiser*; Fillinham Collection. For comments on the Duke of York's visits to Carlisle House: Mary Coke, *The Letters of Lady Mary Coke*, Edinburgh, 1889–96. For Teresa's partnership with James Cullen: *GLC Survey of London*, vol. 33, p. 174; *Cullen v. Fletcher*, C12/114/26, PRO.

For Augustus Hervey's attempts to divorce Elizabeth Chudleigh: Beatrice Curtis Brown, *Elizabeth Chudleigh, Duchess of Kingston*, Gerald Howe, London, 1927; Elizabeth Hervey, *The Life and Memoirs of Elizabeth Chudleigh . . . commonly called Duchess of Kingston*, London, 1788; Doris Leslie, *The Incredible Duchess: the life and times of Elizabeth Chudleigh*, Heinemann, London, 1974; Elizabeth Osborn Mavor, *The Virgin Mistress – A Study in Survival*, Chatto and Windus, London, 1964; Charles E. Pearce, *The Amazing Duchess: being the romantic history of Elizabeth Chudleigh*, Stanley Paul and Co., London, 1911; Sir Leslie Stephen and Sir Sidney Lee, *Dictionary of National Biography*, Oxford University Press, Oxford, 1949–50; Marchioness de la Touche, *Les Aventures trop amoureuses, ou Elisabeth Chudleigh . . . et la Marquise de la Touche sur la scène du Monde, etc.*, London, 1776; Thomas Whitehead, *Original Anecdotes of the late Duke of Kingston and Miss Chudleigh by Thomas Whitehead, Many years a servant to the duke of Kingston*, London, 1792; *An Authentic Detail of particulars relative to the Duchess of Kingston*, London, 1788. For Mrs Harris's letters: James Harris, Earl of Malmesbury, *A Series of letters of the first Earl of Malmesbury, his family and friends from 1745 to 1820*, Richard Bentley, London, 1870.

For description of the royal galas held at Carlisle House: *Public Advertiser*, Fillinham Collection. For John Wilkes: *Dictionary of National Biography*. For contemporary attitudes towards masquerades: CR of CCC, Oxford, *The Danger of Masquerades and Raree-shows, or the complaint of the state against masquerades, opera's, assemblies . . . and several other irrational entertainments*, W. Boreham, London, 1718; A. Betson, *Miscellaneous Dissertations Historical, Critical, and Moral, on the origin and antiquity of masquerades, plays, poetry &c.*, T. Meighan, London, 1751; Johann Jakob Heidegger, *Heydegger's letter to the Bishop of London concerning a sermon preached by the latter condemnatory of Masquerades*, London, 1724.

Sixteen

For the Pantheon: for information on the building itself, on the birth of Turst's plans and on the relationship between Margaretta Ellice and Elias Turst: PRO C107/149; C12/387/19; and C12/408/29; Robert Elkin, *The Old Concert Rooms of London*, Edward Arnold, London, 1955.

For James Wyatt: Edward Brayley, *Historical and Descriptive accounts of the Theatres of London*, J. Taylor, London, 1826; Anthony Dale, *James Wyatt, Architect, 1746–1813*, Basil Blackwell, Oxford, 1936; Christopher Reginald Turnor, *James Wyatt, 1746–1813*, Art & Technics, London, 1951.

For the Licensing Act: Vincent J. Liesenfeld, *The Licensing Act of 1737*, Madison, London, 1984; Curtis Price, Judith Milhous and Robert D. Hume, *Italian Opera in Late 18th Century London*, vol. 1, Clarendon, Oxford, 1995.

For reports of the Carlisle House masquerades in February: February 1771 editions of the *London Chronicle* and the *Gentleman's Magazine*. For the poem on the coffin of the 'Walking Corpse': *Middlesex Journal*, February 1771. The best sources of information on the Guadagni affair are Patricia Howard, *Guadagni in the Dock: a crisis in the career of a castrato*, Early Music, February, 1999; and the chapter entitled 'The Hobart Management' in Ian Woodfield, *Opera and Drama in 18th Century London*, Cambridge University Press, 2001. In addition: Charles Burney, *General History of Music from the earliest ages to the present period*, London, 1776–89. For Hobart's undercover investigations into the Harmonick Meetings and Mrs Cornelys's trial: Sessions Rolls of the Middlesex Justices MJ/SR 3240, held by the Metropolitan London Archives; Ronald Leslie-Melville, *The Life and Work of Sir John Fielding, with a foreword by Sir Rollo*

F. Graham-Campbell, Lincoln Williams, London, 1934; *The Case of the Opera House disputes, fairly stated, etc.*, London, 1784. For contemporary reports of Mrs Cornelys's trial: *Daily Advertiser*, February 1771; and *General Evening Post*, 12–14 February 1771; *Annual Register*, 18 February 1771; *London Magazine*, March 1771, pp. 121–2; *Oxford Magazine*. For the charge of Teresa keeping a disorderly house: *General Sessions of the Peace, Middlesex*, MJ/SB/B/0207, February 1771; *Middlesex Journal*, 14 February 1771. For Simon Slingsby's ruin: *Morning Post*, 1 January 1785.

Seventeen

Mrs Boscawen's letter to Mrs Delaney: *The Autobiography and Correspondence of Mary Granville, Mrs Delaney, Edited by Right Honourable Lady Llanover*, Richard Bentley, London, 1862. For the rising cost of the Pantheon and Turst's disintegrating relationship with Margaretta Ellice: Records held by Chancery, C107/149, C12/387/19, C12/408/29, PRO. Most of the newspaper reports on Carlisle House in this chapter were taken from the *Public Advertiser* for January and February 1772 or from unattributed cuttings held by Westminster City Archives and the Fillinham Collection. For Fanny Burney's quote: her novel, *Evelina; or, the History of a young lady's entrance into the world*, Newman, London, 1815.

For description of the Pantheon: *GLC Survey of London*, vols 31 and 32. For reports of the *Threnodia Augustali* in Carlisle House: James Harris, *A Series of letters of the first Earl of Malmesbury, his family and friends from 1745 to 1820*, Richard Bentley, London, 1870. For Teresa's arrest at the orders of John Berger: *Cornelys v. Burger* (1772) PRO C12/392/28. For her petition to George III: State Papers Domestic of George III, 1760–1783, Memorial of Teresa Cornelys, 1770 (?), PRO. For details of Teresa's plea to stop the sale of Carlisle House: *Cornelys v. Chamberlain* (1772) PRO C12/1518/6. Notice of Teresa's bankruptcy was posted in *London Gazette*, 3–7 November 1772. The *Westminster Magazine*, 1773, carried a two-part satire on the sale of Carlisle House.

Eighteen

For Sophie in flight from the scandal: John Taylor, *Records of My Life*, Edward Bull, London, 1832; for details of Mrs Cornelys at the Polygon, Southampton, and the Polygon development, I am indebted to original fieldwork by Stuart Robertson, Archaeological Consultant Services, London E1; A. T. Patterson, *A History of Southampton 1700–1914*, vol. I, Southampton, 1966; *The Southampton Guide*, 4TH edition, 1787.

For an account of the 1775 Venetian regatta, its races and prizes: 'A Circumstantial Account of the Ensuing Regatta; comprehending the plan, directions &c, relating to that entertainment, etc.', *The Author*, London, 1775; *Gentleman's Magazine*, 1775, p. 315; W.W. and A.E. Wroth, *London Pleasure Gardens of the 18th Century*, Macmillan, London, 1896. For Mrs Lynch's letter to Dr Johnson of 24 June 1775: Hester Lynch, *Letters to and from the Late Samuel Johnson*, London, 1788. For reports of Teresa's comeback at Carlisle House and her rural masquerades: Fillinham Collection.

Nineteen

For accounts of the Duke of Kingston's death and the trial of the Duchess of Kingston: Beatrice Curtis Brown, *Elizabeth Chudleigh, Duchess of Kingston*, Gerald Howe, 1927; *The Life and Memoirs of Elizabeth Chudleigh, commonly called Duchess of Kingston*, London, 1788; Elizabeth Hervey, *An Authentic Detail of particulars relative to the Duchess of Kingston*, London, 1788; Doris Leslie, *The Incredible Duchess: the life and times of Elizabeth Chudleigh*, Heinemann, London, 1974; Elizabeth Osborn Mavor, *The Virgin Mistress – A Study in Survival*, Chatto and Windus, London, 1964; Charles E. Pearce, *The Amazing Duchess: being the romantic history of Elizabeth Chudleigh*, Stanley Paul and Co., London, 1911; Sir Leslie Stephen and Sir Sidney Lee, *Dictionary of National Biography*, Oxford University Press, Oxford 1949–50; Marchioness de la Touche, *Les Aventures trop amoureuses, ou Elisabeth Chudleigh . . . et la Marquise de la Touche sur la scène du Monde, etc.*, London, 1776; Thomas Whitehead, *Original*

Anecdotes of the late Duke of Kingston and Miss Chudleigh by Thomas Whitehead, Many years a servant to the duke of Kingston, London, 1792. Elizabeth Chudleigh's letters to the Dukes of Portland and Newcastle are contained in the *Catalogue of Papers of the Third Duke of Portland*, held by the University of Nottingham; they are numbered PWF 2800–2805, and are reproduced with their permission.

In addition, the following publications provided particular details of the trial: Lewes Melville (ed.), *Trial of the Duchess of Kingston*, W. Hodge & Co., Edinburgh and London, 1927; *The trial of R. F. December 1706 . . . With the proceedings . . . in the prerogative Court. To which is added an appendix relating to the indictment against Elizabeth Duchess of Kingston*, London, 1776.

For the Duchess's letters to the Duke of Portland: PWF 2800, PWF 2802, PWF 2803, PWF 2804, PWF 2805, Papers of 3RD Duke of Portland, Nottingham University.

The Duchess's spat with the playwright Samuel Foote was widely reported in the papers, and his play, *A Trip to Calais*, was published in London in 1778.

Twenty

For William Hickey's description of Carlisle House: William Hickey, *Memoirs of William Hickey (1749–1809)*, Hurst & Blackett, London, 1913. For the Gordon Riots: William Vincent (pseudonym for Thomas Holcroft), *A Plain narrative of the late riots in London, Westminster and Southwark*, London, 1780; and Records of the King's Bench Prison, PRIS10/136, held by the PRO.

For Amicus's letter defending Mrs Cornelys's name: *The Times*, May 1792. For Teresa's life at Knightsbridge Grove: Edwin Beresford Chancellor, *Knightsbridge and Belgravia: their history, topography, and famous inhabitants*, Pitman and Sons, London, 1909; Henry George Davis and Charles Davis, *The Memorials of the Hamlet of Knightsbridge*, J. Russell Smith, London, 1859; *GLC Survey of London*, vol. 45; John Taylor, *Records of My Life*, Edward Bull, London, 1832. For quote on asses' milk being for sale at Knightsbridge: *Post Boy*, 6 December 1711.

For the dates of Teresa's imprisonment: *Fleet Commitment Files*, PRO. For conditions in prison in the eighteenth century: John Ashton, *The Fleet – Its River, Prison, and Marriages*, T. Fisher Unwin, London, 1889; Anthony Babington, *The English Bastille: A history of Newgate gaol and prison conditions in Britain 1188–1902*, Macdonald, London, 1971; John Coackley Lettsom M.D., *Hints respecting the prison of Newgate, Extracted from the fourth volume of memoirs of the Medical Society of London*, London, 1794; William Eden Hooper, *The History of Newgate and the Old Bailey, and a survey of the Fleet prison and Fleet marriages, the Marshalsea and other old London jails*, Underwood Press, London, 1935; John Howard, *The State of the Prisons in England and Wales*, London, 1791. For poem: 'Humours of the Fleet', Roger Lee Brown, *A History of the Fleet Prison, London, The Anatomy of the Fleet*, Edwin Mellen Press, Lewiston, New York, 1996; *Petitions, Addresses, etc. to the House of Commons – To the Honorable the Commons of Great Britain in Parliament assembled. The humble Petition of the Debtors confined in His Majesty's Prison of the Fleet*, London, 1789. For Mrs Sumbel's autobiography, in which she writes about her meetings with Teresa, Sophie Cornelys and Teresa's death: Leah Sumbel, *Memoirs of the Life of Mrs Sumbel, late Wells, of the theatre-Royal, Drury-Lane, Covent-Garden, and Haymarket, written by Herself*. C. Chapple, London, 1811.

Epilogue

Teresa's obituary appeared in the *Gentleman's Magazine*, October 1797. The record of her burial appears in the parish registers of St Sepulchre-without-Newgate, held by the City of London Archives, Guildhall Library, London. Sophie Williams's comments on her mother's death were reported by Mrs Sumbel in her *Memoirs of the Life of Mrs Sumbel, late Wells, of the theatre-Royal, Drury-Lane, Covent-Garden, and Haymarket, written by Herself*, C. Chapple, London, 1811. The report on Sophie's character and later life comes from John Taylor, *Records of My Life*, Edward Bull, London, 1832. For other details of Sophie's later life: obituary in the *Gentleman's Magazine* 1823, vol. XCIII, supplement I; *Notes and Queries*, 7 July 1894. For details of Angelo Pompeati's death:

Giacomo Casanova, *Histoire de Ma Vie, op. cit.*, *Biographischer Index des Wiener Opernballets von 1631*, Vienna, 1994.

For the last days of Carlisle House: Edwin Beresford Chancellor, *The Romance of Soho*, Country Life, London, 1931; Fillinham Collection; Anthony Pasquins (John Williams), *An Elegy, written in Soho Square, of seeing Mrs Cornelly's house in Ruins, Monthly Mirror*, October 1789.

For Samuel Curwen's description of Carlisle House: Samuel Curwen, *Journal and Letters of the late Samuel Curwen*, Wiley and Putnam, London, 1842. For the decline of Soho in the nineteenth century, I used my own book, *Soho, A History of London's Most Colourful Neighbourhood*, Bloomsbury, London, 1989. For Miss Chudleigh's later life and death, I used all the books on her cited above and, in addition, papers of Miss Elizabeth Chudleigh held by the National Library of Wales, Aberystwyth; Henriette Louise d'Oberkirch, *Mémoires de la Baronne d'Oberkirch*, Paris, 1853.

For Casanova's old age and death, I used the books on Casanova listed above (page 307), in particular, J. Rives Child, *Casanova*, George Allen and Unwin, London, 1961; Edouard Maynial, *Casanova et son temps*, Paris, 1910. In addition: Prince Charles de Ligne, *Mélanges anecdotiques littéraires et politiques*, Paris, 1833. Teresa's letter to Passano appears on pp. 222–4 of Charles Samaran, *Jacques Casanova, Vénitien*, Calman-Levy, Paris, 1914. Details of the removal of human remains from St Sepulchre-without-Newgate to Epping were given to me by David McCarthy of the Corporation of London. The later history of St Sepulchre's church and its association with Sir Henry Wood came from the church's website: *www.st-michaels.org.uk/sepulchre/history.htm*.

Index

balls – *cont.*
237, 238, 239, 251, 253, 255, 259, 268, 287, 301
bankruptcy 165, 175, 179, 238, 241, 242, 246, 247, 249, 250, 284, 285
Banqueting Hall 199
Baraque, Theâtre de la 62
Barbarigo, Princess 193
Barbon, Nicholas 104
Barrington, William Shute 2nd Viscount 207, 239, 265
Barrymore, Earl of 207, 219
Bartolozzi, Francesco 128, 250
Bateman, Lord 207, 219
bautta 10
Bayreuth 46–51, 54, 56
bear-baiting 96
beau monde 207, 268
Beauchamp, Lord 207
Beaufort, Duchess of 286
Beaufort, Duke of 207
Beccheroni, Gaspera 43, 44
Beckford, William 14, 105
Bedford, Duchess of 176
Bedford, Duke of 89
Belisario 5, 13
Belshazzar 33
Bentinck, Lord Edward 251
Berger, Albert 178, 238, 240
Berger, John 178, 238, 240
Berkeley, Countess 219
Berkeley, Earl of 219
Bernasconi, Andrea 55
bigamy 257, 260, 262, 263, 266
Bill of Rights Society 203
Blackfriars 251
boat-trips 96
Bodycoate, Henry 136, 137, 140

Bolingbroke, Lord 127, 219
Bolton, Duchess of 127, 205
Bolton, Duke of 219
Boorder, John *see* Fermor, John
Boruwlaski, Count 289
Boswell, James 234
Botany Bay 275
Bow Street court 88, 227
boxing 96
Brackstone, Mary 137, 139, 194, 242
Bradshaw, George Smith 106, 107
Bragadin, Matteo 53
Brandenburger lake 48
Brewer Street, 38, 98, 169
Bristol, 3rd Earl of *see* Hervey, Augustus
Bristol, Duchess of *see* Chudleigh, Elizabeth
Briton 202
Broad Street pump 291
Brockhaus, F. A. 295
Brosses, Charles de 7
Brussels 61
Buccleuch, Duchess of 201
Buccleuch, Duke of 219
Bucintoro 26
Buranella, La *see* Casanova, Zanetta
Burghersh, Lord 207
Burgtheater 42
Burney Charles 33, 35, 98, 213
Burney, Fanny 127, 206, 234
Bute, Earl of 202

Caduta dei Giganti 34, 35, 36, 37
Calabria 53
Calshot Castle 248
Camden, Lord 235

St Sepulchre-without-Newgate Church 284, 302

St Stephan's Cathedral 28, 287, 297

Salisbury, Bishop of 105

Sammartini, Giovanni 27

San Giovanni Cristostomo theatre 33, 52, 169

San Nicola del Lido Church 26

San Samuele Church 16, 21, 300

San Samuele theatre 2, 3, 4, 5, 9, 13, 14, 20, 26, 27, 53, 169, 296, 298

Sandwich, Earl of 127, 202, 219

Sant'Angelo theatre 28, 52

Saunders, Paul 106, 107, 122, 138

Savile, George 270, 271

Savoir Vivre Club 250

Saxony, Electress of 293

Scalabrini, Paolo 42, 46

School of Eloquence 288, 289

Seingalt, Chevalier de *see* Casanova, Giacomo

Semiramide riconosciuta 41, 42

Serenissima, La 9, 11, 12

shooting 96

Sidney, Viscountess 286

Simpson, Matthew 218, 224

Sinclair, Patrick 240

Siprutini, Emanuel 117

Siroe, re di Persia 169

Slingsby, Simon 215, 229

Smith, Frederick 272

Smith, Lewis 240

Smith, Mrs *see* Cornelys, Teresa 272

Smith, William 240

Smithfield market 277

Smollett, Tobias 99

Society in Soho-square xix, 111, 113, 114, 115, 117, 125, 126, 127, 128, 151, 153, 168, 172, 174, 198, 200, 222

Sofonisba, La 33

Soho Square xv, xvi, xvii, xviii, xxiii, 105, 108, 109, 110, 114, 131, 132, 133, 136, 160, 168, 169, 170, 177, 185, 201, 202, 204, 210, 211, 227, 228, 230, 234, 240, 242, 243, 246, 269, 272, 283, 286, 289, 302, 303

Soho xv, 30, 38, 97, 102, 103, 104, 105, 126, 148, 154, 173, 197, 201, 204, 217, 231, 235, 240, 249, 252, 253, 257, 269, 270, 288, 291, 302, 303, 304

Sons of Liberty 203

South Sea Company 77, 78

Southampton 248, 249

Southwark 171

Sparsholt, Winchester 85

Spencer, Earl of 219

Spencer, Lady 127, 193, 219, 286

Spencer, Samuel 241, 243

Spitalfields 104

Stable Yard 247

Stamitz, Johann, 59

Stampiglia, Louis 55

Stanhope, Lady *see* Harrington, Countess of

Stanley, Hans 248

State of Prisons in England and Ireland 277

Stavendale, Earl of 219

Stavordale, Lord 207

Story of My Escape 60

Story of My Life 285

Strawberry Hill 192